BROADCASTING HOLLYWOOD

BROADCASTING HOLLYWOOD

THE STRUGGLE
OVER FEATURE FILMS
ON EARLY TV

JENNIFER PORST

RUTGERS UNIVERSITY PRESS
NEW BRUNSWICK, CAMDEN, AND NEWARK,
NEW JERSEY, AND LONDON

Library of Congress Cataloging-in-Publication Data

Names: Porst, Jennifer, author.
Title: Broadcasting Hollywood: the struggle over feature films on early TV / Jennifer Porst.
Description: New Brunswick: Rutgers University Press, [2021] | Includes bibliographical references and index.
Identifiers: LCCN 2020052283 | ISBN 9780813596228 (hardcover) | ISBN 9780813596211 (paperback) | ISBN 9780813596235 (epub) | ISBN 9780813596242 (mobi) | ISBN 9780813596259 (pdf)
Subjects: LCSH: Television broadcasting of films—United States—History—20th century. | Copyright—Broadcasting rights—United States. | License agreements—United States. | Motion pictures—United States—Distribution. | Motion picture audiences—United States. | Television viewers—United States. | Motion picture industry—United States—History—20th century. | Television broadcasting—United States—History—20th century.
Classification: LCC PN1992.8.F5 P67 2021 | DDC 791.45/750973—dc23
LC record available at https://lccn.loc.gov/2020052283

A British Cataloging-in-Publication record for this book is available from the British Library.

♾ The paper used in this publication meets the requirements of the American National Standard for Information Sciences—Permanence of Paper for Printed Library Materials, ANSI Z39.48-1992.

www.rutgersuniversitypress.org

Manufactured in the United States of America

For Asher, Madison, Griffin, Stella, Ellie, and Mikey

Contents

ABBREVIATIONS

ABC	American Broadcasting Company
AFL	American Federation of Labor
AFM	American Federation of Musicians
AFRA	American Federation of Radio Artists
AFTRA	American Federation of Television and Radio Artists
AGVA	American Guild of Variety Artists
ASCAP	American Society of Composers, Authors, and Publishers
BBDO	Batten, Barton, Durstine & Osborn Advertising Agency
BOA	Bank of America
CBS	Columbia Broadcasting System
COMPO	Council of Motion Picture Organizations
DGA	Directors Guild of America
DOJ	Department of Justice
FCC	Federal Communications Commission
Four A's	Associated Actors and Artists of America
FRC	Federal Radio Commission
HUAC	House Un-American Activities Committee
IATSE	International Alliance of Theatrical Stage Employees
IMPPA	Independent Motion Picture Producers Association
JWT	J. Walter Thompson Advertising Agency
MCA	Music Corporation of America
MGM	Metro-Goldwyn-Mayer
MPAA	Motion Picture Association of America

MPPDA	Motion Picture Producers and Distributors of America
NAB	National Association of Broadcasters
NARTB	National Association of Radio and Television Broadcasters
NBC	National Broadcasting Company
O&O	owned and operated
PCA	Production Code Administration
RCA	Radio Corporation of America
RKO	Radio-Keith-Orpheum Pictures
SAG	Screen Actors Guild
SCTOA	Southern California Theatre Owners Association
SEG	Screen Extras Guild
SIMPP	Society of Independent Motion Picture Producers
SWG	Screen Writers Guild
TBA	Television Broadcasters Association
TOA	Theatre Owners of America
TVA	Television Authority
U.A.	United Artists
WGA	Writers Guild of America

BROADCASTING HOLLYWOOD

INTRODUCTION

MEDIA DISRUPTION AND CONVERGENCE

When Disney launched their streaming platform Disney+ in November 2019, the strength of the service's content library, which includes properties from Lucasfilm, Marvel Studios, Pixar, Walt Disney Studios, Disney Channel, and National Geographic, and the optimistic projections of the platform's subscriber numbers resulted in Disney's stock closing at its highest price ever, at $152 a share.[1] The launch may have seemed to be an overnight success, but in fact, it was the culmination of decades of attempts by the conglomerate to establish itself in the digital world. They first created their Disney Online unit in the summer of 1995, but while digital native companies like Google, Amazon, and Facebook thrived and grew, many legacy media companies like Disney struggled to adapt to the digital world. In 2010, Bob Iger, former CEO of Disney, who was largely responsible for seeing Disney+ to fruition, explained, "I have tried to keep two obvious philosophies. First, that our current business not get in the way of adopting new technologies, and second, that our business belongs on these new platforms."[2]

The emergence and proliferation of digital technologies and the internet in the 1990s and the first decade of the twenty-first century led to the theorization of these processes as convergence, which, as defined by Henry Jenkins, describes the ways that content flows across multiple media platforms, the cooperation between multiple media industries, and the migratory behavior of media audiences.[3] This framework becomes particularly relevant when a new technology or medium emerges because the "old" media must find ways to engage with the new media. Oftentimes, as Disney experienced, that transition is not particularly smooth, and as Netflix acknowledged in a July 2016 press release, "disrupting a big market can be bumpy."[4] In the wake of the many successful media companies that struggled or failed in the face of digital media, many observers asked why the legacy media industries— film and television in particular—failed to take advantage of the potentials of digital media by not making more extensive, and timely, efforts to converge. It appeared as though the existing titans of media had their heads in the sand when it came to digital technologies, and when they finally stole a look, it was too late.

Take, for instance, the transformation of Netflix from a DVD-by-mail company that demolished the home video rental industry (let us lower our flags to half-mast for Blockbuster Video and the many local video stores left in Netflix's wake) to a streaming video platform whose aggressive push into the development and production of original content on a global scale reportedly had media titans like Disney scrambling to launch their own streaming platforms. The press spilled a lot of ink over the fact that Disney was supposedly caught unawares when it came to their challengers in the streaming space, but companies like Disney and the people who lead them did not achieve success through ignorance or a lack of intelligence. That is not to say they have never made a bad decision, but it does prompt the question, Why have companies like Disney struggled to successfully defend their market dominance in the face of these new innovations? What prevented them from quickly adapting and taking advantage of these new technologies?

Although the recent academic interest in convergence would imply that it is a digital native phenomenon, the notion that the seemingly distinct industries of film, television, and digital media work cooperatively is neither new nor exclusive to the twenty-first century. Earlier struggles between old and new media bear an uncanny resemblance to those occurring between legacy and digital media today. In looking back at the period of technological change when television emerged as a viable, commercial media form, we can see that many of the same questions and issues of convergence were at play. Analyzing the moments throughout the history of the media industries when a disruptive technology was introduced and the existing industry either adapted or failed to innovate can help us understand those important moments in history and illuminate the issue of contemporary media innovation and disruption. William Uricchio has argued for the importance of this kind of work by claiming that in this moment when contemporary media is undergoing transitions wrought by digital technologies, scholars should adopt a new view of media that benefits from considering other moments of media in transition, and one that demands new sorts of conceptual focus.[5] That conceptual focus should move away from the isolated study of specific media (e.g., film) and toward a view of media as a "web of pre-existing, competing, and alternative media practices," which would enrich the possible meanings that the study of an isolated medium can generate.[6] Similarly, Mark Williams outlined the need for new work in media history that he called "intermedial studies," or the "examinations of relations between and across specific media at significant historical junctures."[7] Williams, like Uricchio, sees the rise of digital culture as an impetus to "reunderstand" the history of media and media culture, and he argues there is an emerging emphasis on the "fissures, discontinuities, and synecdoche" of history.[8] One of those significant historical junctures occurred in the 1940s and 1950s when television disrupted the film industry. Over the past few decades, media scholars have worked to illuminate the tumultuous relationship between the film and television industries in that period. For example, Christopher Anderson, Tino Balio, Michele Hilmes, William Boddy, Edward Buscombe, Robert Vianello, and Douglas Gomery advanced the understanding of Hollywood's relationship with early television through examinations of Hollywood's ownership of television stations, theater and subscription television, and production for television.[9] More recently, David Pierce, Michele Hilmes, Amy Schnapper, and Eric Hoyt offered analyses of the attempts to license or sell feature films to television through overviews of the activities of the major film studios in relation to television and a focus on what happened when feature films were eventually released to television.[10] However, scholars have not yet explained the struggle over the licensing and sale of Hollywood's feature films to television, and have not examined it through an analysis of the many different industrial agendas involved in the negotiations. *Broadcasting Hollywood: The Struggle over Feature Films on Early TV* builds on their work by investigating the efforts made by the film and television industries in the 1940s and 1950s to work toward feature films appearing on television. Through extensive archival research, I argue that it took until 1956 before Hollywood's feature films appeared on television, not because of the long-held assumptions that the film industry was either apathetic or hostile to the nascent television industry, but rather as a result of a complex combination of industrial, social, legal, and governmental forces. Ultimately, this book demonstrates that those issues that prevented Hollywood's feature films from appearing on television before 1955 also characterize other key periods of media industry disruption and convergence, and in particular, the contemporary film and television industries and their relationship to digital media. This analysis will show that periods of media industry disruption are ultimately resolved according to the flexibility (or lack thereof) of the industrial, economic, and regulatory structures of each medium; the strengths and weaknesses of labor; the power of law and regulation; and changing social and cultural norms that affect exhibition and audience consumption.

To more clearly understand both the historical and contemporary periods of media industry disruption and convergence and the behaviors of those involved, we can look to economic theory for some key concepts. Joseph Schumpeter, one of the most influential economists of the twentieth century, articulated a theory of innovation called "creative destruction," which views the process of innovation and disruption as one where new technologies can render older technologies, and thereby the companies that produced and sold them, obsolete.[11] Ironically, as economist Orly Lobel points out, "Schumpeter did not coin the phrase *creative destruction*. He borrowed it from an earlier (and rather unknown) economist, popularized the phrase, and received the glory of its splendid simple truth: knowledge flows and humanity progresses by breaking down barriers and merging separate ideas."[12] The concept of creative destruction frames capitalism as a kinetic system where innovators sustain economic growth even while they destroy the value of established companies. Contemporary economist Clayton M. Christensen developed the concept of the innovator's dilemma in order to look more closely at the reasons why dominant companies often fail in the face of disruption. Christensen argued that even the most successful, well-managed companies that pay close attention to their markets, listen to their customers, and invest in new technologies can still manage to lose their market dominance in the face of new, disruptive technologies.[13] One of the central reasons for that failure is rooted in the distinction between sustaining and disruptive technologies. Sustaining technologies foster improved product performance, much like the invention of sync sound film, which was not a wholly new medium and did not compete with film, but offered an improvement to the existing technology. Disruptive technologies, on the other hand, bring something very different to the market than was previously available. Products based on disruptive technologies are often cheaper, simpler, smaller, and, frequently, more convenient to use.[14] Disruptive technologies alter the business or social landscape, disrupt the status quo, change the way people live and work, and rearrange value pools.[15] This definition helps clarify the distinction between change, which is inevitable and ongoing, and disruption, which fundamentally alters the ways in which media is produced, distributed, and consumed. When existing media is faced with a disruptive technology like digital media or television, they often struggle to adapt and take advantage of the opportunities presented by the newer technologies. In order to understand their behavior, as economist Andrew Currah has argued, "we must examine the *incentives* they face, as well as the organizational and institutional *context* in which executive decision-making takes place."[16] Those incentives and contexts, in both the 1950s and now, include the legal rights to the content, the geography of windows and deals, fiduciary duties to shareholders, the powerful interests of and contracts with successful retailers and exhibitors, the high risks inherent in producing costly films, contractual obligations with labor organizations, the government's attitude toward the regulation of industries via antitrust law, and more.

The Struggle over Hollywood's Feature Films to Television

For a long time, traditional discourse about the relationship between the Hollywood studios and early television has fallen into two camps: (1) Hollywood studios were antagonistic to television until the late 1950s, when they realized television was not going away, at which time the studios grudgingly tried to find a way into an industry already dominated by three main networks (National Broadcasting Company [NBC], Columbia Broadcasting System [CBS], and American Broadcasting Company [ABC]); or (2) Hollywood always desperately wanted to get into the television business, but government regulations, and specifically the actions of the Federal Communications Commission (FCC), thwarted Hollywood's efforts until the mid-1950s, when studios finally gave up on their dreams of owning networks and accepted the role of producers of content for the new medium. Those long-held beliefs about Hollywood's apathy/hostility to television in the 1940s and 1950s have their roots in statements published in the industry trades during that time, such as one in *Radio Daily* on 4 May 1949 by Mal Boyd, the president of the Television Producers Association: "Most of the major film companies are allowing their fear of television as a competitive medium to stand in the way of effective exploitation of their product by video means." That assumption about Hollywood's motivation was then used to explain why studios could not make successful inroads to television until the mid-1950s. These trade storylines carried over into academic scholarship such as James L. Baughman's work on ABC in the 1950s, which states, "As television sharply reduced box office receipts, Warner and others adopted a public pose of hostility toward the home screen. In the early 1950s, studio head Jack Warner had been one of the most vocal proponents of the colony's TV 'boycott.' He had banned TV sets from the lot and forbade them from appearing in any Warner films."[17] Tino Balio made the argument for Hollywood's antipathy by saying, "As TV began to make inroads into movie audiences, Hollywood's first impulse was to maintain a strictly stand-off attitude toward the new medium. Television was a novelty whose attraction for the public would quickly wane, the hypothesis being 'They'll get tired of it soon enough.'"[18] Christopher Anderson echoed Balio's claim and acknowledged the "movie industry's legendary antipathy" toward television.[19] All of those works, and others since the 1980s, have acknowledged the *antipathy* or *hostility* storylines, and while many have attempted to complicate those storylines, their zombie-like persistence often exemplifies the argument made by Robert C. Allen that "many assertions about the cinema have been passed from one historian to another without ever being verified or challenged."[20]

The relationship between Hollywood and television in the late 1940s and early 1950s was, in fact, tumultuous and complex. As television grew, Hollywood dealt with fundamental industrial shifts motivated by the consent decrees that resulted from the Supreme Court's decision in the antitrust case against Paramount et al.[21] As a result of those challenges and the changes occurring in American society, such as the baby boom, suburbanization, and postwar reacculturation, Hollywood saw its box office returns drop from wartime highs to all-time lows. During the war, people had disposable income but fewer goods to spend it on, so they often spent that money at the movies. Over time, as Hollywood studios watched that income slowly fade, it would make sense that they should happily take advantage of the potential new revenue stream from licensing or selling their films to television. In 1948, television stations suddenly found themselves with many hours of programming to fill and inadequate resources to meet that demand. The television industry even deliberately cannibalized radio to feed what Michele Hilmes described as television's "gaping maw."[22] Many television stations then called on Hollywood studios looking for films with which to fill their television schedules. If you consider that between 1935 and 1945 the Hollywood studios produced 5,380 feature films and 7,636 short subjects, totaling approximately 9,342 hours of entertainment, they certainly had enough content in their vaults to supply television.[23] If each medium could benefit from the other, why were the only feature films that appeared on television before 1955 foreign or independent films, or films that had been repossessed by agents like Bank of America? Why did those feature films appear on television while the major Hollywood studios' features took almost a decade or more to make their way to television? By analyzing the complex play of institutional, cultural, and economic forces at work in the struggle over the licensing and sale of Hollywood's feature films to television in the late 1940s and early 1950s, we can more clearly understand the relationship between Hollywood and the emerging television industry, as well as issues common to all periods of media industry disruption and convergence.

CONDUCTING HISTORICAL MEDIA INDUSTRY STUDIES

This book certainly follows the emerging profile of media industry studies, which Michele Hilmes has defined as the study of "those texts and practices that are *not* included in the study of literature, art, music, and drama as they have been structured in the academy over the last hundred years or so." Such studies call "into being a radically different conception of the entire process of creative production and reception."[24] Completing a study that focuses on those texts and practices that have traditionally been left out of the histories of film and television requires a consideration of the many different interests and factions at work in the media industries in the mid-twentieth century. As such, this is neither a network focused television history such as William Boddy's *Fifties Television: The Industry and Its Critics* nor a major studio-centric film history like Christopher Anderson's *Hollywood TV: The Studio System in the Fifties*. Rather, it gets into what Charles Acland described as the "dirt and depth of economic systems"[25] and deals with all of the sloppy spaces, emerging partnerships, intermediaries, and organization *between* the two mediums. By analyzing the issue of feature films on television before 1955 from a variety of perspectives, such as those of the film studios, unions and guilds, exhibitors, and theater organizations, this work follows in the footsteps of Jennifer Holt's *Empires of Entertainment*, which highlights the roles of various stakeholders, interests, and agendas as part of a "complex dialogue and negotiation of forces that all combined for striking consequences in a relatively short time frame."[26] This book is also informed by Eileen Meehan's analysis of television as "media constructed as industries through the active involvement of corporations and the state. From this perspective, the state sets in place economic rules, incentives, and protections that foster the privatization and commercialization of technologies of mass communication. Analytically, this creates a picture of television in which the foreground is filled with individuals, corporations, trade associations, non-profit organizations, and government entities pursuing their particular interests against a background of institutional structures, rules, policy processes, and political agendas that together constitute the state."[27] Meehan advocates for a multiperspectival approach to the study of media history that produces more complex, holistic, and adequate explanations of both the how and the why of historical events.[28] This book is also inspired by Michele Hilmes's use of what Michael Werner and Bénédicte Zimmerman called the *histoire croisée*, or a history that takes into account the "diversity of transactions, negotiations, and reinterpretations played out in different settings around a great variety of objects" using records from Congress and the FCC, creative texts and records of producers, corporate reports and marketing plans, and press coverage.[29] Approaches such as Holt's, Meehan's, and Hilmes's allow for a complete understanding of the dynamics of negotiation and change during periods of disruption, and provide an opportunity for telling the histories of many largely marginalized groups such as unions and independent television station owners. Including these stories allows for a more complete history of television itself. Moving away from a history of television that focuses primarily on the networks demonstrates the multifaceted nature of television both in terms of television as an industry and in terms of the texts it produces and broadcasts.

The inclusion of different stakeholders, interests, and agendas in this study not only makes it possible to have a complete understanding of the industrial structures of the film and television industries at that time, but also fleshes out the complicated and symbiotic dynamics between them. Douglas Gomery, in "The Centrality of Media Economics," argued that "one needs to hypothesize and understand how a particular form of industrial structure leads to certain corporate conduct."[30] The understanding of industrial structures and corporate conduct then allows for the comprehension of the texts that an industry produces. The analysis of the conflict between the industrial structure of established Hollywood and the flexible and growing structure of television provides further insight into many of the decisions made by those in charge. For example, the simple fact that the film industry was a dominant and successful industry whereas television was a young upstart led some studio executives to view working with television as somehow beneath them. The relative chaos of the early years of television also caused uncertainty in the film industry as people questioned how best to move forward and feared taking a wrong step. As Michele Hilmes argued in *Hollywood and Broadcasting*, the relationship between the film and broadcasting industries has been an "ongoing process of conflict, compromise, and accommodation" that shaped the "economic and expressive structures of both media."[31]

David Hesmondalgh's work in *The Cultural Industries* complements Holt's, Meehan's, and Gomery's methods and provides a cultural-economic framework for this book. As opposed to focusing on the change and continuity in the texts produced by the cultural industries or in the ways that audiences understand those texts, Hesmondalgh analyzes the patterns of change and continuity in the cultural industries themselves. He also suggests we look at the overall place of cultural production in economies and societies, the ownership and structure of cultural industry businesses, and the organization of production. He advocates for that approach because industries produce culture, but culture also produces industry. He argues that it is important to look not only at the industry itself but also at the larger American culture during that time period and the ways the changes and continuity in the culture at large affected the industries.[32] This echoes the argument of Brian Winston in "Breakages Limited," wherein he asserts that patterns of change in the media can be understood as a field wherein three elements—science, technology, and society—intersect.[33] In the cultural industries of film, television, and digital media, simply studying economics, industrial structures, science, or technologies will result in a limited understanding of the industry and its products. Considering the culture in which the industry and its products circulate allows for a more nuanced conception of the economics, industry, science, and technology of film and television. In this study, for example, the Communist witch hunts and conservative legislation of the 1950s affected the ability of unions to more forcefully lobby for residuals, and the change from the more liberal politics of the Roosevelt and Truman eras to the more conservative Eisenhower years affected the outcome of one of the central conflicts in this story: the antitrust lawsuit *U.S. v. Twentieth Century-Fox, et al.*, which alleged the studios refused to license or sell their feature films to television.

Because Hollywood's feature films did not appear on television before 1955, the subject has understandably received little attention compared with other aspects of the relationship between film and television in the 1950s, such as Hollywood's ownership of television stations, theater and subscription television, and production for television. The scant scholarly attention paid to this subject is due in large part to the often-impossible task of showing something that did not happen. Because Hollywood's feature films did not appear on television before 1955, there are no contracts for their sale or lease, and there are no television schedules or ratings information to help scholars describe their appearance on television. If there is no historical record of something happening, there is no way to *show* it, and historians are left to guess. However, the archive created by the antitrust case against Twentieth Century-Fox et al., as well as other lawsuits that made their way through the courts over the issue of films on television, provides the evidence to allow a rendering of what happened during this period. In analyzing these significant legal cases, this work also follows in the footsteps of scholars like Jane Gaines, whose seminal work *Contested Culture: The Image, the Voice, and the Law* analyzes intellectual property law not just as practical law but as an object of culture. She argues for an understanding of media law as a "discourse of power, one that restrains persons and regulates other objects of culture," and she points out that legal cases often arise during moments of "conflict-irritants," which require the legal system to perform its "ameliorative and conciliatory functions."[34] The introduction of television in the mid-twentieth century was one of those conflict-irritant trouble spots, and the lawsuits that arose to resolve those conflicts provide a means to better understand the conflicts, the industries, and the larger processes at work during times of media disruption.

This methodological approach required accessing the files related to those cases that were archived across the country, and the information in those archival materials demonstrates the value of legal files as an archive for media scholars. In these files, many important histories previously considered lost to the ages can once again be found. The many legal documents available in related case files made it possible to investigate this significant moment in history from the perspective of various stakeholders through the vast number of primary documents they left behind. Gathering those documents required extensive travel to archives across the country in search of the files of studios, unions, theaters, and television networks; trade publications, house organs, and unions' and theater organizations' communications with their members; and legal documents from court cases. As such, the antitrust case *U.S. v. Twentieth Century-Fox, et al.* plays a central role in this book for two reasons. First, although it is certainly less well known than the *U.S. v. Paramount Pictures, et al.* antitrust case, it was extremely significant in terms of its effect on the relationship between the film and television industries. Second, it resulted in the creation of a vast archive of materials related to the struggle over feature films on television before 1955. For the case of *U.S. v. Twentieth Century-Fox, et al.*, which was filed in 1952 and went to trial in 1955, the Department of Justice (DOJ) had the Federal Bureau of Investigation search the defendant companies' files and make copies of every document related to the issues of the case. As part of their preparation for trial, the DOJ's lawyers also conducted numerous interviews, studies, and surveys with persons in the industries who had knowledge of the issue of feature films and television. Those materials, over 30,000 pages of documents, are all housed in the National Archives, and additional files were found in studios' archives and other archives around the country. The transcript from the antitrust trial alone consists of over 3,000 pages of testimony from the people most involved in these negotiations. Scholars rarely have the opportunity to study a web of densely intersecting documents as complex as this collection, and the available files include the whole range of documents that existed, not just the polished versions of stories that studios often fed to the trades. In addition to painting a detailed portrait of many of the players involved in the industries at that time, the supporting materials in the government's and studios' case files highlight the difficulties the film and television industries had to overcome before the appearance of Hollywood feature films on television in late 1955. All of these documents have their own rhetorical purposes and, particularly where a lawsuit was involved, were often created by persons working for their own personal gain. But just as it is important to understand these types of complex industrial negotiations not only from the studios' viewpoint but also from the various perspectives of the multiple parties involved, so too is it important to analyze these issues using a wide range of data from a variety of sources. While no single document can provide a complete and accurate statement of any truth, one can gain a richer understanding of the workings of the television and film industries at this time in the dialogue between these multiple interests and perspectives.

The focus on primary documents, as opposed to secondary accounts, made it possible to piece together a firsthand account of what happened from the different players involved. The documents collected in the process of a lawsuit are particularly valuable, especially in this case, in that they contain the voices and stories of people left out of other histories and archival collections. In many cases, people even testified in court about erroneous information they had seen in the trades. Although the laws of time and space would not allow for participant observation, by working to understand this historical period from the point of view of the participants and including their own voices as much as possible, this book incorporates ethnographic methods. The thousands of pages of transcripts from the various trials over feature films on television are essentially interviews of the persons involved. In an effort to allow those people to tell this history in their own words, longer quotes have been used more frequently than they would have been if this study relied solely on secondary sources or more conventional archival materials. By analyzing the transcripts of trials to understand the range of people's thinking and behavior in regard to these issues, this book takes the unique approach of using ethnographic methods like those mobilized in the work of media industry scholars such as Sherry Ortner's *Not Hollywood* (2013) and John Caldwell's *Production Culture* (2008) and applying them to history.

When I was analyzing the many sources utilized in this book, it was critical to keep in mind what Caldwell has argued—namely, that trade accounts are often scripted for some form of vested self-interest, and scholars should understand the industrial reflexivity in trade expressions as a form of local cultural-economic negotiation.[35] This book also considers the fact that, as William Uricchio has pointed out, the ideological implications of these archival documents are particularly important when considering moments of change and contention in media history.[36] As a result, many of the archival documents used in this research should be understood as local negotiations of their larger cultural and industrial context. That is not to say that it is impossible to find any truth in documents, but simply that we should recognize that every document and utterance comes from a certain perspective and makes a particular argument for a particular purpose according to the situation and audience. Every piece of information has a certain bias, but comparing and contrasting the transcripts from trials along with other primary documents that exist from the time enables a more accurate portrait of this time period than might have been possible if relying heavily on secondary sources. By considering the different perspectives of the many players involved, this book tells a more complete history of this important period in media history.

A Complex Web of Stakeholders

Because the analysis in this book involves manifold factors, it is useful to clarify the difference between many of the players, formats, and entities involved before jumping into the meat of this struggle. Adding to the complexity of this analysis is the fact that trade and industrial terminologies can be slippery ground. Particularly in this period when television was new and people were still establishing clear terminology for the new medium, the vocabulary was somewhat fluid and often confusing. Reviewing the central terms in this case, even those that many scholars take for granted at this point, will allow us to ensure clarity before we begin.

First, although it may seem self-evident, we should consider the basic concept of feature films. Herein, feature films are defined as multireel films that typically ran for approximately ninety minutes in length and were originally intended for theatrical exhibition. This is distinct from films that were made for television, or "spectaculars," as Pat Weaver, president of NBC from 1953 to 1955, called them, wherein networks would air film clips in a television show, sometimes giving the television program the same name as the theatrical film, as an advertisement for the theatrical release.[37] During the early years of television, the fluidity of these terms was a bit confusing because people who worked in the industry and for the trades used the word "film" for filmed content that appeared in a variety of platforms. For example, there was a distinction between live television and filmed television, but they often just called filmed television "film." That made distinguishing between film for feature films in theaters and film for television a difficult task, and made research portals' search functions virtually useless. For this book, the focus is not on live television or on the film that was produced specifically for television broadcast, but rather on the feature films that the studios originally produced for theatrical exhibition in the 35mm format.

Another term that becomes particularly murky in the postwar period is "Hollywood" and who is included under that umbrella term. Rather than simply including the major studios, for the purposes of this book, "Hollywood" includes all of the studios that were member studios of the Motion Picture Producers and Distributors of America (MPPDA): Columbia Pictures Corp.; Loew's, Inc.; Metro-Goldwyn-Mayer (MGM); Paramount Pictures, Inc.; Radio-Keith-Orpheum Pictures, Inc. (RKO); Samuel Goldwyn Studios; Twentieth Century-Fox Film Corp.; Universal Pictures Co., Inc.; Republic Productions, Inc.; Hal Roach Studios, Inc.; and Warner Bros. Pictures, Inc. For reasons ranging from the fallout from the *Paramount* antitrust case to the specific requirements of the major studios' contractual obligations to labor unions, these major Hollywood studios approached the challenges of this time and particularly the issue of feature films on television very differently than did independent studios. Therefore, it is also important to clarify the distinctions between Hollywood and independent producers and studios, as well as between the different kinds of independent producers and studios. Independent films at this time were defined as any films not produced by member studios of the MPPDA. Within that group, however, there are two different groups of independent producers. There are the producers that were independent from the MPPDA studios but were members of their own association, the Society of Independent Motion Picture Producers (SIMPP). Included in that association were Vanguard Films, Inc.; Edward Small Productions, Inc.; Sol Lesser Productions, Inc.; Hal Roach Studios, Inc.; Majestic Productions, Inc.; Empire Productions, Inc.; Comet Productions; Embassy Productions; Nero Films, Inc.; Cagney Productions, Inc.; California Pictures, Inc.; Walt Disney Productions; Chaplin Studios; and Story Productions. Like the MPPDA, SIMPP entered into contracts with the unions and guilds in Hollywood and was therefore limited in their ability to distribute their films to television. Finally, there are those independent producers that were not members of SIMPP and thereby not subject to the terms of the agreements between that association and the unions and guilds.

There are many unions and guilds in Hollywood whose function is to collectively bargain with the Hollywood studios on behalf of their members. Although the members of the unions and guilds are employed by the producers, and the unions and guilds have contracts with the producers that guarantee minimum requirements for the employment of their members, the unions and guilds are often at odds with the producers when it comes to agreeing on the basic terms of those contracts. The unions and guilds in the film and television industries that play a large role in this story include the American Federation of Musicians (AFM), the Screen Actors Guild (SAG), the Screen Writers Guild (SWG), which was later known as the Writers Guild of America (WGA), the International Alliance of Theatrical Stage Employees (IATSE), and the American Society of Composers, Authors, and Publishers (ASCAP).

There is also the very fundamental distinction in this context between production, distribution, and exhibition. Histories of Hollywood and television have at times conflated the three activities into one broad category—the film industry's relationship to television—that tends to obscure many of the complexities of the film studios' approaches to television. During the early days of television, both the FCC and the consent decrees resulting from the *Paramount* antitrust case prevented the Hollywood studios from becoming involved in the exhibition of television (i.e., owning networks and stations) but did not stop them from being involved in production and distribution. Other factors prevented the studios from producing for, or distributing to, television, and while both subjects could benefit from further investigation, the focus of this book is on the distribution of Hollywood's product (older feature films in particular) to television in the 1940s and 1950s.

Despite the monolithic term, television is not one thing. Just as it is important to clarify the distinction between film production, distribution, and exhibition, it is also important to understand the differences between television networks, independent stations, affiliate stations, and owned and operated stations. They all have different loyalties and responsibilities, and those differences play a role in their varied attitudes toward feature films on television. The major television networks at this time were ABC, CBS, NBC, and DuMont, and they broadcast their program schedules not directly to viewers but to their affiliated and owned and operated stations. They produced much of their programming in New York and earned their revenue from deals with advertising agencies and sponsors and the sale of commercial time during their programs.

Independent television stations were small local operations and were often owned by regional media companies or local businesses such as newspapers or radio stations. They were licensed by the FCC to transmit a television signal within a specific market, and in return for the use of that broadcast spectrum, they promised to operate in the public interest. If a station was not affiliated with or owned and operated by a network, they had to produce, purchase, or license all of their own programming. In the early days of television, many stations remained independent because doing so offered them a wider choice of programming. For example, if there were only one or two stations in a given city, and four networks were offering them their programming, the stations could choose whichever network's programs they liked best. This competition incentivized the networks to produce better, more original content. But it also required either coaxial cables or the delivery of kinescope recordings to distribute that content to the stations, and in the early years of television, neither of those means was practical. As a result, the independent stations, particularly those in more remote geographical locations or smaller markets, found themselves with a great deal of airtime and not enough content to fill it.

Although affiliate stations are extremely common in contemporary television, in the 1940s and early 1950s they were less so. Affiliate stations are local stations that have an agreement with a network that they will broadcast the network's programming. The network provides their affiliates with a schedule of programs, with national or regional commercials included, and payment for the station's airtime. The affiliate station does not necessarily have to air the network's programs, however, and if they choose not to, the network can offer their programs to another station in that area. Just as it was with the independent stations, distributing network content to affiliate stations was challenging in the early years of television. Therefore, many stations chose not to affiliate with networks until the higher-quality coaxial cable system was available to them.

Owned and operated (O&O) stations were stations that, as the name implies, were owned and operated by one of the networks. This was in contrast to affiliate stations, which are contracted with a network but not owned by them. Regulations prohibited networks from owning stations in every market in the United States, so O&O stations were, at the time, relatively rare. But since they were owned and operated by the networks, they almost always carried the network's programming. The different relationships of these station types to the networks affected the amount of original programming they needed in order to fulfill their FCC-mandated minimum broadcast hours, and thereby influenced their need for feature films to help fill their schedules.

Finally, even the government could not be viewed as one unified force. The two major players in this case were the FCC and the DOJ, and it is important to understand the distinctions between them because their different allegiances and motivations often placed them in conflicting roles vis-à-vis the film and television industries. The FCC's mission, as outlined in the Communications Act of 1934, was to make wire and radio communication services available to the people of the United States, and a central part of their job was licensing radio and, eventually, television stations. The FCC's primary allegiance was to the radio and television industries, so they took steps to thwart Hollywood control of broadcasting by declining to approve studios' applications for networks, stations, and frequencies. The DOJ, however, had different interests. The DOJ is responsible for enforcing the laws of the United States, and, as part of that duty, they are required to investigate and pursue companies suspected of violating the 1890 Sherman Antitrust Act. This led them to engage in legal action against the film studios that attempted to force the studios to work with television by making their films available to the new medium. While the distinction between these two agencies and their interests may seem self-evident, it is actually quite important because the FCC and the DOJ differ markedly in their intended functions and actions, particularly in this case of the relationship between the film and television industries, and the struggle over feature films on television.

Although this book focuses exclusively on the relationship between the film and television industries in the United States, the struggles detailed herein also confronted media industries in countries around the world. The distinct laws, policies, industrial structures, and labor conditions for film and television in each country resulted in unique circumstances and different timelines for the processes of industrial convergence in each of those locations. To fully analyze these struggles around the world would require several book-length studies, and, particularly given the increasingly global media industries, this presents fertile ground for scholars of media industries and media history to research these phenomena in non-U.S. contexts.

BROADCASTING HOLLYWOOD

The chapters herein are organized topically, with each focusing on the central catalysts of and obstacles to change related to the struggle over feature films on television. Then, in order to mobilize the argument that the histories of film and television should be considered and told as an aggregate, integrated media history, the internal organization of each chapter is roughly chronological. This provides a bird's-eye view that allows us to better see and understand the complex cross-institutional dialogues between the different factions involved in the struggles over the licensing and sale of Hollywood's feature films to television and clarifies the intermedial practices at work in this period. Although this is largely a narrative historical account of who did what when, it turns the tables on normal narrative explanations of history by telling the story of what prevented the Hollywood studios from getting their feature films on television.

Chapter 1, "Systems of Authority and Evaluation," focuses on the ways in which disruption forces existing institutional structures and regulatory bodies to define new media and reconceptualize the function of existing media. As scholar Des Freedman has argued, "How media industries 'work' is connected to how they are structured in relation to the various policy frameworks to which they are exposed. In order to fathom the dynamics of these industries, therefore, one of our tasks is to research media policy environments and pressures."[38] In this case, one of the central players is the FCC, whose early decisions defined the structure of the film and television industries and proscribed the kinds of behaviors the film industry was allowed to pursue in television. Self-regulatory bodies like the National Association of Broadcasters (NAB), the MPPDA, and the Council of Motion Picture Organizations (COMPO) also played key roles in the relationship between film and television and the content that appeared in each medium. This chapter also outlines some of the ways that film studios evaluated their options in the new medium of television, and the institutional and regulatory obstacles that thwarted early efforts to license or sell their films to television. It provides a broad overview of the media's industrial structures and economics in the 1940s and 1950s in order to clearly show why Hollywood's feature films were so desired by some in the television industry, but withheld by Hollywood's major studios. The different approaches by government, industrial self-regulatory bodies, studios, and television networks and stations to the issue of new technologies and regulation highlight the many different perspectives at work.

Chapter 2, "Exhibition, Audiences, and Media Consumption," considers the key fact that industrial disruption changes not only the nature of production but also consumption, and looks at the changing audience in the mid-twentieth century and the role of theaters in the struggle over feature films on television. Even without the introduction of television, the film industry experienced significant change as a result of the *Paramount* antitrust case, which emancipated many theaters from studio ownership. In this changing landscape, exhibitors often felt most threatened by the notion of feature films appearing on television. While some theater owners attempted to use their expertise in media distribution and exhibition in the ownership of television stations, other exhibitors collaborated with the studios to find a foothold in television via the development of theater television. Many groups in the film industry undertook studies of audience behaviors in an attempt to determine the effects of television on the box office and the best way forward in an industry in flux. This chapter also investigates technology's influence on audience consumption, and the influence of the adoption of color and widescreen formats on the sales of television sets and the kinds of content that were available where and when.

Chapter 3, "Contracts, Rights, Residuals, and Labor," focuses on the complex debates over who held the rights to content in a new medium. Those debates not only determined the ways in which media texts could flow between platforms, but also significantly affected the ways in which laborers were compensated for their work. Accordingly, this chapter looks at the major unions and guilds in Hollywood, their concerns about the technological displacement of human labor, and their early struggles over residual payments for their work appearing in other media. While unions and guilds like SAG, the Directors Guild of America (DGA), and the WGA are most prominent (at least in the minds of the public today), the AFM was one of the strongest unions in the media industries in the mid-twentieth century. This chapter looks at their role in the struggle over feature films on television and uncovers that the AFM was on the cutting edge of fighting for residual payments and ultimately forged the structure for residual payments that is still in use today. The chapter also steps back to contextualize these labor struggles within some of the larger political and cultural forces of the day, such as the communist witch hunts undertaken by the House Un-American Activities Committee (HUAC) and the changing political tides that were becoming increasingly hostile to organized labor.

Chapter 4, "Roy Rogers, Gene Autry, and the Intervention of the Courts," looks at the ways in which intellectual property and contract law circumscribe certain aesthetic forms and play a crucial role in the social production of meaning. The case studies of the lawsuits brought by B-Western film stars Roy Rogers and Gene Autry against Republic Studios to try to prevent Republic from releasing their films to television highlight the power of contract law and intellectual property rights, the ways that they determine what appears onscreen, and the ways that stars worked to build multimedia brands in the mid-twentieth century. Ultimately, these cases not only put the industries on hold for years while everyone awaited their decisions, but also played a central role in defining the nascent medium of television and thereby circumscribed the ways that the mediums of film and television would relate to each other for decades to come.

Chapter 5, "Antitrust, Market Dominance, and Emerging Media," considers antitrust law in the mid-twentieth century and the ways its enforcement affected the film and television industries. It begins with the seminal antitrust case, *U.S. v. Paramount Pictures, et al.*, and the ways in which this case laid the groundwork for many of the changes and legal challenges navigated by the Hollywood studios in the 1940s and 1950s. It then considers another important but often overlooked antitrust case that took place in the early 1950s: *U.S. v. Twentieth Century-Fox, et al.*, wherein the studios had to defend themselves against the DOJ's claims that they were engaging in anticompetitive behavior against the television industry by withholding their feature films from television. The development of the case illustrates how emerging media like the subscription television service Phonevision, the contract demands made by unions like the AFM, and complaints made by independent theater owners can all lead to legal action that takes years to resolve. Ultimately, the antitrust cases had the power to effect massive industrial change with both hoped for and unintended consequences for every aspect of the industry.

Chapter 6, "Feature Films Make Their Way to Television," details the last steps in the licensing and sale of Hollywood's feature films to television. It focuses on the economics of the deals and the ways in which factions of the film and television industries positioned themselves to make the largest possible financial gain from the transactions. It highlights the media industry's bottom line and the ways that economics and basic industrial structures influenced the texts that audiences were able to consume. The distinction between independent producers and the major and minor Hollywood studios played a significant role in the ways in which the companies valued their product in different mediums and their ability to be flexible in the face of industrial disruption. This chapter takes a more detailed look at RKO and their approach to these negotiations in light of the fact that they, more than any of the other major studios at the time, were struggling to keep their head above water. The transition of feature films to television also necessitated aesthetic changes to accommodate for the basic differences between the mediums, including visual quality of large screen film versus small screen television, the interruption of commercials, and television's thirty- and sixty-minute program structure. The role of advertisers in television, and their enthusiasm for the involvement of Hollywood stars in the promotion of their products, added to the complexity of the negotiations, and distributors of film to television sprang up in all different shapes and sizes. All of these distinct interests ultimately determined who released what feature films to television and when, which meant that the landscape of early television programming existed as a result of complex industrial negotiations that played out over more than a decade.

Although the struggle over the licensing and sale of Hollywood's feature films to television had largely been resolved by 1960, the same obstacles would come back to haunt the media industries at future points of industrial disruption, and the conclusion turns to the twenty-first century to sort out the many ways this historical case study might inform our understanding of contemporary industrial processes. What we will find is what economists James Manyika, Michael Chiu, and colleagues have argued: "Leaders cannot wait until technologies are fully baked to think about how they will work for—or against—them. And sometimes companies will need to disrupt their own business models before a rival or a new competitor does it for them."[39] This book demonstrates that the Hollywood studios were, in fact, making concerted efforts to capitalize on the new television medium, including exhibiting their feature films on television; but their efforts were thwarted by a constellation of practical obstacles including prohibitive contracts with unions and guilds, an inability to determine and monetize the value of the nascent television medium, questions about the aesthetic quality of television, industrial inertia, and the protestations of theaters.

As David Thorburn and Henry Jenkins have argued, "In our current moment of conceptual uncertainty and technological transition, there is an urgent need for a pragmatic, historically informed perspective that maps a sensible middle ground between the euphoria and the panic surrounding new media, a perspective that aims to understand the place of economic, political, legal, social and cultural institutions in mediating and partly shaping technological change."[40] This study of the struggle over the licensing and sale of feature films to early television provides the analytical groundwork that allows us to better understand any period of disruption and convergence. It enables us to see that convergence is a historical as well as a contemporary phenomenon, and through the application of contemporary theories of convergence and innovation to this historical case study, it helps us better understand where the media industries were in the mid-twentieth century and how those industries evolved into the twenty-first century.

CHAPTER 1

Systems of Authority
and Evaluation

By the middle of the first decade of the twenty-first century, the internet had developed to the point that it became another site for the distribution and exhibition of moving-image media, and legacy media faced the challenge of figuring out how to utilize the new technology to exhibit its older content. Similarly, in the mid-twentieth century when television was developed, the film industry had to determine how they could realize the potential of its films on television. As scholar Christopher Anderson argued, "The motion picture industry during the 1950s was less an empire on the verge of ruin than one struggling, under unsettling conditions, to redefine its frontiers."[1] Those struggles actually began decades earlier, which Philip W. Sewell described as "a long period during which television existed as an object of conversation and imagination rather than a device in the home for (most of) the public."[2] The conversations and conflicts that arose during that time between the film and television industries demonstrate "the roles that culture and language—particularly as manifested in systems of authority and evaluation—play in making and managing a social, technical, and economic phenomenon such as television."[3] In this case, the systems of authority and evaluation included the industrial structures and regulatory bodies whose decisions would play a crucial role in the evolution of the media industries in the mid-twentieth century. Those bodies primarily included the FCC and industrial organizations such as COMPO, the NAB, and the MPPDA. The FCC in particular played a significant role in shaping the television industry and the texts it produced, even to the extent that scholar Timothy White has argued, "The failure of the studios to establish themselves as forces in television broadcasting was a result of FCC policy, not Hollywood incompetence."[4] This chapter examines the way that FCC policies such as the 1948–1952 freeze and their rulings against studios owning television stations shaped the television industry and affected the studios' approach to films on television. Other influential policies related to the regulation of television and film content as instituted by industrial organizations such as the NAB and the Production Code Administration responded to audience and government concerns about film content and its suitability for the broadcast audience. That industrial self-regulation effectively shaped the landscape of what was possible on television, and technological differences as basic as the conflict between the adoption and use of 16mm film and 35mm film also determined what audiences saw on-screen. Finally, studios and theatrical organizations spent a great deal of time and resources studying television to determine how best to take advantage of it, and those processes influenced the film industry's approach to television and affected the manner in which films made it, or not, to television. Ultimately, this begins the story of what happens when a new medium is introduced and different industrial and economic models collide.

EARLY TELEVISION AND THE FCC's FREEZE

Since television has its roots in radio, many of these struggles began decades before television got its commercial start. As Michele Hilmes outlined in *Hollywood and Broadcasting*, the federal regulation of radio played a key role in the relationship between the film and radio industries.[5] Hilmes argued that the "radio and film interests coexisted fairly peaceably during the 1930s and 1940s, each side gathering strength and making preparations for the confrontation that would finally take place in 1947 with the advent of regular commercial television broadcasting."[6] Those earlier decades integrally tied broadcasting to the principle of private ownership of the public airwaves. It created an uneasy public-private partnership where private corporations and advertisers acceded to regulation of the industry by the Federal Radio Commission (FRC). Just as the FRC, which would later become the FCC, discouraged radio programming that duplicated materials such as phonograph records, so too did they discourage duplicated materials like feature films appearing on television. The FRC/FCC's emphasis on public service programming and freely available radio content for all who could afford a receiver created significant roadblocks for the Hollywood studios hoping to own radio, and later television, stations.

Although television as a technology was invented decades before it had its commercial start, its early development was complicated by, among other things, the fact that the FCC did not, until 1941, authorize licenses for commercial television. Those licenses were crucial because they authorized stations to make money.[7] But the United States' entry into World War II in 1942 quickly hamstrung that growth. While domestic industries focused on supporting the war effort, the commercial development of television slowed to a crawl.[8] Then, in 1947, after the war ended, the FCC gave the "go-ahead" for commercial television to resume.[9] At that point, both CBS and the Radio Corporation of America (RCA) lobbied for the adoption of their color television technologies, and that competition led to a wait-and-see period after the war when new station construction and set sales stalled. No one in the television industry wanted to commit to a color system without the FCC's official approval. Nor did they want to move forward with investments in black-and-white production and distribution infrastructure or television sets if the promise

of color television was on the horizon. In 1947, the FCC's decision to avoid autho-
rizing either color system effectively committed television to black-and-white content for the foreseeable future.[10] The FCC also failed to resolve the many issues of
scale, cost, value, and screen formats that would play a significant role in delaying
the migration of feature films to television.

Part of the FCC's inefficiency in the 1940s was due to the fact that they were
experiencing what historian James L. Baughman has described as "postwar leth-
argy" and a turn away from the New Deal commitment to business oversight. Since
Congress controlled the FCC's budget, the commission was beholden to Congress's
goodwill, and at that time Congress was divided over broadcast regulation. As
Baughman detailed, "A majority of conservative southern and western Democrats
sided with their Republican colleagues in opposing, sometimes vociferously, more
vigorous regulation. More liberal Democrats uniformly championed greater oversight. The commission was torn between these two congressional sensibilities."[11]
It was also the case that the U.S. president appointed FCC commissioners, and neither President Truman nor President Eisenhower gave commission appointments
high priority. Eisenhower, for example, often delegated the task to his staffers, who
outsourced it to the Republican National Committee. As a result, his commissioners were often decidedly conservative, as evidenced by the statement of one of
Eisenhower's appointees, George C. McConnaughey: "My personal views on government regulation are quite simple. I favor as few controls as possible."[12] For better or worse, the introduction of television forced the FCC commissioners to take
on a whole raft of technological, economic, and content-related issues.

In September 1948, the FCC issued a report and order, which has commonly
become known as the "freeze order." It provided that no new or pending applications for the construction of TV broadcast stations would be acted upon.[13] The
commission believed that they had formulated their rules based on inaccurate
engineering information, and they wanted time to reconcile technological problems such as overlapping frequencies, ultra high frequency (UHF) versus very
high frequency (VHF), and color television. Initially, the freeze was intended to
last a few months, but it dragged on until 1952. That delay affected the studios
because, as Peter G. Levathes, formerly the head of television for Fox, recalled,
"In 1948, let us say, and this is the year that the Federal Communications Commission placed a freeze on the construction permits that were offered, we sort of
suspended consideration of [feature films on television] because there weren't
stations going on the air."[14] The studios believed that only when the freeze was
lifted would stations and markets increase enough to pay sufficient advertising
dollars for films.[15]

The operational stations, however, needed more programming, and as Wayne
Coy, head of the FCC, explained in 1948, "Both the quality and the quantity of television programming leave much to be desired at the present time."[16] Despite those
challenges, some industry leaders like David Sarnoff remained optimistic, and in
his address to RCA stockholders at the company's annual meeting in 1949, he
reported that the previous year had been RCA's most successful yet. He explained,

"Television is not just something added to broadcasting. It is a new industry calling for development of a new art form and for new conceptions in entertainment as well as in equipment. While these problems present great challenges, they also present great opportunities for progress. Therefore, we look forward to the future with confidence."[17] Some of that confidence was rooted in the fact that the number of sets in homes and the income brackets of television viewers had increased, as did the number of available channels and operating stations.[18] The networks expanded their coaxial cable and radio relay capabilities, and by the end of 1950 they had approximately forty-two cities and metropolitan areas connected to the networks.[19]

As the industry grew, advertisers spent more money on television not only because of expanded audience reach but also because the industry shifted from single sponsorship to what was called "shared" or "participation" sponsorship. In August 1949, NBC announced the opening of the three-hour timeslot on Saturday nights to a "new video programming concept whereby the three top Saturday night program hours will be offered as a block for participation sponsorship by 12 noncompetitive advertisers."[20] NBC described the programming as "consistent with the activities of American families on a typical Saturday night out," and they explained that their goal was to offer advertisers with smaller budgets an opportunity to get into "attraction" television.[21] According to a J. Walter Thompson (JWT) Television Department report, "The 52-week concept of single sponsorship as accepted in the radio industry, was initially changed in television due to rapidly increasing costs. However, as results of the shared type of advertising became available, the efficiency of the method became apparent. Because the impact of a television commercial is so much greater than that of a radio commercial, regular frequent exposure for a single product is not only unnecessary, but can be an uneconomical use of commercial time."[22] Shared sponsorship allowed for greater flexibility for programmers and sponsors and had the potential to increase the amount of money available to pay for programming like feature films.

Despite the fact that networks were expanding and advertisers were increasingly willing and able to pay more for television, network sales departments still could not charge as much for advertising as they would have liked because of the limited number of stations in many markets. The coaxial cable network had expanded, but as a result of the FCC's freeze on new stations, many cities still had only one or two stations. For example, AT&T had connected twenty-one cities, but thirteen of them had only one station. New York, Chicago, and Washington were the only cities with four or more stations, which was enough for full-time affiliation for each of the four networks. Most other cities were like Boston, which had two stations, and their station WBZ-TV broadcast only NBC shows; the three other networks, meanwhile, shared time on the other station.[23] In 1950, many stations did not necessarily want to carry network programming, because doing so meant that they would make less money from commercials. Income from commercials airing on network programming went to the network, whereas income from commercials airing during programming that originated from the station went to the station.

However, the high costs of producing original programming forced stations to give up "free" time to the networks. As Dean Fitzer, general manager of *Kansas City Star*'s station WDAF-TV, explained, "The problem becomes even more vicious when considering that network programming consumes most of an affiliate's best time."[24]

In April 1952, the FCC finally adopted the Sixth Report and Order, which, among other things, lifted the "freeze" on the authorization and construction of new television stations.[25] This step allowed manufacturers to move forward confidently with the production of new television sets, and also restarted the process of approving licenses. Those moves by the FCC finally made the expectation of a large increase in the television audience a reality, and led to the hope that the growth would substantially increase the commercial value of, and thereby profits from, releasing any films to television.[26] This significant expansion of the television landscape excited many people in the film industry, as evidenced by the fact that shortly after the FCC lifted the freeze, the chairman of Republic Studios, board of directors expressed to the board a great deal of optimism about the prospects for their activities in television.[27]

THE DECLINE OF CLASSICAL HOLLYWOOD

As television enjoyed the promise of an optimistic future, the film industry transitioned from a period of dominance and stability to a period of profound change and uncertainty. In 1946, the film industry raked in their highest box office grosses ever, and motion picture attendance hit 4.127 billion.[28] By 1947, however, the tide had turned, and the seven majors (Paramount, MGM, RKO, Warner Bros., Twentieth Century-Fox, Universal, and Columbia) experienced a decline in attendance. That decline, however, was only 8 percent in gross returns, while net profits fell a more serious 25 percent, which showed that the business may have suffered more from rising costs than from slipping revenues.[29] By 1948, weekly attendance had fallen almost 10 percent, and because television had grown during this time, some observers blamed it for the box office decline. Statistical evidence, however, told a different story. In 1948 there were only a few hundred thousand television sets in homes, while the weekly attendance at theaters had dropped by 12 million tickets a week.[30] Those numbers would indicate that television had only a slight influence on the theatrical box office, but television provided an easy scapegoat for what were very complex problems.

Some studio heads who had close ties with the nascent television industry looked to the potential the new industry held for their businesses. For example, Ned Depinet, president of RKO from 1942 to 1952, recalled that David Sarnoff, having previously owned a controlling interest in RKO, "sent me over a television set for my office, and said, 'Ned, watch this. We have to watch the development of this thing.' And he sent me one for my home so I could keep informed. I have been looking at television since it started."[31] Sarnoff and RCA owned a controlling interest in RKO until 1939, and Sarnoff, the Rockefellers, and Floyd Odlum each owned a very large interest in RKO for many years after 1939.[32] Spyros Skouras, president of Fox from 1942 to 1962, had an intense interest in television since 1936 and "spent a great deal of time and effort in studying and working with the problem."[33] Herbert Yates, the president of Republic Studios, remembered that as early as the period between 1937 and 1940, "I was pretty close to the companies that were promoting [television]. . . . There was a good deal said about it among members of the industry and general opinion was, if I remember correctly, that it would very likely be a factor in the entertainment business."[34] Yates recalled talking "many times" to Deke Ailsworth at NBC about "the future of television as he saw it."[35] Then, when television began its commercial development in 1947 and 1948, members of the film industry more seriously investigated ways to gain a foothold in television. For example, Yates asked Morton Scott, vice president and general manager of Hollywood Television Service, a subsidiary of Republic Studios, to start familiarizing himself with the television industry so that "when the time came for Republic to get into the industry, they wanted [Scott] to be an expert on the subject."[36] Fox also made their interest in television official when, in 1947, their head of television, Peter G. Levathes, was "instructed by management to devise ways and means by which Twentieth Century-Fox could get into the television business."[37]

By 1948 television had become a central topic of conversation for the film industry both in public and in private. Ned Depinet, president of RKO, recalled that the MPPDA had regularly discussed plans to obtain television channels from the FCC, particularly for theater television. He explained, "We didn't know but what the day might come when you would broadcast a picture into a theatre onto the screen and eliminate the necessity of having a booth and an operator. Then we talked of augmenting the entertainment in the theatre, showing a picture and also some sort of a live performance that could be broadcast [on television]."[38] Depinet's statement reflected the film industry's early view of television as a tool to be used in service of film, and the idea to use the television broadcast of feature films into theaters to eliminate the theater booth and operators also indicated a desire to phase out the costly distribution of film prints to theaters, which studios finally accomplished with the introduction of digital technologies a little more than a half century later. However, that thinking also reflected the studios' view of television as a technology that could serve the film industry. For example, Jesse Lasky, one of the founders of Paramount and another early proponent of television, argued in 1948 that "the picture industry better get very close with television soon, somewhere, somehow." He saw television as a medium for publicizing new stars and films, and said that film, "instead of viewing video as an enemy, should consider it an adjunct."[39] Lasky's prediction eventually proved correct, and television became the most effective way to promote theatrical feature films. In September 1949, Eric Johnston, president of the Motion Picture Association of America (MPAA), attempted to buoy the spirits of the exhibitors through an address to the annual Theatre Owners of America (TOA) convention: "Nobody knows where this sprawling young giant is going, but I do know this: We as an industry aren't going to be caught short by television. We feel honestly and deeply that the motion picture industry has so much to contribute to the usefulness of television in its service to the public. The motion picture theater is already a great center of service to the community. Television would immensely expand the horizon of the community theater. It would add a new dimension. Television and motion picture exhibition are natural allies. And we intend to see that they become allies."[40] That year, the MPPDA's new television committee approved a continuing study of television as it affected the film industry, and authorized a paid aide who worked full time on the association's television activities.[41] In addition to surveys conducted by different groups in the film industry that tried to identify the effect of television on the box office, other investigations were done to ascertain the best use of film on television. In 1949, for example, Fox had their television department investigate the prices being paid for feature films, but they decided that "prices were so pitifully low that it would be improper for [Skouras] as a trustee of his stockholders' money or his stockholders' assets to toss Twentieth Century-Fox' tremendously valuable film library to the television market."[42]

Warner Bros. also held firm against releasing their films to television and publicly claimed that they had taken that position with their theaters in mind. In order to refute stories to the contrary, in July 1950 Jack Warner announced at a Warner Bros. sales meeting, "And, for the benefit of a few irresponsible gossips, I want to say that the only screens which will carry Warner Bros. productions will be the screens of motion picture theatres the world over."[43] The theaters were incredibly important to the studios because over 85 percent of their revenues were derived from theatrical exhibition, and the economic stability of that source of income was vital. As long as the financial benefits of television remained uncertain, the studios were not willing to risk their box office grosses on the bet that television might someday provide as much revenue as the theaters.[44]

United Artists (U.A.) was not burdened by the ownership of theaters, but they held the other studios' position against releasing their films to television. They did, however, hedge their bets a bit. In March 1949, Myron Blank and Stan Prenosil of the TOA met with Paul Lazarus at U.A. to discuss the exhibitors' concerns regarding the competition of 16mm films with established 35mm theaters. Lazarus told Blank and Prenosil that "a contract was being negotiated with Film Classics which would grant that company a franchise for exclusive distribution of U.A.'s 16mm films but with U.A. retaining control of the prints and not allowing them to be shown in competition with established theatres."[45] Lazarus pointed out, however, that this would apply only to future product, as many of their older films had already been sold outright with no strings attached. U.A. had also developed a policy of not selling any motion picture films to television while the films were still in theatrical distribution. However, the company retained its right to sell other films not in theatrical distribution to television, and they did not want to be restricted by any agreement to keep their product off television for any specified length of time.[46]

STUDIOS SET THEIR SIGHTS ON TELEVISION STATIONS

One of the studios' first strategies was to own television stations, and before the FCC instituted its freeze, many studios had submitted applications for station licenses. This was a natural fit because they could use the stations as another exhibition outlet for their existing libraries, and they had the labor, physical resources, and production experience to create original content for television. In the early 1940s, Barney Balaban, then president of Paramount Pictures, and John Balaban, his brother, then secretary-treasurer of the Balaban & Katz theater circuit, announced that Balaban & Katz was going to pioneer in the television medium just as they had in theaters, and Balaban & Katz owned one of the first television stations, WBKB, in Chicago.[47] By 1944 they owned and operated two stations, and in order to provide content for those stations, they established the New York Film Procurement Office to purchase film for broadcast.[48] By June 1948, Paramount, Fox, . and Warner Bros. had applied to the FCC to purchase or build television stations across the United States.[49] In all these cases, the FCC contacted the DOJ as to their opinion of the qualifications of the studios to hold broadcast licenses, particularly as they related to the Supreme Court's decision in the *Paramount* antitrust case.[50] In that case, the studios were found guilty of violating antitrust laws and restraining trade by the power they wielded as vertically integrated studios that functioned as an oligopoly. One of the primary remedies the studios agreed to in their consent decrees was that they would divest themselves of their ownership of their theaters. The DOJ and FCC were concerned that in light of the studios' impending divorcement from their theaters, they would simply substitute television stations for theaters and continue their oligopolistic behaviors via the new technology. When Gael Sullivan, executive director of the TOA, inquired to Wayne Coy, chairman of the FCC, about members of the film industry owning television stations, Coy responded, "The Commission has no policy against the issuance of television permits or licenses to motion picture exhibitors, provided they are legally, financially, technically and otherwise qualified to become broadcast licensees. However, I am sure you are aware of the fact that the Commission is considering the questions raised by the court decisions involving violation of the antitrust laws by certain motion picture exhibitors."[51] Coy clearly implied that the members of the film industry would have an uphill battle in terms of gaining approval for television stations, and as a result, many studios, including Fox and Warner Bros., withdrew their applications for stations.

TV's GAPING MAW

Meanwhile, the television industry desperately needed content to fill their broadcast hours, and feature films provided a natural solution. As Morton Scott, vice president and general manager of Hollywood Television Service, explained, "The running of pictures is probably about as cheap a way for a station to stay on the air as anything else they could use. . . . They have to stay on the air a certain number of hours every day."[52] That was the case from the earliest days of television, and in 1944, Sidney N. Strotz, vice president in charge of the Western Division for NBC, said, "I don't think there is enough talent in the world to supply the demand that would have to be met if all television entertainment were put on a live basis. Rehearsal hours, memorizing lines and staging live productions, to say nothing of the mechanical factors like sets and scenery, would make it a formidable if not impossible problem."[53] To help meet their need for content, stations and networks looked to Hollywood.

The relationship between the networks and stations and the difference between independent, affiliate, and owned and operated stations determined their attitudes toward the use of feature films on television. The networks preferred live programming because it made the network the primary source of higher-quality content, which syndicators and independent producers and distributors had difficulty competing with. Networks offered larger, national audiences to advertisers, who then provided higher budgets for network programs. By offering higher-quality live programming, the networks strengthened their ties with their affiliates, and, as Michele Hilmes has argued, "it behooved the networks to promote the superior value of live over recorded programming because the ability to transmit live belonged to the networks and to the networks alone."[54] Live television also differentiated the medium from film, and networks used their live programming and "quality" anthology series as evidence for the FCC of their service of the public interest.[55] Serving the public interest was a primary concern of the FCC when it came time to grant and renew broadcast licenses, and as scholar Alison Perlman explained, "The award of a broadcast license, and thus the ability to use what Congress had deemed a scarce public resource (the airwaves), ostensibly has obligated licensees to serve the public interest, as defined by U.S. regulatory agencies, in exchange for this privilege."[56] At that time, content like live programming that was unavailable elsewhere was considered to be in the public interest, whereas theatrical films that appeared in theaters and then aired on television were less so. In July 1949 it was reported that the FCC was going to "crack down" on television stations whose programming was "not entirely in the public interest." The FCC cited as particularly problematic the use of test patterns to fill airtime requirements and the repetition of feature films that had already been shown to local television audiences.[57] In many instances, however, the networks still had no choice but to use films to meet their programming needs. As Jack Van Volkenburg, head of television for CBS, explained, even though CBS preferred live programming, they would use feature films in prime time since it took them "time to build up enough programs of good enough quality to fill up the prime-time evening hours."[58] Even the major networks lost tremendous amounts of money in the early years of television as a result of producing their own live programming. The head of ABC, for example, had to invest millions of his own funds, and the corporate parents of NBC and CBS had to rely on income from other sectors of their businesses to offset the losses of the fledgling networks.[59]

If the networks struggled to produce enough live content to fill their broadcast schedules, independent and unaffiliated stations had it even worse, and they "inevitably suffered by comparison to the expensive, big-name productions sent out by the networks."[60] They had significantly less income than the networks since they had only small local audiences to offer to potential sponsors. In order to keep their licenses, however, they had to meet the FCC's minimum requirements for broadcast hours.[61] Although in later decades most television stations affiliated with networks and picked up their network's programming for their prime-time hours, during the early years of television that was not the case. The need for filmed programming was especially strong in 1947–1948 when television was expanding but the nationwide coaxial cable system had not yet linked the major markets.[62] Local stations could either produce all of their own live programming or find films to license or purchase. In such an environment, as Peter Levathes, the head of television at Fox, described, "films were usually used on a local basis. A station would buy the film and usually program it either early or late in the evening, because the network programs that came through from New York, or from Hollywood, preempted the choice time, so that the use of films was relegated to a secondary position."[63] Roswell Metzger, of the Rutrauff & Ryan Advertising Agency, explained that many stations used features to help build their audiences because "the television industry was developed on a pattern similar to the radio. . . . First lots of sustaining time on stations, stations bought features and developed features trying to peddle them, trying to get the listening audience to a size where it was a commercial entity to the advertiser, and they have gradually gotten over the hump, like they did in radio."[64] In March 1950, Frank Mullen, partner in Jerry Fairbanks Co., told the Hollywood Ad Club of "the devouring appetite of TV for filmed shows," and he argued that "Hollywood's current output of pictures would only scratch the surface."[65] In May 1950, *Variety* reported that "Eastern TV stations will buy practically everything Hollywood has to offer providing the price is right. If the cost can be kept within the range of what local and national spot advertisers can afford, orders will come through with every mail delivery."[66]

Since the major studios had not released their feature films to television, networks and stations relied on films from independent and foreign producers. Despite a limited supply, as reported in *Television* in February 1950, "about 25% of local sponsored time is film programs. Most popular are the Westerns edited to 60 minutes running time. To split the cost of sponsorship, many stations break their full length features into three 'acts' with the intermission providing space for commercials."[67] Some stations were even borrowing programming techniques from the theaters. In July 1949, for example, WJZ-TV in New York inaugurated a weekly "bargain bill" of double-feature films on Tuesdays from 7:30 P.M. to 9:30 P.M. The films were reportedly going to be "light comedies deemed suitable for summer entertainment, mainly 'B' pictures produced between 1940 and 1945."[68] Los Angeles stations in particular were heavy users of feature films, and by the end of 1950 they were forecast to spend approximately $1 million on feature films. By this time, many of the stations had exhausted the first runs of feature films that were available for television, and were in their third or fourth runs. An article in *Variety* described the demand: "No other market in the country is laying out this much coin for old footage, which dates back to 1931 and runs to 1945. Big reason for extensive use of old pictures is fact there is no cable from the east nor any connection with Frisco stations here, isolated, must supply own programming other than kinescopes fed to the four stations with web affiliations."[69] Despite the large numbers of films being shown on Los Angeles stations, Milford Fenster, film manager for television station WOR-TV in New York, which was owned at that time by General Teleradio, Inc., explained that on his station in 1950, feature films constituted only a "minor portion of station programming." When they used feature films they would air them "during segments other than what is known as Class A. In other words, they were used in what we call fringe time, early in the afternoon late at night." Class A time was the "major time," or similar to what is today known as prime time. B time was generally the hour or two before prime time, and C time included all the rest of the broadcast hours.[70] The discrepancy between Fenster's use of film and that of the stations in Los Angeles highlighted the difference between cities like Los Angeles that did not yet have network connections or easy access to kinescope recordings, and stations in cities like New York, where their physical location made it easier to rely on live network programming for their Class A time, and use films in their Class B and Class C time.

Regardless of the time of day they were broadcast, feature films earned some of the highest ratings on television. In April 1950, WPTZ in Philadelphia earned a 27.1 rating for their *Hollywood Playhouse* show, which aired feature films during the day. The station had analyzed radio ratings and found that although soap operas were successful during the day, they were too expensive for independent stations. WPTZ noticed the success of matinees at the local theaters and decided to try that model on television.[71] To find enough films to program every day of the week, WPTZ searched for a package of good-quality films at a price they could afford. Associated Artists Productions, a film distributor that had a library of films big enough to assure advertisers of a consistent supply, offered WPTZ a choice of over 200 features.[72] WPTZ waited until the number of television sets in the Philadelphia area exceeded 400,000 and offered advertisers what was at that time a unique rate setup. Six different advertisers were rotated through six different time slots in the program, so by the end of the show, each advertiser had six different brand and title identifications for the cost of a single participation advertisement.[73] The success of WPTZ's programming and their incredibly high ratings garnered a great deal of attention from both television programmers and advertisers. It reinforced the notion that feature films on television could be successful, and supported the transition to multiple sponsorship for advertisers. Although the shift in television sponsorship from single sponsors to multiple, participation, or "magazine-style" sponsorship has often been attributed to Pat Weaver and his NBC spectaculars,[74] local television stations had implemented that strategy years before the networks did.[75] The fact that local stations were early adopters of multiple sponsorship makes sense particularly in light of the fact that one of the main reasons the networks moved to participation sponsorship was to mitigate the ever-increasing costs required to produce television content. Spreading the production costs among a group opened up television advertising to a whole new range of sponsors, and that same approach could make it possible for a greater number of stations and advertisers to purchase and license feature films for television.

FOREIGN AND INDEPENDENT FILMS ON TELEVISION

Although the major studios had not made any deals for their features on television, some films made their way to television through other means. In 1946, Paul Alley, television film editor at NBC, wrote a piece for *Radio Age* wherein he explained, "Although many outstanding Hollywood features have been presented on NBC, the major film companies have not as yet released their product for television. But working through independent producers, NBC is able to present an amazingly high standard of motion picture features and short subjects."[76] Many independent producers wanted to sell or license their feature films to television in order to either make up for disappointing box office runs or simply increase their grosses, and they were able to because they were not constrained by the many contractual and legal limitations that encumbered the major studios. In March 1948, for example, Hal Roach made a deal with Regal Television Pictures Corp. of New York to license thirty-two of his films for television.[77] Then, in April 1948, WPIX, a television station owned by the *New York Daily News*, purchased the television rights to twenty-four Alexander Korda films for $125,000.[78] CBS was also reportedly close to a deal for a series of Monogram's films. The network was not sharing details, however, in fear of exhibitor resistance.[79] David Sarnoff and RCA/NBC negotiated with Arthur Rank for a ten-year deal, which would include swapping the television rights for Rank's films for RCA/NBC playing trailers for Rank films for free. In an attempt to assuage exhibitors, RCA proposed that Rank make his films available for television broadcast after an arbitrary amount of time had passed from their theatrical release dates.[80] As CBS explained to Mrs. Frank J. Lowell, of the Scarsdale Movie Council, in response to her inquiries in January 1950, most of the films on television had little, if any, theatrical value, which was a major reason they were available. Even though the films had little remaining theatrical value, the network still chose the available films with the best "entertainment value, quality of production, and quality of technique" as well as films that had the "broadest appeal to all age groups." CBS further explained, "The age limit [of the films] depends upon the producers of motion picture films who are reluctant to release pictures of recent vintage because of their theatrical value. There are other limitations imposed by contractual relations between producers and organizations like ASCAP and AFM."[81] When the CBS-TV film department got the rights to air feature films, they offered the films to their affiliates. In March 1949, for example, they offered their affiliates first-run rights in their areas to four film packages totaling eighty-two features and shorts.[82] Some still complained, though, as Pat Weaver did

in 1949, that "currently the Hollywood groups simply do not understand there is
no magic in film, that a crumbly B picture half-hour TV show will be terrible. The
fact that it's on film will not help it."[83]

FILM CONTENT AND AESTHETICS

In addition to the quality of the films, another issue was the suitability of the content and aesthetics of theatrical feature films for television's all-ages family audience. In the early years, the FCC required that when airing a motion picture on
television, the station had to announce somewhere in the introduction to the program that it was a motion picture, so that anyone who wanted to avoid the more
risqué content of feature films could change the channel.[84] Even so, in one instance,
older motion picture serials that KTLA televised drew protests from audiences who
thought the content was "too rough" for younger audiences. In response, the station decided to program more cartoons and fairy tales.[85] Many television networks
and stations relied on the fact that feature films would have had to pass through
the MPPDA's Production Code Administration (PCA) before they were granted a
theatrical release.[86] Particularly for films that had gone through the PCA's rigor-
ous screening, stations were more confident that the content would be suitable for
television's family audiences watching at home. That confidence would not apply,
however, to foreign and independent films that appeared on television without
having obtained approval by the PCA or Hays Office. The lack of a clear system of
regulatory standards led to a patchwork of censorship processes and oversight that
sprang up in the television industry. Advertisers had some say in the content if
advertising appeared with the film, and the FCC could revoke a station's license if
they showed films whose content was obscene or indecent or not deemed in the
public interest. In one instance, Harry Bannister, general manager of WWJ-TV,
Detroit, in a memo to his staff, outlined some guidelines for their programming:

> [It] must be so meticulously correct that no portion of our schedule will give
> offense in the slightest degree to anyone at any time. There must be no use of
> "blue" material or of anything susceptible to double entendre. There must be
> nothing in our schedule which will cause the lifting of an eyebrow by even the
> most strait-laced in our audience. Appearance, language, intonation, gesture—
> must all be beyond reproach. Racial comedy types must be avoided. References
> to God or religion must always be reverent. Crime and drunkenness, when used,
> must be condemned. A list of all taboos would be too lengthy. In all cases, good
> taste, propriety and the avoidance of offense must be the ultimate criteria.[87]

The censorship issues that popped up in different states and localities were remi-
niscent of the issues the film industry faced before the adoption of the MPPDA's
code for theatrical films.[88] In one case, the Pennsylvania State Board of Censors
moved to require its seal on all films aired on Pennsylvania television stations. In
response, the JWT advertising agency threatened to eliminate films entirely from
their television programs. It was a significant enough problem that five Pennsyl-

vania television stations brought a lawsuit against the Board of Censors to halt this action. John W. Reber, vice president of JWT, complained that another half dozen outside organizations imposed even greater restrictions on television content than the censor boards. Other plaintiffs in the lawsuit cited the greater costs entailed by censorship, especially if each state board insisted on showing their seal of approval. It also posed a problem in terms of how to manage the timing and placement of the censor board seals.[89] The patchwork system of television censors and audience concerns not only caused headaches for stations and networks but also led to threats of further government oversight. To head off those threats, in December 1951 the NAB instituted their Code of Practices for Television Broadcasters, which, as scholar Deborah L. Jaramillo explained in *The Television Code*, was "a fascinating yet dull document, full of the anxieties and consensus politics of the 1950s, the appeasements of a defensive commercial industry, and the standardization of quotidian business deals" that "regulated both program content and stations' dealings with advertisers."[90]

Another issue for films on television was that the aesthetic quality of films broadcast on television remained poor. For starters, screens averaged only twelve inches, and for the television broadcast of feature films most television stations used standard 16mm projection prints that had the high contrast and wide brightness range necessary for theatrical exhibition but, when used on television, resulted in empty shadows and monotonous highlights. As Robert E. Lee, a writer and producer of television, described, "We can't afford the luxury of low-key emotional lighting that has become so fashionable in motion-picture production in the past five years, because this just comes over on television like mud, and the only way it can be presented on television . . . is by completely reprinting the projecting positive and taking out and in effect producing a television-lighted film."[91] James Gordon, an engineer for Twentieth Century-Fox, presented a paper to the American Society of Cinematographers TV research committee wherein he recommended the use of 35mm low contrast, fine grain positive film for television broadcast. This type of film, he argued, would considerably improve the reproduction quality of motion pictures on television and give films on television more definition.[92] The problem, however, remained that most television stations had projection equipment for 16mm films and could not afford to equip their stations with the projectors and fireproofing necessary for the 35mm nitrate film that was common in the film industry at that time.

HOLLYWOOD'S LOCKED VAULT

Although the television networks and stations obtained feature films from independent and foreign sources, in these early years the networks did not make serious inquiries with the major studios as to the availability of their features for television. As Jack Van Volkenburg, the president of the Television Division of CBS, later explained, "We just never have solicited from the majors, because in the early days we had a very distinct feeling that if we could obtain them at all, that we just would not be able to afford the price."[93] That did not mean that television stations and advertisers never inquired with the major studios as to the availability of their films. As Peter Levathes of Fox recalled, in 1947 "they wanted films for the purpose of using them as a way of programming themselves during the early times, when they were operating at a loss, and they needed films as filler. . . . That was the spirit of most of the inquiries, and most of the discussions I had with television people, to make films available as incidental programming to the main programming that stations were offering."[94] Despite the fact that Levathes observed stations using films only as filler, he seriously investigated the amount that Fox might earn for the use of their films on television. Following those inquiries, Levathes advised Skouras to "abandon any further consideration of films for TV."[95] At that time, Fox had between 700 and 900 feature films in their vault, and they believed that they had only one chance to get the sale or licensing of them right. They thought that once television spread nationwide, they could demand more money for their films.[96]

Faced with offers they found unworthy of their feature film content, Fox dipped their toes in the television waters in the fall of 1947 by negotiating for their newsreels with the William Etsy Agency, and they eventually agreed to release their newsreels to Camel cigarettes and NBC. They packaged the content into a show, the *Camel News Caravan*. As Peter Levathes recalled, "It was the first time that films in such large quantities became available to television. We put on the air a 10-minute news presentation on film five nights a week, and this brought into play the entire international organization of Twentieth Century-Fox, involving 176 locations throughout the world that supplied film for this project."[97] The newsreels Fox provided for television differed from the ones shown in their theaters. When their camera crews filmed events around the world, they used parts of that footage in a shorter newsreel for theaters and aired a longer version on television. If, for example, the president of the United States made a speech, the theatrical version of the newsreel would contain only highlights from the speech, whereas the television version would show the speech in its entirety.[98] Fox produced the television newsreels for broadcast five days a week, and in so doing created one of the first television newscasts.[99] That Fox supplied content to television upset Fox's exhibitors, but Fox had a larger game plan. They not only wanted to earn income from television but also wanted to ingratiate themselves with the FCC since they still had applications for stations and channels pending the FCC's approval.[100]

Fox's experience with the television newsreels was ultimately negative, however, and the rumors of that bad experience made other studios reluctant to deal with television. For example, in an April 1948 memo to Jack Warner regarding Warner Bros. possible entrance into the television newsreel business, Norman Moray, short-subject sales manager for Warner Bros., explained that they should not "tie up" with one sponsor because they could end up at the mercy of that sponsor, just as Fox was with Camel. Moray continued, "The Fox people tell me that they are fighting constantly and they are not too happy with their deal. Fox's original deal provided that Camel and NBC would automatically take on the Fox Television News in every affiliated station, as rapidly as these opened up, which ultimately would bring in a pretty fair return. However, it has since developed that NBC can not control their affiliates and at the moment Fox [is] holding the bag."[101] At that time, the studios enjoyed the power they amassed in what is now known as the Classical Hollywood studio era. They controlled every aspect of their business, and entering a relationship like the one that Fox had with Camel, wherein they had to relinquish, or even share, control, sounded like a headache they neither needed nor wanted at that time. Moray's memo also makes it clear that the very different industrial structure of television versus the film industry—namely, the power of advertisers in television—and the somewhat chaotic nature of the developing television industry also made the film studios uncomfortable.

While some leaders in the film industry worked to take advantage of television, others were determined to avoid the new medium because they saw it as the source of their economic woes. Jack Warner was one of the staunchest critics of television, and in a telegram he wrote in March 1948 to Samuel Schneider at Warner Bros., he made it clear that he had no interest in selling his films to television, regardless of the price: "Policy we have adopted here at studio and you do same at home office re television is that we will not at any time give any of our productions shorts cartoons or features to be used for television broadcast irrespective of price they are willing to pay for same. Please be sure this adhered to unless contrary decision made by HM or myself."[102] A few years later, in 1955, Warner attempted to clarify his true intention behind that telegram by citing the decline in box office revenue Warner Bros. experienced at that time. He attributed that drop to the "serious inroads" made by television, and he further explained, "People were asking for television what they call clips from the films, scenes from our pictures, or pictures themselves, in one form or another, short subjects, and so forth, that they could run on television, and . . . we came to the conclusion that a wire like that was necessary to bring a halt, and stop the exhibition of Warner's products on television at that time, rather than injure our income, which it had."[103] Although many of the studios balked at what they considered low prices offered for their films, by the end of 1948, Wayne Coy, the head of the FCC, remained optimistic about television's ability to pay higher prices for Hollywood's features. As he declared to the TOA's national convention, much to the theater owners' dismay, "Everyone knows that television is going to get the very best and the most movies it can buy. Whether its advertiser-sponsors can ever afford the first-run feature films of today remains to be seen. Advertising over television is going to be extraordinarily effective. It should be able to pay accordingly."[104]

STUDIOS' TV SUBSIDIARIES

Another strategy some studios adopted was to create a subsidiary for their television business, and Columbia established one of the first and longest-running subsidiaries in Screen Gems. Columbia originally started Screen Gems not to handle their television business but to handle their 16mm business, which was a format they began using in 1944. They entered the field more seriously in 1948 and 1949 and often distributed their 16mm films to nontheatrical locations such as schools, hospitals, and the military. The format became the default for television largely because it was safer than the flammable 35mm nitrate film in use at the time.[105] That Screen Gems initially focused on 16mm and was later considered a natural fit to take over Columbia's television business shows how connected those two fields were in the minds of the film industry during this period.

In early 1949, Columbia asked Ralph Morris Cohn, son of Jack Cohn and nephew of Harry Cohn, to examine the possibility of buying television stations, making films for television, and licensing their library to television.[106] He presented a report to Columbia that proscribed three phases: (1) develop technical knowledge about production for television by making television commercials, (2) determine how to make Columbia's library of theatrical product more valuable in television, and (3) subsequently, produce programs exclusively for television.[107] Columbia liked Cohn's report and asked him to run Screen Gems in order to implement the plan.[108] Cohn's report found that television stations were too expensive, so Columbia decided not to acquire any.[109] They also decided against selling or licensing their feature films to television because, as Cohn argued, "exhibitor reaction would be extremely unfavorable."[110] When asked whether they used a different name, Screen Gems, to hide from exhibitors the fact that Columbia was pursuing business in television, Cohn explained, "That was considered. But obviously, since we were quite freely identifying ourselves with Columbia Pictures, and there was no secret about it, and every trade paper that carried any news of our activities identified us as such—if this were to have been done for purposes of subterfuge, it would have been a weak and foolish subterfuge."[111] Cohn later explained that he had not recommended that they refuse to sell their films to television, but rather "that to sell motion pictures in the form in which they were originally made and released to television was a shortsighted policy which would not create the kind of values for Columbia that I believe should be created in terms of a long-range program for television. . . . I also recommended the creation of forewords, beginnings, middles, and ends to be applied to these pictures. New production which would be made to fit these pictures within a framework, so that a property would be created, rather than just the use of old movies on television."[112] Cohn had determined that television and theatrical films were different art forms, and testifying in 1955, Cohn explained his reasoning as based on the distinct qualities of the two mediums—for example, television screens were significantly smaller than theater screens, and feature films were shot with the larger theater screens in mind. Another point was an early articulation of John Ellis's glance theory, which contends that the viewing conditions in the home are very different from those in the theater.[113] Cohn argued, "The audience approach to the television entertainment is considerably different from the audience approach to motion pictures. The sympatic response of a person sitting back in a darkened hall, with other people absorbed by the skill of the actors and what is going on is completely different from the response of a person sitting in the living room, free to go to the kitchen or the bathroom, free to talk without disturbing anyone else."[114] For those reasons, Cohn concluded that content produced for television had to be "materially different" than theatrical content. Cohn's observations also echo William Boddy's description of the critical debates about the distinct natures of live and filmed programming on early television. As Boddy noted, "The opposition between film's 'feel of the past' and the immediacy of live television created different putative audience paradigms for film and live programs, in which viewers of a live performance were seen as more highly involved than those of film programs."[115] As Pat Weaver, an executive at NBC's television operations from 1949 to 1955, argued, "Television is not movies. It is show business in the living room."[116] Ultimately, their conclusions were the same: the nature of filmed and live programming and the audience's experience of each were materially different and required producers to approach each differently.

As a result, instead of selling or licensing their film library to television, Columbia decided to exploit their older feature films by making them into "original" films for television. They planned to rework the older features by adding new material, and thereby make quality television programs at a low cost.[117] But in order to rework their older films for television, they had to make sure that they owned the rights to do so.[118] Cohn identified two westerns and two one-reel cartoons for which the rights were clear, and he proceeded to adapt them for television as a trial run. They cut the films down to twenty-two minutes each, and filmed a beginning, middle, and end to serve as a framework that would create a "property." As Cohn later recalled, "What we had hoped to do was to build something of continuity, because in my explorations in television and the advertising field, I learned that one thing that advertisers looked for, and which has a great value to them, is the idea of continuity. So that if you see something this week you will come back to it next week. And this was the one ingredient that we didn't feel that the movies had, as such, and we felt that we could enhance their value to a point where we could get more money for them."[119] In the end, Cohn concluded that his plan was only a "beautiful dream," because in test screenings with broadcasters, advertisers, and advertising agencies, they found that the cost of making the test films far exceeded the value they created.[120] So, in 1950, they abandoned the project of reworking their older films for television, and Columbia's board of directors appointed a committee to revisit the possibility of releasing their feature films to television. They had, since 1949, asked for continuous reports from Screen Gems on the subject, and in a signal that there were internal disagreements, the board wanted this committee to check those reports for accuracy. Eventually, after a "thorough review and investigation," the committee confirmed Cohn's earlier conclusions against releasing their older films to television at that time.[121]

THE COUNCIL OF MOTION PICTURE ORGANIZATIONS

Although Twentieth Century-Fox ran a two-page ad in *Variety* in May 1950 proclaiming, "Business is Better Than Ever!," as Herbert Yates, president of Republic, recalled, "It was in '49 and '50 when we found we were losing business. I was afraid to go on television and aggravate exhibitors."[122] Spyros Skouras felt the downturn more personally and described television's impact as causing the demise of over 6,000 theaters in a three-year period. He explained, "During this period I received letters from the Middle West, from many old friends who lost their theatres. People that owned two and three theatres. Their families and their children, that was their life, that was their career, and their theatres closed. Now, that was a tremendous impact of television on the motion picture industry."[123] Even though exhibition was divorcing from production and distribution, Skouras's passionate tale of the exhibitors' woes demonstrated that the ties between the different segments of the industry remained strong. The Warner brothers, for example, were leaving their theaters in the hands of one of the brothers, and Charles Skouras, the head of National Theatres, was Spyros Skouras's brother. Those close ties would mean that many of the studios resisted actions that might harm the theaters—including releasing feature films to television. This was not the case for all of the studios, however. At the end of 1950, RKO Radio Pictures' substantial circuit of about one hundred first-run theaters was put in a separate company.[124] Ned Depinet, then president of RKO, explained that RKO considered the effect of furnishing their films to television on the box office of their own theater chain a "very important factor up to the end of 1950 when the theatres were placed in another company and we had nothing whatsoever to do with them. But up to that time it was a very important factor."[125] That did not mean, however, that RKO did not care about the theatrical box office, and in fact, Depinet still claimed to be unwilling to gamble their theatrical revenue for what they could make in television.[126]

Regardless of family ties, declarations of loyalty, or whether the studios and their theaters had officially divorced, a great deal of unrest existed in the industry, which was exacerbated by the financial difficulties they faced. Spyros Skouras observed of the intra-industry discord, "Many times we have seen producers disparaging Hollywood and speaking unfavorably of their competitors or rival productions. Many times we have heard exhibitors speaking ill of their brother exhibitors across the street. This self destructive criticism by producer, exhibitor and distributor has done more to hurt us than all outside criticism."[127] Skouras also noticed the "avalanche of lawsuits" brought by exhibitors against distributors. He observed, "These suits have become so numerous and the amounts involved so vast, that if something constructive is not done by each branch of the industry, working in cooperation with each other branch, to solve this problem, there is not going to be anything left for any of us."[128]

In 1949, steps were taken to broker peace, and COMPO was organized as an "all-industry public relations body embracing all segments from production and distribution through exhibition. . . . For the first time, with a judicious, forward-thinking program spearheaded by Ned Depinet, the motion picture industry has an instrument for its common weal."[129] The organization was formed, as Depinet, acting president of COMPO, recalled, "because business was not too good."[130] The purpose of the organization was "to fight discriminatory entertainment taxes, to plan a comprehensive public relations program, and to allow a free exchange of ideas among the various elements of the motion picture world."[131] This was one of the few moments in film history when virtually every member of the industry, from unions to studios to exhibitors, came together to overcome the challenges they faced. The organization included members from all areas, including production, distribution, exhibition, the unions, and even the trade press. They were a professional cultural effort to construct a common film identity on a larger scale, but they also focused on more specific concerns that affected multiple areas of the film industry.[132] At a COMPO meeting in August 1949 in Chicago, Arthur Lockwood, president of the TOA, remarked, "The mere fact of our presence here is in itself an indication of the desire of all of us to improve the relations among ourselves and with the public which we serve."[133] The range of topics that COMPO expected to handle was illustrated in the points Lockwood proposed on behalf of the TOA as issues for discussion: a campaign for eliminating admission taxes, a united front against restrictive legislation such as censorship, the more extensive use of television trailers to advertise feature films, the elimination of unfair competition and the granting of special favors to other forms of entertainment (i.e., television), the necessity of an all-industry public relations program, the development of a plan to increase Americans' movie-going habits, and establishing a system to provide the industry with accurate information to repel legislative attacks.[134] When COMPO's executive board reconvened in New York City in August 1950, they commissioned what they called "Project Box-Office" in order to "find out why our industry is getting less and less of America's amusement dollar, why our box office has not reflected the increase in population in recent years, and why attendance is off."[135] The committee recommended that they pay particular attention to an analysis of the effects of TV. They believed that continuing studies of television would provide the industry with "bench marks" so that an intelligent appraisal of trends could be made from future studies.[136]

In late July 1951, COMPO held a three-day meeting at the Beverly Hills Hotel. Spyros Skouras was unable to attend the meeting, but a telegram he sent was read to those in attendance: "The COMPO seminar marks the first time that men of production, distribution, exhibition and advertising departments have met together in the history of our industry, and to me there is no meeting that has greater validity and greater opportunity to unify all elements to promote welfare of our business. The need has never been as great as it is today, because all through the country there is better public and press attitude being shown towards motion pictures. Now is the time to strike and get the benefit of this improved state of mind."[137] It was a closed-door meeting, but digests of the talks were made available to reporters. The secrecy was intended to prevent any "dirty linen from being washed out in public," a delegate explained.[138] COMPO did, however, make an audio recording of the proceedings, and from those transcripts, and the testimony given later by those in attendance, a clear picture of the events and discussion that took place at the conference emerges.

Representatives from many parts of the film industry attended, including exhibitors, producers, writers, and directors, and the conversations covered a wide range of concerns. As B. B. Kahane later recalled, the meeting was convened because business was "quite bad." A "dozen or more" subjects were on the agenda, which included advertising, the quality of films being produced, and television.[139] As Ned Depinet later testified, the meeting "was an effort on the part of all units in this industry to find ways and means to protect ourselves from unfavorable publicity, from confiscatory taxation, from censorship. We wanted to build up good will, we wanted to stay in business."[140] The conference organizers dedicated a full day to the discussion of television. Sidney Meyers of Wometco Theatres in Florida and Ronald Reagan, who was the head of SAG at the time, were co-chairmen.[141] In his opening comments, Reagan attempted to inject some pragmatism and levity into the proceedings, saying, "Regarding the greatest menace which television has to offer, which is the fact that it is free, and it is in the home, I still can't help but realize that there is a kitchen in every house built in America, and restaurants are still doing a hell of a business."[142] Although Reagan's joke may have gotten a laugh, the mood changed when the exhibitors took the microphone.[143]

The exhibitors' statements generally fell into one of two categories. Some of them thought that television, like radio before it, would contribute to the success of films in the theaters. Others thought that actors appearing on television would negatively affect the value of motion picture stars in theatrical films.[144] As a moderator, and in the midst of the expressions of dire concern, Reagan again attempted some optimism, saying, "Television has more problems to worry about than we do. . . . Because the best effort they can put forth on a program on the biggest television shows still cannot command a sizable majority of audience against the ancient, old and cheap motion pictures that they are able to secure for television showing. So we're worrying about this great vital television, which, like radio when it was a novelty, has made inroads, and yet we are worrying about competition which is coming from the worst and the oldest of our product as being the best thing that television can offer."[145] When Fred Schwartz of Metropolitan Theatres in New York took the microphone, he noted the growing tendency of distributors and producers to release their films to television. He continued: "Up to this particular point only the old pictures, really old pictures have been released, but the pressure mounts and there is talk of Republic and there is talk of Monogram, and other distributors have mentioned to us that if they go the way of television it will be difficult for them to resist, so in exhibition circles there is naturally a great deal of concern about being forced to compete with motion pictures when those motion pictures are being served for nothing into the home and we have to charge for them."[146] Schwartz acknowledged that "marginal" producers might be more tempted to sell their films to television to "recoup a quick dollar," and clarified that his remarks were not intended for them. He also argued that releasing feature films to television would harm the overall value of feature films because of the experience of watching television in the home. Films, he argued, were "carefully nurtured" and deserved to be "carefully exhibited." He described watching a feature film on television at home as an experience where "the man has to go in every once in a while and maybe diaper the baby or his wife is bothering him about something here and the doorbell rings, the telephone rings. It's not conducive to enjoying the picture and he doesn't blame it on his surroundings, he just says, 'Well, the pictures are no good,' and if he's part of the lost audience you have a hell of a time getting him."[147]

Finally, Rotus Harvey, an owner of theaters in California, interjected and said, "I have heard enough about the pros and cons about television, let's find out what the Hollywood producers are going to do about it."[148] Y. Frank Freeman from Paramount was the first of the producers to respond. He explained:

> The two mediums have got to develop in their own way, separate and apart. I do not believe that the personality who devotes himself to television can ever succeed in motion pictures if he continues his services on television. I do not believe that the personality who devotes his time and effort to motion pictures can ever go on television, . . . and succeed in motion pictures. He so dilutes himself with the public that his peculiar talent or her peculiar talent in the motion picture will have been destroyed, and for that reason . . . we are going to devote our time and talents to the making of motion pictures for theatre exhibition.[149]

Freeman's statements received enthusiastic applause, and he later explained that he could not release feature films "for dollars to television for free showing to the public and at the same time deny to the individual who is a part of that picture the right to go dilute himself on television."[150] Freeman concluded his remarks by reassuring the exhibitors that he spoke for the majority of the people in Hollywood when he said that they would remain loyal to the exhibitors because they had built the industry along with producers and distributors into the "greatest industry the world has ever known."[151]

B. B. Kahane of Columbia took the stage next and explained that the theaters were his primary interest.[152] He hedged his bets a bit, however, and reasoned that "obviously no company or no individual representing a business can make a statement that never will we go into the television field. I can say, though, that in the foreseeable future there is no plan, no intention of any kind for our company to get into the production of pictures except for theatres, primarily."[153] The exhibitors disapproved loudly, and Kahane attempted to reassure them by saying, "No, no, our business is the making of motion pictures and we have no thought or intention, as I said, of making pictures for television."[154] Creighton "C. J." Tevlin held the floor next on behalf of RKO. As historian Richard Jewell documented, Tevlin was an associate of Howard Hughes's and "one member of a managerial triumvirate which controlling owner Hughes had placed in charge of studio operations in 1948."[155] Tevlin opened by saying, "I'll tell you very clearly what our attitude is on television. We are violently opposed to it. I think actions speak louder than words. We do not permit any of our personalities to appear in any way connected with television. We have had very substantial offers from the sponsors from material that we own . . . but I can assure you we're thinking of nothing but straight motion picture business."[156] But as we know from RKO's ongoing negotiations over their feature films on television, Tevlin was talking out of both sides of his mouth. Ned Depinet later confirmed that duplicity when he recalled of the discussions: "[The exhibitor] has never got any assurances from me that I wouldn't sell my pictures to television if the opportunity presented itself. I have always said that for the time being we were not licensing our pictures for television, and we didn't intend to in the immediate future. That is because they never had a price worth a tinker's dam."[157]

At the conference, however, Depinet focused on ways that television could work in service of the theaters, specifically, using television to advertise theatrical feature films. Both Depinet and Tevlin tried to shift the focus of the conversation away from the threat of television and toward a discussion of the steps exhibitors could proactively take, which included advertising feature films on television. As Tevlin said, "I think the exhibitors here should not look to Hollywood entirely for the solution to this television problem. It isn't our battle. Television is in competition with theatres, with the motion picture theatre as an institution. Television isn't in competition with RKO and Metro, only indirectly, and you cannot put this burden on us, you have to get in, advertise, use every means to bring people into the theatre. . . . [If theatres] are unwilling to spend say the profit they make out of concessions [on advertising,] then they are in trouble. Hollywood will not be able to help you."[158] Tevlin's comments received some applause from the audience, but the exhibitors may not have been among those clapping. Si Fabian offered a rebuttal wherein he pointed out all of the "ballyhoo" the theaters had undertaken, such as special presentations, vaudeville, orchestras, and Bank Night. He argued, "We were always selling something in addition to the motion picture, but our primary and most important commodity was and will continue to be the motion picture."[159] Fred Schwartz then offered the producers an ultimatum: "You have to make up your mind, we believe, that you have to choose one thing or the other. We think if you play both ends to the middle, you'll be coming out on the short end of the stick in the long run."[160]

Shortly after Schwartz threw down the gauntlet, the day ended abruptly when Steve Broidy of Monogram took the microphone to explain that his company sold some of their films to television because they needed additional revenues to resolve their financial difficulties. Broidy complained that the reason he had to turn to television was that the exhibitors "didn't give him a fair break in the showing of his pictures." According to Howard McDonnell, "Immediately several theatre men got up and tried to smooth that over and talk it down, but he said the fact remained that he didn't in his opinion get a fair break, and he had to turn to television to get the extra revenue. The meeting then adjourned almost immediately."[161] With that, the conference closed without any resolution of the issue of feature films on television.[162] The exhibitors received assurances from the major producers that they were not, at least for the foreseeable future, planning to release their features to television. However, those promises often contradicted the fact that many studios had for years been investigating the possibility of releasing their features to television. The details of the conference proceedings were supposed to be confidential, and no transcripts of the talks were to be made available to the press or public. But the producers' strong statements, which they thought they were making behind closed doors to a room full of agitated exhibitors, would later return to haunt them.

SUBSCRIPTION TELEVISION

In addition to pressure from exhibitors, another reason many studios declined to release their films to television was that they believed that theater and subscription television held greater economic promise and that their feature films played an important role in those formats. For example, at the meeting of Columbia's officers in August 1951, they discussed whether to release their feature films to television, and as Ralph Cohn recalled, "We had been told a great many exciting things about subscription television, and at that time comparatively little was known about it. But we were aware of the possibility then that some of these motion pictures could conceivably have a much greater value in subscription television, and had to take that into consideration in making any decision."[163] Many film studios hung on to their libraries in the hope that they might take greater advantage of airing those films on pay television. In 1951, Paramount purchased International Telemeter, a subscription television service that functioned using a coin-to-box machine that was connected to a television set and unscrambled the signal once money was deposited into the box. It remained unclear, however, whether the FCC had jurisdiction over pay television—especially pay television that was transmitted via cable instead of the broadcast airwaves—and since the FCC had not been kind to the studios, the studios hoped the FCC did not have that jurisdiction.[164]

In the early 1950s, there were two main competitors in subscription television. The first was Skiatron's Subscriber-Vision. Skiatron had an experimental license from the FCC and awaited their approval for a trial run in 300 homes in the New York area in cooperation with station WOR-TV. In their efforts to acquire films for the test, Skiatron appealed to Eric Johnston, head of the MPAA, for help in obtaining "quality" films.[165] Johnston suggested that Skiatron contact each producer and distributor individually, and so in December 1951 Skiatron sent letters to the studios asking them to respond by January 15th with a list of what features Skiatron could expect from their companies. For example, Skiatron's letter to Barney Balaban at Paramount read as follows:

> It is for this purpose, and to prove to you and others what we already know— that in subscription television Hollywood may tap a fabulous and much-needed new source of revenue that can enlarge the movie audience to an extent undreamed of in the past—that we are appealing for your help. We need motion picture product that is either new or fairly recent, otherwise the true attraction and drawing power of these films, as expressed in the viewers' willingness to pay to see them, will not be clearly established. . . . Skiatron knows and appreciates your reluctance to circumvent the motion picture exhibitor, and we already have made it clear that we are willing to cut him in for his fair share of the profits. Many of the theatre-men reportedly are actually in favor of subscription video which, they feel, gives them a better chance to compete than free home TV.[166]

It was not the case, however, that all of the exhibitors supported subscription television, and in fact, Skiatron likely exaggerated the point to make their case. The

comments of Fred Schwartz of Metropolitan Theatres at the COMPO meeting in
1952 more closely reveal the exhibitors' true feelings:

> There is a much bigger difference between a first and subsequent run as it exists
> today than there would be in the future between the first and subsequent run if
> subscription television was the subsequent run. I wouldn't like to compete with
> a subsequent-run theatre who charged five cents, which is what it might be on a
> per-person basis, . . . where the person didn't have to get dressed up in the eve-
> ning, didn't have to go down town and didn't have to worry about parking an
> automobile, where their natural lethargy would keep them at home. I wouldn't
> like to be faced with that type of competition. I don't think any theatre can exist
> if subscription television comes into being.[167]

There were larger issues, however, with the Skiatron proposal, including the fact
that the FCC had not yet authorized the company's test.[168]

The FCC had, however, authorized a test of the Phonevision system, another
subscription television service that was owned by Zenith Radio Corporation. Since
the studios had been under pressure from both the DOJ and the FCC because they
had refused to make their films available for earlier Phonevision tests, they reluc-
tantly agreed to provide films produced between 1936 and 1948 for a test of Phonevision in Chicago that ran from January to March 1951.[169] *Fortune* described the
test as follows: "Most of the ninety films were two years old, quite a few had been
made a decade ago, and not many were of the quality that would have lured father
to the neighborhood theatre on even a hot summer's night."[170] Although the films
may not have been the studios' best, the test was still relatively successful. A survey by the National Opinion Research Center at the University of Chicago showed
that on average 7,200 *nontest* television-set owners regularly watched the scrambled films in the evening.[171] As *Fortune* observed, "Considering that they could get
nothing more than an idiotic mélange without an unscrambling device, it is easy
to guess that most of the bootleg audience symbolized both a hunger for something better than TV now offers and the frightening 'wantlessness' that character-
izes many devotees of the medium."[172] Despite *Fortune*'s low opinion of television
and its audience, the fact that over 7,000 television sets tuned in to watch a scrambled version of a feature film demonstrated the desire television audiences had to
view those films at home.

Ralph Cohn later recalled Columbia Screen Gems used their participation in
the Phonevision test as a way to learn more about the potential of subscription television. He recalled that based on the numbers in the limited test, a larger audience of 10 million households would have earned Columbia $1,650,000.[173] Cohn's
calculations, if correct, showed the potential for Phonevision to provide the studios with the revenue for their films on television that they hoped for. And actually, Phonevision was more of a competitor to broadcast television than it was to
the film industry because it would compete with advertisers for limited prime-time
viewers, and the prices that Phonevision could pay for content would potentially

be much greater than what advertisers could afford. As E. F. McDonald, the president of Zenith Radio Corporation, explained, "If only 25 percent of the existing television sets in Chicago were equipped with Phonevision, and if these Phonevision homes patronized a 9:30–11:00 program in the same percentage [13 percent] that our test audience did, the station broadcasting the service would get more net revenue than the gross time charges for these hours of all four existing Chicago television stations combined."[174] In order to move forward, however, Phonevision required the approval of the FCC, and federal attorneys were not sure whether the Communications Act would allow for stations whose programming was even partially denied to the general public except on payment of a fee. The fee itself posed a problem as it might require the FCC to regulate the fees and thereby take responsibility for the economics of television in the same way the Interstate Commerce Commission was responsible for the economics of land transportation.[175] In their Nineteenth Report and Order in 1953, the FCC outlined the questions they faced regarding subscription television. They included whether subscription television was in the public interest, legal questions such as whether it falls within the definition of "broadcasting" as defined by the Communications Act or whether it is a common carrier or other radio service, and engineering questions of where the service could fit in the already crowded radio spectrum.[176] Rather than providing answers, the FCC's statement merely identified the unresolved problems related to subscription television. Regardless of the FCC's indecision, Skiatron's Subscriber-Vision and Zenith's Phonevision continued working to move forward.[177]

By December 1953, the studios were looking into ways around third-party providers like Skiatron and Zenith and investigating subscription television for themselves. Other subscription television services relied on either phone lines or existing broadcast frequencies and were therefore subject to the FCC. Particularly since the studios witnessed the FCC dragging their feet in the Skiatron and Zenith cases, they began looking into subscription television that was transmitted into homes via cables, thereby, the studios hoped, bypassing the FCC.[178] By February 1955, the FCC had still not made a decision regarding subscription television, and they invited comments as to whether their rules should be amended to allow television stations to provide subscription service. They noted that "any such authorization involves a basic change in the American system of broadcasting and raises substantial questions of a legal, technical and policy nature."[179] By the time the comment period ended in September 1955, the FCC had received more than 25,000 formal documents, letters, and postcards. This was the largest response that the FCC had received for any case; thus, they required even more time to process the comments and decide how to proceed.[180]

Meanwhile, the theaters were fighting subscription television in all forms. The TOA's Television Committee, for example, hired a group of professional lawyers, public relations firms, professors, and researchers in early 1955 to help them in their campaign against subscription television. By October of that year, the Television

Committee reported that "newspapers from coast to coast ran our views; every trade paper was sent weekly summations on the latest polls; and television and radio programs were used as forums to present the facts. And wherever the facts were presented, our position became stronger and stronger."[181] Members of the committee debated people from Zenith on television and radio shows and engaged in letter-writing campaigns to the FCC and Congress. They believed that through those efforts they had turned the tide against subscription television.[182] They may have been correct, at least in part, because by the end of 1955, the FCC had not granted any channels for Zenith's or Skiatron's subscription television service, and the studios had been stymied by the fact that they had been unable to make subscription television via cables profitable. AT&T controlled the existing cable infrastructure, and they were willing to lease those cables to the studios, but only at exorbitant rates. Only decades later, with the introduction of satellite technologies that enabled the large-scale adoption of cable television, would subscription television in the form the studios envisioned become a reality.

Just as the law played a fundamental role in shaping the media industries and their content, so too did governmental agencies' policies regarding the media. Not only did the FCC make decisions that affected the film industry by thwarting their aspirations of television station ownership, but the commission's actions in the imposition and lifting of the "freeze" significantly affected the growth of the television industry and thereby the release of feature films to television. Even something as seemingly innocuous as the FCC's rules as to the minimum number of hours of programming a station had to broadcast every day played an important role in the issue of feature films on television, because in order to meet those minimums, stations had to find content they could afford and that had already been produced elsewhere. Feature films were one of the best solutions to that challenge. Just as the FCC's decisions today regarding net neutrality will largely determine the future of media via the internet, so too did their decisions in this early period of television determine the course of that medium.

Ultimately, the behaviors of industrial organizations like COMPO and the MPPDA illustrated scholar William Lafferty's observation that "rather than springing from some fit of pique over the apparent ascendancy of television as the nation's most popular entertainment medium, the film industry's policies and attitudes concerning the broadcast potential of its feature film libraries arose from the most pragmatic factors, determined by shifting economic patterns within the film and television industries, the evolving programming policies of the networks and, ultimately, the challenge presented by new communication technologies such as videocassettes and cable television."[183] While new technologies can introduce opportunities for industrial change, public and private decision-making about how the industry will or will not utilize that change greatly influences the ways that the technologies are adopted. The question of the value of content in one medium versus another is central to this process of convergence, and it would take years for the film and television industry executives and laborers to get on the same page as to the value of their feature film work in television. The media industries, their economic structures, and their regulation by forces both internal and external all determine what films appear on television when, why, and how. But those questions are also largely determined by audiences and the ways in which they interact with any new medium or technology. In this case, the role of the audience and the changing nature of exhibition in the mid-twentieth century played a significant role in the struggle over feature films on television.

CHAPTER 2

EXHIBITION, AUDIENCES, AND MEDIA CONSUMPTION

At the heart of disruption is a change not only in how something is made but also, crucially, in how it is consumed by users or audiences. Today, we see this in people moving from watching films in theaters and broadcast on their TVs to streaming media on a range of devices often while on the go; and the linear flow of legacy film and television programming has shifted to à la carte curation via apps and Over-the-Top services, which bypass traditional cable, broadcast, and satellite platforms to distribute content directly to audiences. Similarly, in the late 1940s and early 1950s, disruptions related to shifts in the media industry, technology, and regulation happened alongside changes related to exhibition and the consumption of media. As scholar Lynn Spigel argued in *Make Room for TV*, during the years following World War II, "the primary site of exhibition for spectator amusements was transferred from the public space of the movie theater to the private space of the home. . . . Between 1948 and 1955, television was installed in nearly two-thirds of the nation's homes."[1] As Spigel meticulously documented, "advertisements for television variously referred to the 'home theater,' the 'family theater,' the 'video theater,' the 'chairside theater,' the 'living room theater,' and so forth. A 1953 Emerson ad went one step further by showing an oversized television set that appears on a movie theater stage as a full house views the enormous video screen. The caption reads, 'Now! A TV picture so clear, so sharp . . . you'll think you're at the movies.'"[2] That kind of rhetoric illustrated the shifting patterns of audience behaviors. It drew on the audience's familiarity with the theatrical experience and conflated the movie theater with watching television in your living room, which might have been effective at selling sets, but also drove theater owners to harden their stance against the release of Hollywood's films to television.

In 1950, as television made its way into American homes, different factions of the industry prophesied an imminent breaking point between film producers, exhibitors, and television. The TOA was one of the largest associations of theater owners in the United States, and that year Gael Sullivan warned in a letter to TOA members, "We are fast approaching the crossroads in the relationship of television

46

to the Motion Picture Industry."[3] *Variety* reported that a "top industry figure," who wished to remain anonymous, had speculated that a "showdown between exhibitors and motion picture producers over television will come inside of the next 12 months." The article concluded saying, "Sooner or later, one of the majors will break loose and peddle its own old product to video sources. Once this happens, the dam will break wide open and the battle between exhibs and distributors will be on in full force."[4] Although this suggested that the studios worked together in a common front against television, as we saw in chapter 1, they were all engaged in their own investigations and posturing to gain the most financial advantage from their feature films on television as possible.

The erosion, whether real or imagined, of theater audiences as a result of the introduction of television was a serious concern to the studios, but even more so to the theater owners themselves. This anxiety was not new, however, and had plagued many theater owners since the introduction of radio. As Michele Hilmes outlined in *Hollywood and Broadcasting*, when Hollywood studios became more involved in radio production in the 1920s and 1930s, exhibitors' complaints intensified.[5] Hilmes argued, "Throughout the history of film industry participation in radio, and later television, broadcasting, it is invariably the exhibitors who have the least to gain and the most to lose by this sort of experimentation."[6] In 1939, the Hays office of the MPPDA created a report on television for the studios that argued that of all the branches in the film industry affected by television, the exhibitors would be affected the most.[7] Feature films on television was a case study in the pattern that Hilmes outlined: "It is the production-distribution forces that, historically, have had the more roving eye, being less firmly wedded to theatres as their only outlet than the exhibitors who depend on film as their sole source of profits."[8] We must also bear in mind Janet Staiger's argument that "the history of the alliances [in Hollywood] is one of combination and disintegration as each member calculates what policy will yield optimum profits."[9] As a result, "it is difficult to generalize motives for actions across large interest groups; each group may contain elements within it that, often because of local legal or business circumstances, may act in ways dissimilar with, or even contradictory to, goals of affiliated or parent organizations."[10] Exhibitors, perhaps more than any other segment of the industry, are prone to a difference of opinion, and the inability to coalesce behind one singular plan contributed to their difficulties. They faced challenges on a number of fronts, and ultimately, for all segments of the film and television industries, one of the central, but often overlooked, challenges of the time was determining exactly who their audience was, and how best to serve them.

THE DECLINING BOX OFFICE

While more money poured into television's coffers via set sales and increased ad spending, the theatrical box office continued to drop. Television sets in use had increased from 200,000 in 1948 to about 4 million by 1950. However, the weekly theater attendance had fallen by 6 million, and in total, between 1946 and 1954, motion picture attendance declined from 4.127 billion to 2.52 billion.[11] Those numbers threw further doubt on television being solely responsible for the decline in theater attendance, but television continued to draw much of the blame. Ned Depinet complained that the "box office has already gone down from television competition. The pictures that are on television right now are hurting us very severely."[12] On his recent trip around the world to promote CinemaScope, Spyros Skouras observed that "where there is no television the attendance of theatres is as great as was in the United States during the years of 1946 to 1948. Where is television, for instance, where it has made its appearance, as presently in the United Kingdom, the attendance has declined. If it was not for the television, . . . the motion picture industry today would be equally as prosperous as other great American industries."[13] Although Skouras had reportedly seen those conditions for himself, the data on the effect of television on the theatrical box office was still a point of contention. As Mitchell Wolfson, chairman of the TOA's Television Committee, acknowledged, "You can hear and read all sorts of opinions about what television broadcasting has already done to motion picture attendance. It is hard to rely on the many polls and statistics, since they so often appear in conflict."[14] The drop in theater attendance, even if only partially due to the influence of television, made exhibitors nervous and increasingly territorial, and their new competitor, television, drew most of their ire. Any suggestion of television encroaching on the theaters' domain by broadcasting feature films was met with increasing hostility.

In the late 1940s, one of the biggest changes to affect the film industry, and theaters in particular, happened as a result of the antitrust case *U.S. v. Paramount Pictures, Inc., et al.* Until the Supreme Court's decision in that case, and even for years after, the studios remained vertically integrated, which meant that the theaters were not simply important sources of revenue for the studios; they were owned by the studios. Even though the antitrust case had initially gotten its start in the 1930s in response to theater owners' complaints about the studios' anticompetitive behaviors, by 1948, when the case was decided against the studios, many theater owners began to regret their role in the case.[15] After the studios sold many of their theaters and changed their distribution practices, exhibitors saw their box office revenue steadily decline, and they faced the threat of television. By that point, many theater owners were less happy with the prospect of divorcement from the studios than they were with the vertically integrated system they had complained about earlier. For example, in September 1948, Herman M. Levy, the TOA's general counsel, presented a report at the association's annual convention wherein he complained about the outcome of the *Paramount* antitrust case: "These are some of the well nigh disastrous results that have come from that decision: competitive bidding, the loss or splitting of treasured runs, the end of the 'closed' situation, the upheaval of clearance, the restriction against distributors using past relationship as an element in doing business with exhibitors, the possible body blow to buying and booking combines, etc."[16] In an issue of *Daily Variety* from May 1948, editor Arthur Ungar published "Keep Step or Fall Out," wherein he warned the film industry to find ways to work with television. He even suggested that the studios look at the divorcement from their theaters as an opportunity to become more active in television.[17] Postdivorce, the studios' relationship with the theaters would significantly change, but the studios continued their allegiance to theaters that remained their primary source of product and thereby income. In fact, one of the central reasons the studios claimed that they kept their feature films from television was to protect the theaters' financial well-being. That may have been true, but it was also the case that as long as the theaters remained subsidiaries of the studios, the studios had even greater interest in ensuring a robust income for the theaters. If the studios, however, were divorced from their theaters, it could level the playing field somewhat for the two sites of exhibition: theaters and television.

Fox was one of the first studios to separate from their theaters, and by the end of September 1952, they had officially divorced their production and exhibition businesses. Spyros Skouras, Darryl Zanuck, and Joseph Schenck remained with the production company, while Charles Skouras took over the newly independent National Theatres, and George Skouras took over the Metropolitan Playhouses, United Artists Theaters, and Skouras Bros. Theaters. Spyros Skouras kept his shares of Skouras Bros. Theaters but put them in a blind trust, which meant that a third party took over day-to-day management of business related to the shares in order to avoid any conflict of interest.[18] This kind of division of the company's assets was commonly adopted by the studios, and the theater chains often remained unofficially tied to production and distribution through the close, and often familial, relationships between the heads of the companies, which contributed to the allegiance that studios often felt toward exhibitors.

Regardless of their divorcement, the theaters remained incredibly important to the studios because, as Columbia argued in 1955, over 85 percent of their revenues were derived from theatrical exhibition, and the economic stability of that source of income was of the utmost importance.[19] In May 1948, Barney Balaban, president of Paramount, told *Daily Variety* that Paramount had no intention of offering their old films to television either for licensing or for sale. He said that even though the television networks had expressed a desire for those films, the interests of the exhibitors were Paramount's first concern, and he believed that the current reissue value of their films "far outweighed" what they could make from television.[20] Jack Warner echoed Balaban's reservations when he testified in 1948: "It is a simple deduction, if you can see something free, I see no reason why anybody should want to pay for it, irrespective that maybe the films may not be quite as good, or maybe they are even worse, but nevertheless if you can get something free, I see no reason why somebody should want to pay an admission at the box office to a theatre to see the picture."[21] When asked how important he considered the theaters, Spyros Skouras explained, "That is our existence. The theatres are our main outlets."[22] Skouras predicted that if the studios were to license their films to television, "definitely the majority of the small theatres of America would close their doors. At least eight to ten thousand. . . . Also the development of the wide screen, such as Cinemascope of the Twentieth Century-Fox people, plays such a great part. It revived interest of the people to go [to] the movies. It helps somewhat, but not sufficient that we can say that the small theatres of America can be saved if the entertainment that they sell with admission later on is offered to the public gratis."[23] Skouras argued that Fox would be "in the red" if those small theaters closed.[24] His dire warnings were reinforced by articles that appeared even in the popular press. For example, an article in *Fortune* described the Hollywood studio heads' attitude toward television as "plain scared. The major-studio executives by and large are afraid of what will certainly be a bare-knuckle scrap. Part of their reluctance is over the risks involved; their personal fortunes are made and they have little desire to increase them at the peril of being wiped out."[25] Many of the reigning studio heads had been in the film business for decades and had yet to retire. By the 1960s there would be a significant turnover in that power structure with many of the old guard stepping down, but in the early 1950s they largely still ran the show. Rather than seeing the licensing and sale of their vaults to television as a source of additional revenue, the studios saw it as a lose-lose proposition. This fear of cannibalizing their current, still profitable business led the studios to delay their pursuit of television as a platform for their feature films.

THE TELEVISION EFFECT

In order to assess with confidence the cause of their woes, exhibitors joined forces with the studios to survey audiences. Different groups with different motivations and methods undertook these surveys in a variety of locations across the nation, so they all produced slightly different data and conclusions. In 1950, Paramount conducted a survey in metropolitan New York that concluded that television owner-ship cut family theater attendance by 20–30 percent. Those figures differed, how-ever, from a survey sponsored by motion picture theater owners in Washington, CBS and NBC, DuMont, and the *Washington Star* that was released shortly before the Paramount survey. This earlier survey was conducted in Washington and cited a 74 percent drop in theater attendance. Paul Raibourn, Paramount's vice presi-dent in charge of television, argued that the Washington figures were "erroneous and misleading."[26] Herbert Yates at Republic also commissioned a survey to deter-mine the extent to which television had encroached on the theatrical box office nationwide. The salesmen in each of Republic's thirty-two film exchanges made weekly reports on how many "video" sets were sold in their cities and towns, and then compared the box office revenues of theaters in those areas with theater grosses from previous years.[27] As demonstrated by these wildly different methods and results, all of the surveys offered conflicting information as to television's effect on the theatrical box office; and to add to the confusion, *Variety* reported in 1950 that the drop-off in box office revenue was a worldwide problem, and not limited to countries or areas where television had been introduced.[28] In the midst of this conflicting evidence, some theater owners argued against assigning all of the blame for the declining box office on competition from television. As Gael Sullivan stated in a speech at the annual TOA convention in May 1950, many factors affected the theatrical box office. He said this was particularly true considering that television was still not nationwide, and noted that Charles Skouras had observed that even theaters in non-television areas had experienced a significant drop in attendance. Sullivan also cited a United Paramount Theatres report that could not clearly identify television as the dominant factor in their declining grosses. Sullivan concluded with the argument: "It is significant that every survey has shown that television has a mule-kick effect on the movie attendance of those who acquire television sets. The surveys differ only by how hard and high the mule kicks."[29]

Even though, or perhaps because, the results of previous studies had been inconclusive and often contradictory, many of the studios and exhibitors continued to hire researchers to produce new studies. Alexander Kenneth Beggs, a senior economist at the Stanford Research Institute, completed one of the largest and most comprehensive studies. In March 1955, he began a study of the "economic facts with relationship to the television market for feature films and the attractiveness of these films for motion picture producers-distributors for the period 1945 through 1954."[30] The study identified what Beggs called a "severe decline" in the level of the average monthly attendance of theaters in Los Angeles and Denver, and an "even more severe decline" in the net operating profit per theater. He found that the dates when television stations were established in those cities corresponded to the decline in attendance and profitability of the theaters. For example, the first television station in Los Angeles was established in 1947, and the first television station in Denver was established in 1952. Beggs and his team observed a decline in theater attendance in Los Angeles beginning in 1947, but theater attendance in Denver remained constant until 1952, when the television station started broadcasting and theater attendance began declining.[31] As Judge Yankwich, the judge in the antitrust case *U.S. v. Twentieth Century-Fox, et al.*, remarked, "People have just so much time to devote to being entertained."[32] In the postwar years, there were, in fact, a number of different leisure activities competing for the audience's time, and, as scholar Lynn Spigel has shown, television was only one of them.[33]

Beggs and his team also conducted extensive studies of film and television audiences in order to determine the extent to which their television viewing affected their film attendance, and vice versa. They interviewed people in Denver, San Francisco, Portland, and Lubbock, Texas, and ultimately, their results showed that the vast majority of the American audience was an audience for both film and television.[34] Of those people who watched television and attended movie theaters, approximately 23 percent reported that they would attend movie theaters less if higher-quality older feature films were shown on television. Approximately 77 percent, however, indicated that showing higher-quality older feature films on television would not affect their moviegoing habits. The percentage of people who would attend movies less often if higher-quality films were on television reported that they attended movies more often than did the average population, but they also expressed greater difficulty in going to the theater. Some of the obstacles they cited included babysitter problems, the distance to the theater, and the high price of theater tickets. Almost half of those people said that they would go to movie theaters more frequently if the ticket prices were lower. Given the choice of a favorite

television show, a good Hollywood movie, or that same movie shown on television, 60 percent of respondents said they would prefer to go to the theater to see
the Hollywood movie. Eighty-two percent of them said that they wanted an opportunity to rewatch old movies that they liked. Ultimately, Beggs and his team concluded that there would be a saturation point for the losses the film industry might
suffer if their films were shown on television. He argued that the closer the country got to saturation in terms of the ownership of television sets, the lower the
potential level of financial loss the film industry could see.[35] The trick then became
determining when that saturation point might hit. Because if the studios made a
move too early or too late, they feared they would lose potential revenue in the theaters and for their films on television.

Exhibitors' Woes

Amid all of the prognostication and uncertainty, the theater owners demanded that
the studio heads clarify their positions on the release of their films to television.
In 1948, Robert Coyne, an executive with the TOA, called on the studios to inquire
about their plans and to advise them to discontinue any activities that might injure
the 35mm theaters. Coyne reported back that he had met with "great success" in
his mission, but later Peter G. Levathes, Fox's head of television, described a different recollection of the encounter: "When the TOA, or other such organizations,
made contact with film companies they have tendency to exaggerate their effec-
tiveness in dealing with film companies, and Mr. Coyne, . . . wanted to tell the boys
back home . . . that he had really done a great thing. In reality, he had accomplished
nothing, and I had held his hand for a couple of hours, as any businessman would
do when his customers come to him and complain."[36] Although Levathes would
make it sound as though the theaters were not as important to the studios as the
theaters believed themselves to be, by that time, the exhibitors remained a major
factor in many of the studios' decisions. The studios' concern for the theaters' well-
being sprang in part from the fact that by the late 1940s, many of the men running
the studios had gotten their start in the industry in exhibition. Barney Balaban of
Paramount, for example, had spent much of his life running the Balaban and Katz
Theatres in Chicago.[37] Nate Blumberg of Universal and Spyros Skouras of Fox also
got their starts in the theater business.[38] Those roots in the theater business made
the studio executives sentimental about the theaters in a way that often blinded
them to the realities of the larger industrial landscape. This does not, however,
mean that the theaters did not deserve some of the considerable clout they wielded.
By the late 1940s, the TOA represented approximately two-thirds of the theaters
in the country; and since, at that point, the theaters were not yet divorced from
the studios, the studios had something of a once-removed membership in the theater organization. For example, Fox's National Theatres subsidiary and Paramount
Theatres were both members of the TOA. The TOA wanted to further solidify this
close relationship by getting even more studios officially involved in the organization, and Gael Sullivan of the TOA approached Spyros Skouras and Barney

Balaban and asked them to talk with Nicholas Schenck, the Warner brothers, and RKO to persuade them to join as members.[39] The TOA was certainly not shy about communicating their interests to the studios, which, at that time, were primarily related to the issue of feature films on television. In early 1948, for example, the Southern California Theatre Owners Association (SCTOA) began a protest of the potential sale of Alexander Korda's films to television, and encouraged the nationwide TOA to join the protest. SCTOA argued that films that still had theatrical potential or that were contracted for future dates in theaters should not be licensed for television, because such action would cut into the revenues of the theaters and, thereby, of the producers.[40] This kind of protest caused the studios to fear incurring the wrath of the theaters. In January 1948, during negotiations between Republic Studios and B-western film star Roy Rogers for Rogers's new contract, Rogers expressed an interest in having time off to participate in television programs. Robert Newman, then vice president of Republic, stated that the "exhibitors would never let them get into television," and Newman believed that Herbert Yates, president of Republic, would not allow Rogers to appear on television "because of the exhibitor pressure."[41] Even the television networks hoped, as much as possible, to avoid crossing the theaters. For example, in 1948, CBS was close to a deal for a series of Monogram's films, but the network refused to share any details of the deal, reportedly out of fear of exhibitor resistance.[42]

Before 1948, the theaters, despite their strong protests against films on television, were largely positive about television—especially in terms of its potential to advertise theatrical feature films and get audiences into the theaters. Those hopes were rooted in the theaters' experiences in the late 1920s, when theater owners collaborated with local radio stations to publicize films or to introduce audiences to vaudeville and feature stars.[43] By May 1948, however, as more films began making their way to television, Ted Gamble issued a statement on behalf of the TOA proposing a moratorium on deals for films on television "until television finds itself and its place in show business generally."[44] Gamble argued that television was riding the coattails of the film industry. Many theater owners believed that they were the studios' moneymakers, and what "we support financially is being used against us."[45] The statement was a shift in rhetoric from the association and signaled a more trenchantly negative position, particularly on the subject of films on television.

By September 1948, the theaters were in fact so nervous about television that the TOA invited Wayne Coy, the chairman of the FCC, to speak at their convention regarding the future of television and its impact on the theater business.[46] Although the TOA likely hoped for some reassurance from Coy, his speech only increased the audience's fears about the rising tide of television. Rather than providing comfort, Coy practically taunted them by asking, "Can the nation's 18,000 commercial movie houses hold their own with 39,000,000 home theaters?"[47] He continued to paint his bleak picture: "You are pondering how you can compete with a diabolical, fiendish screen in the living room that miraculously produces vaudeville, motion pictures, news reels, musical comedy, drama, opera, grand opera, soap opera, circuses, prize fights, football games, world series games, air races—news and history in the making. You are wondering who will stand in the queue, buf-feted by the wind, the rain and the snow to see your show when he can see all that without stirring from his easy chair."[48] Coy also implied that the theater owners had missed out on the television juggernaut, and tried to explain the FCC's position by saying, "So you see it is not that we love the theater business less, but that we are bound by law to love the broadcasting business more. Pursuant to that responsibility, I must tell you frankly that we are going to create just as much tele-vision competition as possible."[49] It was no surprise, then, that in October 1948, one month after Coy's address, Arthur Lockwood, the president of the TOA, sent a letter to the heads of all the studios alerting them to the fact that the TOA mem-bership had adopted a resolution that "all producing and distributing companies be requested by this Association to completely eliminate the release to television, of all motion pictures of any length, which were made for theatrical exhibition."[50] In the months after the letter was sent, individual theater owners contacted the studios to encourage them to continue to withhold their product from television. Spyros Skouras's response explained, "So far as Television is concerned, Twenti-eth Century-Fox is not producing any motion pictures of any length for both theatrical and television release. We have up to this time, not released any of our theatrical shorts for use in this medium."[51] A subsequent TOA Special Bulletin in November 1948 outlined the responses they had received from the studios regard-ing their policies on films to television. In addition to Fox, Paramount, Warner, RKO, Loew's, Republic, Columbia, and Selznick had all assured the TOA that they were not releasing 16mm films to any locations that might compete with 35mm theaters with some exceptions such as the Red Cross, hospitals, sanitari-ums, prisons, and some schools or camps for children.[52] These policies were strikingly similar to the systems of theatrical clearances and runs that the stu-dios had recently been enjoined against using as a result of the antitrust case *U.S. v. Paramount Pictures, et al.*[53]

Despite the written assurances that studios would not release their feature films to television, many theaters remained concerned. Peter Levathes at Fox described how unpopular his television department was with the theater organizations: "They were not happy about our engaging in these activities, but we felt that television was an art that was very closely related to motion pictures, and that we had to gain experience in it, and that we had to stay in it to the extent that we could, to explore it, to keep informed about it, and to evolve ways of utilizing it for our financial advantage."[54] Gael Sullivan, in a speech at the annual TOA convention in Atlanta, further illuminated the theaters' attitudes toward television through the follow-ing colorful metaphor: "I have heard it said that the honeymoon in the film busi-ness is over. Getting down to the business of a day in day out marriage with a declining box-office is a difficult thing. It is particularly difficult for the theatre exhibitor, when his wife—the film producer, and all the helpers, the stars, writers, directors and skilled technicians—are being coveted by a vigorous, young third party, television."[55] That Sullivan compared the relationship between the theaters and studios to that of husband and wife reveals the extent to which the exhibitors believed their ties with the studios to be intimate and exclusive. Mitchell Wolfson, head of the TOA's Television Committee,[56] advised theater owners that they should applaud producers and distributors that refused to make their films available to television. He continued, "All producing and distributing companies should be counseled that a grave danger and injustice would be presented should television be provided with motion picture film designed and created for exhibition in motion picture theatres. The 'giving away' of the industry product on television is economically indefensible from the point of view of the theatres, as well as the producers and distributors who would soon find that they have jeopardized their own income as would be evidenced by the diminishing returns at the box office."[57] Wolfson further proposed that the TOA keep track of any feature films that appeared on television, so that they could maintain a list of the producers and distributors of those films and the "damage that may be accruing" to the theaters by those "unfair practices." By keeping track of that information, he suggested that theaters would have the option of taking legal action against the producers and distributors.[58] He later clarified that his position on television was not an entirely negative one. He explained, "I feel positive that television definitely can be used to help the motion picture theatre, provided motion pictures made expressly for motion picture theatre exhibition are restricted to motion picture theatre use."[59]

Theater owners kept an eye on television in a number of ways, and they were helped by the fact that by 1949, most exhibitor trade magazines contained sections on television.[60] They included information on the effects of television on theaters, reported films that had run on television, and contained information about which studios had licensed or sold those films to TV.[61] The theaters did not just keep track of the studios' activities regarding films on television. They also monitored and communicated with the networks. For example, in March 1949, Stanley W. Prenosil, assistant executive director of the TOA, contacted the director of the Publicity-Television Department at ABC, asking to receive advance copies of television programs.[62] Later that year, Harry Vinnicof, head of the SCTOA, wrote to Gael Sullivan, president of the TOA, inquiring about their "advice and action" in regard to an article that ran in *Variety* the day before, reporting the following: "WCBS in NY is televising two feature films on Saturday nights, with short subjects in between. Prior to the screenings, an announcer on the CBS outlet reads the following: 'If you were planning to go to the movies tonight—don't. Stay at home in the comfort of your own living room and see two full-length motion pictures and three short subjects.'"[63] These kinds of advertisements had been used by broadcasting since the days of radio. For example, as historian Michele Hilmes documented, "in February 1932, *Variety* reported that an RKO broadcast had seriously angered theater interests when the announcer had gone so far as to conclude the broadcast with 'Aren't you glad you stayed home this evening to listen to the 'RKO Theater of the Air'? Stay home every Friday night for it.'"[64] Many radio, and later television, stations used similar advertisements to attract viewers for their programming, and they played right to the theater owners' greatest fears. For example, in September 1950, Bob Rains at Universal wrote to Duke Wales at the MPPDA, alerting Wales to a commercial that aired on KECA-TV and told viewers that KECA-TV planned to schedule films as selected by the audience. The commercial ended by saying, "Why go to the movies and pay your money when you can sit at home, enjoy yourself and still see top films." Rains also noted a statement in *Variety* that the television industry planned to adopt the expression "Old movies are better than ever" to combat the film industry's slogan, "Movies are better than ever." Rains saw this as a trend in the television industry, which he believed made it "imperative that a committee be formed to meet with the television industry and see if such statements can't be done away with."[65] This marketing tit-for-tat increased the sense that television was in competition with film, and it reinforced the notion that if feature films appeared on television, audiences would no longer make a trip to the theaters to see them.

By June 1949, some exhibitors were so nervous about the competition from feature films on television that the threats that were previously veiled became explicit, and theaters threatened boycotts of the film producers' product. The president of Pictorial Films complained that exhibitors had threatened that if the distributors gave their features to television stations, exhibitors would refuse to play them in their theaters.[66] Most exhibitors stopped short of publicly threatening a boycott, but they did not hesitate to express their negative opinions of the release of feature films to television. Many theater owners believed that they were responsible for the fame and fortune of Hollywood's stars and studios, and that running feature films on television would constitute a betrayal.[67] In 1950, *Variety* reported that prominent exhibitors were "plenty sore about the television stations buying up these old films. They say the American exhibitor will never forgive or forget the film producer who sells his product to television after it makes the rounds of the theatres."[68] Fred Schwartz of the Century Circuit said releasing features to television would simply be a stupid and foolish stunt on the part of the producer. Leo Brecher, president of the Metropolitan Theatre Association of New York, said simply that he "would not like it." The Allied board, along with Walter Reade Jr. of the Reade theater circuit, claimed they would be "amazed and resentful." An editorial in *Showman's Trade* called the question a "matter of honor" and came close to explicitly threatening a boycott of such a producer.[69] Many exhibitors privately admitted that they would "get back" at any producers who released their films to television. Trueman Rembusch of Allied, for example, had stated, "I for one am not going to play any producer's pictures who is so traitorous to the motion picture industry as to sell his productions, new or old, to television or Phonevision. I imagine that a great many exhibitors feel as I do."[70] Theater owner Sam Pinanski stated, "Hollywood will have to make up its mind whom it wants to serve."[71] The exhibitors' concerns about feature films on television had in some cases progressed from anxiety to outright hostility between the theaters and the studios. Walter Reade Jr., president of Walter Reade Theatres, for example, had made comments to the press disparaging Republic Studios and their dealings with television—specifically their having offered their films to television. In response to a letter from Herbert Yates, head of Republic, wherein Yates outlined Republic's attitude toward television, Reade indignantly stated that he and his theaters had been one of the main supporters of Republic over the years and had always given Republic "top terms" and "top playing time" for their films. He continued: "If Republic was going to be in the big league, I felt you should act like big league and not fly by nights, which in my opinion is the way films found their way to Television before your company made large numbers available. Whether I am right in my contention, or you are right in your contention, I guess only history will tell. I . . . feel that we cannot support you so long as your policy concerning TV is as indefinite and ambiguous as I feel it is at the present time."[72] Although the exhibitors' threats were somewhat hollow because they did, in fact, rely heavily on the major studios' films, their motivation was to make this conflict a zero-sum game for the studios wherein the studios had to decide between the theaters and television. From all of those threats, both public and private, the studios were keenly aware of the theaters' feelings on this subject. For example, in 1949, when Robert Newman, former vice president at Republic Studios, was asked what impediments kept them from releasing their films to television, Newman answered, "Always the exhibitors . . . The opposition of the exhibitor . . . When you are in business and they are your chief customers, you watch their desires pretty carefully."[73]

The theaters certainly agreed that they were the studios' chief customers, and they took that claim even further by arguing that they were responsible for the studios' success. In March 1950, the TOA asked Herbert Yates, president of Republic, if he would meet with Joseph H. Corwin, a representative of the TOA, to discuss Republic's releasing their films to television and the question of Roy Rogers, one of Republic's biggest B-western stars, making a deal to star in a television series. Yates asked Roy Rogers and Arthur Rush, Rogers's representative, to join the conversation.[74] Corwin said it was a mistake for any of the studios to play their films on television, and he believed any important star going on television would hurt his box office. Yates asked what Republic was supposed to do when their income from their theaters was declining, and although Corwin acknowledged that issue, he requested that "inasmuch as the Theatre Owners of America were largely responsible for the success of Republic and Roy Rogers that [Republic] should hold the line a little longer." Yates responded by pointing out the hypocrisy in the theaters' stance toward television: "In the meantime I notice that exhibitors all over the country are putting in television screens as rapidly as possible, and a number of them are entering permits for telecast stations."[75] Yates said he believed that Republic had to make films for both theater and television, and he thought both industries could work together to the profitable end of all concerned.[76] The finger-pointing did not stop there, however. The theaters also accused the studios of not producing enough high-quality product to attract audiences to the theaters. As Gael Sullivan of TOA complained to *Variety*, "There is an urgent need for more and better pictures in order that the exhibitor may provide consistently good entertainment. This is the responsibility of the producers and if they fail to meet it, exhibitors have no alternative but to encourage, if necessary, help finance independent production. Exhibition has an investment of approximately two and one-half billion

dollars in the industry which must be protected."[77] Sullivan's statement added a
new threat to the exhibitors' arsenal: that of funding their own independent productions to ensure content for their screens. In another move designed to allow
the newly independent theaters to turn television into an ally and circumvent the
studios, United Paramount Theatres (UPT) purchased ABC in 1953. Despite concerns about UPT's record of antitrust violations as part of Paramount Pictures
before the 1948 divestiture order, the FCC approved the deal. Leonard Goldenson,
president of UPT, assured the FCC that "the real vitality in the future of television
is in live television." He did push ABC to embrace filmed programming, but programming that was filmed specifically for television and not theatrical films.[78] The
theater owners already considered themselves the financiers of the major studios'
films, and in the wake of the *Paramount* antitrust decision, the threat of the theaters' further independence through owning stations and networks and financing
their own features made the studios nervous.

Another thing that upset the theaters and complicated the matter of feature films
on television related to the issue of 16mm versus 35mm film. As discussed in chapter 1, most television stations were only equipped with the technology to broadcast films on 16mm rather than 35mm film. Another effect of the boom in the use
of 16mm film after the war was that those prints began to show up as "unauthorized showings" in places like hotels, and the TOA, for example, complained to
United Artists about the "unfair competition" of 16mm prints of features that had
originally been released in 35mm.[79] Most studios that released 16mm prints of their
films had a standing policy not to release those films to any locations that competed with their 35mm theaters. Abe Montague of Columbia explained their policy regarding 16mm films as follows: "We decided that in no case where there was
reasonable opposition, 16 or 35, would we want to serve our films in 16mm. . . . Our
main business, naturally, is the supplying of 35mm to legitimate theatres, and we
didn't want in any way, shape or manner to endanger that, in the smallest or in
the largest way."[80] Before their divorcement from the studios, many theaters enjoyed
protection from competition, so the introduction of rivals from 16mm prints and
television was anathema to most exhibitors. Correspondence between theater
owners, theater organizations, and the studios described the unauthorized showings of 16mm films as everything from unethical to obnoxious to parasitic.[81] In
order to deal with what the theaters viewed as the "scourge of 16mm," the TOA
encouraged the theaters to not only monitor the broadcast of feature films on television, but also practice "vigilance on the part of each and every exhibitor." They
suggested what sounded like a spy network of exhibitors who would, upon hearing that a 16mm film was screening in a venue that was "harmful" to their theater,
attend the screening to count the attendance and assess the admission price. Then
they would write down the information on the cast and detail any advertising material for the screening. The TOA warned that the exhibitor should record the title
of the film because "many times titles are changed from the original release." The
TOA then assured the theater owners that if they took those steps and forwarded
the information they collected to the sales manager of the company that originally

released the film, "action will be forthcoming."[82] Then at the TOA's annual meeting in 1950, Abram F. Myers, chairman of the National Committee of the Allied Theatre Owners, congratulated producers and distributors who, "after careful consideration of all the factors involved have voluntarily determined and announced it is to the best interests of the film industry not to license their films for nontheatrical exhibitions on such media as television, Phonevision, and 16m showings."[83] That the theaters combined television, Phonevision, and 16mm showings, however, is notable because while they were all largely based in the 16mm format, the theaters' putting them in one category would return to haunt them in the form of an antitrust suit, which will be discussed in detail in chapter 5.

THEATERS EYE TV STATION OWNERSHIP

While studios had attempted to acquire television stations and channels, the exhibitors—one of the most natural fits for television station ownership, in part because of their existing relationship with audiences and their local communities, and in part because they had no restrictions from the FCC or the DOJ in terms of station ownership—largely ignored that opportunity. In September 1948, at the annual convention of the TOA, Marcus Cohn, a lawyer-specialist in television, discussed some of the problems of television as they affected the motion picture industry, and he commented specifically on the exhibitors' failure to secure a share of the limited number of television stations available. He observed, "It is shocking how few exhibitors have taken measures to protect themselves in this matter."[84] When Wayne Coy, chairman of the FCC, addressed the convention on the future of television and its impact on the theater business, he warned the attendees: "Suppose the theater owner reasons that he was the pioneer in both the visual and aural mass entertainment fields and that he might now try to become a broadcaster himself? If he had had that idea a year or so ago, it would have been a sound one. But today he will find that practically all the channels not assigned are involved in hearings before the FCC. The competition is intense."[85]

On this issue, as with so many others, opinion and strategy were divided, and in May 1949, Gael Sullivan of the TOA wrote to James Coston of Warner Bros.: "I was—to put it mildly—shocked to learn that Warner Bros. filed a petition with the [Federal Communications] Commission to withdraw its television application for a construction permit in Chicago. As I have told you privately on several occasions and as I have stated publicly on numerous occasions, I am absolutely convinced that exhibitors and producers must get into television. They must get in it to protect their present investments and to expand the scope of their present business."[86] Sullivan had recently been in Washington discussing with "key government people the question of producers and exhibitors going into television." He left convinced that "the motion picture people will get as good a break as anyone else on their applications," and he concluded his letter saying, "I tell you frankly that I would consider it catastrophe if Warners turned a 'cold shoulder' to television."[87] By 1949, some theater owners, albeit a small number, already owned and operated television stations. Wometco Theatres in Florida, for example, owned the only television station in the state, WTVJ-TV, Channel 4 in Miami.[88] Mitchell Wolfson, who was also the chairman of the TOA's Television Committee, owned Wometco.[89] Wolfson explained his motivation for purchasing the station: "It seemed just as logical to us at Wometco for motion picture exhibitors to become television broadcasters as it was for radio broadcasters to enter into television. After all, we are the experts in what is good visual fare for the people in our communities."[90] The TOA's Television Committee, under the direction of Wolfson, hoped that exhibitors owning and operating television stations might solve the exhibitor's television problems. The committee believed that an exhibitor who was also a licensee of a television station had the potential to receive and distribute special events not only to the home but also to the theater. Owning a television station would also allow the exhibitors to use that station to advertise the films that were being shown in their theaters.[91] Wolfson faced considerable resistance to those views, however, as evidenced in the manner in which he began his discussion of television broadcasting with the members of the TOA: "Now I shall reveal the other side of my split personality. From now on you will be hearing from Mr. Hyde Wolfson, that terrible broadcaster, instead of Dr. Jekyll Wolfson, that nice motion picture exhibitor."[92]

LURING AUDIENCES BACK TO THE THEATERS

To bolster their theatrical revenue, many of the studios tried to use television through, what Jack Warner called, "hooks" or "come-ons" for their films. As Warner described: "We found it successful to show a short teaser or commercial on other programs throughout the year. And we do that on the Ed Sullivan show as often as we can. . . . We do that with all programs, television programs [and] we grasped at this idea as a good business move in the matter of making and distribution of film, and in advertising our pictures to let the public know about our contemplated and public productions."[93] Running ads and promotions for feature films had worked well in radio, and studio heads believed that the addition of visual elements that television made possible would only make those ads and promotions more successful.

A new challenge was that theater owners had noticed shifts in the volume of their ticket sales that paralleled the television programming schedule. As S. H. "Si" Fabian, one of the top exhibitors in the nation and a leader of the TOA, observed in July 1952, "Last summer the theatres of this country had a very fine business, without exception in all areas we did a great business, and like a knife cutting right through a piece of cheese, in the middle of September when the big shows came back on television our business went to hell. Why? It just so happened, it's coincidental probably, there was a bad run of product, nothing to play, nothing to keep those people coming to our theatres."[94] Fabian believed that if better-quality films of the kind the theaters had in the summer were available through the fall, the theaters could compete with those big new television shows and recapture the audience they lost to television. So, the film industry tried to improve the quality of their product by developing bigger and better visual and aural systems than what television offered in the home. One of the ways they did that was through the increased production of color film. Photographic color had first become possible in film in 1897, but the film industries did not adopt its use until much later because, as historian Brad Chisolm explained, it was "cumbersome, expensive, and gave less-than-perfect results."[95] In 1949, the studios released thirty-one color feature films, which constituted almost 18 percent of the total releases; and by 1952, the five major studios had released sixty-two feature films in color (34% of total releases).[96] This number would only continue to grow as the studios moved further into the 1950s. It was not until June 1951, when the Supreme Court upheld the FCC's decision to approve the CBS color television system, that the industry could finally move forward with the production of television sets and programming in color. As Ralph Cohn of Screen Gems explained, "It played a part insofar as in [Columbia's] library there was a certain number of color films, and we realized that until there was widespread use of color television both from a broadcasting standpoint and a receiver standpoint the value of those color films couldn't be truly realized on television."[97] While the FCC had dragged their feet on the authorization of color television technologies, the studios had moved forward with increasing the number of color films they produced. In 1946, the studios released only 9 percent of their films in color; and by 1953, the studios had released seventy-eight feature films in color, which constituted 50 percent of their total releases. The following year, the major studios released ninety-seven feature films in color, which was almost 70 percent of the total releases.[98] Even though NBC declared 1954 "The Year of Color" and featured a schedule of color broadcasts, those programs were few and far between.[99] Until there was a steady stream of color programming, audiences were not going to buy expensive color television sets. Until that happened and color television became a reality, however, color films were destined for theatrical release only. It would be at least a few years before color television set production and ownership overtook the numbers of black-and-white television sets on the market, and until that occurred, Hollywood's color feature films would remain in their vaults.

That theatrical releases were increasingly color films also meant that the value of black-and-white films to the theaters and theatrical audiences had decreased. As a result, the studios sensed a sweet spot in the lag between the development of color film and color television, when enough theaters would have color, widescreen films that they would not mind older black-and-white films being sold to television, and before color television had developed enough that television no longer had interest in black-and-white films. Jack L. Warner recalled that at some point between 1954 and 1955 his studio made a deal with a company called Guild Films for a series of approximately 190 Warner Bros. black-and-white cartoons for television. Warner, who had previously spoken out against television, explained the rationale: "I thought it was all right at that time to sell the cartoons to television, for a very simple reason. Color television was here, it was advancing by leaps and bounds, and unless we got these black and white cartoons sold at that time, we figured they would be valueless in a matter of years."[100] Other studios followed suit, and in 1954, Columbia, for example, released over one hundred black-and-white one-reel cartoons to television. They also released about sixteen westerns and two or three British features.[101] These small steps to release some films on television represented the best the studios could do at that time, and it also signaled their willingness to release their films to television as soon as they were able.

In addition to color films, the studios moved forward with developing wide-screen technologies like CinemaScope, Cinerama, Vista-Vision, and Todd-AO. As B. B. Kahane, vice president of Columbia, testified, "We strive to present our pictures in the largest size we can. We have recently gone from small screens to large screens, to get a better presentation. And of course we don't think there is any comparison between a picture shown on a large screen in a theatre and a 10 or 12 or 21 or even a 27 inch screen in a house."[102] These larger-format films not only would be less suitable for viewing on a smaller television screen, but also would help differentiate television from film and, the studios hoped, attract audiences to the theaters. As Ned Depinet recalled, "The trend has been to give the public a larger picture on the wall to counteract as best the industry can the effects of the small postage stamp effect of television. . . . And I think that the tendency of the industry is going to be to develop these methods in order to improve the pictures on the screen and cover a larger vista, and that is one of the major improvements in the last few years, spearheaded by Cinerama."[103] This expansion also served to, as historian John Belton argued, redefine "the motion picture as a form of participatory recreation (as opposed to passive entertainment) . . . against the background of its competition for audiences with other leisure-time activities. The motion picture sought a middle ground between the notion of passive consumption associated with at-home television viewing and that of active participation involved in outdoor recreational activities."[104] Adopting these systems, however, required a large investment on the part of the theater owners, and studio heads like Skouras worked hard to encourage theaters to improve their systems in order to draw audiences away from their free home television. As Skouras explained, "Better projection, better sound, and better entertainment to the public. As I believe only by superior entertainment of the movies that they could bring back the people from their homes, from free home television. Otherwise you have to give them better entertainment than the home television."[105] Some theater owners were convinced, however, that 3D, which required a smaller investment from theater owners, was the best option. N. A. Taylor, an operator of a sixty-theater Canadian theater circuit, agreed, saying, "The third dimension process is the answer to television."[106] Even more so than larger-format films, 3D films could not play on television screens.

It appears, however, that the studios were interested in developing these new technologies not only so that they could differentiate Hollywood films from television and lure audiences back to the theaters, but also so that they could play one partner, the theaters, against the other, television. The studios recognized that once these new widescreen and 3D technologies became standard for the theaters, the theaters would not object as much if the studios' older, black-and-white films appeared on television. Then the studios would have more freedom to distribute their older, less-in-demand films to television without the concern of retribution from the exhibitors. This possibility came to light in the spring of 1953, when, in response to the financial downturn experienced by Fox, some of the Fox stockholders challenged the management. Charles Green was one of the stockholders who carried a proxy on that challenge, and he approached Skouras and demanded that Fox immediately sell their films to television. Skouras refused "point-blank" on the grounds that if they did that, the theaters would be put out of business because of the "unfair competition of free Television." He "added, however, that once CinemaScope and other new systems for improved theatre entertainment are installed in all of the theatres and the old type of motion pictures become obsolete, that these films could be made available to Television without injury to anyone."[107] Skouras reasoned that they still wanted to protect their exhibitors, who were their main source of income, but once the theaters had installed the CinemaScope system, they would no longer be interested in showing older, black-and-white "flat" films. At that point, Fox could sell their "flat" films to television without upsetting the theater owners or affecting their income.[108] Skouras and Fox continued to work on CinemaScope, and by 1955 they had made significant progress. Out of 23,000 theaters in the United States and Canada, 16,000 of them had installed the Cinema-Scope system. As Skouras testified, "So in time, when all the theatres and all the producers will use the new techniques, and the flat will be outmoded, out of style, probably the flat pictures will be available to the television."[109] Although there was the possibility that Skouras was using his desire to wait until all theaters had CinemaScope installed as an excuse to delay the release of Fox's films to television, there were others in the film industry who had similar plans.

THEATER TELEVISION

Although television station ownership by the film studios provided a clearer route for distributing their feature films to television, theater television also held promise in terms of creating a new system of distribution that would compete with nascent broadcasters and give studios a slice of television's profits. Perhaps more importantly, studios hoped that it had the potential to deliver films directly into homes via technologies that did not require FCC approval or rely on cables controlled by companies like AT&T. As historian Timothy White explained, "They hoped theatre television would allow them more control over the distribution of their own television product, and would differentiate their product from that of broadcast television."[110] By 1949, many of the studios and theater organizations were working to move full speed ahead with theater television.[111] They planned to project original programs transmitted by directional microwave relays or closed circuit coaxial cables to theaters for paying customers. Theater television would have higher production values and be more exclusive than content available via television broadcast to much smaller television screens in homes. The studios still did not quite understand (or perhaps they were in denial) that a significant part of the appeal of television was that their customers, the audience, could stay home to enjoy the programming. The studios, and certainly the theaters, were determined to force those audiences back to the theaters—even if that meant spending a great deal of money on developing and installing new systems for theater television. Even as early as the late 1930s, RCA conducted tests of their own theater television system. RCA developed a practical large-screen television projector, and in the spring of 1941 they demonstrated the system to the members of the FCC at the New York Theatre in New York. Although those tests built great excitement, the development of theater television was put on hold for the duration of World War II. By 1944, those who had invested in theater television systems were getting restless, and Paul Raibourn of Paramount addressed the Theatre Panel Meeting at the First Annual Conference of the Television Broadcasters Association (TBA), saying, "If the broadcasters are economically unable or don't want to further television, I assure you that within a few years the theatres will have it and the broadcasters will be far behind, which all present would be very happy about."[112] By 1948, the FCC had granted Paramount an exclusive theater-television channel at 7,000 megacycles— far beyond the range of home receivers, so home sets would not be able to pick up the signal—and Paramount tested the system in their Paramount Theatre on Broadway.

Spyros Skouras was one of the most dedicated proponents of theater television, and his dedication was rooted in his belief that home television would not affect the theaters as long as theater television existed.[113] That was in part because Fox planned to pick up television broadcasts and screen them in theaters via their theater television systems, thereby using the free television broadcast to charge admission to the theaters for audiences to watch the programming on the large screen. People in the television industry were predictably unhappy about that prospect, and NBC's Frank Mullen stated publicly that the network would resist any attempt by theaters to pick up television shows for theater television.[114] This jockeying for control of content sowed seeds of distrust and competition between the industries, which inhibited the potential for cooperation and collaboration.

The film industry kept pushing the FCC to consider their applications for the allocation of broadband frequencies for theater television channels, and the FCC finally agreed to hold hearings on the matter in September 1950. Although the television broadcasters had initially shown themselves amenable to theater television, some of them, including the NAB, the TBA, and CBS, had since changed their stances and publicly stated their opposition to granting channels for theater television.[115] The TOA understood the challenge they faced and in an internal memo acknowledged, "We look for a tough fight to gain the channels required to develop theatre television into a nation-wide system. This FCC hearing, we feel, is crucial to the television future of the motion picture industry, and if we fail now, theatre owners will have lost their last chance to compete in the television picture."[116] If the broadcasters and networks voiced their opposition to theater television, the MPAA had pledged to mount a "strong public relations job" to "overcome such opposition, in addition to the showing at the theatre TV hearing itself."[117] The MPAA public relations facilities would be made available for that work, and they would use "movie shorts, press releases, and so forth."[118] The TOA created the Theatre-TV Research Bureau[119] and even asked their members for loans of $500 each to pay for the association's activities in relation to theater television.[120] The ongoing fight for theater television was extremely costly, and was exacerbated by the film industry's financial struggles.[121] Despite all of the time and money invested in theater television, at the completion of the FCC's hearings at the end of 1950, the FCC still declined to approve the channels needed to get theater television up and running. Spyros Skouras complained, "I believe we have failed to persuade the FCC to license us with the channels we deserve because . . . we have not a common clear understanding of the value of this new medium for our theatres, and because we lack harmony and coordination."[122] The theaters' hopes of finding inroads to television were, at least temporarily, thwarted, and the expenses they had incurred in the process of their applications were seemingly for naught. The promise of theater television had given the exhibitors hope for a profitable future and had provided something of a welcome distraction from the fight over feature films on television. With those hopes at least temporarily quashed, the exhibitors' sense of the tenuous nature of their position in the industry increased, as did their ire toward their competitor: television.

Despite those setbacks, one of the primary objectives of the MPAA's Television Committee during this time was the rise of theater television, and committee members devoted a great deal of time and money to preparing their case for the FCC hearings on the matter that were scheduled for the fall of 1952.[123] The hearings, which focused on deliberation of the allocation of part of the UHF spectrum for theater television, continued until the spring of 1953.[124] They became a forum for members of the television industry to act on any ill will they harbored toward the people in the film industry. For example, the National Association of Radio and Television Broadcasters (NARTB) was upset about "malicious and unprincipled" statements some exhibitors had made to the press about television broadcasting, and the NARTB was planning to use the FCC's hearings as an opportunity to "strike back" at the exhibitors.[125] The hearings ended with the FCC once again denying the studios' petitions on the grounds of their previous monopolistic practices.[126] The FCC formalized their rationale for those decisions through their Nineteenth Report and Order, issued in June 1953, which determined that theater television was "essentially a service which should be performed by communications common carriers. It further determined that there is nothing in the Communications Act or the Commission's rules which would prevent a common carrier from rendering this specialized type of service on frequencies set aside for general common carrier use."[127] The FCC said they would consider applications for the use of those frequencies, however, on their "individual merits," and would include in those considerations, among other things, whether the applications met the standards of public interest, convenience, or necessity.[128] The FCC's decision did not mean, however, that the studios gave up their efforts. In late 1955, Fox, for example, was still working to get their Eidophor system off the ground, and hoped to hold public tests of the system within a few months. As Skouras recalled, "We feel through this system we will be able to supply a number of theatres throughout the United States with such superior entertainment that the public will return to the theatres. . . . It took Twentieth Century-Fox over 18 million dollars to launch CinemaScope on a world-wide basis. And, also, it will take equally as much to launch the Eidophor. But we feel that the large screen theatre television . . . will be of great service to the theatres of the world."[129] Fox invested large sums of money in the CinemaScope and Eidophor systems and asked their exhibitors to do the same. During a period when the studios and theaters continued to struggle, these gambles would ultimately not provide the return on investment that Skouras hoped for. As historian Timothy White concluded, "More expensive than broadcast television, and lacking the quality of the motion picture image, theater television could compete with neither."[130]

THEATRICAL REISSUES AND RERELEASES

Another of the studios' hesitations in terms of licensing their films to television was that they still did not want to relinquish what they believed to be a highly lucrative market for the theatrical reissue and rerelease of their films, and they did not want to destroy that potential income by releasing the films to television. In one example of this from early 1950, National Comics offered Columbia $250,000 for the rights to distribute their serials to television. Since Columbia was unsure of how the value of their serials in television compared with their value in the theaters, Columbia decided to rerelease the serial *Wild Bill Hickock* to theaters as a test of the potential of the theatrical reissue market. The rerelease of this one serial made $275,000 for Columbia, which they considered a success—especially when compared with the lower offer from National Comics for Columbia's entire catalog of serials. Shortly thereafter, Columbia began rereleasing more of their serials to the theaters.[131] Other studios and filmmakers also turned down sales of their films to television in favor of theatrical rereleases. For example, Fox tried to wring money out of their film vault through gimmicks like the February 1950 "bonus drive" for salesmen to "liquidate" the older product. Salesmen and branch managers would get a 10 percent commission on all theatrical rentals from the group of films that included many of Fox's independently made releases, such as British filmmaker Alexander Korda's *Karenina* and *Ideal Husband*.[132] Harold Lloyd had received an offer of $250,000 from NBC in New York for a package of seventy of his older films. Lloyd turned down that offer, as well as an offer from a major studio for the story rights to *The Freshman* (1925), citing the potential theatrical rerelease value, and that he had "too many exhibitor friends to peddle pictures to video."[133]

Studios repeatedly pointed to a few examples of the potential success that their films could find if rereleased to the theaters. The "Realart Deal," for example, was a deal Universal made with the Realart Company in June 1947, in which Universal licensed the films they had produced between 1933 and 1946 to Realart, so Realart could rerelease the films theatrically. In other words, Realart was carrying out a reissue function for Universal rather than Universal carrying it out themselves.[134] Realart licensed the films for an immediate cash payment to Universal of $1,750,000 as well as a percentage of the profits.[135] Between 1947 and early 1955, Realart made approximately $21 million from the rentals of these films to theaters. Of that revenue, Universal was paid almost $7 million, which averaged out to about $20,000 per film for Universal.[136] As Ned Depinet, former president of RKO, explained, "RKO reissued or re-released a number of its pictures. That is a custom that has been in vogue almost since the beginning of feature films, and from 1946 on RKO relied very substantially on reissue revenue to maintain its organization and to keep it in business."[137] Approximately 25 percent of RKO's total releases from 1946 to 1954 were reissues, and approximately $15 million of revenue was derived from the reissue of those eighty-some odd features.[138] RKO's most successful reissue was *King Kong* (1933), which in 1952 grossed $1,361,000, or almost twice as much as it had originally grossed in its theatrical run. RKO claimed that their reissues averaged between $100,000 and $500,000 per film, which was significantly more money than they had been offered by television.[139]

Many of the films that succeeded as theatrical rereleases did so because at that time there were no other ancillary markets like VHS or DVD available, so a rerelease offered new audiences and existing fans a unique chance to see the film. Ned Depinet explained that no one could predict for certain what the exact life of the theatrical distribution of a feature film was or why one film had a longer and more successful life than others:

> Society dramas and namby-pamby pictures don't reissue as well as hard hitting sensational pictures, but for anyone to say that a picture has completed its theatrical exhibition does not know what he is talking about. Mr. Goldwyn had quite a library some years ago, and he sold a license for three years for them to be reissued, and somebody paid him a substantial sum of money. They were reissued, and the license expired, and now Mr. Goldwyn is reissuing them himself and taking in more money than he took in the first time. I don't know what the life is. On our KING KONG, the fourth time it went out it did more business than the three previous times put together, absolutely.[140]

Fox also used their profits from theatrical reissues as a reason not to license their films to television. As Spyros Skouras explained, he had refused to offer Fox's films to television because television offered films to audiences for free, whereas a theatrical reissue could gross eight to ten times the amount that Fox was offered for their films on television. Skouras claimed that since 1946, Fox had earned almost $20 million from their theatrical reissues, and he did not believe television could match that amount.[141]

Beyond the financial comparisons, Peter Levathes believed that releasing feature films to television would make it impossible for the films to be reissued to theaters because "the public would have seen the films, and they wouldn't pay admission to see something that they had received on the air free of charge."[142] Levathes argued that changing conditions in society and culture made it impossible to forecast which films might one day have resonance with an audience. He explained, "For example, a picture called OX BOW INCIDENT, when it was released, it did not do very well, but it had certain sociological implications, and it was released later, and it did very well."[143] Ralph Cohn of Columbia agreed with Levathes that once a film had been played on television, it had no further theatrical value, because once an audience had seen it once, or multiple times, on television, they would no longer be interested in seeing it in the theater. He believed this scenario was compounded by the fact that if an audience could see a film at home on television for free, they would never pay to see it in the theater. Cohn testified that theatrical reissues had earned Columbia "substantial sums of money."[144] He explained that this was because the income was nearly all profit, and "because they were amortized films, films that had been almost completely amortized, and all we had on them was print costs. So they played a very important part in the final result of our operation."[145] In light of this almost pure profit the studios earned from their theatrical reissues, Alexander Beggs, of the Stanford Research Institute, concluded in a study financed by the studios that as far as he could calculate, the income that would have been available from the studios' exploitation of the films in their vaults on television would not have compensated for the loss they would have incurred through destroying the reissue and rerelease value of their old films.[146]

The potential value of remaking an older feature film for theatrical release was another source of potential profit that the studios did not want to give up by releasing their films to television. In each of the years 1946 through 1954, remade feature films constituted anywhere from 4 to 12 percent of the studios' total production,[147] and Spyros Skouras testified that Fox was remaking three or four of their older films a year.[148] If the studios released their films to television, they argued, they would be relinquishing their rights to remake that story. As Jack Warner explained, "Instead of having to purchase a story for X amount of dollars, you have the story there gratis, because those are the terms under which we buy stories, the right to remake them. So you see there is a tremendous amount of money sometimes in the actual buying of a story. If you will give this particular story to television, I feel in my judgment, and the judgments of the men who run our company, that you would lose the possibility of remaking that film again."[149] Warner's argument does not consider that the studios, as owners of the copyright on those motion pictures, could have included in their contracts the fact that they retained the story rights for theatrical remakes. It appears, however, that Warner may have willfully excluded that option because some of the studio heads actually wanted to remake their old films—not for the theaters, but for television. In May 1954, for example, Jack Warner and Benjamin Kalmenson went to the ABC offices in New York and discussed a deal for Warner Bros. to produce thirty-nine one-hour television programs based on three of the studio's older feature film properties: *Casablanca* (1942), *Cheyenne* (1947), and *King's Row* (1942). By the end of 1955, Warner Bros.

had produced almost twenty of the thirty-nine programs they were calling *War-ner Bros. Presents*. It aired on ABC every Tuesday night from 7:30 P.M. to 8:30 P.M. As Jack Warner argued, one of the primary motivations in producing those programs was to drive audiences back to the theaters by including segments in those programs that they called "Behind the Camera," which showed how the studios' new features were made and included clips from coming attractions.[150] This example highlights one of the key ways to successfully manage disruption, which involves "finding a better way to meet a *fundamental need* that the customer has, not just replacing an existing process or outcome with something similar but slightly better."[151] In this case, there was a fundamental difference between the perceived and actual customers for both the film and television industries. Practically speaking, the studios considered the theaters to be their primary customers, and, as economic theorist Clayton Christensen warned, "There are times at which it is right *not* to listen to customers, right to invest in developing lower-performance products that promise *lower* margins, and right to aggressively pursue small, rather than substantial, markets."[152] Although the public bought the tickets to see the films, the theaters rented the films from the studios and paid studios a share of their box office. If the studios had thought of the public as their customers, then perhaps they would have been more in tune with what those customers were willing to pay for. The studios had blinders on to some extent, and those were reinforced by the fact that the film industry enjoyed its oligopoly status until well into the 1950s. The market dominance they enjoyed through that arrangement, however, caused them to falter in the face of innovation.

Further complicating those matters, however, was that exhibitors, like many other segments of the film industry, often had a difficult time agreeing on the best way forward. As media scholar Deron Overpeck has demonstrated, "Throughout its history, the exhibition sector of the film industry has been torn by internecine disagreements about the appropriate relationship with production-distribution and even about who should be allowed to join exhibitor trade organizations. Indeed, exhibition could reasonably be described as the most chaotic aspect of the American film industry due to this long history of internal and external fighting."[153] Although the exhibitors remained a force to be reckoned with, they may have wielded greater power if they had successfully united behind proactive ways to manage the industrial disruption, rather than, as so often happened, digging in their heels in opposition to change. Ultimately, what lay at the heart of these issues was the fact that, as William Boddy has described, "the shifting boundaries between analogue and digital, cinema and television, and broadcasting and the Internet, throw into question traditional critical oppositions between domestic and public media reception, active and passive scenarios of consumption, and authored and non-authored texts."[154] Those shifting boundaries and their resultant ruptures often required the intervention of the courts before the parties involved could move forward.

CHAPTER 3

Contracts, Rights, Residuals, and Labor

The collaborative nature of the media industries poses a particular problem when negotiating the rights to media texts and the compensation for laborers' work. Without clearly identifiable, singular authors for films and television series, the questions of how to credit those who participated in their creation, and who determines how, when, and where the texts appear have proved sticking points at each moment of disruption. Copyright law assigns legal authorship of a text and thereby officially governs who has the right to determine the use of that text and who deserves compensation for that use. The studios typically hold the copyright to the content they produce, and that is a tradition rooted in an uneasy deal between studios and the many laborers involved in making that content. Residual payments were one way the unions and guilds ensured that even though they were not the legal owners of their work, they would still be properly compensated and credited for their contributions. As legal scholar Catherine L. Fisk has detailed, "Since 1938 all Hollywood motion pictures and scripted television shows—now including shows created by Netflix, Amazon, and Hulu for streaming on the internet—have been produced by workers where everyone from the director, actors, and writers to the gaffers, grips, and drivers belong to a union."[1] Unions and guilds have played a central role in Hollywood since the 1930s. Their contracts with studios define the terms and conditions under which a large part of Hollywood labor functions, how they are credited and paid, and where, when, and how media is exhibited. The introduction of television in the mid-twentieth century was the first period of industrial disruption when unions and guilds were a strong force in the industry, and the early battles over the reuse of their work in another medium set the stage for every negotiation and labor strike that has since taken place. This chapter focuses on the role played by the unions and guilds in the film and television industries, and the AFM in particular, in the early struggles over what later became a bedrock of labor contracts in Hollywood: residual payments. It will also more broadly consider the question of rights to content in a new medium, and the conflicts over who held those rights. The history of those struggles illustrates the ways in which contract law and long-term contracts can tie up existing media industries for years, and how legal and regulatory frameworks fundamentally influence the relations between labor and management and the texts they produce.

CLEARING RIGHTS

In order for feature films to appear on television, the rights to those films had to be cleared, and the complex questions related to exactly what rights were held by whom caused confusion and delay. Typically, the studios owned the copyright to their films, which included the right to, as scholar Catherine L. Fisk described, "rewrite it, throw it in the trash, produce the story into a movie or TV show, or attribute it to anyone or no one."[2] Even though most of the studios started incorporating television rights into their contracts in the 1930s, the exact meaning of "television" and the definition of what those rights included became points of contention.[3] Earl R. Collins, president of Hollywood Television Service, a subsidiary of Republic Studios, explained that when the first television stations went on the air in the mid-1930s, there were, in fact, many people in the film industry who believed that feature films would eventually be exhibited on television. Collins said that as a result,

> substantially all talent, story purchase and other motion picture contracts thereafter prepared were prepared with provisions granting to the producer or distributor all television rights of every kind whatsoever in and to the motion pictures and the appearances of all artists therein. It was and is understood throughout the motion picture industry that such so-called "television rights" provisions were designed to and in fact did give to the producer and/or distributor of the motion picture the exclusive right to license such motion picture for television exhibition freely and without contractual or other restriction, upon whatever terms and conditions and under whatever circumstances were deemed proper by said distributor.[4]

Meyer Lavenstein, general counsel for Republic, recalled that their policy had been to include in all contracts Republic made for the employment of actors, and in all contracts for the acquisition of literary material, "a provision confirming that Republic had the right to exhibit and produce and transmit motion pictures by any device, method, or means now or hereafter known, including television as now or hereafter known, and the word 'television' appeared in every contract of that kind made by Republic since the summer of 1935."[5] Just because they had that right, however, does not mean that it went unchallenged, and rights restrictions that had made their way into Republic's contracts caused a great deal of uncertainty. In 1954 and 1955, Republic's legal department was working through the contracts for their films to determine "whether and to what extent there existed legal objections to the use of the sound track which included music in connection with television exhibition of the pictures."[6] In early 1955, the department discovered, for example, that when editing films for television broadcast, for some of those films the studio was contractually obligated to "retain at least one visual, vocal, musical number by 'The Sons of the Pioneers', exclusively, although others in addition to the Sons of the Pioneers may be photographed in the respective scene or scenes in which said musical number is used."[7] That contractual provision meant that if Republic wanted to license or sell those films for use on television, and needed to edit the films for time or content, the scene or scenes featuring the Sons of the Pioneers had to remain in the film, and it was Republic's contractual responsibility to ensure that they did.

When asked whether he was aware of the difficulties of clearing film rights for television, Creighton Tevlin, vice president of RKO, explained, "Well, I was very conscious of that, and so were other executives, our legal department, and the complications that might arise with respect to an individual picture were so many and so diverse in character, that I just couldn't possibly remember all of the items that would have to be taken into account."[8] For instance, some authors of literary material had retained the television rights, but other authors had only retained the rights to the material on live television. Music rights were particularly complex because some composers had retained the rights to the musical score for television, but in other instances the copyrights had expired or were set to expire soon. In those cases, the studio had to determine when exactly the copyrights would expire and who was then vested with the right of renewal. Tevlin recalled that RKO attempted to make a complete survey of all of their rights, but "the work was so voluminous that we never actually completed a full survey of the whole library."[9] As a result, RKO had to deny many requests to license or purchase their films because they did not have clear ownership of all of the rights for reuse on television.[10] Tevlin explained that it was those complex factors, in addition to the possibility of negotiating better deals with the unions, that led RKO to determine that the best course of action would be to attempt a bulk sale of their library, thereby more easily eliminating those complications.[11]

In 1948, in order to determine exactly what television rights they had and what rights were held or denied by different unions, actors, producing partners, or others, Columbia undertook a survey for each of the feature films in their library. The survey was later described by Columbia's lawyers as a "Herculean task" since a minimum of twenty contracts had to be examined for each of the more than 1,000 features the studio had produced before 1948. Columbia also had 1,700 short subjects with similar contracts, and the total task was considered "overwhelming."[12] Screen Gems was still working through their library, and by 1955 they had been able to clear the rights for television to over one hundred westerns and a number of other features.[13] They were then able to release seventy-two westerns to television, in addition to two or three released the year before.[14] They made the move to release some of their films to television in 1955, the westerns in particular, because of a number of factors, of which Ralph Cohn recalled: "First, the beginning of a leveling off process in the prices that were being received for certain pictures . . . that were playing on television. Secondly, the fact that the large network shows were beginning to use up more and more of what had been known as local station option time, which meant that there would be less playing time on the television stations for feature pictures, and, as a consequence, the demand for them could considerably lessen, plus the fact that the sales department of the company advised us at that time that the reissue value of these pictures was comparatively negligible."[15] Even though they had determined the time was right to release some of their films to television, they would not be able to release the rest of the films until the remaining issues over television rights had been resolved. Conflicts over rights to the use of films on television were widespread and led to many court appearances to assert or defend rights. In August 1955, Judge Yankwich in the District Court in Los Angeles commented that his court "had all sorts of litigation relating to who has television rights as to what, and we have quite a series of decisions which rule on certain specific contracts. So whatever they say in the contract doesn't mean anything, except their own doubts as to what their rights are."[16]

Union and Guild Contracts and Residuals

An additional obstacle to Hollywood's feature films appearing on television was the unions and guilds and their claim to rights and what later became known as residual payments for their work appearing in other media. Macklin Fleming, lawyer for Columbia, Screen Gems, and RKO, explained that foreign films and independent films appeared on television in the late 1940s and early 1950s because these types of films were not restricted by union agreements. He argued, "From the point of view of a major producing studio, however, they can't tell the unions to go whistle, because if they sell their pictures to television, and license them on television, and do not reach an agreement with the unions, then they are faced with the possibility of a major strike. . . . [If] all of the demands of the crafts and Guilds are accepted at face value, over 100 percent of the television receipts would go to those sources."[17] Whether or not the studios were interested in selling their feature films to television, rereleasing them in theaters, or remaking them for television, they still had to deal with the union and guild demands for the reuse of their performances. As Creighton J. Tevlin, vice president of RKO, explained, "The pattern in connection with all of the Guilds we dealt with was that they were entitled to some compensation in the event these pictures, or pictures they worked on or contributed to, were exhibited on television in addition to being shown theatrically."[18] By this time, the International Alliance of Theatrical Stage Employees (IATSE), which represented some nineteen or twenty different unions including the carpenters, camera operators, editors, set designers, and many others who were employed in the physical production of films, had begun making demands for television.[19] The musicians in the AFM demanded 5 percent of the gross proceeds from sales of films to television, plus rerecording fees for the musicians. SAG had demanded anywhere from 12.5 to 15 percent of gross proceeds of sales to television, and the directors, writers, and craft unions were also demanding extra compensation for their theatrical films that were broadcast on television.[20] New groups like the Screen Producers Guild, which was formally organized in 1950, also had the potential to make demands.[21] According to CBS, the contracts and demands of the

American Society of Composers, Authors, and Publishers (ASCAP) presented yet another obstacle to getting films on television.[22] As Saul Rittenberg, a lawyer for Republic, outlined in an interoffice memo on the use of music on television, no problems existed related to the use of music that had been purchased outright from outside sources or that employees of Republic had written for their productions; however, "in connection with music specifically licensed for use in particular pictures, there are, in general, two types of problems. One concerns the copyright status of the property, and the other the form of the license."[23] In terms of the copyright status, although Republic had licensed perpetual rights to the music from the publisher, in some cases the copyright of the composition may have expired. In that case, if the publisher did not renew the copyright, then any use of that music by Republic could have constituted an infringement of the copyright owner's rights. In regard to the form of the license, most of the licenses granted synchronization rights only for the performance of the film in theaters that held valid performing licenses from the performing rights societies. If the synchronization rights were not extended to television, Republic would have had to pay additional fees for that use. There was obviously some risk involved in each of those potential problems, and Republic had to decide whether they were willing to tolerate those risks in order to move forward.[24] As Fleming explained in late 1955, "The problem is that the unions say that the television is a new and different medium from motion pictures, and that when their work is performed on television, they are entitled to added compensation,—more pork chops."[25] The producers continued to hold their position that they had paid everyone once, and since the producers owned the exhibition rights, they believed they could exhibit the films as they pleased without having to make additional payments for those showings.

With unions and guilds making demands for payment for the use of their work in the new medium of television, there arose the question of exactly what organizations had the right to demand payment and for whom. In 1949, for example, the AFM faced competition from a new guild, the American Guild of Variety Artists (AGVA), which claimed jurisdiction over musicians who performed on stage and sang, danced, or performed in any way other than playing an instrument. At the 1949 AFM convention in San Francisco, James Petrillo, president of the AFM, complained that "someone got the crazy idea that when a musician plays under a spotlight it makes him an actor and he must belong to AGVA. No musician anywhere, any time need belong to another trade union. . . . We are going to stop this raiding at the outset because we won't give ground."[26] Meanwhile, the Screen Writers Guild (later renamed as the Writers Guild of America), which represented writers of theatrical films, faced a similar jurisdictional dispute. Three of the four branches of the Authors League—the Dramatists Guild, the Radio Writers Guild, and the Screen Writers Guild—were trying to claim jurisdiction over the writers' work in television. Then some writers formed the Television Writers Association, which further complicated the matter.[27]

SAG faced similar jurisdictional problems. Although Ronald Reagan later recalled that in 1949 SAG was not paying serious attention to television, because

"TV was live and we didn't really think it was our baby,"[28] his account was complicated by the emergence of a competing guild that forced SAG to pay attention to television. In 1949, George Heller, the executive secretary of the American Federation of Radio Artists (AFRA), formed the President's Committee of Television Authority (TVA) in New York. The TVA was composed mainly of members of East Coast live talent unions and wanted jurisdiction over all of live and filmed television, including films on television. SAG disagreed and argued that they had the rights to film in all forms. As Reagan recalled, "We girded ourselves for battle, but so we could be completely secure in the knowledge our cause was just, we did a lot of soul searching and were reassured in our belief that we had no basis for even pretending a claim to live TV. Among ourselves we came to the conclusion that logically AFRA (the radio union) should expand and take in TV, and the other guilds and unions would do well to follow our lead in forsaking any claims. After several years of expensive bickering, this is of course what happened, and AFRA became AFTRA—the American Federation of Television and Radio Artists."[29] In October 1949, Reagan presented SAG's proposed resolution in regard to the TVA, which was based on his conclusion that there were two areas in TV, one on film and one live, in addition to a third, gray area of film spot commercials and film inserts. SAG proposed that "1) TVA be established by the International Board of the Four A's [Associated Actors and Artists of America] to have jurisdiction over live TV including simultaneous kinescopes of such shows; 2) that SAG and SEG [Screen Extras Guild] have jurisdiction reaffirmed by the Four A's over filmed TV; and 3) the 'gray areas' be submitted to mediation."[30] Despite SAG's proposal, in April 1950 the International Board of the Four A's agreed to give the TVA authority over all of television—filmed and live.[31]

SAG was not giving up so easily, however, and in June 1950 they mailed to their members a detailed comparison of SAG's contract proposals for televised motion pictures and the proposals of the TVA. SAG argued that the TVA wanted jurisdiction over actors in televised motion pictures, and outlined the ways they believed that the TVA's proposals would seriously undercut working conditions for motion picture actors. SAG stated that problems with the TVA's proposals were "the result of TVA's complete lack of experience in contract negotiations for actors in motion pictures and TVA's ignorance of the problems of such actors."[32] In September 1952, SAG argued to the International Board of the Four A's that since the Four A's had given the TVA authority over television in 1950, the TVA had been unable to secure a single contract for their members, except for contracts covering actors' work in live television. SAG asked the Four A's to rescind its gift of authority over television to the TVA and to pass a resolution giving SAG authority over motion pictures—including motion pictures for television. The resolution passed without dissent.[33] Once those disputes were resolved, SAG could move forward confidently with contracts with the film producers, and the TVA eventually became a part of AFRA, which became AFTRA. Internal disputes between the actors and writers unions over television would continue, and, for both unions, those disputes would require the intervention of the National Labor Relations Board to resolve.[34] In the meantime, the basic confusion over jurisdiction between and among the unions presented a fundamental problem that even if the studios wanted to negotiate for their films to appear on television, it was unclear who had the authority to participate in those negotiations.

ACTORS, WRITERS, AND DIRECTORS

The issue of rights also extended to actors appearing on television in personal appearances, in roles on a television show, and in feature films. In September 1947, the MPPDA jumped into the fray and announced an edict against actors appearing on television in any capacity, because "it was agreed that in the present stage of development television appearances are likely to be harmful."[35] The policy did not, however, restrict Paramount on its own station. The MPPDA explained that they were going to keep a "close check" on the development of television so that they could formulate a policy at a later time.[36] In line with this blanket ban on actors appearing on television, many studios included similar restrictions in their contracts with actors. For example, the contract that Mickey Rooney signed with MGM in August 1933, to act in the film *Fire Chief* (released as *The Chief* in 1934), prohibited the reproduction or transmission of the film on "all other improvements and devices which are now or may hereafter be used in connection with the production and/or exhibition and/or transmission of any present or future kind of motion picture production."[37] In 1933, this ban was primarily intended for radio as a part of the "so-called radio ban of December 1932," but it carried over to television.[38] Complicating matters even further was that many actors were still working under long-term contracts with studios, and so they had to sign a loan-out contract for any work they did for another studio. Often the loan-out contract contained language restricting the sale or licensing of the film to television. These clauses were the studios' way of controlling all current and future rights to their films in all media, and whether or not the signatories fully understood television at the time the clauses were agreed to, the contracts served to ensure that the films did not appear on television.

The battle over actors appearing on television was not only a matter of the studios trying to keep their actors off television screens. Actors also began pushing back against their films being broadcast and sued their studios to keep their films off television. In April 1948, in one of the first legal actions related to this issue, actress Blanche Mehaffey filed suit against Paramount Pictures and Guaranteed Pictures, claiming that they did not have the right to broadcast the film *The Mystery Trooper* (1931) on Paramount's station KTLA without her permission or without her receiving payment. She asked for $100,000 for "distorted and uncomplimentary likeness of Miss Mehaffey and damage to her future value in network television."[39] Mehaffey's suit was eventually dismissed, but as we will see in chapter 4, this question of the actors' role in television rights would soon reappear and have its day— or more accurately, years—in court.

Although some actors had enough power to negotiate their own terms of employment with the studios directly, many actors relied on the basic standard agreements between SAG and the studios for the terms of their labor and compensation. When SAG was formed in 1937, they signed a ten-year contract with the producers, and that contract had not included any clauses dealing with television. So, when the union began contract renegotiations with the studios in 1948, there was a significant amount of pent-up dissatisfaction and a great deal to discuss. The negotiations began in March 1948, and Ronald Reagan, who was the president of SAG at the time, led the negotiating committee.[40] He later explained that in the matter of feature films on television, "our contention had been, and still is, that if a producer wants to use a film in theaters and then sell it to TV, the actor has a right to set a price for the two uses, or even refuse to sell TV rights. It is possible that a performer might have an exclusive TV contract and be legally unable to permit use of his screen performance on TV."[41] Thus, the actors not only claimed that they had the right to additional payment for the use of their performance in the television medium, but also asserted a claim to the right to televise the work at all. Because most of the major studios had included television rights clauses in their contracts with individual performers since the 1930s, they were not happy with SAG's assertions. In April 1948, SAG members were notified that the contract negotiations had broken off, but the guild could not strike until 1 August, when their previous contract expired. The points of contention included restrictions on reissues of old films to curb the unemployment of actors, a stopgap clause to preclude the use of theatrical films on television (this clause is identical to the television clause in the producers' contract with musicians), no loan-outs of contract players without the actors' consent, the right of actors to work in other areas of entertainment such as radio and television, and a reduction in the length of term contracts.[42]

The guild argued that the producers did not have the legal right to sell or license to television their feature films made for theatrical exhibition. As the newsletter for SAG members explained, "The Guild will take the position in such negotiations that film made for motion picture theatre exhibition may not be used for television without compensation to the actors to be agreed upon between us as part of a collective bargaining agreement."[43] The producers, on the other hand, claimed that their previous contract specifically retained television rights for producers. The producers said that if they agreed to SAG's demands, they would be giving up rights they already held.[44] SAG, however, argued that there was no major clause covering television rights in their basic agreement.[45] B. B. Kahane, vice president of Columbia, recalled:

We very firmly took the position that, having paid an actor for his services in the theatrical picture, the actor was not entitled to any additional payment, that we were entitled to the results and the proceeds of the services; that there was no difference between an actor or anybody else who was paid for a job that was done. They took the position that at the time those contracts were made for their services in theatrical pictures, television was not contemplated, that that was a completely new medium of entertainment, and that for that reason they felt that the compensation that was paid the actors for the theatrical pictures should not be deemed the only payment to be made.[46]

The contract negotiations ultimately lasted five months, but since SAG and the producers remained at an impasse, they decided to move forward with the contract without resolving the terms for feature films on television. Reagan later recalled that "we had wearily agreed to a stopgap clause that settled nothing with regard to movies someday being reissued on television—but then everyone said they'd be crazy to sell their movies to a competing medium."[47] The stopgap clause stated that the studios were not allowed to release to television any of their films made after the 1 August date of the new contract. If any studio moved forward with releasing those post–1 August films to television, SAG had the right to cancel the contract.[48] Although this stopgap clause left the door open for releasing pre-August 1948 films to television, the AFM had a ban on all feature films to television that remained in place and meant that the pre-1948 films would stay in the studios' vaults.

SAG, like the AFM, was concerned at this time about declining employment for their members, and they feared that using films on television would further eliminate jobs for actors. The guild blamed the Taft-Hartley Act for a significant loss of jobs to non-guild members. Reagan commented at the meeting of COMPO in 1951 that even though "the greatest pool of acting skill and talent that has ever been assembled in the world is right here in Hollywood, seven thousand Screen Actor Guild members," in the fourteen months preceding, 4,000 non-guild members had been given jobs that should have gone to members.[49] By 1954, the union, along with the Hollywood AFL (American Federation of Labor) Film Council, also had to contend with the issue of employment lost to runaway productions. The Film Council issued a press release outlining Senator Thomas Kuchel's pledge to the Film Council to "do everything within his power to help the unions solve a growing unemployment problem caused by 'runaway' foreign production of movies by American producers who go abroad to take advantage of lower wage rates."[50] At SAG's annual meeting in November 1953, Leon Ames, SAG's first vice president, echoed the AFL's concerns, arguing, "The most serious problem facing the actor is lack of employment—the great decrease in available acting jobs, caused by a decrease in the number of pictures being produced in this country."[51] The anxieties about the loss of employment resulted in the unions taking a harder line in negotiations over residual payments for films on television than they might have otherwise.

Another reason actors felt nervous about employment stability was that in the early 1950s, studios' seven-year contracts with actors were going by the wayside. Although there were many things about those long-term contracts that actors found objectionable, they did provide stable income over a period of years. For those actors who still worked under long-term contracts, if they wanted to make a film with another studio, they needed a loan-out agreement from their "home" studio. If the actor's home studio included in the loan-out contract any stipulations restricting the film's appearance on television, the borrowing studio was bound by that limitation. For example, a 1953 agreement in which Columbia would borrow Rock Hudson from Universal to play "Ben" in Raoul Walsh's *Gun Fury* (originally titled and contracted as *Ten Against Caesar*), co-starring Donna Reed, stated that Columbia could not "cause or authorize said photoplay to be televised until such time as it is your practice to televise or permit the televising of your other feature photoplays of comparable class and quality produced by you during the same period that said photoplay was produced."[52] Not only did Universal want Columbia to assume responsibility for clearing the various rights and consents for the film with the unions and guilds, but Universal also wanted to make sure that Columbia would not at some point dump the film on television while withholding from television their own stars' films.

The comment in Hudson's contract related to "comparable class and quality" points to another of the actors' concerns: the negative effects of the often lower-quality aesthetics of television. In the late 1940s, Abe Montague, vice president and general sales manager of Columbia, viewed a private Phonevision screening of *Gilda* (1946) and found the results "disturbing. The artistic and photographic values of the picture were completely destroyed in telecasting. The important Columbia star, Rita Hayworth, did not televise well."[53] In 1951, Darryl Zanuck wrote to Spyros Skouras regarding a request he had received from Tyrone Power for Power to appear in a short film for television. Zanuck stated he did not believe it was a good idea for any of Fox's stars to appear on television until Fox was sure that television could photographically serve both the star's and the company's best interests.[54] Indeed, for a time, female artists were not permitted on television at all because the studios were "afraid that the photography for the female [was] very bad in television and could do nothing but hurt the personality."[55] However, as technologies improved, the studios' and actors' fears subsided, but the studios' desire to feature their stars and films in only the best aesthetic conditions lingered far into the 1950s.

Writers for film struggled with many of the same challenges, and as legal scholar Catherine L. Fisk detailed:

> The issue of profit sharing was a logical one to raise in 1947 because the rapid growth of television, the studios' drastic reduction in the number of movies made, and the studios' increased reissue of old films were causing widespread unemployment of writers. The SWG Executive Board received a report showing that only 466 writers were employed in July 1947, down by 80 since the year before and 100 in two years. At the same time, writers knew their old scripts were being reused as radio dramas and anticipated that studios would soon license their huge catalogues of films to be shown on TV. Writers felt entitled to share in whatever wealth the studios made from the reuses of their work, in a way that theatrical reissues and radio already offered and television promised.[56]

By that time, some writers had negotiated profit sharing in their individual contracts, and the SWG along with the other guilds representing writers, including the Radio Writers Guild, the Dramatists Guild, the Authors League, and various committees of writers in television, made profit sharing and licensing, rather than the sale of scripts, the writers' top priorities in bargaining for new collective agreements.[57] In September 1947, the members of the Writers Guild met to discuss the guild's demands with respect to payment of percentages of the gross. As Fisk argued, "This was an important meeting at which the members had the chance to forever change the way they were paid and also to come up with a plan to assert the rights of TV writers to have the claims to credit, creative control, and compensation for which movie writers had fought in the 1930s."[58] Unfortunately, the meeting happened at the moment when the House Un-American Activities Committee (HUAC) ramped up their investigations of suspected communists in Hollywood. The committee's intense focus on unions as instruments for communist propaganda distracted the Executive Board and weakened their bargaining position in negotiations over the Minimum Basic Agreement in 1949. In June, the guild proposed "that writers be paid at least 10 percent of the gross revenue derived by producers for rerelease of film in another medium (including television and radio) and that if more than one writer had been employed on film, that percentage would be divided in proportion to each writer's compensation (not their contribution) on the picture. Again, the producers objected."[59] At least one of the studios countered that writers would be given profit sharing only if they agreed to wage cuts. Just as with the actors, the most contentious issues in the negotiations were payments for reissue or reuse of work and the separation of rights.[60] The Screen Directors Guild was also renegotiating their contract in 1948, and later that year, both the Directors Guild and the Writers Guild entered into agreements with the studios that were similar to SAG's.[61] So the studios were locked into contracts that allowed for films that had been theatrically released before August 1948 to be sold to television without further compensation to the guilds. For any films released after that date, however, producers had to negotiate a compensation deal before releasing any films to television. The contracts effectively prohibited the licensing or sale of their feature films to television and would not be up for renegotiation for another few years. With these restrictions written into the labor contracts, the prohibitions on feature films appearing on television were adding up.

THE AMERICAN FEDERATION OF MUSICIANS

One of the most prominent unions in this struggle was the AFM. While unions such as SAG, the Directors Guild, and WGA may have in recent years become more powerful and well known, in the mid-twentieth century the AFM was one of the strongest forces in Hollywood, and they often led the way in establishing terms that other unions adopted in their subsequent contract negotiations. The AFM was organized in 1896, and by 1947 it had 216,000 members.[62] James C. Petrillo was president of the local chapter of the Chicago Federation of Musicians, and in 1940 he became the president of the AFM.[63] Petrillo was largely beloved by his union's membership, in part for the flack he endured while fighting on behalf of his members. Petrillo was frequently demonized in the press and often referred to as a "czar" and "the big bad wolf."[64] Many of those with whom he negotiated also expressed what might politely be described as less than favorable opinions of Petrillo. As Ed Fishman, a former orchestra booking agent, explained, "In all my years there has been a fear built up for Mr. Petrillo and for the union, and you do it their way or you don't do it at all."[65] Justin Miller, president of the NAB, agreed, saying, "Mr. Petrillo has absolute and dictatorial power over his union and over the ability and opportunity of American musicians to obtain employment. So thorough has been this monopolistic control of the A.F. of M., that virtually no professional musician in the United States or Canada has been able to pursue the field of musical employment without membership in the union."[66] Allen Weiss, chairman of the board of directors of the Mutual Broadcasting System and vice president and general manager of the Don Lee Broadcasting System, recalled that at the time, "we realized the helplessness of the broadcasting industry under the despotic control of one man."[67] J. N. "Bill" Bailey, the executive director of the FM Association—a nonprofit trade organization composed of FM broadcasters, manufacturers of FM equipment, and others whose business related to FM broadcasting—compared Petrillo to Stalin, Hitler, and Mussolini.[68] Since he had such an outsize reputation, coverage of the AFM often appeared in the press, and the struggles with the AFM were referred to among studio heads as the "Petrillo problem." By reducing their conflicts with the AFM to a personality issue with Petrillo, the studio heads and industry press efficiently marketed the obstacle as an individual problem and avoided demonizing either the performers or the union as a whole.

Petrillo saw his demonization in a slightly different light, and when asked why he had the reputation as a "czar," Petrillo placed a large amount of the blame on what he called the "propaganda machine" of the NAB. Petrillo explained, "No one was ever more vilified than I have been in the press. I have 260 cartoons in my office from the press of this country, and when I get a little time I read them, and I have a few laughs. If they would spend half of the money that they spend on cartoons vilifying me as the president of this organization, if they would give it to the musicians, we would all be happy. But, that is not the system of the National Association of Broadcasters. . . . Every time I see them, they say: 'Oh, Jimmy, my pal.' And 'You are the squarest guy we ever did business with.'"[69] Despite the AFM's power, before 1944 no formal written agreements existed between the film producers and the federation; however, contracts were in effect in the form of the printed regulations of the federation relating to wages, hours, working conditions, and so forth, which the AFM circulated after negotiations with the producers.[70] Then, in 1946, the so-called industry contract with Petrillo was completed.[71] The agreement included such regulations as a guaranteed minimum number of film recording musicians that the studios would employ each year.[72] It also contained extensive language regulating the use of music and musicians in feature films and television. In a newsletter to AFM members, Petrillo announced that they had successfully added a clause in the contract that, as Petrillo explained, "practically freezes the sound track already made on the shelves. The producer is not permitted to use this sound track in any way except for its original purpose during the term of this contract or after the contract has expired. This means, in effect, that the sound track cannot be used for any other purpose for all time."[73] The AFM also included a clause that stated that those restrictions would be passed on to anyone who purchased the films. So, this contract not only prohibited the use of a film soundtrack in any way other than accompanying the film itself (the AFM had been struggling with the sale of recordings of film soundtracks and the "bootlegged" use of film soundtracks on television and radio as background music for other programs[74]), but also explicitly forbade the use of the soundtrack, and thereby the film, on television. The AFM argued that the films made between 1928, when sync sound was introduced, and 1946 were intended for theatrical exhibition only and that the musicians who performed in those films were paid on a wage scale created for that limited theatrical use. They asserted that if the films were to be broadcast on television, the musicians should be further compensated by additional payments.

Charles Boren of Paramount recalled that both Barney Balaban and Nicholas Schenck had vigorously opposed the television clause, and it was such a point of contention that "[it] was kept in suspense, and when we came to the final drafting of the contract . . . when it came to the television clause, at that time we were still in an impasse, for this was not up to our committee to draft the television clause or anything else, and it was referred actually to the principals. By the principals, I mean the presidents of our companies."[75] However, Burton A. Zorn, special labor-relations counsel for the majors during their negotiations with the AFM in 1946, recalled that although the television provision may have been contentious, it was never really up for negotiation: "Petrillo made it very clear from the beginning to the end of the negotiations that these television restrictions were an absolute 'must'; that no contract would be signed by the federation without them; that unless they were agreed to and incorporated in the 1946 labor contract, there would be no music in Hollywood until such time as these provisions were put into a contract, regardless of how long that might be."[76] Zorn explained that the producers made every effort to avoid the inclusion of the television clause, but they finally signed the contract to avoid having the studios shut down by a musicians' strike. According to Zorn, Petrillo argued that he did not know enough about television at that point to feel comfortable agreeing to terms. He did say, however, that "when [Petrillo] felt he knew enough about the development of television to determine how to protect the interests of his members, he would then be willing to sit down and negotiate some arrangement."[77] In the meantime, the negotiators ended up with contract provisions that restricted the use of film music and musicians on television.[78] All the studios eventually capitulated to the AFM's demands and signed the contract, which was to expire at the end of August 1948.[79] The AFM did, however, agree that if a producer desired in the future to use their films on television, the AFM would negotiate with the producer individually to see if they could agree on terms.[80]

The Society of Independent Motion Picture Producers (SIMPP), which existed between 1941 and 1958 to advance the interests of independent producers in the studio-dominated industry, had substantially the same contract as the one negotiated by the majors.[81] Although the SIMPP members signed the contracts containing the AFM's clause against feature film soundtracks appearing on television, independent producers disliked the clause even more than did the majors.[82] Before signing the contract, Isaac Chadwick, president of SIMPP, organized a meeting for the thirty-three member companies to discuss the contract. At that meeting, Steve Broidy, president of Monogram Pictures, raised the question of films on television. Chadwick recalled, "Our members had considerable interest because a substantial amount of our revenue had, prior to the making of this contract, been derived from the rental of our pictures to television stations for broadcasting. Broidy then stated that with respect to that clause, if we must sign it, we must, but we felt that it was harmful to our interests and a substantial loss to us."[83] Later, when asked whether SIMPP objected to the clause restricting their films on television, Anthony J. O'Rourke, chairman of the Labor Advisory Committee for SIMPP, said, "No; there was no protest. The matter had been already agreed to by the major motion-picture producers, and we could hardly expect to get any less than they had granted, and so it was not contested."[84] Charles Bagley, then vice president of the AFM, remembered the negotiations slightly differently: "I don't recall that there was any particular dispute at all. They seemed to realize that [television] was a new project, of which they were all ignorant, and they were willing to go slow at it and find out what it was. . . . It was a realm of uncertainty we were all peering into."[85]

Although some scholars have argued that these restrictions and negotiations were based on a disagreement over residual payments for the work of individual performers, from all of the records available it is clear that the AFM's restrictions had more to do with maintaining employment for as many members of the union as possible. If the musicians had agreed to allow recordings to be used, or for films to appear on television, Petrillo predicted "ruination for the musicians," and he feared that in one year 50 percent of his musicians would "be on the streets."[86] Petrillo explained the cause of his concern in a congressional hearing in 1947 on the activities of the AFM: "Overnight we lost 18,000 musicians because of Movietone and Vitaphone. . . . We make the Movietone and the Vitaphone. We make the progress that puts us out of business. . . . We are giving those people the instrument to knock our brains out, and we are trying to find ways and means of not giving them that instrument. . . . [The studios] have a right to protect themselves. I do not criticize them for it. But why can't we protect ourselves?"[87] The broadcasting industry had promised Petrillo that if he eased his restrictions on the musicians in television (not just in feature films but in television and radio more broadly), it would lead to increased employment for the musicians. Petrillo disagreed, however, and argued, "If they [in television] are able to go to Hollywood and buy those films from Hollywood, there would be no need to employ musicians in the studios."[88] Petrillo also recognized that studios like Paramount and RKO already had significant interests in television, and he was especially suspicious that they wanted to use their films on television. As long as he had the restrictions in their contract, the AFM would have recourse to stop any studios if necessary.[89]

While the ban on the use of feature film soundtracks on television was in force, the studios continued to try to find ways around it. Republic Studios even went so far as to fundamentally change the ways they recorded and mixed soundtracks. Before November 1948, Republic, as well as many of the other studios, would destroy the individual dialogue and music soundtracks once a film was dubbed. They explained that it was mainly an issue of not having enough storage space for all of those tracks. The problem they eventually ran into was that if all of the music and dialogue were mixed together on one track and the individual tracks had been destroyed, it was impossible to separate the music from the dialogue. So even if Republic had been interested in releasing their films to television without music, they could not do so unless they were willing to rerecord all of the other dialogue and sound for the film. But once the AFM ban went into effect, Republic found storage space under one of their stages and began keeping individual tracks.[90]

Congress and the DOJ, however, suspected that through this clause restricting the use of films on television, the AFM was actually conspiring *with* the studios. Carroll D. Kearns, chairman of a congressional subcommittee that conducted hearings on the AFM, asked, "Did you feel there was any motive here that the moving-picture industry may have really down deep liked this clause in that contract?"[91] And an internal DOJ memo stated, "Those producers which were integrated with theatre ownership and which feared that television would have an adverse affect on the theatre box offices probably clearly felt it was to their benefit to have such a contract provision to hide behind."[92] Irving G. McCann, general counsel to the Congressional Committee on Education and Labor, recalled a conversation he had with Donald Nelson, the president of SIMPP: "I said to Mr. Nelson over the phone, 'I understand that you have entered into a contract with the A.F. of M. to conspire against free trade and that you have blocked television from the country,' or words to that effect. He laughed and said, 'We haven't conspired with anybody. We were just forced to sign the contract.'"[93]

The investigations of the AFM and Petrillo by Congress and the DOJ were indicative of the growing antiunion sentiment in the government at that time. In addition to the HUAC investigations, in the mid to late 1940s a number of laws were passed to curb the power of labor unions. For example, during World War II, a number of bills were passed that limited the ability of unions to strike in industries that had been taken over by the government for the war effort. After the war, industry leaders, in conjunction with some members of Congress, worked to extend those limitations to private industry. Their efforts resulted in a wide range of legislative acts that were intended to "combat racketeering." These acts included the Lea Act (which, in evidence of the animosity felt for the AFM's leader, was nicknamed "the anti-Petrillo" bill), the Hobbs Act (1946), the Case Bill (1946), and the Strike Curb Bill, to name a few. The bill that most upset the AFM (because of the ways that it restricted the power and activities of unions), however, was the Taft-

Hartley bill, otherwise known as the Labor Management Relations Act of 1947. As Joseph Padway, the lawyer for Petrillo and the AFM, explained, "We say there are a few provisions that are good, of the many, in a very bad bill."[94]

In February and March 1947, as the House Committee on Education and Labor conducted hearings on proposed labor legislation, including the Taft-Hartley bill, members of the committee made various allegations against Petrillo and the AFM for unfair business practices. In April 1947, Fred A. Hartley Jr., chairman of the committee, explained that "our attention was called to the fact that Mr. Petrillo and the American Federation of Musicians exercise monopolistic control over all commercial phases of musical production, including recordings, radio, movies, and television, and have used their great power to block the technological development of FM radio and of television."[95] In response to those allegations, Hartley appointed a subcommittee to investigate the complaints against Petrillo and the AFM. The subcommittee conducted hearings in Washington, DC, and Los Angeles and filed an interim report in December 1947. Then, in January 1948, the committee began a full hearing in Congress. One of the charges the subcommittee levied against the AFM was that they had "engaged in a concerted effort to hold back the technological improvements in radio and in television. That you have denied the use of live music through the networks to FM broadcasting stations. That you have forced the movie industry to sign contracts denying the use of any sound track made by members of your federation to television."[96] Hartley stated that if the committee found evidence that warranted it, he would have the DOJ and other federal agencies take "appropriate steps" to punish the AFM for acting "against the public interest."[97] The findings of fact from the 1947 hearings stated, "By virtue of recent labor legislation exempting unions from the restraints which control the activities of private individuals and corporations, James Caesar Petrillo has successfully created a small kingdom within our Republic, over which he rules."[98] Irving G. McCann, general counsel to the Committee on Education and Labor, wondered "whether such a contract comes within the power of a regular labor organization to make, and whether a contract of this character made by business interests and by a labor leader is not, in effect, a violation of the Sherman Act."[99] This question took aim at the heart of the unions' power and questioned the rights given them in the Clayton Act of 1914, which exempted organized labor from antitrust enforcement and allowed them the right to collectively bargain and strike for things like compensation and working conditions.

The allegations that Petrillo and the AFM had blocked the development of radio and television were made primarily in response to the ruling by the International Executive Board of the AFM in February 1945 that members of the AFM should not play for television in any form until further notice.[100] Petrillo explained in an issue of the AFM's *International Musician* that the International Executive Board had concluded that television presented the same threat to employment of musicians as did the change from silent to sound movies because it offered another example of the potential use of recorded music to supplant live musicians.[101] The AFM was concerned that as television progressed, movies would play a greater part in its future, and the majority of television programming would be produced in "canned," or filmed, form, thus eliminating all live radio and television employment. The AFM was determined to avoid a loss of employment, and until they had a better idea of how television might affect employment opportunities, they were simply not going to participate in the medium. Petrillo wrote to the musicians, "We have been fooled so many times and misled by the employers so many times by their saying that every new invention would help us, that if we permit ourselves to fall in line again with that kind of talk, we deserve consequences."[102] Petrillo testified that he was opposed to new technological developments like recordings and television because they were hurting his musicians, and the AFM often referred to the problem as "the technological displacement of human labor."[103] Petrillo said that the iceman would not have approved of the Frigidaire if he had thought it was going to put him out of business, and that the man who drove the horse and wagon would not have gone into the trucking business if he knew the automobile was going to throw him out of a job.[104] The AFM's objections to these new technologies had to do with the "centralization" and "mechanization" that they saw taking away their main source of employment: playing live music.[105]

Members of the broadcasting industry strongly disagreed with Petrillo and his union and believed that Petrillo and the AFM were holding the industries hostage. J. R. Poppele, president of the Television Broadcasters Association, director of the Mutual Network, and vice president, chief engineer, and secretary of the Bamberger Broadcasting Service, complained to Congress: "The present situation is both tragic and absurd."[106] Allen Weiss, chairman of the Board of Directors of the Mutual Broadcasting System and vice president and general manager of the Don Lee Broadcasting System, explained, "I understand the motion-picture studios, who made sound film and had such film they were willing to lease to us, or rent to us, or sell to us, were deprived by some condition in their contract with the musicians' union which prohibited the sale to or the use by television stations of any film on which any music was had."[107] Additionally, Frank E. Mullen, executive vice president of NBC, testified that there were three restrictions the AFM had imposed and against which NBC had to struggle. The first was the AFM's ban on live television. The second was the ban on the use on television of films containing a motion picture soundtrack. The third was the prohibition of the duplication for telecasting of any sound-broadcasting program (i.e., reruns of content from either radio or television) containing instrumental music.[108] Since the broadcasters were aware of the restrictions in the AFM's contract with the studios against feature film soundtracks appearing on television, they believed it was a fool's errand to attempt to purchase or license films from the major studios.

Ultimately, the congressional investigation determined that the behavior of the AFM was unfair, but was unable to find that the union had violated any existing laws, so Congress passed the Taft-Hartley bill in order to officially limit the power of the unions. According to historian Murray Forman, President Harry Truman, who was good friends with Petrillo, attempted to veto the act but was unable to stop its passage after an extended Senate filibuster.[109] One of the problems the Taft-

Hartley bill created for the AFM was that it interfered with the system of royalty payments the AFM had established for recorded music. In 1942, when records were used on the radio, many musicians who performed live music lost their jobs. In an attempt to stop the further loss of musician employment, Petrillo banned recorded music. He came under pressure from Congress and the DOJ and was compelled to work out a deal with the record companies that had the potential to serve as a possible model for future royalties for feature films appearing on television. In 1943 and 1944, Petrillo negotiated a deal with the record labels whereby the companies would pay royalties from recorded music to a general "welfare" fund for all the musicians of the AFM. As the AFM's trade magazine *International Musician* reported to the members, "The recording industry was to bear part of the burden of unemployment created by the use of mechanical devices by providing for direct payment to the Federation of money, the amount of which was to be gauged by the number of records sold. This is of course a method unique in the annals of labor organizations, and is so because the musicians' situation was unique, namely that of their manufacturing the very instruments which were causing their slow death."[110] This was the first time that royalty payments were negotiated for the reuse of a performer's work or the use of that work in another medium. It was also unique because it was not meant for the benefit of the musicians whose performances were being reused, but for the benefit of all the musicians who lost their jobs as a result of the reuse of work.

The Taft-Hartley Act, however, prohibited royalty payments to musicians who did not participate in the making of the records or whatever media was subject to the royalties. At that time, royalties that were paid to the general welfare fund were not subject to income taxes, whereas royalties paid directly to musicians were taxable as income. It was suggested in congressional hearings on the activities of the AFM that one of the reasons Petrillo insisted on this general fund was because he wanted to avoid paying those taxes.[111] Regardless, Taft-Hartley's prohibition of the payment of royalties to a general fund for musicians caused a serious problem, which the union had to find a way around. So in December 1948, the AFM reached an agreement with the major recording companies in which the companies would create a Music Performance Trust Fund and would pay a trustee for phonograph records that were pressed, manufactured, and produced or reproduced, in whole or in part. Although it was largely the same structure as their previous royalty plan, by virtue of it being a trust, it was allowable under the law; and if it was successful, it could serve as a model for royalty payments for feature films on television. General David Sarnoff, chairman of RCA and NBC, had helped Petrillo figure out this solution to the threat from the Taft-Hartley law.[112] Sarnoff had an interest in keeping a fund for musicians operational because the alternative was that the recording industry would be faced with another AFM strike.[113] The money in the fund was to be expended "in a manner to contribute to the public knowledge and appreciation of music, on the sole basis of the public interest."[114] All concerts were to be free to the public and were to be in connection with activities that were "patriotic, charitable, educational, civic and general public nature."[115]

These conditions were largely the same as those outlined in their original record-ing fund, and the only substantial difference was that a public trustee rather than the AFM managed the trust.

Since Petrillo, during the negotiations for the AFM's 1948 contract with the stu-dios, had promised that the restrictions on feature films appearing on television did not forbid further negotiations on the matter, some studios began individu-ally testing the waters with the AFM to see what kind of deal they could make. In 1949, Monogram, for example, entered negotiations with the AFM over residual and royalty payments for 144 of their feature films made before 1948 that they wanted to release to television. As historian Michele Hilmes detailed, the AFM

> called a strike, refusing to work for Monogram until all 144 films could be rescored using the same number of musicians employed for the original, plus a payment of 5 percent of the fee for the film. Monogram also negotiated an agree-ment with the Screen Actors Guild whereby an actor would receive 12.5 percent of his or her original salary for films sold for less than $20,000, and 15 percent of those grossing more than $20,000. The Screen Writers Guild bargained for a similar arrangement, which became known as the "Monogram formula." Mono-gram finally sold a block of films to CBS in 1951, which used them on its "Film Theatre of the Air" program, an 8:00–10:00 P.P. Tuesday program feature. Earlier, in 1949, Universal had announced the intended television release of some of its own films, but the AFM provisions made the cost of release unmanageable.[116]

Despite some individual compromises with studios like Monogram, the AFM was still concerned that television was headed the same way as radio and would use records and film soundtracks in lieu of live musicians whenever possible. In April 1951, after two months of negotiations, the AFM finally reached a deal with the four major radio and television networks (NBC, ABC, CBS, and Mutual) wherein the networks agreed to pay 5 percent of their gross revenues derived from their use of television film to the AFM's Music Performance Trust Fund. This did not cover feature films originally produced for theatrical exhibition—those were still restricted under the AFM's contract with the studios—but it did cover any film made for television that was later rebroadcast. The AFM declared that clause the "most important part of the contracts."[117] The AFM hoped not only that the trust fund would accrue money that could be used to pay musicians to perform in con-certs that were free to the public, thereby providing employment for musicians who had lost work because of the use of mechanized music, but also that the fees the networks had to pay to the fund for the use of film might provide a disincentive to use film at all. They hoped that the royalty payments might make the use of live talent more competitive with the use of films and kinescope recordings on television.[118]

At the AFM's annual convention in 1951, Petrillo was optimistic about the net-works' payments to the fund, but he recognized that the Lea Act and the Taft-Hartley Act were "hamstringing the Federation's efforts to decentralize live music, and blocking all efforts to insure a more equitable country-wide distribution of employment opportunities."[119] By July 1952, one of Petrillo's concerns was that even though the AFM had negotiated a deal with the networks for royalty payments for the use of recorded music on radio and television, TV film producers and radio and television networks and stations had, in an effort to avoid those payments, imported recorded incidental music, themes, bridges, and cues that were produced in other countries by foreign musicians who were not members of the AFM and therefore not subject to the AFM's contractual obligations.[120] So Petrillo turned his attention at that point to urging the creation of a federal Department of the Arts, which would "administer to the needs of the arts and artists just as the Department of Agriculture protects the future of agriculture and the farmers."[121] The movement in government by representatives like Taft to limit the power of unions continued, in part as a response to rising concerns about communism and its link to the unions; the AFM hoped that by creating a Department of the Arts and encouraging their members to vote for pro-union representatives in government, they might at least have people in power who lobbied on their behalf.[122]

In January 1952, the AFM's 1948 contract with the producers was about to expire, and they began negotiations for a new contract at the Hotel Lombardy in Miami Beach, Florida. On the first day of negotiations, the AFM presented their proposals to the studio representatives. The next morning, the studios agreed to a two-year contract extension, and although they had come to terms on some changes (like a 15% increase to musicians' wages), they did not resolve the issue of the use of theatrical feature film soundtracks on television. That meant the ban on feature film soundtracks on television from the 1948 Basic Agreement would remain in place for another two years.[123] One of the reasons that the AFM and the studios were unable to reach an agreement was because the studios did not want to agree to an undesirable deal, in large part because other unions were waiting and watching to see what kind of deal the AFM would get, so that they could demand the same terms. IATSE had, for example, demanded the same terms as the musicians because, as Richard Walsh, then president of IATSE, had argued, they were "not going to be treated any differently than the musicians."[124] Walsh had negotiated a contract with the MPPDA in 1953 but had not been able to reach an agreement as to payments for the use of films on television. One of the sticking points at that time for IATSE was that Republic had made a deal with the AFM. Republic had actually begun negotiations with the AFM in early 1950 to find a mutually agreeable solution to the soundtrack ban in their contract. The negotiations continued until May 1951, when they finally reached an agreement.[125] The agreement included the following conditions: Before the first broadcast of a film on television, Republic had to pay each musician ($25), leader ($50), contractor ($50), arranger ($75), and copyist ($25) who was employed in the original production. If Republic was unable to locate any of those people, they had to make the payment to the AFM's trust. If Republic was unable to determine exactly who, or how many persons, had been employed in the making of the original soundtrack, they had to pay the AFM's trust for twenty musicians, one leader, one contractor, one arranger, and one copyist.

In all cases, Republic had to write the check to the AFM, which would disburse the money to the musicians. Additionally, Republic agreed to pay the AFM's trust 5 percent of the gross time charges for any advertising during the films, and 5 percent of gross revenues from all other uses on television of the film or soundtrack.[126] The contract further acknowledged the possibility that Republic had produced, and might still produce, "dummy soundtracks." Since the AFM had refused to back down on their restrictions on the reuse of their musicians' performances on television, studios like Republic realized that if they wanted to move forward with releasing their films to television, they would either have to completely rerecord the music and sound for their films or release the films to television without any music at all.[127] In the cases where the studios had kept only the composite soundtrack, and not the individual tracks, rerecording all of the sound and music was their only option. If a studio had the composite track but not the individual tracks, the only way to avoid having to completely rerecord all of the sound for a film, which would have involved the actors rerecording their lines as well, was to hire a "dummy" band to rerecord the music for the film. The musicians would go to the studio and rerecord the music tracks, as a "token for the musicians' union," and those musicians would be paid. The studio would then take that new recording and send one copy to the AFM along with a check, put another copy on the shelf, and go ahead with the use of the original composite soundtrack for the film on television.[128]

Not surprisingly, many of the studios decided that this practice did not make financial sense. In 1951, for example, Republic estimated the costs to re-edit, rescore, and redub films for television as $6,500 to $7,000 per film. Two-thirds of that cost was for re-editing, and the other third was for rescoring and redubbing. Herbert Yates explained that for Roy Rogers's early films, for example, a fairly small orchestra had been used, but after Republic's 1946 contract with the AFM, the studio was obligated to hire thirty-five full-time musicians. Since Republic paid for the musicians whether or not they used them, all thirty-five musicians were used to record the scores for all of the films. If Republic rerecorded the music in 1952, and had to pay the going rate at that time for musicians, it was almost twice as expensive as it had been for the original recording with the same number of musicians.[129] After the new dummy soundtracks were produced, Republic sometimes chose to use the original soundtrack for "various operating reasons." In such cases, the contract outlined that "if, after the new sound track has been made, it appears to you that use of the old sound track would be preferable for some or any television broadcasts, you shall have the option of using either the old or the new sound track on any particular television broadcast, as you may choose."[130]

To this point, Republic was the only member studio of the MPPDA to reach an agreement with the AFM, and the other studios were not pleased that Republic had made the deal on their own. B. B. Kahane, vice president of Columbia, expressed his opinion of Republic's deal as follows: "In my mind, there is no validity or justification for any demand of any amount as a repayment for the use of a theatrical film on television, or any other medium, but the demand for five per cent of the gross, or the station charges, in addition to paying the musicians the same amount they were paid when they originally rendered their services in the pictures makes the demand utterly absurd, and, certainly, economically unsound."[131] Other studio heads were unhappy with Republic's deal because, as Republic was a member of the MPPDA, they were supposed to negotiate their contracts together with the other member companies, and not strike out on their own.[132] Clearly, Republic had not followed those rules, and even though the other studios thought Republic's deal was a bad one and were uninterested in it for themselves, they still did not like Republic's maverick behavior. Republic went out on that limb because, as we will see in chapter 4, they, unlike many of the other studios, already had concrete plans to offer their films to television in the very near future.

The deal the AFM reached with Republic set a precedent and IATSE was demanding to get, at least from Republic if not the other studios, the same terms that had been granted the AFM.[133] Since the other producers disliked the deal when Republic made it with the AFM, they certainly were not going to embrace it now. B. B. Kahane described Columbia's negotiations in October 1955 with IATSE as follows: "They started way back a number of years ago to take the position that if any payment was made to . . . other Guilds or Unions, that they were not to be treated, to use the language of the president of the International Union, as stepchildren, but that they expected a similar payment. We have not resolved that question. As a matter of fact, there was a negotiation just concluded last Friday with the IATSE for a new contract, a three-year contract, and the question was brought up, the issue discussed, and tabled."[134] A few months later, the AFM board met with representatives from Universal, Columbia, and RKO who also looked to Republic's deal as a sign that they might be able to reach some sort of agreement with the AFM. They discussed making motion pictures for television and said they were only interested in new productions and not in releasing their old films for television. The studios asked for a two-year "moratorium" from the conditions of their current contracts so that they could do a trial run of production for television, and then come to an agreement on terms for moving forward. The AFM board did not agree to the moratorium.[135] At that same meeting, Mr. Chadwick and Mr. Arnstein, representing the Independent Motion Picture Producers Association (IMPPA), explained that they produced lower-budget films, and proposed a deal wherein they would pay the 5 percent on the making of new television pictures, but they wanted to negotiate for a fair price for releasing their older films to television. The AFM had previously suggested that the studios pay the musicians the full amount of their salaries from the original recording of the music if their performances were to be replayed on television. Chadwick and Arnstein were asking, instead, whether they might pay the AFM 12.5 percent of the original cost for the musicians upon the reuse of their films on television. Unfortunately, the AFM was unhappy with Monogram Pictures at the time because Monogram was selling their films to distributors without having paid the AFM any monies for the reuse of the films. Since Monogram was a member of the IMPPA, the AFM asked the association to first make sure that their members were going to follow their existing agreements.[136]

    In January 1954, the AFM's two-year contract with the studios expired, and the
members of the AFM board met again in Miami Beach with studio representatives to negotiate a new agreement. Seven studios (Loew's, Inc., MGM, Warner
Bros., Twentieth Century-Fox, Paramount, Universal, and Columbia) agreed to
continue the existing contract for four years, starting in February 1954, with a
5 percent increase in wages throughout. RKO hoped to find some arrangement with
the AFM for their films to appear on television, and so they negotiated separately.
In that case, Petrillo handled the negotiations on behalf of the AFM on his own.[137]
It is unclear what exactly happened during the AFM's negotiations with the studios to precipitate this, but in the minutes of the meeting of AFM's International
Executive Board from February 1954, it noted that "President Petrillo mentions that
Nicholas Schenck of MGM has always been very cooperative with the Federation
and feels it would be a nice gesture in recognition and appreciation of his attitude
if the Board would elect him an Honorary Member of the Federation."[138] The board
agreed, and they decided to present Schenck with a gold membership card.[139]
Although the AFM left the negotiations with the studios feeling very happy (with
Nicholas Schenck in particular), the fact that they had not been able to agree on a
way forward for films on television meant that the studios were stuck with the
agreement they had reached with the AFM in 1946: that the studios could not use
the musical soundtracks for their films on television.[140]
    The funds the AFM had developed to help mitigate the loss of employment
among their members still operated, and in 1954 the AFM renewed the Trustee
Administrated Music Performance Trust Fund and the Television Film Fund for
another five-year term.[141] Those funds received 5 percent of the gross revenues from
television soundtracks and tape recordings from the four major networks. In 1954,
the funds spent almost $2.5 million for 17,000 public performances in which nearly
200,000 musicians took part.[142] Disputes arose, however, within the AFM as to how
to spend those funds. The L.A. musicians who had been paid for "rescoring" the
music for films appearing on television were unhappy when the AFM's International Executive Board changed its policy with respect to these rescoring fees and
resolved that they should be made to the trust fund instead of to the individual
musicians who originally were employed to make the film.[143] That change was
meant to eliminate the complications inherent in trying to coordinate and distribute any rescoring fees the AFM had previously tried to procure for their members.
The musicians in the AFM's Local 47, which represented the musicians in Los
Angeles (many of whom were employed in the making of the soundtracks for Hollywood's films), were particularly unhappy with that arrangement. In the AFM
Executive Board's midwinter meeting in 1956, Cecil F. Read, vice president of Local
47, appeared and argued that the money should revert to the musicians who made
the recordings rather than going to the trust fund. He threatened that the Local
and their musicians would take the AFM to court if the board did not do as they
asked.[144] The board responded by reiterating that the trust funds had been established to reduce the loss of employment caused by the use of mechanical music.
The board explained, "To grant the requests of Local 47 would wipe out the Fund,

thereby depriving musicians all over the country of this little employment, and turn the money over to the already well-paid musicians who do the recording and produce the mechanical music. It is therefore, on motion made and passed, decided not to grant the requests."[145] After that meeting, the members of the Local 47, unhappy with the board's decision and with what they viewed as ineffectual leadership by those in charge of their Local, attempted an ultimately unsuccessful coup of their local board members. The members involved were charged with violating the union's bylaws and called to a hearing in front of the AFM Executive Board in May 1956. In the board's decision, they quoted a letter Petrillo had sent to the Local 47 members in October 1955, which explained that the clauses in the contracts the AFM had with the studios that restricted the use of feature films on television, as well as all negotiations and deals they made since then, were made for the benefit of all AFM members and not just those who were employed in the making of the films. The board found the leaders of the coup guilty of violating the bylaws of the union and expelled them from the AFM. They were, however, eligible to reapply for membership after a period of time.[146]

Studio Libraries in Limbo

By 1955, the language in contracts between unions and studios for the bulk sale of film libraries usually placed the responsibility of clearing rights and residuals with the buyer of the films and relieved the seller studios of their responsibilities to the unions with regard to the films. Although in 1947 and 1948 there had been some effort by television stations and networks to check that the people distributing films to television actually held the rights to televise the films, by the early 1950s television stations and networks took a warranty of the rights and an indemnity with respect to the rights. As Don Tatum, in charge of television in the Pacific region for ABC, explained, "Where we have any reason to question or suspect the lack of right, we either make investigations or drop consideration of the pictures. And in most cases we are influenced by the reliability and the standing and the credit of those persons and concerns with whom we are doing business. We normally do not attempt to check individually each case."[147] Those people or companies that purchased the rights to televise the films often had agreed in their contracts with the films' producers that they would pay any royalty payments due to the actors in the films.[148]

Although the AFM had made an agreement with some of the studios for the release of their pre-1948 films to television, the Writers Guild, Directors Guild, and SAG had not made any agreement regarding their pre-1948 films, and all of those union and guild contracts gave the labor organizations the power to cancel their contracts with the producers if the studios released any of their post-1948 films to television. Republic had, for example, released some of their pre-1948 features to television, and they paid the AFM according to the deal they had struck, but Republic had not made any residual payments to the Directors, Writers, or Screen Actors Guilds.[149] Creighton J. Tevlin, vice president in charge of studio operations for RKO from 1948 to 1955, testified, "I have heard of agreements that were made between the Screen Actors Guild and an independent producer, and I had the detail of that. But I know of no agreement that has yet been reached that defines the terms that a major studio would pay the Screen Actors Guild, or the members, in the event the major studio backlogs are put on television."[150] RKO continued to pursue a bulk sale of their films to television because they hoped doing so would allow them to strike a better deal with the unions and thereby earn better lump sum compensation for the loss of any potential theatrical reissues.[151] As RKO's Tevlin explained, "We certainly felt that in dealing with the Musicians Union on the basis of any bulk sale that we made, which would involve millions, we felt that we were not only entitled to, but would receive very important considerations as to terms."[152] RKO hoped that if, for example, the AFM demanded 5 percent of the gross revenue per musician per film, and RKO made a bulk sale and dealt with one large lump sum, they could talk the union down to an amount that would equal a lower percentage per film. RKO continued to explore this option, but it would be years before they were finally able to sell their films to television.

The unions also had the option of bringing lawsuits against the studios in the event the studios moved to put their films on television without first reaching an agreement with the unions. B. B. Kahane explained that they had received notice from attorneys for the guilds warning the studios that they reserved their right to bring suit against the producers if their films were released to television.[153] Kahane recalled an independent company called Lippert Productions that released to television feature films that had been produced after 1948, and was then threatened by SAG with the cancellation of their contract unless the company agreed to make additional payments to the actors. As Kahane explained, Lippert eventually agreed to pay "12½ per cent of the original salaries they received on the picture if the income from the television medium was $20,000 or less, and 15 per cent if the income was more than $20,000. Later I understand that Allied Artists also released several pictures to television and made a similar arrangement with the Actors Guild on the same terms."[154] In interoffice memos from Republic, they also cite the Lippert case as a sort of canary in the coal mine for them to watch for, and noted, "Lippert is now sparring with SAG for a deal to permit him to release new theatrical pictures on TV."[155] To further complicate matters, SEG, the sister guild of SAG, was also asking the producers to make additional payments of 5 percent to extra players when films produced for theatrical distribution were televised or reissued.[156]

Even though negotiations between the unions and guilds and the studios had been ongoing for years, it wasn't until 1960 that many of the important issues related to royalty payments for work appearing in other media like television were finally resolved. To get to that resolution, however, many of the unions and guilds, such as the SWG, went on strike over their right to royalties. As scholar Catherine Fisk detailed:

The Guild's ideal was that writers would either own or be entitled to profit sharing for all uses of their work, including the first use. (If a film was a huge success in its theatrical run, the writers would share in the profits.) What they ultimately settled for was residuals: the writers did not own their works or share in the profits from the first use (theatrical release or the original TV broadcast), but they got residual payments only for reuses (for reruns of TV programs, or when a movie was rereleased in theaters or, for movies released after 1948, when the movie was shown on TV.) In the end, the Guild got producers to agree to residuals for some reuses but gave up on claiming the right to payment for broadcast on television of pre-1948 movies. Instead, the Guild agreed that some of the money the studios made would be used to create a pension plan. [The licensing and sale of the studios' pre-1948 film libraries] was a huge source of revenue for the studios, and the writers got none of it in residuals."[157]

These industrial shifts toward what is today more broadly called the gig economy required Hollywood labor to unite and bargain collectively through their unions and guilds. In the less stable employment environment of New Hollywood, residuals were all the more important because, as entertainment lawyer Jonathan Handel has explained, "the industry needs residuals because talent—especially actors, writers, and TV directors—survive on them between gigs. In fact, residuals make up on average about one-third of the typical SAG actor's income. Without these payments, the industry's professional talent base would evaporate."[158] Today, laborers in the media industries face challenges posed by de-industrialization and globalization, and once again the question of who owns the rights to, and should be compensated for, the products of their labor in different media platforms. The territorial intra-union disputes of the 1940s and 1950s also have parallels in other moments of industrial convergence, as when unions disputed credits for work performed in digital media. The conflicts over whether online media was considered marketing or content, and the creation by the producers' guild of a new credit for a "transmedia producer," continue to illustrate the difficulties posed by technological disruption at even the most basic levels. The disruptions wrought by digital technologies have created a contemporary paradox described by scholar Mark Deuze as follows: "As people engage with media in an increasingly immersive, always-on, almost instantaneous, and interconnected way, the very people whose livelihood and sense of professional identity depend on delivering media content and experiences seem to be at a loss on how to come up with survival strategies."[159] One of the ways to ensure the rights of anyone involved in the production of media is to clearly define those rights in employment contracts. But the language of a contract is always open to interpretation and dispute and sometimes requires the intervention of the courts to help resolve those disputes and move forward.

CHAPTER 4

Roy Rogers, Gene Autry, and the Intervention of the Courts

Contractual rights and copyright determine not only what content appears where and when, but also who can claim authorship and compensation for those works. Even the most clearly written contracts, however, often require the courts to step in and settle legal disputes over their interpretation. Media scholar Jane Gaines has described the law functioning as a discourse of power that "restrains persons and regulates other objects of culture."[1] That is certainly borne out in the central cases in this chapter and the following chapter: the antitrust case *U.S. v. Twentieth Century-Fox, et al.*, and the cases brought by B-Western stars Roy Rogers and Gene Autry to prevent Republic Studios from releasing their feature films to television. In those cases, the courts played a central role in defining the mediums of television and film and outlining the ways in which content and people could move between them. The cases that Rogers and Autry brought against Republic Studios highlight the slippery nature of stardom and personhood, and of contractual claims to ownership of performance, likeness, and creative works. They also served to legally define the television medium as advertising, which had ripple effects in terms of the interpretation of contractual rights to images and content in different spaces. As Gaines has further argued, studying these legal debates "tells us things about the ideological construction of the star image that we could not have known even after years of close textual analysis."[2] These studies also tell us more about the workings of the film and television industries and demonstrate the ways in which the law directly impacts and largely regulates how and what appears on our screens. In the early years of television, when the exact definitions of core concepts like advertising and even of television itself were still being determined, the courts ultimately established those definitions and thereby circumscribed the ways that the industries would relate to each other for decades.

Hopalong Cassidy, Roy Rogers, and Gene Autry

In the late 1940s and early 1950s, some of the most popular and commonly televised films were B-Westerns. Many of them transitioned to television first through locally aired reedited film serials, and eventually through national syndication and network distribution.[3] By May 1950, KTLA, Paramount's station in Los Angeles, was one of the heaviest users of B-Westerns, airing almost thirteen hours of the genre every week. Since the FRC's 1927 Radio Act and 1934 Communications Act mandated that broadcast stations operate in the public interest, they did not enjoy First Amendment protections and could not broadcast material that might offend their audiences. If they did, they risked losing their broadcast licenses. As historian James L. Baughman described, "Precisely because radio [and later television] could enter *every* home, and was assumed to have enormous power over listeners, broadcasters did not enjoy the artistic (or marketplace) freedom exercised by the avant garde artist or burlesquer house proprietor."[4] That presumed power over domestic audiences made the appropriateness of film content a central concern for television broadcasters and audiences. As a result, B-Westerns were perfect film fare for the imagined television audience of suburban families.

Hopalong Cassidy was one of the most popular stars of the genre, and his films commanded the highest prices, with even the third run of his films on television bringing in $1,000 per showing.[5] Unlike most stars, William Boyd, the actor who played Hopalong Cassidy, was able to release his films to television because he owned the rights to the films. In the 1930s and 1940s, he starred in fifty-four hour-long films that had been produced by Harry Sherman for Paramount. After Boyd had a series of contract and production disputes with Paramount, he self-produced another twelve films in 1946 and 1947, which United Artists distributed theatrically. When, in 1948, Boyd believed that the theatrical value of the films had been depleted, he successfully negotiated to purchase the television and nontheatrical rights to the films that had been produced by Sherman, as well as the rights to any future uses of the Hopalong Cassidy character.[6]

When Cassidy's films first appeared on television, Cassidy did not have many endorsement deals, or what people at the time called a "commercial tie-up business." After his films had successfully aired on television, however, a very extensive commercial tie-up business developed.[7] One of his promotional kits told potential sponsors: "Hoppy is probably the only 'personality' with such all-over power in ALL FORMS of advertising such as TV, radio, newspaper comics, magazines, books, records, movies, etc. . . . Make sure that if Hoppy comes to your town that he is endorsing your products and not your competitors."[8] The extensive publicity Cassidy received through his work in film, television, and endorsements made him a huge star. So much so that in 1949, Hopalong's popularity reached dangerous proportions when one of his personal appearances turned into a riot. He had been scheduled to appear at the local department store, John A. Brown Co., to pass out "lucky pocket pieces" to his young fans. The organizers of the event had expected 300 to 400 children to attend, but they ended up with a throng of thousands of kids. Reports in *Television Daily* described the melee: "The police escort soon lost control of the situation as the wild-eyed small fry overturned showcases and turned the store into a shambles in their enthusiasm. Plans for Hopalong's grand entry into the store auditorium were dropped hurriedly. He was obliged to sneak up an alley, like a cattle rustler, and enter the store by fire escape." Cassidy later proclaimed, "This is the most wonderful thing that ever happened to me in 30 years in show business. I never dreamed television would do this to me."[9] This rabid fandom may be at least in part a result of the process that scholar Christine Becker has described as follows: "for film stars moving to television in the 1950s, their star identity was already established, but the intimate and routine quality of early television, as well as its small visual dimensions, presentational genres, over commercialism, and lesser cultural standing in relation to film, enforced a recrafting of that [star] identity away from the extraordinary."[10] This transition of film star to television created a new kind of star that combined the power of Hollywood with the unique liveness, intimacy, and familiarity of television.

By early 1950, the business of distributing Cassidy's films to television had grown enough that he contracted with Toby Anguish's Television Pictures Distributing Corporation for Television Pictures to control the distribution of Hopalong's films. At that point, "Hoppy's" films were grossing $1,000,000 per year through television and were broadcast in forty-eight of the fifty-eight available television markets.[11] When other studios saw how well westerns, and the Hopalong Cassidy films in particular, were performing on television, they began investigating the westerns they had stored in their vaults and "sounding out" their exhibitors as to their reaction to the possibility of selling older westerns to television.[12] Monogram had already sold 250 of their old westerns to Teleinvest, Inc., a distributor in New York, but other studios had reservations about selling the old films of stars they were actively filming with, "for fear of rousing exhibs' ire."[13] And for good reason, as the studios had learned from instances such as one in September 1950, when Allied Exhibitors, a Midwest chain of theaters, refused to show Gene Autry films because he had appeared on television in films produced directly for television.[14]

Hopalong Cassidy's success in television was one of the central reasons that Gene Autry and Roy Rogers, both stars at Republic Studios, became interested in the new medium. Both Rogers and Autry, like Cassidy, had extensive merchandising and licensing deals, which were relatively rare during a time when studios still largely controlled actors' merchandising and licensing rights.[15] One of the reasons Rogers and Autry decided to get into television was to combat the competition Cassidy posed to their merchandising and licensing deals. Rogers's representatives had discussed with Republic the possibility of putting his films on television, but Republic, at the time, "on account of the exhibitors," said that no films could be aired on television.

The lead-up to the Rogers and Autry lawsuits began in early 1950, when William Arthur "Art" Rush called Republic and asked to meet with Republic's president, Herbert Yates. In that meeting, Rush explained that he had studied the popularity of Hopalong Cassidy, and called Yates's attention to the extensive advertising campaigns run by Cassidy's sponsors. Rush outlined the ways that department stores were selling Cassidy's merchandise, and explained that he and Rogers were concerned that they were losing some of their own merchandising business as a result of Cassidy's success. According to Yates, Rush's plan to combat that competition was to have Republic put Rogers's films on television. Rush had suggested that his company, Art Rush, Inc., could manage the distribution of Rogers's films to television, and he suggested that he would take on all of Republic's films—not just Rogers's.[16] In a letter to Yates, Rush explained that Quaker Oats was "ready and willing" to sponsor the films on television and provide local and national advertising for them. He described the transmedia marketing campaign that they planned to set in motion: "Prior to releases on television, all our newspapers, running the Roy Rogers comic strips, the individual stations, Quaker Oats, our 62 licensees, RCA-Victor, our radio show of 561 stations, etc., would bring everything together simultaneously into one gigantic exploitation campaign to put it over the top."[17]

In Rush's meeting with Yates, Yates explained that if Rogers thought he was losing business to Cassidy, Republic was also suffering because the theaters were booking old Hopalong films instead of Republic's films. Yates offered the example that "Metro, who never handled that type of picture, put a special campaign on in 24 theatres in and around New York on a weekend showing Hopalong Cassidy pictures."[18] The meeting concluded with Yates warning Rush "that it was time for Rogers to make up his mind whether he could make more money from his merchandise business and television than he could continuing making motion pictures. I reminded, or rather I stated to him, that for a number of years 81 of Rogers' pictures were distributed throughout the world with heavy publicity and advertising campaigns and his popularity as it stood today was due to those pictures and that publicity and advertising. And I told him that I think that the matter is serious and I advised him to watch his step."[19] Sometime shortly after that meeting, Robert "Bob" Newman, then vice president of Republic, called Petrillo at the AFM to inquire as to the possibility of the AFM relaxing their restrictions against films on television, and Rush happened to overhear the conversation. Rush asked Newman if his inquiry was in regard to Rogers's films, and Newman confirmed that it was.[20] After that conversation between Rush and Newman, Newman met with Frederic Sturdy, a lawyer for Rogers, and told Sturdy that Republic was going to make ten films available to Sherman & Marquette for Quaker Oats. At that point, Sturdy warned Newman that he needed to check the commercial rights to the films because he believed Republic did not have the rights to release the films to Sherman & Marquette or Quaker Oats. This was the first time that Rogers had argued that Republic did not have the commercial rights to his films, and, according to Art Rush, it prompted a great deal of "colorful" language from Newman.[21] Then, in February 1950, Rogers had a meeting at Republic Studios with Yates, Newman, Rush, Saal (in charge of Rogers's publicity for Republic), and a man named Corwin from the TOA. They discussed whether to put Rogers's films on television to combat the competition from Hopalong Cassidy. Yates had asked Corwin to attend the meeting so that he could share the exhibitors' opinion of motion picture stars whose films were in theatrical release appearing on television. Yates wanted Rogers to understand why Republic had lingering questions about releasing Rogers's films to television.[22] Among those questions was concern about the AFM in terms of the "exorbitant standby pay" Republic would have to give the union for the music in the films.[23]

Republic, as one of the "Poverty Row" studios, did not have the deep pockets of the larger Hollywood studios.[24] Poverty Row studios were so named because their office spaces were clustered in proximity around Gower Street and Sunset Boulevard in Hollywood. They specialized in B films and often provided content to independent theaters that were not contracted with the major studios. Republic produced some of the highest quality and most expensive of the Poverty Row films. When the 1940 Consent Decrees in response to the 1938 antitrust suit *U.S. v. Paramount Pictures, et al.* prohibited block booking and blind bidding, the major studios could no longer package their A and B films together in the same way and phased out the production of B films. This created a need for B films that studios like Republic were happy to fill. The final decision in the *Paramount* antitrust case in 1948, however, eroded the market for B films by eliminating the existing systems of distribution and exhibition, which put all studios—major, minor, and Poverty Row alike—in direct competition.[25] As we have seen, the box office was struggling in the early 1950s, and these industrial shifts hit studios like Republic particularly hard and forced them to consider all possible revenue sources, including television.

In one of Republic's earliest attempts to take advantage of potential income from television, Yates met with Music Corporation of America (MCA) representatives to discuss the possibility of having them represent Republic in the sale of some of their Rogers and Autry films to television.[26] MCA wanted to handle the sales of Rogers's pictures for a "substantial percentage in the deal." Yates declined the deal with MCA because "he had to check the distributors and know where he was headed in the television field before he was going to make a deal with anybody."[27] Yates explained that although MCA did try to buy the television rights to Rogers's films, the amount they offered was not enough to interest Republic. He recalled, "It was a million or a million five hundred advance and then we participated in the gross income. It was that sort of a deal. . . . Well, they were to take over the television rights outright."[28] Although the deal fell through for MCA, it was an example of their early negotiations in their eventual rise as a prominent packager of film and television.

Then, in February 1950, things escalated when Gene Autry read an article in *Variety* that reported that Republic had offered his films to television for $1 million. The article stated, "For the asking price, the buyer gets the pictures exclusively and in perpetuity for television. Several networks are reported to have entered bids but hold that $20,000 per picture is too high a price to pay for old westerns. Republic's package price is said to be based on what the Hopalongs have brought."[29] Autry himself had previously offered to buy the films, not for television, but to "get them off the market because they were hurting our newer pictures made at Columbia."[30] Autry asked Yates if he could have an opportunity to meet any other offer for the films, and Autry claimed Yates agreed to that. Autry never actually made an offer of his own, however, because he understood MCA's offer to be that of a partnership with Republic rather than a sale of Autry's films outright, and he believed that he could not compete with that.[31] By that time, Autry was already exploring his opportunities in all aspects of television and had, for example, become a television station owner. He bought a 50 percent interest in station KOWL in Santa Monica, California, during its construction in 1947.[32] In 1949, he bid on station KTSA in San Antonio, Texas, but eventually withdrew his bid when faced with competition from the *San Antonio Express*.[33] He continued to purchase television stations, however, and developed a significant business in that field.

As Autry developed his multimedia empire, Republic continued to search for ways to get their feature films on television. In late 1950, Sturdy received a phone call from Herbert Yates, which was, as Sturdy recalled, "I think everybody will agree a most unusual occurrence."[34] Yates told Sturdy that he was working to resolve the issues related to Republic's feature films on television, and he had checked in with the exhibitors to gauge their feelings on the subject. From those conversations, Yates believed that the exhibitors might not complain if Rogers's television appearances were infrequent. He asked Sturdy what Rogers had in mind and how often he expected to appear on television.[35] At that time, Rogers was negotiating a deal with cereal company Quaker Oats for a television show that would include his older films.[36] Sturdy explained that they had discussed Rogers appearing on television through those shows about once a week. Yates expressed concern that once a week was still too often and was afraid that this would meet with exhibitor opposition.[37] In another meeting in late 1950, Rogers's representatives discussed a new deal for Rogers and the fact that television presented a problem. Robert Newman, vice president of Republic, stated something to the effect that Republic had been working on putting Rogers's films on television, and Sturdy, Rogers's lawyer, responded by saying they had a "theory" that might prevent Republic from doing so. Newman later testified, "I told him we owned all of the rights in those pictures for every type of exhibition, that they were our property entirely, and there was nothing he could do to stop us from putting them out when we decided to do so."[38]

HOLLYWOOD TELEVISION, INC.

By October 1950, Republic had formed a subsidiary, Hollywood Television, Inc., to handle their larger television business. In those early days, Hollywood Television had about a dozen employees with offices located at Republic Studios in North Hollywood. Their primary responsibility was to negotiate with the advertising agencies' television directors in the matter of sales of feature films for television, for the production for television, and the leasing of Republic Production's facilities for television productions.[39] Although Hollywood Television used the term "sell" in regard to their films, they would actually only rent or lease the films. There was no set price for the films, and every deal was up for individual negotiation.[40] Republic would license the pictures, and the television stations would handle the advertising within the limits of the license that Republic gave them, which indicated that the television station had no right whatsoever to use any of the names or the members of the cast in their advertising or commercials or anything else.[41]

Consolidated Film Industry, a subsidiary of Republic in Fort Lee, New Jersey, processed Republic's films for television and had a significant role in determining what audiences actually saw on their television screens. Since there were time restrictions related to commercials and scheduling for films shown on television, Consolidated had the responsibility of cutting Republic's films down to time. Many of Republic's B pictures had a shorter theatrical running time than did A features. That shorter running time made them an easier fit for television's programming schedule, but they still had to be re-edited. In terms of maintaining the integrity of the story, Morton Scott, Hollywood Television, Inc.'s vice president and general manager in charge of production and distribution, explained, "for example, you may have a picture which runs an hour which has an extraneous sequence in it which will come out without having anything at all to do with the story, in which case one fast chop will take care of it. You may have another story which, in order to retain the story line and interest, you may have to make several dozen smaller cuts."[42] There were also difficulties presented by the varying conditions of the prints, as well as the need to negotiate cuts in a print that had composite audio and video tracks. In those cases, finding a spot to make a cut where both the audio and video could be cleanly cut was a great challenge. As Scott explained, "Some pictures edit very easily, others are very difficult."[43] In terms of the form in which feature films appeared on television, this example of Consolidated taking on the responsibility of editing the films for television demonstrates the lack of an institutionalized structure and process for films making their way to television. In some cases, as with Consolidated, these labs were tasked with re-editing films for television, and in other cases that responsibility lay with the television stations or networks, local censorship boards, film agents or mangers, distributors of films to television, and even individual producers or actors who had purchased the rights to their films. This patchwork system for editing films for television raises questions about claims to authorship and medium specificity, and highlights that in these early days of television, for example, a person watching television in Chicago and a person watching television in Denver might see two completely different versions of the same film.

Roy Rogers and Gene Autry versus Republic

Things came to a head for Rogers, Autry, and Republic in February 1951, when Yates, president of Republic; Sturdy, lawyer for Rogers; Rush, agent for Rogers; Newman, vice president of Republic; and Jack Baker, an executive at Republic, met to discuss a new contract for Roy Rogers.[44] In that meeting, Yates said that the situation had not changed sufficiently for him to take chances putting Rogers's pictures or any of their old pictures on television, but he thought the time was coming very soon. He argued that Rogers should make up his mind whether he wanted to work on television or in motion pictures, because Yates did not believe that Rogers could successfully do both. He said that undoubtedly in the very near future Republic would put its entire inventory of old pictures on television, and if exhibitors continued their opposition, it might be more profitable for Republic to devote the entire time and energy of the studio to making pictures for television.[45]

Sturdy then said it might be more profitable for Rogers not to make pictures for television, but to make some sort of deal with Republic whereby he would get part of the income that Republic would get from televising his old pictures. Yates argued that they owned all of the pictures, "lock, stock, and barrel," and had the right to exhibit them any place they wanted.[46] As Robert Newman recalled, "Sturdy leaned over to me and whispered, he said, 'Remember, Bob, I have a theory that might stop you,' or words to that effect. And I said, 'Look, Fred, there is your man [Yates], tell it to him.' And Mr. Sturdy did. . . . Mr. Yates said that we owned those pictures, and when and if we wanted to release them we would release them, that Rogers had nothing to do with it."[47] Rush then said it would be impossible for Rogers to get a sponsorship deal for anything that he would make for television if his old films had been offered to television.[48]

Yates was not alone in his opinion that actors could do either films or television—not both. Fred Schwartz of Metropolitan Theatres argued, "I think the use of personalities on television should be carefully guarded for the benefit of the star, for the benefit of the producer, for the benefit of the exhibitor. They're very valuable and important assets, and they shouldn't be dissipated."[49] He believed that if actors appeared on television weekly, the audience would tire of them, and their value in films would disappear. Schwartz spoke from the theater owners' perspective, but other people in the industry held the same opinion. For example, Ronald Reagan, then president of SAG, argued, "I don't know of any motion picture star that can go on the screen 26 weeks in a row and get people to come back to see him [in the theater]. I've been shouting that for a long time."[50]

Rogers had actually had a very successful radio show with Quaker Oats on the Mutual Network since August 1948,[51] and in early 1951, Rogers began negotiations with Quaker and Sherman & Marquette, the advertising agency behind the show,[52] for the terms of a new contract, which was to include television.[53] Quaker would have been happy to continue with just the radio show, but Rogers and Rush wanted to do radio and television together.[54] Quaker wanted to do a half-hour television show called *The Roy Rogers Television Show*, which would air in the Quaker time slot on NBC at 5 P.M. EST.[55] In March 1951, as Rush recalled, Yates wanted to shoot Rogers's show on the Republic lot, which interested Rush and Rogers because they could use the same crews that had worked on Rogers's films. Rush further described his conversation with Yates: "I told him that I felt that we should do 26 on the initial production year, and he said that . . . I could tell Quaker Oats and Sherman & Marquette that he would not release the old films on television against us for a period of a year. . . . I believe this was in connection with the reaction that he might have gotten from the distributors that a half-hour series of Roy Rogers television films would be a test in the eyes of the theatres throughout the country."[56] Yates had a different recollection of the conversation, and later said that he told Rush

that he could make no promises that he would not release Rogers's old films to television for a year. He did, however, have another offer he thought might interest
Rogers. He said Republic would make four films a year with Rogers for theatrical
distribution. Rogers could appear on television, and either Rush or Republic would
produce those shows for Quaker Oats. Republic would put up half the money for
both groups of pictures, Rush would put up the other half, and they would enjoy a
50–50 split of the profits.[57]

The problem with Yates's refusal to guarantee that Republic would not release
Rogers's films to television for a year was that, as Arthur Marquette explained,
Quaker wanted exclusivity with Rogers on television—especially in light of the
investment needed for Rogers's proposed new television pictures.[58] And since Sherman & Marquette had only a thirty-minute time slot on NBC, they did not want
to purchase Rogers's old films, which were too long for those time slots. When
Quaker Oats wanted the guarantee from Republic that they would not put Rogers's pictures on television for at least a year, Yates reportedly said, "No, we won't
do that unless we can participate in Rogers' earnings from Quaker Oats on television, have some sort of an interest in his merchandise company."[59] Later in March,
Rush met with Yates again and told him that he had seen Frank Folsom, the president of RCA, and Joe McConnell, the president of NBC, who were in negotiations
to broadcast the Rogers/Quaker show; Rush thought that as long as Yates was going
to New York and knew both Folsom and McConnell, Yates should stop in and see
them.[60] Yates met with McConnell, and according to Yates, "McConnell was quite
cute about the whole affair. I asked him quite a few questions, and his answers indicated to me that there was such a deal going on [between NBC, Quaker Oats,
Sherman & Marquette, and Rogers] but he didn't see why in any way Republic Pictures should be interested."[61]

The negotiations for a new deal between Rogers and Quaker fell apart in
April 1951.[62] Then, in May, Marquette and Quaker chose not to renew Rogers's existing contract for the Quaker Oats radio show, and chose not to move forward with
a television show because "they were worried about the old pictures then, what
would be done."[63] Marquette later testified that they did not renew Rogers's radio
contract because their negotiations over television had collapsed. He said, "It was
our best judgment that going either route with Rogers on television was a bad business risk."[64] By "either route" he meant "either hoping to sponsor the old pictures
some time at Republic's price or making special TV pictures in the face of the fact
that the old pictures might some day become available."[65]

After the Quaker Oats deal fell through, Rush traveled to New York again to
discuss with RCA/NBC the possibility of another deal for Rogers. The proposed
deal was for radio and television and was similar to the one they had tried to work
out with Quaker Oats.[66] In the new deal, NBC would employ Rogers for ten years.
They also discussed an "escape clause" in the event that Republic put Rogers's films
on television, which would give NBC the right to terminate the contract at any time
if the films were put on television.[67] Although Rush was in talks with NBC, the
show itself would be sponsored by General Foods and their Post cereal division,

and General Foods wanted to deal directly with Rogers. Benton & Bowles was General Foods' advertising agency, and as Walter Frank Craig, vice president in charge of radio and television for Benton & Bowles, explained, "We wanted to buy this program from an independent packager, we didn't want to buy it from NBC. Therefore we didn't want Mr. Rush to sell himself or sell Mr. Rogers to NBC and then we would buy it from NBC. We wanted to buy it direct."[68] Just as Quaker had balked at the possibility that Rogers's old films might make their way to television, Ed Ebel, of General Foods, and Phil Cleland, of the Benton & Bowles advertising agency, explained to Rogers and Rogers's wife and costar, Dale Evans, over dinner at La Ruc's on the Sunset Strip, that they also wanted to reserve the right to cancel their contract in the event that Rogers's old films showed up on television.[69] Craig explained that Benton & Bowles estimated that time and talent of the television show would run a little over $2 million a year, and close to $3 million total would likely be spent on the program.[70] They did not want to jeopardize the success of that kind of investment with competition from their own star. The deal was potentially very lucrative for Rogers because once NBC had recouped the money spent to produce the show, Rogers and NBC would divide the profits from syndication.[71]

Then in June 1951, in the midst of those negotiations, Hollywood Television, Inc., sent out a letter to the directors of various advertising agencies throughout the United States offering to license Rogers's motion pictures for television exhibition.[72] One of the reasons Republic felt free to make that offer was that negotiations with Rogers over the renewal of his contract had fallen through the month before. The main stumbling blocks were that Rogers asked for the right to make a film with another studio and he wanted to go on TV, and Yates would not give in to either of those demands.[73] After Hollywood Television sent out the letter offering their films to television, Republic had a preview screening of some of the films for representatives from the advertising agencies and networks. Hollywood Television's sales pitch to the approximately twenty-five men who showed up each day included the argument that the films being offered were of better quality than those available earlier, and that they were new films to television with personalities who had not previously appeared on television. Hollywood Television also asserted that their catalog represented a greater number of films than perhaps the agencies and networks could obtain from any other distributor, which would make it more convenient for ordering because they would have to do business with only one firm rather than half a dozen.[74] They offered fifty-two of Rogers's films that had been completed before January 1942.[75] The number fifty-two was chosen because, at that time, films were sold for television in groups of thirteen, twenty-six, thirty-nine, and fifty-two. That was the case, in part, because of the number of weeks in a year and, in part, because operating in quarterly segments based on thirteen made it easier for stations to coordinate their programming.[76]

The price Hollywood Television asked for licensing a group of thirteen Roy Rogers's films for national exhibition was $30,000 per run for one run, and $25,000 per run for two runs. Republic also offered Gene Autry's and Red Ryder's films, but they were offered for less than Rogers's films. For example, for Autry's films, Hollywood Television asked $20,000 per film for one run, and $17,500 per film for two runs. As a condition of the deal for any films, the purchaser would have to pay the 5 percent fee to the AFM in addition to the licensing fee to Hollywood Television.[77] Even though Hollywood Television offered their films to television, the minutes from a meeting of Republic's board of directors in June 1951 show that they were still unsure about following through with any sale. The minutes report that the directors concluded the following: "To proceed with caution before making any commitments; that all phases of the television business, including the desirability of producing directly for television, were being thoroughly studied."[78]

They would have to proceed cautiously because in June 1951, Rogers filed a suit against Republic Productions and Hollywood Television Service and asked for a temporary restraining order to prevent them from selling or licensing his feature films to television.[79] The next month, the judge issued a preliminary injunction restraining and enjoining Republic and Hollywood Television Service, pending the outcome of the trial, from leasing, selling, licensing, or permitting others to use the voice or likeness of Rogers or his horse Trigger or any of their motion pictures for advertising purposes. They were, however, allowed to use them for the purpose of advertising the motion pictures themselves.[80] In the meantime, Hollywood Television had received an offer for Rogers's films that was, as Yates argued, "extremely favorable and productive of substantial profit."[81] The terms of the deal were reportedly as follows: "An offer from a highly reliable distributor of motion pictures on television to license said fifty-two motion pictures for television exhibition at the rate of one picture per week per television station for a period of three years, no picture to be exhibited more than . . . once per year. . . . The total consideration payable under this offer would have resulted in the present receipt by defendants of the total sum of $3,900,000.00, exclusive of commissions, advertising or other sales expenses."[82] Wayne Tiss, vice president at the advertising agency Batten, Barton, Durstine & Osborn (BBDO), disagreed with Yates's assessments and did not believe that any experienced advertiser would make an offer "remotely approaching" the $3.9 million Yates claimed he received for Rogers's films, "unless the sponsor of said program expected to indicate to the public that Roy Rogers in fact approved of or endorsed the product of the sponsor."[83] As favorable as the terms of the offer may have been, Republic was not able to accept because of the lawsuit and the restraining order against them.[84] Yates actually believed that he could have made an even better deal for Rogers's films if he had a chance, because of the popularity of westerns on television at the time, and because Republic was among the first of the larger studios to release their westerns to television. He feared that "the television market for 'Westerns,' and particularly 'Westerns' starring [Rogers], is presently at its zenith, and that the demand therefor and the available return therefrom will decline substantially in the very near future."[85] Not only was Republic enjoined from accepting any offers for Rogers's films for television, no one was interested in buying the television rights to the films once Rogers's suit had been filed, because, as Yates explained, "they don't want to get involved in lawsuits."[86]

Meanwhile, Rogers moved forward with negotiations for his television show. In June 1951, Rush went with Rogers and Dale Evans to New York, where they met with advertising agencies in an effort to sell their half-hour television show.[87] Every agency asked Rush what would happen if Republic released Rogers's old films to television, and Rush explained that they would likely go into litigation about it. Even though none of the agencies specifically said they would decline the proposed television show because of the possibility of Rogers's old films appearing on television, their interest reportedly diminished because of it.[88]

Although Hollywood Television could not move forward with releasing Rogers's films to television, they had licensed 170 of their other films to KTTV for a local license, and KTTV began showing those films five or six weeks before the Rogers trial began. Neither Rogers's nor Autry's films were included in the films licensed to KTTV.[89] The films on KTTV were shown with spot commercials at the beginning, middle, and end of each film from a variety of sponsors. KTTV had the right to three runs within a period of eighteen months for each film, and at the end of those eighteen months or the completion of the third run, whichever happened first, Hollywood Television could sell the films again. An effort was being made to establish as a custom of the trade that one station in an area would be similar to a first-run theater, where they would get the first license to show a particular film, and during that license, other stations would be precluded from licensing or exhibiting that film.[90] Such an arrangement did not necessarily mean, however, that the price went down for each run. For the Hopalong Cassidy films, for example, the first run got $250; the second run, $500; the third and fourth runs, $700; and the sixth and seventh runs were $1,000 all in the same market on different stations. The bulk of the runs in that instance were on KTLA, but the last run or two were on KNBH, which was the NBC station in Los Angeles. The prices went up because of Hopalong Cassidy's increased popularity and the increased number of television sets in the area.[91]

In order to make their films suitable for use on television, Hollywood Television would reprocess the films and cut them down to a length of fifty-three and a half minutes; but often, films were licensed to television stations in their original length. In those cases, the television station would cut the film down to fifty-three and a half minutes in their own editorial rooms, or occasionally run them at their original length. The shortened film length allowed for six minutes of advertising at the beginning, end, or middle, and half a minute for the station break.[92] Even though Hollywood Television was enjoined from releasing Rogers's films to television, they moved forward with reprocessing twenty-six of Rogers's films for television. Generally, in order to get these films down to the limit of fifty-three and a half minutes, chase sequences or fight scenes would be shortened. Apparently, for the theatrical release it was common for Rogers's films to be "padded" for extra time by extending chase and fight scenes in order to make sure the films were long enough. According to Republic, the cost of reprocessing or recutting these films was estimated at $6,500 each. That included re-editing, recutting, and rescoring the music, and one answer print (the very first print that is struck). Each additional print cost approximately $150.[93] If those figures are correct, and if they are combined with necessary payments to unions and guilds, they do support the studios' claim that they needed to hold out for higher payments for their films on television if they hoped to recoup the costs necessary to reprocess their films, much less make any profit.

The trial for Rogers's case against Republic began in September 1951, in the District Court in Los Angeles with Judge Peirson M. Hall presiding. Not only did the judge say that he was "not much of a picture fan," but also that he did not own a television set and had seen "very few television programs."[94] There were quite a few points during the trial when the lawyers, judge, and Rogers spent considerable time trying to define television and wrestle with how it worked technologically, formally, and economically. For example, Herman Selvin, one of Republic's lawyers from the firm of Loeb & Loeb, a major entertainment law firm that represented all the major studios including Republic,[95] at one point noted, "I think I understand the general principle of a television set, and what is actually referred to as the screen, that is the thing on which you see the image, is actually the business end of a very large tube which is called a cathode ray tube. . . . And which, if I understand it, if I remember some earlier experiences properly, is actually the thing which is also the basis of what we know now as radar. Television and radar are substantially the same thing, actually."[96] As ridiculous as these debates might sound today, in these deliberations about the rights to content in a certain medium, they first had to figure out what each medium was. These discussions worked to clarify the difference between exhibition on television and exhibition in the theaters, and were only one of the complex issues the judge had to wrestle with in this case.

Republic's defense was relatively simple. They argued that their contracts gave them the perpetual right to use Roy Rogers's name and likeness for the purpose of advertising the films, which they owned. They also argued that during the contract negotiations, Republic wanted, and Rogers agreed to, "unqualified television rights."[97] Rogers signed his first contract with Republic in October 1937, which ran until he signed his second contract in February 1948.[98] The 1948 contract lasted until May 1951, and from 1937 to 1951, Republic continuously employed him.[99] In Rogers's earliest contract, Republic had specifically claimed television rights to the films. In 1937, as Selvin, Republic's lawyer, explained, Republic was "contracting for the future" since they did not know what form television might take.[100] Selvin drew a parallel to films made before and after the introduction of sound film, and noted earlier cases wherein it had been decided that before sound film existed, and before the parties involved had even contemplated sound films, the rights nevertheless had included sound film.[101] Since most actors at the time still worked under long-term contracts with the studios, the fact that the studios claimed blanket rights to an as yet unrealized medium demonstrates the power balance, in favor of the studios, inherent in those long-term contracts.[102]

Not only did Republic claim the television rights to their films, but they also held copyright for all of the films in question. As Selvin argued, "The proprietor of a copyrighted composition or production, to which the services and efforts of employees contributed, is the absolute and unqualified owner of the results of that employee's services and is unlimited in the right which can be made of that material under the copyright law."[103] Further, Republic argued that in their most recent contract negotiations with Rogers in 1948, as Saul Rittenberg, an attorney for Republic, recalled, "the conversations were that we were to have unlimited, unqualified television rights. . . . There was no discussion of what that meant or what that included in its scope. We said unlimited and that is what we meant."[104]

Rogers's argument was more complicated. In response to Republic's claim that, according to their contracts, they held the television rights to Rogers's films, Rogers said that he had never considered television when he was making his films.[105] He testified, "I think it was experimental right up until '48, before it really got going, and there wasn't any sponsored show, I don't think, up until that time, or I hadn't heard much about them. I think it is experimental until it starts getting—becoming commercial."[106] He claimed that in 1937 he was just happy to have a job, so he signed the contract without examining it in any detail.[107] Rogers argued that he first considered television in early 1948, and he talked with Rush before his 1948 contract negotiations about whether his films could appear on television. Rogers claimed that he did not remember whether his representatives discussed with Republic the issue of his films appearing on television.[108] As the judge observed, "Everybody in making a business deal lets sleeping dogs lie until they start barking. And here television started barking and everybody started looking at the contract."[109]

The central problem of the case, however, was not whether Republic held television rights, because, according to Rogers's contracts, they clearly had those rights. The problem was that television was, by its nature, a medium funded by advertising, and the role of advertising in television and its relationship to the actors and feature films that appeared on television was the actual point of contention. As Sturdy, Rogers's lawyer, explained, "This lawsuit had nothing to do with television, it had to do with the right to use Mr. Rogers' name or likeness or voice for advertising purposes."[110] Typically, studios retained monopoly rights to characters' likeness and image in all media,[111] but since no one held the monopoly rights to "Roy Rogers" name and likeness, the judge had to first define the television medium in order to then distinguish whose rights applied in that space. In Rogers's contract, Republic had given Rogers the right to his own name and likeness except in the films themselves and in the advertising for the films. Rogers argued that Republic, by virtue of their contracts, only held the rights to use Rogers's name and likeness for the purposes of advertising the films themselves; but Republic, by offering the films to television, was claiming the right to license the films for the purpose of advertising products other than motion pictures.[112]

Rogers argued that under the terms of his contract, Republic would have been allowed to use the films on television, just not on any program that had commercial sponsorship. As the judge explained, "The lawsuit is here over not the right to telecast the pictures, but the right to telecast them for commercial purposes."[113] One problem arose, however, when the judge and lawyers tried to define commercial television and, in the course of that discussion, had to wrestle with the distinction between commercial and sustaining programs. In a sustaining program, as Rogers described, "there appears at the beginning an announcement, which might be in the form of a sign or a spoken announcement, to the effect that the particular station or the particular network, as the case may be, presents such-and-such a program. So, for example, it would start out with an announcement saying, 'KTTV now presents Movietime. Our feature for tonight is such-and-such a star in such-and-such a picture.'"[114] The sustaining programs did not have the backing of a sponsor and were paid for by the station in order to meet the FCC's required minimum number of broadcast hours. They included programs like news shows or other programs intended to fulfill the FCC's requirements for providing programming in the public interest. Rogers's lawyers ended up arguing that even "sustaining programs," or a program paid for by the television station itself, were still effectively commercially sponsored because the broadcast of the film served as an advertisement for the station.[115]

Republic's lawyers tried to rebut Rogers's arguments by offering that the majority of movie theaters presented advertisements in advance of their films. Even as far back as 1940, of the 19,974 theaters in operation in the United States, 11,500 sold space for advertising; and by 1952, of the approximately 23,026 theaters in the United States, 17,680 sold advertising space.[116] Selvin asked, "Is there any difference, aside from the fact that in one case the audience is seated in front of their respective television sets and in the other case they are seated inside the theatre, between that type of presentation and the presentation in a theatre where all that happens is that the theatre, say the Ritz Theatre now proudly presents Roy Rogers in Apache Rose?"[117] Rogers, in turn, argued that the fundamental difference between film and television audiences was that "in the motion picture the picture is furnished to the patrons by the patrons themselves paying for it, whereas on a television broadcast the picture is furnished to them by the sponsor."[118]

The problem of advertising also encompassed the issue of implied endorsements and possible conflicts with Rogers's existing endorsement deals. Rogers claimed that starting in 1938 Republic encouraged him to license his name, voice, and likeness for various commercial purposes such as advertising, rodeos, personal appearances, and radio.[119] As Rogers recalled, during that time he struggled to make a living, so when he talked with Yates one day, the subject of a salary increase came up. In response to Rogers's request, Yates suggested that Rogers develop some outside income from things such as radio, commercial tie-ups, and personal appearances.[120] At that time, stars who successfully reserved the right to negotiate these matters for themselves were the exception.[121] Rogers believed that Yates's suggestion was in lieu of an increase in salary from Republic,[122] and he was likely correct because Republic, as one of the "Poverty Row" studios, did not have deep pockets.[123]

By the time of the trial in 1952, Rogers, having been encouraged by Republic to develop outside income, had some sixty or seventy licenses out.[124] During 1950 alone, those licensees had sales of over $20 million worth of merchandise by some seventy-four manufacturers.[125] Since Republic had encouraged those enterprises,

Rogers believed that Republic should not dilute his business by "throwing a lot of his old pictures on, because obviously, if other people can get pictures, or people can see pictures free, or if they can see a feature that may have cost anywhere from . . . $50,000 to $200,000 or $300,000, that you cannot compete with those on your modern specially made T.V. films, all of which are less expensive."[126] Further, Rogers's lawyers argued that sponsors for television wanted exclusivity, and argued that they felt "that if [Rogers's old films] are permitted to go out to any and all stations throughout the country on what they call a syndication basis or a series basis, to be sponsored by anybody that will pay the money, that he would be irreparably damaged. A man's name is something you cannot measure in money, your Honor, and once it is gone, it is gone."[127] As Wayne Tiss, vice president of BBDO's Hollywood office, argued, if Rogers's films were shown on television under commercial sponsorship, it would limit his ability to license his name or likeness for advertising purposes. Because, as he explained,

> if a Roy Rogers picture was sold, let's say, in Ames, Iowa, to be used on a television station on which there may be three or four commercials cut into this film . . . even though Roy Rogers was not involved in those commercials, and let's say one of them . . . is on for a bread that is made in Ames, Iowa, if at the same time Roy Rogers was attempting to sell a television show of his own . . . to the Wonder Bread Company or the Continental Baking Company, they would not find it quite a good idea to sponsor that program because they would never know when another bread would show up on a Roy Rogers show over which they had no control.[128]

Both Yates and William Golden, in the publicity department at MGM, argued, however, that if Rogers's films aired on television, he would gain exposure to larger audiences and increase the sale of any of the products he was associated with.[129]

This case was further complicated by the fact that in granting the rights to the name and likeness of Roy Rogers, those rights also included Rogers's actual name, because for most of his career Rogers played himself. In other words, the character that the actor Roy Rogers portrayed was a cowboy called Roy Rogers.[130] Before Rogers joined Republic, he appeared under his birth name, Len Slye. Shortly after joining Republic, Rogers used the name Dick Weston; but just before he started his first film, Republic gave him the name Roy Rogers.[131] In 1942, he legally changed his name as well, so his film credits read, "Roy Rogers played by Roy Rogers."[132] Playing a character with the same name as his own made Rogers what is known as a "person brand," because a person, rather than a static product, is at the core. Hence, a person brand is more difficult to manage because of the self-within-a-self construction.[133] By collapsing the distinction between Roy Rogers the real person, the star persona, and the onscreen character, Rogers embodied scholar Barry King's theorization of the "personal monopoly" and had perhaps unwittingly made these rights issues more complex.[134]

Because of his status as a person brand, Rogers was concerned that audiences who viewed his old films on a sponsored television program would associate his name and likeness with the product being sponsored, and that television would create a stronger association than radio because television audiences could see and hear him.[135] This concern was heightened because, as Rogers explained, "without the control of the sponsorship, your Honor, they could put it on any kind of a program they wanted to, such as beer or whisky, cigarettes, which would cause irreparable damage to the name, because we have been very careful with that."[136] As scholar Avi Santo noted in his work on the brand licensing of the Lone Ranger, "concerns over commercial exploitation are especially acute when children are imagined as the primary audiences for cultural commodities."[137] In fact, Wayne Tiss of BBDO testified that they had done research that indicated that audiences associated the advertised product with the stars and understood an implied approval by the star of the product. That implied endorsement, or at least the sense that Rogers did not disapprove of the products, even extended to products that appeared in a "spot commercial" situation.[138] Tiss further argued that sponsors were interested in the value of the name, reputation, and sincerity of an actor. He explained that any commercial advertising programs based on a show starring Rogers would want to trade on the name and goodwill Rogers had built up with his audiences over many years. The advertisers wanted to "capture" the goodwill toward Rogers and connect it with their own products.[139] Rogers argued that he had worked hard to maintain a good reputation, and he did not want to dilute the value he had accrued by allowing his films to appear on television without his control over the sponsorship. Further, he argued, "I think the release of my old pictures would dilute the possibilities not only of me making a living, but if they weren't controlled and were run an awful lot of times, it would make your name just like a new song that comes out, it is sung so much that people get sick of hearing it. . . . They have just about ruined Mr. Cassidy through the same idea. They have run his pictures and re-run them."[140] Republic, however, argued that Rogers was less concerned about the effect that televising his films would have on his reputation or his other endorsement deals, and more concerned about his films appearing on television and inhibiting his ability to get another job in television. Republic believed he really wanted to suppress the competition of his films.[141] It was the case that during the trial Rogers was working on a contract with NBC and General Foods.[142] Rogers's radio program, sponsored by General Foods Corporation's Crinkles Breakfast Cereal, began broadcasting nationwide on NBC in October 1951,[143] and Rogers started production on his first television films even earlier, in July 1951.[144] His production company—Frontiers, Incorporated—made western action films that ran in half-hour time slots.[145] Rogers intended the films to appear on a commercially sponsored television program,[146] and by the end of 1951 Rogers had produced four television series, which had yet to air.[147]

After a trial that lasted a little over a month, the judge presented his decision in the case on October 18, 1951.[148] He said that he believed the main question in the case was, Is there a limit on the method by which Rogers's pictures can be exhibited or transmitted?[149] As the judge explained, "The case has been long, and there has been a great deal of testimony, but after all it resolves [sic] around the interpretation of the contracts between the parties. . . . Each one of the counsel claimed the contracts were clear and unambiguous, but as proof of the fact that they are ambiguous is that they each spell out exactly a contrary meaning from what appears to each counsel to be very clear terms."[150] The judge concluded that Republic had the right to televise their films but did not have the right to televise them under commercial sponsorship or to use them for advertising, commercial, or publicity purposes for anything other than advertising the films themselves. He upheld Rogers's right to control any commercial sponsorship, advertising, or publicity to which his name, voice, or likeness was attached for anything other than the films themselves.[151]

Although the judge specified that Republic had the right to televise their films, but not under commercial sponsorship, he complicated that by asserting that sustaining programs were actually commercial in nature. He explained, "Any use by a sponsor of Roy Rogers' name, voice, or likeness in connection with any product, whether that is used as an attention getter or as a direct or indirect endorsement or otherwise, is a commercial use, as the whole purpose is to sell something, whether a tangible article such as a shoe or a boot, or an intangible article, such as a service which is given by radio or television. And hence I must come to the conclusion that the use of the pictures on radio or television on a sustaining program is a commercial use."[152] Perhaps ironically, the judge based his opinion of the commercial nature of sustaining programs on language contained in Republic's contract with the AFM, and he argued that "Republic itself has recognized, by its voluntary execution of that contract, that the use of these films or any films on the sustaining program by the television station itself or by a radio program itself is a commercial use."[153] Through this determination that both commercial and sustaining programs were commercial in nature, the judge essentially legally defined television as advertising. Scholar Jane Gaines argued that "judicial opinions pinpoint cultural trouble spots,"[154] and in this case we see an example of a judicial opinion pinpointing an industrial trouble spot—namely, the trouble posed by the collision of two industries that produced and exhibited similar content, but whose economic structures were significantly different and, in this case, at odds with each other.

Republic filed an appeal to the United States Court of Appeals for the Ninth Circuit in February 1952.[155] However, since the original decision in favor of Rogers meant that the court's injunction against Republic selling or licensing their films to television was upheld, Republic could not offer Rogers's films to television until the appeals court made a decision.[156] Republic continued moving forward with releasing their other films to television,[157] but the lower court's decision had put Republic in a difficult situation in regard to their other contracts. As a result of the *Rogers* case, Republic wanted to revise the language in all of their contracts in order to make sure that in the future they had unqualified rights to exhibit their films on television. However, since Republic was appealing the decision in the case, they were concerned that revising the language in their contracts would signal to the courts that Republic did not believe that their old contracts gave them those unqualified rights, and thereby would extend the limits of the Rogers decision to all of their old contracts.[158]

As Republic moved forward with licensing their non-Rogers films to television, Autry was working to make sure that his films were not among them. In July 1951, Autry sent a letter to Republic Productions and Hollywood Television Service demanding that they withdraw their offers to license his films to television. Republic refused and argued that they intended to exercise the rights they had in regard to their films.[159] Autry then waited for the outcome of Rogers's trial, and when he saw that Rogers had won his case, Autry filed his own suit against Republic for unfair competition, declaratory relief, and an injunction to stop Republic from releasing his films to television.[160] Autry's trial began in March 1952.[161]

Gene Autry versus Republic

In the Rogers trial, the judge had allowed a great deal of discussion about the contracts as well as the negotiations that led to those contracts. Since the language in the contracts was in dispute, the judge thought it pertinent to investigate the different parties' intentions in relation to the language. In Autry's case, however, the judge was not interested in that kind of evidence, and therefore the trial was much shorter than Rogers's trial had been.[162] Autry's lawyers tried to argue that "you can't in every case of interpretation of a contract, particularly a technical contract, as these contracts are, interpret those contracts unless you have evidence concerning the circumstances under which they were executed."[163] The judge remained unconvinced, and that restriction hindered, to a certain extent, Autry's lawyers in making their case.

Republic's argument in the Autry case was substantially the same as it had been in the Rogers case. As Selvin, Republic's lawyer, explained, "We base our case on the rights that we claim we have out of the relationship of employer and employee in the first place, and out of the contracts in the second place."[164] Autry worked for Republic under four contracts between July 1936 and May 1947, and during that time he made fifty-six films for Republic. Selvin argued that Autry, as an employee of Republic, had agreed to render his services in, among other things, the production of films. Selvin further argued that Republic held, by virtue of their contracts with Autry, the sole and exclusive ownership of all the results and proceeds of the services rendered by Autry in the course of his employment by Republic, and likewise had the sole and exclusive right to sell, license, or use, or to authorize or appoint others to sell, license, or use, the films for any purpose and in any manner whatsoever,[165] which, Republic argued, included the right to exhibit the films on television.

Autry's argument was substantially the same as the argument Rogers used in his case. Autry contended that television was a commercial medium, and therefore the use of his films on television constituted commercial advertising.[166] As Martin Gang, one of Autry's lawyer, explained, "Our position is that under no contract does Republic have the right to commercial advertising with reference to

Gene Autry in any way, shape or form except to use his name to advertise the picture in which he rendered services for Republic. That is as simply and bluntly as I can say it."[167] Autry's lawyers echoed the judge's decision in the *Rogers* case and argued that even sustaining programs were commercial in nature because they advertised the station, which had a service to sell and time to sell.[168] Autry, like Rogers, argued that he had signed his contracts with Republic with the understanding that, as he testified, "I was to make those pictures to be shown in theatres where an admission is charged. If they wanted to use my picture to put in a newspaper to advertise the theatre, or the theatre where the picture was showing, they had that right. They never had the right, as far as I was concerned, to ever use my name for any other means of advertising."[169] As in Rogers's case, Autry was concerned about the use of his films on television without any limitation as to who the advertisers might be. Autry saw two potential problems with this lack of limitation: the public might believe that Autry implicitly endorsed those products,[170] and the advertisements might conflict with Autry's existing endorsement deals, which by the time of the trial had earned Autry $1.5 million.[171]

As was the case with Roy Rogers, further complicating the matter was the fact that Gene Autry played a character named Gene Autry in his films. Like Rogers, Autry had worked to cultivate a wholesome image, and he was concerned about advertisements for products like beer, liquor, and cigarettes appearing alongside his films on television.[172] As Autry's lawyers argued, "There is a form of hero worship in the minds and thoughts of many of his fans."[173] Republic countered that the license agreement through which the films were proposed to be exhibited on television expressly prohibited "any advertising [or] any statements which may be understood to be an endorsement of any sponsor by any actor or actress appearing therein or that any such person is connected or associated with Station or any Sponsor."[174]

In addition to Autry's concern about television advertising adversely affecting his image, he believed the necessary re-editing the films would have to endure for television would further damage his image. Just as they had with Rogers's films, Republic wanted to edit Autry's films to approximately fifty-three minutes each in length, thus permitting about seven minutes of advertising in an hour-long television program.[175] Autry's lawyer explained one of the many objections they had to the possible re-editing and reuse of Autry's films on television: "It would be unfair to the public to show vintage pictures cut up in any fashion that Republic decided to cut them up, showing clothes that were out of style, showing old automobiles, showing Mr. Autry wearing heavy make-up, all of which would be to the great disadvantage of Mr. Autry in his present efforts. That these pictures would be sold indiscriminately to advertisers and would do great injury to the audience that Mr. Autry has built up, and to his reputation and esteem with that audience, since he could not control the advertiser or the products."[176] So Republic's lawyers asked whether Autry also objected to the theatrical release of his older films. Gang responded, saying, "Yes, but the economies protect him there, because they have to put on them, 'A re-release,' as will be seen when you see one of these pictures.

The audience knows that, and the theatre owners pay very little money for the old pictures because they are old pictures."[177] It was also the case that if Autry's older features had been rereleased theatrically, they would likely have run in subsequent run theaters. The physical distinction between first and subsequent run theaters helped define films as newer or older. Films that ran on television did not necessarily indicate the year they had originally been produced. For an actor like Autry who was trying to rebrand himself as a "modern" western star, the television broadcast of his older, more traditional westerns could have disrupted those attempts to rebrand himself.

There was also disagreement as to the nature of advertising in television versus advertising in a motion picture theater. According to Roswell Metzger, vice president in charge of radio and television for the Rutrauff & Ryan advertising agency, the advertising in theaters had a different association in the audience's mind than did the advertising on television. He explained that audiences attended theaters for the films being shown there, and films built up the audience for the advertising that ran in theaters. Further, he argued that audiences in theaters did not associate advertising in theaters with the films; rather, they connected them with the theaters and understood they were an additional source of revenue for the theaters. Autry's lawyers agreed and argued that the advertiser on radio and television aimed to associate as closely as possible the star of the program with the product or service being advertised, but that was not true with advertisements shown in motion picture theaters.[178] Another concern expressed by Autry's lawyers was that a part of Autry's income as stipulated in his loan-out contracts was 10 percent of the gross box office receipts. When Autry made this agreement with Republic, the box office was the only source of revenue for the films, but if Republic started earning income from television for these films and it was not included in the loan-out contracts, then Autry would lose that potential income.[179]

Just as in Rogers's case, Autry was extremely concerned about the release of his films to television damaging the income he was making, and hoped to make, from producing films for television. By the time of the trial, he owned at least a couple of television stations and was working on acquiring more. In April 1948, for example, he owned shares of KOWL in Santa Monica, California, and KAPO in Tucson. He was also approved by the FCC to buy station KOOL in Phoenix.[180] He had a radio show on CBS that was sponsored by Wrigley, and he was working on a deal with CBS and Wrigley for a television show that would tie in with his existing radio show.[181] In June 1951, when Hollywood Television Service offered to license Autry's films to television, Autry had already established a production company, Flying A Pictures, to make content for television, and as Judge Ben Harrison noted in his opinion on the case, "Thus Republic, by offering the pictures produced under the various contracts, entered the plaintiff's old pictures in competition with his present productions much to the displeasure of the plaintiff."[182] His older films were viewed as competitive particularly in terms of potential dilution of the stars' value for audiences and advertisers, which both Rogers and Autry wanted to avoid.

The decision in Autry's case was filed in May 1952, and unlike the decision in Rogers's case, Judge Harrison ruled in favor of Republic. The judge ruled that Autry's claim was "untenable" and "unfair" in seeking to prevent Republic "from enjoying the full share of the profits to be derived from said photoplays."[183] The judge's opinion concluded, "Finally to boil this case down to substance, the plaintiff is seeking to prevent Republic from televising the photoplays in which plaintiff starred, his complaint being that sponsored televising of a photoplay is 'commercial advertising'. Plaintiff is attempting to do indirectly what he knows he cannot do directly—i.e. inducing the court to find that the present method of televising motion pictures is 'commercial advertising'. It is my view that television of motion pictures is a form of entertainment and not 'commercial advertising.'"[184] The judge continued that since the broadcast of films on television was a form of entertainment and not advertising, the use of the films on television did not constitute unfair competition, and Republic was free to use them on television. He concluded, "If plaintiff is worthy of his hire, certainly Republic is entitled to the full use of the fruits of his labor."[185] So the judge's decision in the *Autry* case overturned the precedent set in the *Rogers* case by ruling that television was not, in fact, advertising, but entertainment. In an interesting parallel, it was also in 1952 that the Supreme Court overturned the precedent set in 1915 with the *Mutual* case, which had legally defined film as a business, by issuing a decision in the *Miracle* case, which redefined film as art and thereby protected under the First Amendment.[186] The regulation of broadcast content still fundamentally differed from that of film because of the public interest demands placed on broadcasters by virtue of their use of the public spectrum, but the parallel cases point to a larger shift toward the conception, at least in the courtroom, of film and television as art and entertainment, which affords them different protections under the law.

Just as Republic had when they lost the *Rogers* case, Autry filed an appeal in August 1952.[187] When the Rogers's trial began, and throughout the course of both trials, the film and television industries watched with "keen interest."[188] These cases provided a rare instance in which the film studios worked together with the television stations and networks, and a number of television industry personnel testified in Republic's behalf.[189] But the larger importance of the cases was that, as an article in the *New York Times* explained, they "involve[d] a hitherto untried legal issue which might well hold the key to the whole future of the showing on television of movies that were originally made for theatrical purposes."[190] Although the exact lawsuits and the resulting decisions were different, the two cases together posed basic questions about the issue of personal and corporate rights relative to the licensing and sale of films as advertiser-sponsored television programs. For that reason, they held industry-wide importance.[191] With the filing of Rogers's lawsuit, many people in the film industry feared that other actors would follow in Rogers's footsteps and attempt to prevent the sale of their old films to television. Some television sponsors became skittish about licensing old films because of possible legal entanglements.[192] Actors were also paying close attention to the cases, as evidenced by statements made by John Dales Jr., executive secretary of SAG, who said that he believed the outcome of the *Rogers* case to be of great significance to all motion picture stars.[193]

ROGERS AND AUTRY REHEARINGS

It took a couple of years, but Republic's appeal of the lower court's decision in the *Rogers* case finally went to court in 1954. The original decision in the *Rogers* case found that Republic had the right to televise their films but did not have the right to televise them under commercial sponsorship or to use them for advertising, commercial, or publicity purposes for anything other than advertising the films themselves.[194] The court of appeals, however, overturned the lower court's decision and found that on the basis of Rogers's contracts, the restrictions regarding advertising were restrictions on the use of Rogers's name, voice, and likeness, not on Republic's use of Rogers's acting or the motion picture. Judge Bone explained that Rogers "was paid full measure for his services in creating these films, and has specifically relinquished 'all rights of every kind and character whatsoever in and to the same perpetually.'"[195] The court decided that Republic could exercise their ownership and rights to the product of Rogers's employment, whether or not such exercise involved exhibition in connection with commercial advertising. The judge found the restrictions related to advertising in the contract were restrictions on the use of Rogers's "name, voice and likeness," not on Republic's use of Rogers's "acts, poses, plays and appearances" or the product thereof. Judge Bone explained that the fact that Rogers's name, voice, and likeness are contained in and throughout the motion pictures in which he appears was only superficially confusing, and the close reading of the contracts made it clear that the words were used definitively and distinctly in different cases.[196]

Rogers appealed that decision all the way to the Supreme Court, which, in November 1954, sent the case back to the district court to enter judgment for Republic.[197] At the district court's rehearing in December 1954, Republic's lawyer complained that the studio had suffered a significant loss of income from the injunction that prevented them from exhibiting Rogers's films on television for the three years prior. He added that in that same time, Rogers had the benefit of "unfettered competition" on television as a result of the same injunction.[198] It was true that over that period of years Republic had made a significant amount of money from licensing their other films to television and could potentially have made substantially more had they been free to license Rogers's films as well. In 1951, for example, Republic made $208,749.56 from licensing their films to television, and in 1952, the first full year after offering their films to television, they made $1,034,912.17. By June 1953, Republic had been on track to make $1.5 million for the year.[199] Had they been able to release the Rogers and Autry films as well, which were among their highest-quality films, they might have exponentially increased those sums. The court finally dissolved the injunction that had prohibited Republic from releasing Rogers's films to television,[200] but Rogers appealed the decision once again and asked the court to modify or clarify its mandate and protect his motion picture and non-motion-picture (i.e., name, voice, and likeness) rights. So it was not until August 1955 that Rogers had exhausted his appeals, and the matter was finally put to rest in favor of Republic.[201]

Meanwhile, in June 1954, just when the appeals court was overturning the lower court's decision in the *Rogers* case, the appeals court upheld the previous decision in the *Autry* case. In the lower court's decision, Judge Harrison had ruled that Autry's claim was "untenable" and "unfair" in seeking to prevent Republic "from enjoying the full share of the profits to be derived from said photoplays."[202] The judge's opinion concluded that televising motion pictures was a form of entertainment and not "commercial advertising." Therefore, the contracts placed no restrictions on Republic in the use of the films, and their use on television did not constitute unfair competition.[203] Judge Harrison had also granted Republic the right to "cut, edit and otherwise revise and to license others (to do otherwise) . . . in any manner, to any length and for any purpose."[204] The court of appeals upheld the previous court's ruling but included some modifications.[205] They affirmed the district court's decision that Republic should not be enjoined from cutting Autry's motion picture performances and showing them on commercial television, but they disapproved of the parts of the decision where they believed the district court went beyond the issues presented to them. Judge Bone explained that although Republic had the right to edit the films and license others to do the same, it was possible that "such cutting and editing could result in emasculating the motion pictures so that they would no longer contain substantially the same motion and dynamic and dramatic qualities which it was the purpose of the artist's employment to produce. And although appellees unquestionably have the right to exhibit the motion pictures in connection with or for the purpose of advertising commercial products of all sorts, we can conceive that some such exhibitions could be so 'doctored' as to make it appear that the artist actually endorses the products of the programs' sponsors."[206] Judge Bone's concern about the "emasculation" of the film suggests a "view of intellectual property as an extension of one's own body," derived from Enlightenment philosopher John Locke's conception of the right of personal property as a protraction of our own control over our bodies. This link between intellectual property rights to film and moral rights—which, in this case related to Autry's claim that excessive editing and the incorporation of advertisements violated the integrity of his work—"established the judicial formula that would eventually lead to the expansion of moral rights for filmmakers."[207] So, the appeals court prevented Republic from editing the pictures to less than fifty-three minutes of running time, from presenting them as other than feature films, and from permitting them to be exhibited in connection with advertising in a manner that would suggest that Autry endorses the product of the sponsors of the program. Autry was pleased with those modifications and considered them a "substantial victory." The ruling clearly established the right of studios having clear title to films to present them on TV in connection with advertising, but at the same time, the court recognized that actors were entitled to protection against unrestricted exploitation for advertising purposes. These rulings in favor of Republic cleared the way for them to release Rogers's and Autry's films for television exhibition. There were a total of 141 films involved, and Republic immediately began negotiations to televise them in the fall of that year.[208]

These two cases were extremely significant not only because they caused Republic to delay the release of many of their higher-quality feature films to television for almost four years, but also because many of the other studios held off releasing their films to television until the matter was resolved, out of fear that their actors might file similar suits. The cases were also important because they posed basic questions about the personal and corporate rights and privileges relative to the sale or lease of movies as advertiser-sponsored entertainment. Scholar Jane Gaines analyzed Rogers's and Autry's cases as they related to the control of rights to stars' images on- and off-screen and the ways that those rights challenged studios' copyrights in their motion pictures,[209] and Peter Decherney considered the cases as they related to moral rights, or artists' control over their names and works when copyrights belong to corporations.[210] However, as Gaines and Decherney pointed out, copyright protects only certain aspects of any work, and in the *Rogers* and *Autry* cases, questions about those limits became significant in the history of copyright. The cases therefore had industry-wide importance, and the appeals court decisions were regarded as having established precedent.[211] They also demonstrate the ways in which the law via legal hairsplitting has the power to determine what appears on-screen.

Ultimately, the archival materials reveal that there was much more at stake in the ways that these cases determined the relationship between the film and television mediums, defined and limited the star as transmedia mogul in this earlier period, and managed the ways in which texts and images moved across platforms during moments of disruption and convergence. It also complicates other long-held beliefs about this period, such as the fact that stars simply preferred work in film because it was more prestigious. As Rogers's and Autry's experiences demonstrate, more practical interests often resulted in stars participating in one medium over another. The cases demonstrate the power of contract law to restrict the ways in which images, texts, industries, and individuals can move between different media, particularly during a period when an existing medium—in this case, film—was confronted with the new medium of television. These cases also illustrate the ways in which the law, more broadly speaking, functions as an ideological and economic instrument that defines any new medium well before those producing or consuming the medium's content are themselves sure as to what the medium is capable of. This legal history helps to more accurately flesh out this complicated period in media history, and paints a clearer picture of some of the major obstacles that prevented Hollywood's feature films from appearing on television.

CHAPTER 5

ANTITRUST, MARKET DOMINANCE, AND EMERGING MEDIA

The original goal of antitrust law in the United States was to ensure that economic competition exists, that consumers are not taken advantage of, and that corporations can provide the best goods and services in a fair marketplace. The Sherman Antitrust Act was passed in 1890 to prohibit corporations from dominating their industry through abusive practices that exclude competition. It is perhaps no coincidence that Thomas Edison first filed his patent application for his motion picture camera at almost the exact same time in 1891, and the history of the media industry and antitrust law have been intertwined ever since. Antitrust cases involving Hollywood have often set precedents that have changed the interpretation of the law and its enforcement, and, in turn, the law has had a profound effect on the media industry, the content it produces, and the ways in which audiences consume that media. The power of the law allows the courts to restructure entire industries and to define what monopoly and competition mean in different markets. Those powers are evident in the two cases discussed in this chapter: *U.S. v. Paramount Pictures, et al.* and *U.S. v. Twentieth Century-Fox, et al.*, which demonstrate the law's effect on the media industry in the mid-twentieth century. An analysis of the cases' development, resolution, and perhaps unintended consequences helps further clarify the nature of the relationship between Hollywood and the law, the ownership of media rights, and, in particular, the often fine line between the assertion of the legally granted rights of copyright or patent owners and the unlawful use of those rights to destroy competition. Ultimately, antitrust law played one of the most significant roles in the struggle over feature films on television.

One of the factors that significantly determined the decisions and behaviors of the film industry in terms of television was that until the late 1940s, the film industry functioned as an oligopoly. That meant that the handful of vertically integrated studios that controlled production, distribution, and exhibition colluded to dominate the market, and the decisions of one studio influenced the others and vice versa. This structure differentiated them from many other established companies that face industrial disruption in that the apparent stability of an oligopoly

provides those involved with a false sense of confidence. In this case, the Hollywood studios' overconfidence in their market dominance demonstrated what economist Andrew Currah described as "a tendency for oligopolists to neglect or even
marginalize emerging markets, especially those that are seen to threaten the status quo. Therefore, the behavior of oligopolist firms tends to reflect, defend and
enforce the prevailing structure of the industry, making any kind of radical change
difficult to justify or initiate."[1] The strength the studios felt in the market dominance they enjoyed through their oligopoly was about to become their biggest
weakness in the face of the disruptive technology of television. Their false confidence often expressed itself in the dismissal of television as unimportant. For
example, Benjamin Kalmenson, president and domestic sales manager for Warner Bros. Pictures Distributing Corporation, later testified, "As near as I can rec-
ollect, in 1948, in my mind at least, television was in its infancy and meant nothing
to me, so as the result of that I did nothing."[2] On the other hand, as we saw in chapter 1, there were people in the film industry who had been aware of and tracking
the development of television for many years. For example, Meyer Lavenstein, general counsel for Republic, recalled that before 1935, Republic was primarily interested in television as a boon to their film laboratories. They believed that television's
demand for content would result in more business for making and processing films
for theaters and for television.[3] This kind of prognostication highlights the danger
for dominant firms facing industrial disruption of incorrectly forecasting the manner in which consumers will actually use a new technology. Faulty predictions
can lead companies to miss opportunities when they invest in and prepare for a
future that does not ultimately come to fruition. In these early years, one of the
things that prevented studios from working to distribute their films to television
was that their interests in television were often focused elsewhere.

The oligopoly the studios enjoyed during the studio era was challenged, and ultimately dismantled, by the antitrust case *U.S. v. Paramount Pictures, et al.*[4] This
case got its start in July 1938, when trustbuster Thurman Arnold, the chief of the
DOJ's Antitrust Division, filed a suit against the major Hollywood studios charg-
ing them with combining and conspiring to restrain trade unreasonably and
monopolizing the production, distribution, and exhibition of motion pictures.
After years of consent decrees that the studios did not strictly adhere to and that
the government did not bend over backward to enforce, the case was revived, and
in June 1946, Judge Augustus Hand found the defendants guilty of antitrust violations. He wrote that in spite of the defense's argument that business convenience
and long-term use sanctioned their behaviors, "in various ways the system stifles
competition and violates the law[,] and that business convenience and loyalty to
former customers afford a lame excuse for depriving others of rights to compete
and for perpetuating unreasonable restrictions."[5] Despite many historical accounts
to the contrary, the initial decision in the case argued against the studios divest-
ing of their theaters because, as the judge reasoned, that major shift would deprive
the public of the films they had come to expect. The court concluded that ownership of the theaters by producers/distributors was not in itself a problem; rather,

the problem lay in their price-fixing, noncompetitive granting of runs and clearances, unreasonable clearances, formula deals, master agreements, franchises, block booking, pooling agreements, and the discriminatory granting of licenses in favor of affiliates and old customers. Instead, the judge advocated for a bidding system for films that, he argued, would create the kind of competition that had been previously lacking.[6] The studios appealed the decision all the way to the Supreme Court.[7] By March 1948, as the court was writing its decision, many in the film industry waited with bated breath. The TOA's legal committee, for example, prepared data covering as many phases of the anticipated decision as possible.[8] Then in May 1948, the Supreme Court handed down its 7 1 decision in which it strongly suggested the divestiture of theaters, but left the specifics up to the lower courts to sort out. By this point, the studios knew that divestiture was imminent, but they knew not when.

One reason the studios were able to maintain their oligopolistic control in the classical Hollywood era was that their vertically integrated system allowed for them to block book their films in the theaters. Although the decision in the *Paramount* antitrust case had also declared that block booking of films was illegal, buying or selling feature films for television in blocks was common at that time. As Morton Scott of Hollywood Television Service testified in 1952, "In television sales you sell in blocks. That prevents a station from being selective in their buying." And then in a moment of realization that he had perhaps unintentionally admitted to illegal behaviors, he continued, "Perhaps I shouldn't say that. . . . A station is offered a group of pictures and they buy those in groups. They don't buy individual pictures."[9] That the practice of block booking was found to be illegal in the context of the film industry but was permissible in the context of the television industry highlights one key factor in antitrust law: in order to be a violation of antitrust law, a behavior has to have the intended effect of using and maintaining market dominance by a practice that eliminates competition. In the film industry, block booking was a tactic the studios could use by virtue of their market dominance to keep independent producers and theaters at a disadvantage. In the nascent television industry, the studios did not hold the same market dominance, and so the practice did not necessarily have the same anticompetitive effect.

Furthering the delay in the resolution of the case, the Supreme Court decided that the five majors could not be treated collectively, so each studio's fate had to be determined individually.[10] At that point, the case had already dragged on for a decade, and some of the majors predicted it could take another ten years for all of the dust to settle.[11] The studios, led by Paramount and Fox, eventually decided to work on consent decrees rather than endure further hearings. A consent decree is a settlement between parties to a criminal case or lawsuit in which the company agrees to take specific actions without admitting fault or guilt for the situation that led to the lawsuit. Companies often agree to consent decrees instead of continuing the case through a trial or hearing, or in return for the government not pursuing criminal penalties.[12] The effect of the decrees was to dismantle the vertical integration of production, distribution, and exhibition that the Hollywood studio system had used to dominate the film industry for decades. While the studios and theaters grappled with the fallout from the *Paramount* antitrust case and its resulting consent decrees, a new antitrust lawsuit was brewing that would also impact the industry in fundamental ways.

PHONEVISION AS HOME BOX OFFICE

The antitrust case *U.S. v. Twentieth Century-Fox, et al.* got its start, in large part, as a result of Phonevision, one of the most prominent subscription television services at that time. Although the Zenith Radio Corporation had been developing the technology for a while, it was in August 1949 that they asked the FCC to allow a three-month trial run of Phonevision in the Chicago area. Zenith, along with RCA, was one of the major radio manufacturers, and Phonevision was designed as an early pay-per-view system that would allow home audiences to watch feature films that had exhausted their theatrical runs on their home television sets via their phone lines. The plan was to show first-run films, current stage shows, and sports events to approximately 300 subscribers, who would be asked to "contribute" amounts "equivalent to what regular charges for commercial service might be." The voluntary contributions were intended as a tool to better gauge the level of interest in the service, so that when the test period ended and Zenith officially launched the service, they could assign appropriate fees per view. Two hundred and fifty of the subscribers would be in the Lakeview telephone exchange area, and the rest would be scattered around the city. Special telephone lines would be installed, and customers would receive a Zenith receiver and any other necessary equipment. Zenith would use their Chicago station W9XZV for the transmission of the programs, which would be scrambled for viewers who did not have the Phonevision box. When Phonevision subscribers wanted to watch a program, they called the telephone company. The telephone company would send out a special signal that electronically released a key in the Phonevision unit that unscrambled the program.[13]

In February 1950, the FCC granted Zenith approval for a commercial test of Phonevision. As *Variety* described, it "may prove an event that will have the deepest influence on the entertainment business in many decades."[14] E. F. McDonald, the president of Zenith Radio Corporation, then contacted film studios asking for permission to license their films for the trial. E. F. McDonald was a minor celebrity for the wealth he accumulated in the radio and automobile industries. His arctic expeditions, radios in tow, had also brought him and his Zenith radios a great deal of attention. He had been a serious force in broadcasting for decades, and played a leading role when he founded the National Association of Radio Broadcasters in 1922. In March, Cecil B. DeMille appeared at a Phonevision press conference with McDonald. DeMille advised the film industry that "if some way of turning the home into a box office is found, the motion picture industry must go along. Phonevision is home box office. What I am urging this industry to do is not to turn its back on progress. Shake your fists or swear but you can't stop it."[15]

DeMille's comments not only prefigure HBO's successful moniker but also point to the fact that Phonevision was an early attempt to deliver a service to home audiences that only HBO was able to do decades later. DeMille said he would be making his films available for the Phonevision test, but would not specify which ones. He cautioned, "Commander McDonald has asked help from the industry. If the industry doesn't find a way to extend it to him, he will help himself."[16] McDonald stated that he had plenty of films for his test, but he refused to say which films or to specify who had given them to him. That was in part because Gael Sullivan, executive director of the TOA, was reportedly working to determine who had given films and who had not. After the press conference, *Variety* reported that "McDonald prophesied that television will do to motion pictures what films did to vaudeville and legit theatre unless the industry cooperates with the new medium."[17] Those statements concerned the theaters, and according to internal TOA memos, they feared that "the experiments in phonevision or similar developments in home television box office may be disastrous upon movie attendance, should they become effective."[18] Following McDonald's statements, the studios declined his request to use their films for his new service. In response, McDonald filed a complaint with the DOJ regarding the studios' refusal to deal with him, and the DOJ began an investigation into the studios' position on television.[19]

Like the theaters, the FCC was also concerned about the studios' dealings with Phonevision. In April 1950, the studios had a hearing before the FCC to oppose the FCC's policy that excluded antitrust violators, which the studios were very recently labeled thanks to the *Paramount* antitrust case, from entering the television field. During that hearing, commission members suggested to the studios' counsel that the policy of producers making films available to television stations would be given great weight in whether to approve applications for television stations. The television stations were akin to the independent theaters that the studios were so recently convicted of engaging in anticompetitive behavior against. The remedies in the *Paramount* antitrust case were designed to prevent exactly the kind of anticompetitive behaviors the FCC suspected the studios might be utilizing by refusing to license their films to television. The hearing had just begun when Senator Charles W. Tobey (R-NH), a member of the Interstate Commerce Committee, released a letter to FCC chairman Wayne Coy that cautioned, "The commission should know whether another monopolistic conspiracy with respect to the use of motion pictures is being hatched by persons seeking licenses of the public airways. A refusal by motion picture producers to deal with Zenith for purposes of its duly authorized experiment would be a significant factor for the commissioner to consider in the matter now before it."[20] The senator's suspicion that the studios were hatching another monopolistic conspiracy would eventually lead to further investigation of the studios' behavior in relation to television, and in particular, their feature films on television.

That same month, in a speech at a luncheon held by the Society of Motion Picture and Television Engineers, Spyros Skouras attempted to evoke sympathy for Fox's decision to withhold their films from Phonevision, and remarked, "I am sure that you of all people understand what I am trying to do [in refusing to provide films for the Phonevision test] so as to safeguard the interest of the exhibitors and I hope that our industry will realize the importance of this matter."[21] He also prophesied, "Let those who say that theatres will go out of business because of some gadget installed in homes understand once and for all that the motion picture theatres of America will flourish as they have never flourished before."[22] His confidence was rooted in his optimistic views of theater television, and he announced that Fox planned to install large-screen televisions in twenty of their Los Angeles theaters by early 1951. Skouras also advocated the elimination of second, or B, features from theater bills and substituting TV programs for them. In response, Gael Sullivan, executive director of the TOA, announced that the reaction of theater owners was "overwhelmingly favorable."[23] After Skouras's speech, he received a letter from T. R. Gilliam, the manager of Twentieth Century-Fox in Chicago, stating, "I also have spoken to a few of my friends who are not in any way connected with the motion picture business, and your address has made a very definite impression on them, as they seem to have accepted your statements as representing all of the important companies, that important motion pictures will not be given to television for home consumption."[24] Skouras later insisted that his comments were intended solely for the issue of feature films for Phonevision, but he argued that other people had simply misunderstood him to mean feature films to television more broadly.[25] McDonald was in the audience during Skouras's presentation, and afterward he said to reporters, "Theatres are moving into the homes and nothing can stop them. Television, not phonevision, is putting theatres out of business. What hasn't occurred to Mr. Skouras is that theatre TV and phonevision are almost identical except that phonevision will have a bigger audience and will be cheaper."[26] Skouras continued to use theater television as the counterpoint for Phonevision and as his reasoning for not releasing films for the Phonevision tests. In May 1950, in correspondence between Skouras and McDonald, Skouras explained, "I am opposed to Fox's giving pictures to phonevision at this time in order to protect the theatres, until they have installed large screen television."[27] It is telling, however, that Skouras said "until" the theaters had installed theater television. Whether or not he was planning to release his films to television once theater television became operational, he certainly left open that possibility.

Other studios also refused to participate in Phonevision, in large part because of the objections of the theaters. The exhibitor organizations commended the action of Twentieth Century-Fox and other companies, but they also issued warnings as to the consequences if studios changed their position. Trueman T. Rembusch of Allied stated, "Any producer foolhardy enough to furnish film for the Chicago Phonevision test, I am sure will find a spontaneous resistance toward the acceptance of his pictures by a regular theatre."[28] Walter Reade Jr., of the Walter Reade Theatres in New York City, wrote to Spyros Skouras as one of the exhibitors that was completely dependent on Fox's films, thanking him for continuing to take the position as firmly and positively as he did on the matter of films for television.[29] Arthur Lockwood, former president of TOA, viewed Phonevision as a "very serious threat." M. A. Lightman Jr. of Tri-State asserted, "It would hurt bad." Fred Schwartz of the Century Circuit believed that Phonevision and theaters could not exist together, and Rembusch called it the greatest threat to exhibition conceived to date.[30] Dave Wallerstein, of Balaban and Katz Corporation and co-chairman of the TOA's Television Committee, wrote to Marcus Cohn, "I am very pleased that we have been able to make their road a rocky one. . . . [To] me it represents the greatest possible threat to our business, and we should do everything we can to prevent its coming about."[31] Once again, the theaters proved themselves willing and able to effect change through mass letter-writing campaigns and the casting of dire threats.

On two occasions Zenith Radio scheduled trial tests of Phonevision in the Chicago area, and both times the tests had to be postponed—chiefly because no major Hollywood studio would release any films for the test. Universal, for example, had received requests in April 1950 and October 1950 to furnish 35mm or 16mm feature films for Phonevision, but Universal said they could not grant the request.[32] In May 1950, McDonald announced that the test planned for September in Chicago was temporarily on hold because they had been unable to get any films from the major studios. Zenith had even offered "to pay at the same rate as would be charged a conventional theatre of comparable audience." McDonald suggested that if the studios continued to refuse to license their films for Phonevision, the courts might have to get involved. He explained, "Failure of the test because of refusal of film producers to furnish films would unquestionably make it much more difficult to obtain FCC approval to the adoption and use of Phonevision as a permanent commercial television service."[33] But since the studios had in mind the possibility of their own systems to deliver their feature films directly to homes, preventing Phonevision from obtaining FCC approval was actually one of their goals. The studios did not want to license their films to Phonevision because they wanted to keep them for themselves. By the end of May 1950, when it appeared as though Phonevision was failing even before they got started, Trueman Rembusch told exhibitors "there was little danger of Phonevision putting them out of business."[34] At the TOA's convention later that year, Mitchell Wolfson observed, "Then there is Phonevision, which I frankly think is the 'flying saucer' of the television industry—everybody has heard about it, no one has really seen it, and I frankly believe it will quietly fade away without hurting anybody."[35] The theaters certainly had a vested interest in downplaying the significance of subscription television because of the fact that it promised the easiest and most direct way that studios could get their feature films on television. Phonevision would, however, come back to haunt them in other ways.

In response to the studios' unwillingness to release their films for Phonevision, McDonald contacted his friends in Congress and filed a complaint with the DOJ. McDonald's influence innervated the DOJ's investigation of the studios' behavior.[36] The DOJ's prosecution of the studios for antitrust violations in the *Paramount* case had been active for over a decade at this point, and the DOJ took very seriously any suspicions that the studios might have continued their anticompetitive behaviors.

Whereas in later decades the major media conglomerates held significant sway over the DOJ, Congress, and the executive branch, which all adopted neoliberal approaches to antitrust that favored large corporations, the 1950s was one of the last periods when significant antitrust action was undertaken against large corporations in Hollywood on behalf of the complaints of independents.

THE DOJ INVESTIGATES THE AFM

The antitrust suit against the studios and their distributors did not develop only as a result of E. F. McDonald's complaints about the studios' refusal to provide films to Phonevision, however. The DOJ was not immune to the rising tide of antiunion sentiment in the United States government, and the department had been pressured by members of Congress to investigate unions (and the AFM in particular) for possible antitrust violations. As a result, the DOJ had spent years scrutinizing the AFM in an attempt to find antitrust charges that could stick, and the case against the studios actually sprang, in part, from the DOJ's hopes that they could bring antitrust charges against the AFM as well.

As we saw in chapter 3, Congress's concerns also manifested themselves in public hearings conducted as to the behaviors of the AFM as they related to the new broadcasting industry. At the conclusion of the Congressional Committee on Education and Labor's hearings into Petrillo and the AFM in 1948, the committee argued that the AFM was engaged in restraint of trade to impede the technological development and public enjoyment of television and referred the matter to the DOJ to investigate whether any action could be taken against the union for violation of antitrust laws. The DOJ had previously brought a case against the AFM in 1942, when the AFM had first tried to ban musical recordings. In that case, the government contended that the objective of the union was to prevent the competition of recorded music, which the government believed was a restraint on commercial competition within the scope of the Sherman Antitrust Act.[37] The court, however, held that the AFM's ban was nothing more than a form of "closed shop" in which the union sought to prevent not only the broadcasting of music by nonunion musicians but also the broadcasting of "canned" or recorded music in competition with the live music of union members. The court held that this type of activity was not condemned by the Sherman Act, in the light of the Clayton and Norris-LaGuardia Act provisions, which held that as long as a union's activities were related to negotiations for employment, they were not subject to the Sherman Act.[38] The Clayton and Norris-LaGuardia provisions continued to thwart the DOJ's investigations of the AFM, but they persisted nonetheless. The DOJ remained concerned that the union was essentially dictating the conditions under which the product of the producers (film) could be sold to their customers (television). The DOJ prognosticated that this could mean that unions more generally could stipulate the prices and conditions on the sales of, say, automobiles or homes in order to get the wages they wanted for their union members. In an internal DOJ memo from 1954, George Haddock, a lawyer with the DOJ, explained, "I believe it is a dangerous and bad thing for a union to dictate the use which an employer may make of his property, but I think it is doubtful that we could win such a case in the light of the broad phraseology of the Clayton and Norris-LaGuardia Acts and the liberal interpretation of those acts by the Supreme Court."[39]

Independent producers had for years spurred the DOJ on in their investigations by urging them to take action against the AFM. In May 1951, for example, I. E. Chadwick, president of the Independent Motion Picture Producers Association, lodged a complaint with the DOJ about the restrictive provisions of contracts between the AFM and the different motion picture producers' associations, which prohibited the use in television of the music soundtrack containing music made by members of the federation. When Chadwick called the DOJ in July of that year to check on the status of his complaint, he told his contact that although he and his association thought that they had cause to take action against the AFM under antitrust laws, he did not want to file suit because he feared retaliatory action by the AFM. He and other independent producers hoped that the DOJ might act on their behalf.[40]

The DOJ still harbored strong suspicions that the studios had colluded with the AFM to put the clause in their contract that restricted the use of film soundtracks on television in order to protect their theaters from television competition. In a memo from William C. Dixon, chief of the Southern California Office of the DOJ, to H. G. Morison, assistant attorney general, in July 1951, Dixon explained, "It appears that all negotiations between the major producers and the American Federation of Musicians were handled in closed or secret conferences. . . . As you know, 20th-Century-Fox and the major film producers had at the time this provision was originally inserted in the agreement in 1946, extensive theatre holdings, the value of which would necessarily be adversely affected by the opening up to television of all films made by the independent as well as the major producers."[41] By the end of 1951, the DOJ had to put the matter in an "indefinitely deferred status" not only because they lacked the evidence to prove a conspiracy, but also because, as Richard K. Decker, acting chief of the trial section, explained, the DOJ's "appropriations are in such poor shape. The situation does not warrant a very high priority at this time because of that."[42] With the reduction in staff they faced as a result of their inadequate funding, and the fact that they were finding it difficult to deal with matters considered of even greater public importance, the DOJ chose instead to pursue cases they thought had a better chance of success.[43] Only a year later, however, in December 1952, the DOJ reopened their investigations of the AFM. Members of the Independent Motion Picture Producers Association had continued their complaints to the DOJ about the AFM's restrictions, and claimed that they would have released many films to television if it had not been for those restrictions. William Dixon advocated for testing the legality of the contract provisions in court, and argued that doing so would be beneficial regardless of whether the DOJ could prove that the AFM had colluded with the studios.[44]

By 1955, the DOJ had been running in circles on this issue for eight years. They remained concerned that even if the studios "willingly or even joyfully acquiesced in this contract," unless the DOJ could prove that they had colluded with the AFM in the creation of the contract provision that restricted the use of the studios' films on television, the AFM would be exempt from prosecution under the Sherman Act by virtue of the Clayton and Norris-LaGuardia Acts,[45] which, again, protected unions from antitrust prosecution as long as the unions' activities were nonviolent and conducted in relation to securing the terms and conditions for the employment or wages of their members. Haddock argued, however, "it might be considered desirable to bring the suggested case, even if there is serious question about winning it, in order to point to the need for congressional action to limit the scope of the exemptions for union activity directly affecting competition."[46] Finally, in September 1956, after nine years of off-and-on-again investigations, the DOJ concluded for the final time that they did not have enough evidence to prove a restraint of trade against the AFM under the current laws, and closed the case for good.[47]

U.S. v. Twentieth Century-Fox, et al.

As the DOJ's and Congress's investigations into the AFM brought attention to the issue of feature films on television, so too had McDonald's complaints regarding the film studios' refusal to deal with Phonevision resulted in an ongoing investigation of the film industry and their position on television.[48] Rumors also circulated in exhibitor circles that McDonald had bribed his congressman with $50,000 to persuade the DOJ to investigate the studios and force them to release their films for the Phonevision test.[49] Whether or not bribery was involved, in July 1952 the DOJ's investigation led to Attorney General James P. McGranery filing a civil antitrust complaint in the federal district court in Los Angeles that charged twelve motion picture producing and distributing companies with a conspiracy to restrain interstate commerce in 16mm feature films in violation of the Sherman Act. The defendants were Twentieth Century-Fox Film Corporation; Warner Bros. Pictures, Inc.; Warner Bros. Pictures Distribution Corporation; RKO Radio Pictures, Inc.; Republic Pictures Corporation; Republic Productions, Inc.; Columbia Pictures Corporation; Screen Gems, Inc.; Universal Pictures Company, Inc.; United World Films, Inc.; Films, Inc.; and Pictorial Films, Inc. Paramount and MGM were not defendants because at the time of the commencement of the suit, and up to the time of the trial in 1955, they produced 16mm films only for distribution in foreign countries and to the armed forces, and not for general domestic distribution.[50] The complaint contained the actual signature of Attorney General McGranery, and it was unusual that the attorney general would have signed the complaint himself, which indicated that the DOJ was especially interested in this case and thought it was particularly significant.[51]

While the suit cited 16mm films specifically, its primary focus was television. It involved 16mm films, however, since the advent of commercial television had created a tremendous new demand for 16mm feature films. For television exhibition, 16mm film was more feasible than 35mm both technologically and economically, and it had become the primary format for films on television.[52] For example, by 1951, of the 108 television stations in the United States, 67 had 16mm projection equipment. Only twenty-two had both 16mm and 35mm projection equipment.[53] The stations with 35mm equipment were located in larger cities like Los Angeles, Chicago, and Boston.[54]

Much of the scholarship on the historical transition of film to television seldom fully accounts for the role played by the technology of film format or film stock. Yet one of the significant obstacles to Hollywood's feature films appearing on television was that most television stations were equipped to broadcast only films on 16mm and not on 35mm. Charles Weintraub of Quality Films, a distributor of feature films for television, described the reasons why television stations preferred 16mm to 35mm film as primarily economic:

> Firstly, because a station generally pays for the shipping charges. Obviously, a 16mm print, much smaller in size, isn't as expensive a proposition as a 35mm. Secondly, it is much easier to handle, talking now physically, than a 35mm print. Thirdly, it reduces what is commonly known in our industry as the fire hazard in the various projection rooms of TV stations, because most of the 16mm films are on safety stock, as compared to a lot of the 35mm films made prior to 1948 and 1949, which were on nitrate film. Another advantage, in my opinion, would be the cost of obtaining 16mm projection equipment would be far less than 35mm equipment. . . . It is much easier to store 16mm film than 35.[55]

The fire hazards of 35mm nitrate film that Weintraub referred to were perhaps the costliest to mitigate. Nitrate film is extremely flammable, and if any television station wanted to broadcast a 35mm nitrate print, they had to invest in projection equipment that could handle 35mm nitrate films and build a fireproof booth. It was only in May 1948 that Kodak unveiled the first fireproof 35mm film at the convention of the Society of Motion Picture Engineers. Kodak estimated, however, that it would take a total of three years before that type of film was standard in the industry: one year of small-scale experimental use by exhibitors, followed by another one or two years for plant conversion. This meant that until at least 1951, any television station or network that did not want to, or could not afford to, pay the shipping and fireproofing costs of 35mm films had to use films on 16mm.

The 16mm film business started in or around 1935 and grew during World War II, when most major producers, including Fox, Warner, RKO, and Republic Productions, released 16mm versions of their product for showing by the Armed Forces, veterans' hospitals, the American Red Cross, and the United Services Organization, Inc. (USO).[56] The demand for 16mm film by military and auxiliary organizations had diminished by the end of the war, but demand from the civilian market increased to such an extent that total distribution of 16mm films soon became greater than it was during World War II. The major studios did not necessarily like using the 16mm format, as they found the visual quality inferior and the economics of the trade unfavorable, but they produced 16mm prints of their films for locations like those listed above, as well as for schools, churches, and hospitals,

principally to fulfill what they considered their patriotic and civic duty. It also did
not hurt that providing prints of their films to locations such as the Red Cross and
hospitals resulted in good public relations for the studios. Ned Depinet, former
president of RKO, explained that one of the reasons the studios did not use 16mm
for theatrical exhibition was because it required the reduction of the optical from
35mm to 16mm, which, when blown up through projection on a big screen, lost a
significant amount of clarity. Depinet recalled of the development of 16mm, "It
never was supposed to be commercial stock for the theatrical industry. 16 millimeter came along and was developed for home movies, people wanting to make
movies of their children in their homes and on their vacations, and then the war,
the second World War brought 16mm into prominence, because, being lighter, less
weighted, less space required, and projectors being more easily portable, the Army
adopted it."[57]

The studios had never seriously invested in the 16mm film business because it
did not earn substantial profits for the studios, and since the 16mm business was
not nearly as profitable as the 35mm business, it was not as well organized or supplied. Peter Levathes, who had run the 16mm division for Fox, described it as a
"very loosely organized system of distribution," which they considered a source of
"terminal revenue" for their films. He said the 16mm market "was hitting the bottom of the barrel, so to speak, in the liquidation of the product."[58] With the exception of some drive-in theaters "established in cow pastures," commercial 16mm
theaters did not really exist at that time.[59] Sidney Kramer, head of 16mm business
for RKO before 1953, explained that they intended their 16mm business as a sup-
plement to their regular distribution activities and noncompetitive to their 35mm
theaters.[60] In order to ensure that 16mm remained noncompetitive, the studios
would not release 16mm prints to any exhibitor that proposed to show the film
within a certain distance of a 35mm theater. For example, when Bernard Lowenthal, a former 35mm theater operator in Brooklyn, New York, moved to Miami and
attempted to get 16mm prints from the majors to lease to Miami hotels for showings to guests in their lobbies or courtyards, he received "no's" across the board.
Mr. Furst, the salesman for Universal in New York, explained to Lowenthal that
16mm film was unavailable for Lowenthal because "it would be in competition to
the theatres in the Miami Beach area."[61] Because the studios' 16mm business was
so small and disorganized, and because most television stations could project only
16mm films, the two mediums would have to figure out a technological middle
ground before Hollywood's feature films could make their way to television.

Although the use of films on television might have been the primary concern
of the DOJ, their focus on 16mm film necessarily included the other outlets served
by 16mm films. As Newell A. Clapp, acting assistant attorney general in charge of
the Antitrust Division, explained, "According to the complaint, defendants have
imposed arbitrary and unreasonable conditions upon the exhibitions of sixteen
millimeter feature films in hospitals, schools, churches and USO centers, and have
prevented the use of these films on television. This suit seeks to prevent defendants
from continuing their restrictive system of distributing these films."[62] Another

complaint regarding the studios' restrictions on 16mm film had come from a source not mentioned by Clapp: hotels in Miami. Many hotel operators in Miami had shown 16mm prints of feature films free for their guests. The 35mm theater operators in the area had complained vociferously to the studios about these showings, claiming that they stole potential audience members. As a result, the hotel owners contacted their representatives in Congress as well as the DOJ. Their allegations against the studios for anticompetitive behavior, in addition to the complaints regarding Phonevision, and the fact that the dominant technology in television was 16mm, all led the DOJ to make the antitrust case about 16mm film rather than about films on television.

The complaint charged that the defendants and the co-conspirators "engaged in an unlawful combination and conspiracy to limit distribution and restrict exhibitions of 16 millimeter feature films, including the exhibition of such films on television."[63] The purpose of their conspiracy, the government alleged, was to protect 35 millimeter theaters from competition—especially from television.[64] Attorney General McGranery stated in a DOJ press release, "This suit is filed as part of the continuing program of the Antitrust Division to prevent businessmen and others from combining to place restrictions upon what members of the general public may see on their television sets."[65] The DOJ's complaint also included the following restrictions on the distribution and exhibition of 16mm feature films: refusing to license anyone to telecast 16mm feature films; refusing to license the exhibition of 16mm films at locations competitive with established 35mm theaters; limiting the conditions on which licenses for exhibition of 16mm films may be granted, even to approved places of exhibition such as churches, schools, clubs, hotels, drive-ins, or other places of exhibition in theaterless towns; imposing arbitrary and excessive clearances between the first release of a feature motion picture of 35mm width and its exhibition on 16mm width; refusing to license the exhibition of 16mm feature films at free merchants' shows, taverns, in coin-operated machines, and refusing to license roadshowmen; reserving for each of the defendants severally, or for some of them jointly, the right to approve or disapprove locations for the showing of 16mm feature films before or after the licensing thereof, with the right to arbitrarily abrogate any license granted for exhibition at any approved location; and granting or withholding licenses to exhibit 16mm feature films to such approved or disapproved locations.[66]

The complaint further alleged that the defendants, with the assistance of the co-conspirators, had maintained an intricate system to police and enforce those restrictions and blacklisted or boycotted exhibitors that disregarded them.[67] The effects of those actions, the complaint alleged, included the following: the telecasting of the finer feature films to television audiences in the United States has been suppressed; competition in the interstate distribution and exhibition of feature films has been unreasonably restrained; actual and potential exhibitors of 16mm feature films had been foreclosed from significant parts of the United States market; and persons living in theaterless towns or in institutions that prohibit their inhabitants from visiting theaters were denied the opportunity to see other than outmoded feature films.[68] The DOJ wanted the court to order the defendant companies to grant "unrestricted leases and licenses for the exhibition, including telecasting" of the feature films the court "deemed necessary to dissipate fully the consequences of the aforesaid illegal combination and conspiracy."[69] The DOJ was still going to allow for reasonable clearance periods between runs of the studios' 35mm films and 16mm films if the exhibition of the 16mm films was "substantially competitive" with the theaters.[70] So the studios could still have used 16mm outlets, including television, as subsequent run locations, but those allowances did not assuage the studios and the theaters. Shortly after the suit was filed, Skouras wrote an editorial in the *Los Angeles Examiner* that opened with the dramatic pronouncement that "the Department of Justice started last month an antitrust suit against a number of Hollywood motion picture producers to compel them to make their films available to television and TV advertisers. In other words, the motion picture producers are kindly requested to cut their own throats."[71]

Other members of the film industry also issued public complaints about the suit. SAG, for example, issued a press release in August 1952 complaining that the DOJ was attempting to force the studios to give their films to television for free showings, and if that happened, SAG believed the country's theaters would be forced to close and the studios would no longer be able to finance the production of their films. SAG's statement continued, "The Guild Board condemns this action by the Federal Government, which jeopardizes the livelihood of 250,000 workers in the film industry. . . . The Guild Board recognizes that old theatrical films which have exhausted their theatre box office possibilities may go into television provided that (1) the producer of the picture sells the television rights of his own free will and not under government compulsion, and (2) the actors in such films receive additional compensation for their television rights."[72] SAG sent a copy of the press release to the American Federation of Labor (AFL) with a request that they look into the matter, and SAG also sent a copy to the attorney general, James McGranery. Newell Clapp, the assistant attorney general, responded to the letter on behalf of the DOJ, reiterating the DOJ's concerns and rationale for filing the complaint. SAG's response expressed the following anxieties: "We realize, of course, that the antitrust allegations in this matter must be adjudicated in the courts but we are most disturbed over the impracticality of any court setting 'reasonable clearance periods between runs of a particular feature motion picture in a theatre' and exhibitions of the same motion picture for free viewing on television."[73] The guild cited the recent example of the successful theatrical reissue of *King Kong* (1933) as the kind of potential that would be destroyed if films were given to television. *King Kong* was film industry members' go-to example of the theatrical potential that older films still had in the theaters, and they invoked it regularly. It was true that the reissue of *King Kong* had done very well at the box office and had grossed almost $3 million in its reissue. Unfortunately, it was an anomaly, and most films when reissued grossed far less. In response to SAG's request that the matter be investigated, the AFL, at their annual national convention in September 1952, voted to approve a resolution condemning the antitrust suit. IATSE, SAG, and the California State Federation of Labor sponsored the resolution.[74]

The Los Angeles City Council also got involved in the matter, and passed a strongly worded resolution condemning the suit that read "NOW, THEREFORE, BE IT RESOLVED, that the City Council of Los Angeles, . . . recognizing the frightful fact that if by government decree our Motion Picture Industry can be forced to sell its finest pictures to Television Companies and advertisers at reduced low prices, set by government, that such a decree would not only be unjust enrichment of one industry at the expense of another, but that the Motion Picture Industry would soon be without production, which would lead to the closing of theatres and eventual bankruptcy of both studios and theatres across the nation."[75] The full text of the resolution is comically hyperbolic, and the council closes by inviting the leaders of the film industry to confer with them on "ways and means" of how they might exert their influence to protect the film industry's "constitutional property rights." Although both the council's resolution and SAG's press release would make it seem as though the DOJ was forcing the studios to give their films to television for free, that was not the case. The DOJ wanted the studios to make their films available for sale or lease at reasonable prices set by the studios. The confusion existed, however, as another result of the innate difference between the financial models of the film and television industries. Just because television audiences did not have to purchase a ticket to watch television programming, it did not mean that payment was not made somewhere by someone. It was just that in television, the money changed hands behind the scenes, and that relative invisibility caused the kind of tumult seen in the City Council and SAG statements. The hyperbole was not limited, however, to the producers, unions, and city council. The theater owners and their associations were particularly upset by the suit and made their opinions known. Their opinions were so vocal, in fact, that some people began to suspect that it was actually their influence that motivated the studios' allegedly illegal behavior. A *Los Angeles Times* article that ran shortly after the lawsuit was filed argued, "It is the contention of some members of the television industry that the pressure to keep films from TV distribution comes primarily from the exhibitors rather than from the producers."[76] The studios and theaters were afraid of what "the menace to the picture industry of 40,000,000 little home theaters" would do to the income from the theatrical business.[77]

The theaters were, in fact, afraid of the competition from the television home theaters, especially if Hollywood's feature films were made available to them. The theater organizations encouraged all of their member theaters to write letters to the DOJ, their congressmen, and the president, expressing their opposition to the case. One letter from the Strand Theatre in Lowell, Michigan, charged, "Your antitrust suit against twelve distributing companies releasing motion picture films elaborates neatly the amount of corruption existing in your department and the United States Government in general. Free enterprise no longer exists. You are protecting and abating parasites who desire product founded solely for the distribution to motion picture theatres."[78] Another letter from J. C. Mohrstadt Theatres in Hayti, Missouri, made it clear that he would be "very unhappy" if the case was successful and his theater was forced out of business. He wrote, "I am not a lawyer and don't know the legal implications of such a suit, but I was under the impression that the meaning of the Anti-Trust law was to protect small businesses of this United States, not to destroy them. If the suit you have instituted was won, it would seem to me that you would be creating a monopoly of Television stations that would crush in a single blow, these thousands of small theatre owners."[79] Many of the letters echoed concerns that turning over Hollywood's films to television would force the theaters out of business. Then there were letters like the one from Frank Lesmeister of the State Theatre in Blair, Wisconsin:

> I have bin reding in the papers and today I got the box office and after reding it there I tryed to come up whit a ancer but I cant find one. If the Goverment will make all the Film Companyes give there films to T.V. before we get them then there is nothing left for us to but close all are theatres, I will try and give you a small examble we have atowen of 850 Pop here and we have six taverns here and all the rest of the places where thay will be showing FREE.TV. and we are paying the Goverment 20 per cent gross admission tax and thay are able to show the same picture FREE ON T.V. where do you think thay will go. not to the theatre but where thay can see it FREE.[80]

It seems from the number of spelling and usage errors in this letter from Lesmeister that he likely did not compose letters often, so the occasion of the suit must have been significant enough motivation to sit him down at a typewriter to compose and then mail the letter. There are literally thousands of letters like these in the files of the DOJ. Some of them typed, some handwritten, and some signed by all of the employees at a particular theater. The combined effect of that mass of letters is somewhat overwhelming, which was certainly the theater owners' intention.

In addition to sending letters, theater owners also passed resolutions regarding the suit. For example, in the resolution passed by the board of directors of the Southern California Theatre Owners Association (SCTOA), they argued that the DOJ was "badly informed and mislead in filing the suit because the suit appears to be unreasonable and contrary to common business sense."[81] They cited the importance of the 22,000 theaters that were worth an estimated $2.5 billion and employed 2 million people in the United States, and their integral role in the "American Way of Life by affording the general public entertainment, recreation and education at a charge, nominal by comparison."[82] They argued that the money needed to produce new feature films could only be earned through the theaters, and if those theaters were forced into bankruptcy, as they argued would inevitably happen if the DOJ won their case, the film industry would fail. That would, they asserted, in effect encourage monopolistic behavior by the television industry, which would then be left without competition. They complained that "the motion picture theatre industry not only has been adversely affected but on the verge of total destruction because of the subtle unfair competition of the television business," and argued that television broadcasters should be making their own original programming that would be "more suitable for their purpose."[83] The SCTOA promised not to request that the DOJ force films produced by and for television to be sold to the theaters, and requested that their senators, state representatives, and the president urge the DOJ to "end this harmful litigation."[84]

The board of directors of the Allied Theatre Owners of Indiana, Inc., which represented approximately 500 independent theater owners, met in July 1952 in an emergency session to discuss the suit. From that meeting, Trueman Rembusch sent a letter to the attorney general, which asserted, "The motion picture exhibitors of this state have concluded that the suit is so illogical in its pleadings and so drastic in the remedies sought that by its very existence it casts a shadow upon the integrity of the Department of Justice, and implies a definite tie-up between the hierarchy of the Democratic party and the monopoly, television. That conclusion was reached by exhibitors with expert knowledge of production values after making a comparison of the superior television programming given the Democratic National Convention as compared with that given to the Republican National Convention."[85] In this letter, as in many of the other letters and resolutions, the undercurrent of anxiety about hidden political agendas and socialism is evident and reflects the growing anticommunist paranoia of the time.

Despite the outrageous accusations made against the department, the DOJ still took the theater owners' and associations' concerns seriously, and in August 1952, Clapp and Kramer of the DOJ met with representatives from the major theater organizations. The theater groups expressed a fear that a court mandate to license theatrical films to television stations would create unfair competition by practically compelling the producers to accept much lower rentals than those paid by theaters. The DOJ made it clear that if the theater groups' objective was to persuade them to withdraw the suit, such attempt was fruitless. The DOJ did, however, indicate that they would be willing to give the theater owners a hearing, if, at a time a consent decree was negotiated, they wished to come forward with constructive suggestions. The DOJ then pointed out that the relief they sought from the suit provides for reasonable clearances and reasonable royalties, and argued that the legitimate interest of theater owners would be protected by such clearances and payment.[86]

THE TRIAL

Although the suit was filed in July 1952, it did not go to trial until September 1955. The intervening years were spent with various motions, objections, and interrogatories filed by both sides. In October 1954, the government complained to the judge that "under all of these circumstances, there is strong reason to believe that the interrogatories propounded by the defendants some two years after the filing of the complaint, were filed to vex and harass the plaintiff and to cause delay in the ultimate trial of this case on the merits."[87] In December 1954, in preliminary proceedings,

Judge Harry Westover indicated the priority of the case for the DOJ and the courts in saying, "The head of the antitrust department was in here not so long ago, and I assured him that when this case was ready for trial, we would clear the decks and give it priority, I mean get rid of the other cases and give it priority."[88]

Shortly after that, on January 20, 1955, the DOJ named the other major theater associations as co-conspirators in the case. Co-conspirators are charged with agreeing to commit a criminal act and doing something to help facilitate an agreement to commit a crime, which in this case was the violation of the Sherman Antitrust Act by restraining the trade of 16mm films. Since it was the producers and distributors that held the rights to license or sell their films to television and other 16mm outlets, they were the defendants, while the exhibitors, without direct control over the licensing or sale of the films, remained co-conspirators. The DOJ, however, was attempting to prove that the pressure the exhibitors exerted on the producers and distributors was a major factor in what the DOJ alleged was the producers' and distributors' illegal behavior. As the judge commented at one point, "If [the producers] get any more pressure letters from exhibitors, the producers will be appearing in the position of an unwilling bride being forced to act, which is not very usual for a co-conspirator."[89] The TOA had originally been named as a co-conspirator, but now the list was expanded to include Allied States Association of Motion Picture Exhibitors, Independent Theatre Owners Association, Inc., Metropolitan Motion Picture Theatres Association, Inc., Southern California Theatre Owners Association, Pacific Coast Conference of Independent Theatre Owners, and COMPO.[90] The theater owners and their associations were not happy with that turn of events, and at one point, the special assistant to the attorney general, Samuel Flatow, joked to the judge, "Sir, I think I would have to be very careful with my life if I walked into TOA today."[91]

Before the case had a chance to make it to trial, however, some of the defendants agreed to consent decrees. Republic Pictures and Republic Productions were two of the first companies to enter consent judgments in the case in September 1955. The decree required Republic within ninety days to license or offer for licensing on 16mm eighty percent of the films that they had released for 35mm theatrical exhibition in the United States during the second preceding calendar year. It also restrained them from refusing to license said feature films and fixing the conditions thereof.[92] The ninety-day deadline for Republic to offer their films to television would have occurred in mid-December, so for the studios that were concerned about a possible buyers' market, this would have been alarming news. Both Republic and the judge wanted to make sure that the industry and the public understood that just because they had agreed to a consent decree did not mean they had admitted guilt. As the judge noted, "Mr. Flatow came in and stated that some of the defendants were desirous of consenting to a decree. I notice one of them said officially the other day the decree did not mean a thing, that they were not doing anything, they just agreed to it because it was a way of saving lawyers' fees. That was Republic's president."[93] The judge also emphasized that the entering of a consent decree by some of the defendants would not influence him against the remaining defendants.[94]

Pictorial Films was experiencing financial difficulties, and in November 1954, lawyers from Loeb & Loeb told the court that they were withdrawing as attorneys for Pictorial Films because Pictorial had been "unresponsive and uncooperative in communications and access to information" and had not paid Loeb & Loeb for their work.[95] So it was not a big surprise when Pictorial Films, Inc., and Films, Inc., followed Republic's lead and entered consent decrees. The consent decrees for both Pictorial and Films outlined substantially the same terms as the Republic decree, with the one difference being that the former's decrees simply stated, "Said defendant is ordered and directed to license or offer for licensing in good faith, directly or through distributors, to Government and other outlets its feature films available for 16mm exhibition." So rather than specify the studio's license or offer 80 percent of their films, as the Republic decree had, it just said "its films."[96]

Republic, Pictorial, and Films, Inc., were not as financially strong as their co-defendant studios. Republic, in particular, was involved in a number of different lawsuits at that time (the Rogers and Autry suits to name only a couple), which took a significant toll on their finances. It was also the case that all of the defendant companies were seriously concerned that the judge would find them guilty. Their fear was based largely on a statement made by Supreme Court justice Douglas in his opinion in the recently decided antitrust case against Paramount et al. Douglas argued that it was "not always necessary to find a specific intent to restrain trade or to build a monopoly in order to find that the anti-trust laws have been violated. It is sufficient that a restraint of trade or monopoly results as the consequence of a defendant's conduct or business arrangements."[97] Since the studios had endured the long and expensive process of that earlier antitrust case, they had been very careful to avoid anything that could be used as evidence of anticompetitive behavior. Douglas seemed, however, to argue that evidence of a conspiracy or the intention to conspire was not necessary to be found guilty of violating the antitrust act. It merely required that the effects of a company's actions were anticompetitive. Based on that standard, it was even more likely that the studios would be found guilty in the case against Twentieth Century-Fox et al. Faced with the distinct possibility of a guilty verdict and weak financial positions, Republic, Pictorial, and Films wanted to avoid additional, and potentially unnecessary, lawyers' fees for the trial. So they entered agreements with the government that they could negotiate as much in their favor as possible.

One glimmer of hope existed, however, in the fact that Judge Yankwich seriously disliked the DOJ's lawyers who were trying the case. The studios' lawyers had tried many cases before the judge, and their West Coast styles were very different from the styles of the East Coast lawyers from the DOJ. As the judge explained to Flatow, one of the DOJ's lawyers, on the first day, "Listen, you have got to learn one thing, which counsel [for the studios] have learned. Nobody makes a set speech in my court, you see. If you do, you will be deprived of finding out what is in my

mind. And therein western judges differ from eastern judges. That is, we are talk-
ative judges. In other words, you will know before you get through just how I feel
about certain things. In the second place, you deprive us of a lot of fun."[98] About
a month later, the judge was still giving the DOJ lawyers a difficult time. At one
point the judge admonished them, saying that he was upset that the DOJ had not
used more of their West Coast attorneys to try the case, and he hoped that mes-
sage was "transmitted to Washington." Yankwich said he was tired of having to
lecture all the time to the DOJ's East Coast lawyers, who were "unfamiliar with
the rules of evidence and unfamiliar with the local practices."[99] Although the judge
was clearly fed up with the DOJ's lawyers, he remained friendly with the studios'
lawyers. He had heard many cases involving the film industry, including the case
Franchon & Marco, Inc. v. Paramount Pictures, Inc., et al. This was another antitrust case wherein Franchon & Marco, who owned and operated theaters in Los
Angeles and elsewhere, claimed that distributors and other theater owners and
operators had combined to control 80 percent of the supply of films. In that case,
the judge found in favor of the distributor and theater owner defendants and concluded that there had been no combination or conspiracy.[100] Homer Mitchell, a
lawyer from O'Melveny & Myers, had represented some of the studios in the *Franchon & Marco* case, and was again representing the studios in the *Twentieth
Century-Fox* antitrust case. Overall, Judge Yankwich's track record demonstrated
his preference for the studios and his reluctance to find them guilty on antitrust
charges.

This reluctance was due in part to the judge's clear love of Hollywood and his
soft spot for those who ran the studios and held other positions of power in the
film industry. For example, when Spyros Skouras was on the witness stand, the
judge praised him as being a "profound man" and talked with him at length about
films that were remade and made especially for television. Skouras pandered and
told the judge that he would take his "wonderful advice" straight back to his television department.[101] The judge often talked about movies he had recently seen,
and many of the disparaging remarks he made about the East Coast lawyers from
the DOJ seemed to be made in an attempt to ingratiate himself with the studios
and their lawyers. These local cultural affinities between Judge Yankwich and Hollywood directly affected the case, as well as other cases heard by the judge, and
thereby significantly influenced the basic structure and output of the film industry. This influence demonstrates the important ways in which social relations can
impact industry as much as economics and the law itself.

The studios' defense was relatively straightforward: they denied all allegations
and asked for the dismissal of the case and the recovery of their costs from the
government.[102] Many of the studios did admit that their decisions as to whether to
approve the licensing of 16mm films to certain locations had been based on whether
the location in question would be in competition with their existing 35mm theaters. Universal, for example, argued that their denials for licensing 16mm films
for exhibition were based on whether the proposed locations would substantially
and adversely affect theatrical exhibition of their 35mm features.[103] The studios

denied, however, that those decisions were made as part of a conspiracy with the other studios. They all argued that they had acted independently and made decisions based on their own best interests. Some studios tried to lay the blame at the feet of others, like the AFM. Republic, for example, argued that they were not legally free to grant any requests to license their films for television without special agreement with, or written consent from, the AFM.[104] In the years before the case went to trial, the studios also changed their tune in court filings regarding important points such as whether anyone in their company had meetings about the licensing or sale of their films to television. In their initial filings, the studios had, across the board, denied that any conversations of that type had taken place. In the meantime, however, the DOJ had the FBI visit the studios and their co-conspirators and make photocopies of any and all documents they could find related to the issues in the case. What they found was that the studios were, in fact, engaged in numerous discussions about the licensing and sale of their feature films to television, so the studios ultimately revised their responses to answer "yes" they had, in fact, had meetings or conferences regarding selling their films to television.[105]

During the trial, the heads of the studios who appeared as witnesses were all specifically asked what their policies were regarding feature films on television. Their responses, much like their behaviors in regard to feature films on television, varied slightly, but shared certain commonalities. Ned Depinet, who had been president of RKO until October 1952, testified that their policy had been "one of watchful waiting." He explained, "If anybody has ever come forward with a price that we thought was commensurate, we probably would have had a tough decision to make as to whether we want to turn our backs on 20,000 exhibitors who have patronized us over the years, in order to give our product to television. But we have never had to make that decision, because there has never been a price involved that we thought was worth a tinker's hoot."[106] When asked whether he had not put RKO's films on television because he was afraid of reprisals from exhibitors, Depinet answered, "Oh, no. I didn't want to kill the goose that laid the golden egg. . . . I didn't want to trade a known business for one that is unknown. I don't know where television is going. I knew I was getting my revenue from legitimate theatres, and it was a very good business."[107]

Spyros Skouras, when asked what the general policy of Twentieth Century-Fox had been with respect to licensing feature film for use on television, explained that they had opposed the release of their films to television because they could not get prices from television that would compensate for the losses they would experience at the theatrical box office if their films appeared on television. Skouras continued that as a company, they had to make $55–$60 million a year from their "live inventory" and therefore had to protect their main source of income—the theaters. Skouras explained that by "live inventory" he meant the films that had not yet amortized (i.e., paid off their costs), and that it took sixty-five weeks for a film to be completely amortized.[108]

The studios also answered the charge that they were trying to crush the competition of television by highlighting their activities in the television industry more broadly. Those activities included things like producing content for television and theater television. During the questioning of Peter Levathes, he argued, "In view of the nature of the argument that is being advanced that poor little television is being starved by these powerful conspirators, I believe the fact that they are trying to cooperate in some ways, at least, has some bearing upon their relationship, just as the fact that they themselves are now using the medium, as Mr. Skouras testified, bears upon the matter."[109]

Ultimately, the defendant film studios claimed that they had not entered into any agreement with each other as to their films on television, but that they were always aware of and paying attention to what the others were doing with respect to that issue. The judge at one point virtually made their case for them when he stepped in to explain his understanding of the behavior of companies in an oligopolistic industry:

> [Professor Sutherland, an economist] coined this phrase of "monopolistic competition," and he points to the fact that a person in deciding that a man engaged in the production of goods for the market and seeking to sell it is consciously and unconsciously always aware of what the others in the field are doing. But he says that that is not even a tacit agreement, it is merely because, as he explained elsewhere, and as I and others who did not adopt his theory have stated repeatedly, when you are living in an interrelated market, and you are dealing with an oligopoly—we like that word—and that is where the customers are many and the manufacturers are few, at all times you may be conscious of it.[110]

If the studios had any fears that they might be found guilty, this statement by Yankwich should have put those fears to rest. The writing was on the wall: the trial that began in September 1955 was decided on 5 December 1955 in favor of the defendants.[111] The judge found that although the actions of the different studios were similar, the government was unable to prove that the studios' practices were the result of any contract, concert, combination, or conspiracy.[112] As Herman Levy, general counsel for the TOA, noted after the decision was made, "This is a decision of the greatest importance in industry history. The industry was fortunate to have had a jurist of Judge Yankwich's capabilities and conscientiousness sitting on the case."[113] Then, on 27 December 1955, the consent judgment between the government and Republic, Films, Pictorial, and Warner Bros. Distributing Corp. was stayed, which meant that the studios were no longer required to offer their films for licensing within a certain period of time.[114]

Although *U.S. vs. Twentieth Century-Fox, et al.* has not received as much attention in film and television histories as other cases, such as the now-notorious antitrust case against Paramount Pictures et al., it profoundly impacted the film and television industries and the ways they eventually negotiated to broadcast Hollywood feature films on television in the mid-1950s. While it was necessary for the studios to resolve the many obstacles that existed in advance of selling or licensing their feature films to television, the studios' move to sell their films in 1955 directly resulted from this antitrust case and its eventual resolution. The studios' fear of being found guilty and forced to offer their films to television on terms the government specified helped motivate the studios to resolve the issues that were keeping their films off television. It is largely because of this case that Hollywood's feature films showed up on television when they did, and neither sooner nor later. In terms of feature films on television, the resolution of *U.S. v. Twentieth Century-Fox, et al.* closed the door to one of the most significant obstacles that remained between feature films and their broadcast on television. By the end of 1955, the film industry breathed a sigh of relief over the victories they had won in court. With the resolution of the *Rogers, Autry,* and antitrust lawsuits, and the studios' divorcement from their theaters, the studios were free of many of the restrictions that had prevented their films from appearing on television. While there were still many details to be worked out, and some studios would still take time to license or sell their films to television, by 1956 the first announcements were made regarding the major studios' libraries making their way to television.

That these cases took years to resolve demonstrates one of the weaknesses of antitrust law and its prosecution in the mid-twentieth century: the DOJ waited until illegal behaviors had taken place and then worked to prosecute the guilty parties and mitigate their harmful effects. Today, antitrust enforcement has shifted, largely because of the amendment of the Clayton Act in the 1970s, to a system that is much more reliant on requiring corporations to get approval for mergers or acquisitions from the DOJ, FCC, and FTC before they occur. The idea is that the approval process can identify possible antitrust abuses and use consent decrees to outline rules the new entities must follow after the merger or acquisition. The problem is that, much like what happened in the 1940s and 1950s, unless there is someone policing those companies to make sure that they are abiding by the terms of their consent decrees, those decrees are worth about as much as the paper they are printed on. One interesting twist, however, was the announcement in November 2019 that the DOJ was reviewing the consent decrees that resulted from the *Paramount* antitrust case, and the DOJ ultimately decided to terminate the decrees because, as they argued in their brief, they "have served their purpose, and their continued existence may actually harm American consumers by standing in the way of innovative business models for the exhibition of America's great creative films."[115] Clearly this action is related to a concern or interest one of the studios has about future business in the streaming space, but the fact that consent decrees from the late 1940s are raising red flags for someone in the industry today illustrates the long-term consequences of these legal actions and highlights that the introduction of new technologies and media often necessitates a reconciliation of contract terms and legal obstacles, even if they are decades old, before an industry can move forward.

CHAPTER 6

FEATURE FILMS MAKE THEIR WAY
TO TELEVISION

By 1956, although many of the hurdles related to the expansion of television, rights and residuals, and legal questions about competition and contracts had been, at least momentarily, resolved, obstacles remained that prevented many of Hollywood's feature films from appearing on television. The resulting negotiations reveal the different power structures in the film and television industries and the ways in which the players involved affected not only the outcomes but the nature of the negotiations themselves. For example, RKO was one of the first major studios to strike a deal for their films to television, and although they were a major studio, the significant organizational and financial struggles they faced precipitated their willingness to make a deal. Regardless of its financial strength, any studio that had a contract with the unions and guilds still had to consider those agreements and how to resolve the question of residual payments for the reuse of their work in television. This chapter will examine the ways that the studios overcame these kinds of roadblocks to releasing their feature films to television and the means by which the films made it to the small screen.

By December 1955, the television networks were doing so well, and the studios struggling so much, that rumors swirled that NBC and CBS wanted to purchase two motion picture studios in order to have a more robust programming pipeline. As detailed in the *Hollywood Reporter*, "The rumors have not spared any motion picture company, though the most talked-of rumor has been NBC negotiating for MGM control. Films in the vaults, production facilities and know-how, with the possibility of a star roster, would make the first network to gain such control a power that might walk away with the marbles."[1] Although television had expanded at an incredibly fast rate, the facilities and personnel for producing original television content, especially for local stations, had not kept up with that growth. Don Fedderson, executive vice president and general manager of the KMTR Radio Corporation, which operated the KLAC radio and television stations, observed, "Television is like a furnace, you keep throwing the coal in and there doesn't seem to be any saturation point. That seems to be our biggest worry, getting enough product to keep it going."[2]

That television continued to grow meant that expenditures on television advertising were increasing. These included expenditures on broadcast time, program material, and commissions to the agencies involved in the sale of time or program material. For example, in 1952, the total advertising expenditures on television had been $453.9 million, and by 1954 that had almost doubled to $809.1 million. The total costs of all the program material used television-wide had increased 708 percent from 1949 to 1954. One of the reasons costs were on the rise was that the number of television sets in use had increased a whopping 3,350 times between 1946 and 1955. By 1955, there were 33 million sets in use, which represented about 80 percent of the homes in the United States.[3] With more money being spent on advertising and the purchase of television sets, that meant higher revenues for the television industry, and in 1954 the total revenues of the industry were $593 million, which was a 37 percent increase over 1953.[4] Advertising agencies were not always interested in spending their money on feature films, however, especially during network prime-time hours, because advertising agencies made commissions on the shows they produced.[5] Producing original content for television required more labor and funding than if the agencies simply licensed or purchased feature films; but because of those network commissions, there may have been greater profit for them in producing their own original content.[6]

The prices the distributors charged for their films varied widely and for a range of reasons. By 1954, distributors earned an average of $50,000 per feature film as its first-year earnings. That was up from $10,000–$30,000 for the top films in 1952, and from $7,600 in 1949. Distributors reported that the costs of putting the films on television accounted for about 25 percent of their play-off revenue, or the total amount they earned from television stations during the run of the film. Profits to the distributors were about 25 percent, which left about 50 percent of the play-off revenue as the price paid to the sources of the feature films.[7] Charles Weintraub, president of Quality Films, a distributor of feature films to television, explained, "It is a rather ambiguous question, because each film perhaps is a little different. I could get a quarter of a million dollars for *Gone With the Wind*, and couldn't get $25 for some other picture. . . . I think and honestly feel that one of the most important factors is who is the sponsor in the particular local market that is interested in playing motion pictures."[8] In one example of how the prices could vary greatly from market to market, Weintraub had tried to sell films to a television station in Milwaukee, and the station offered him between $200 and $400 per film. He believed he could do better than that since Milwaukee by that time had over half a million television sets in use, so he went to Young & Rubicam (the advertising agency that represented Schlitz Brewery) and made a deal for $1,750 for the same film. As Weintraub explained, "When you talk about price, it is a pretty fluid thing. In Los Angeles, for instance, in 1950 and '51 there was a sponsor known as Hoffman Television. It was the first one to pay any real money for pictures, the first sponsor. And where the general market in this town was around a thousand or eleven hundred dollars a picture, he paid $2500 for just one run. Since that time when other sponsors came on, I was able to obtain as high as $8,000 a picture in Los Angeles."[9] The Wild West nature of these markets and prices in the early days of television was one reason why the film studios, despite their many surveys, were unable to come to any concrete conclusions about the new industry.

The size of a particular market also played an important role. In terms of smaller markets, Weintraub described the pricing per hour as determined by a variety of factors. There was a guidebook called *Standard Rates and Data*, which listed all of the stations in the United States and designated the hourly rates for time that the stations charged their sponsors. Those amounts varied from $100 an hour to $3,500 an hour, depending on the size of the market and station. If a distributor knew from the *Standard* guidebook that a station could afford to spend only a certain amount of money on a film, the distributor would not waste time trying to demand significantly more. As Weintraub explained, "I have found out that in most of the small markets you take what you can get. There isn't much leeway to holler or argue or tell them you have something better."[10] Those sponsors that paid to advertise during feature films on television reportedly found it very profitable. For example, Dr. Ross Dog Food was one of the larger sponsors in the Los Angeles area. They sponsored a program on Channel 13 called *Million Dollar Theatre*, which purported to have the better A films for television. As a result of advertising on television, Dr. Ross Dog Food received so many orders for their dog food that in order to meet the demand, they had to take a break from advertising on television and spend money to expand their facilities. When Dr. Ross's *Million Dollar Theatre*, one of the most expensive programs and ad buys, went off the air, the other stations lowered their offers for feature films from $8,000 per film to $3,500 per film. Channel 5, the Paramount station, was the exception because they had larger sponsors in Barbara Ann Bread and Star-Kist Tuna. Channel 5 would offer $5,000 or $6,000 per film. Weintraub argued that if Barbara Ann Bread and Star-Kist Tuna dropped their programs, the other stations would try to pay even less.[11]

There were also some seemingly random factors that affected particular markets and their rates for films. Weintraub described one example in Chicago of a used car dealer named Jim Moran, who was the biggest user of feature films on television in that area. He broadcast the films on WGN, the *Chicago Tribune* station, and would pay $2,000 to $2,500 for a single run of a film. At one point, Moran and his partner, George Domet, had a fight and Domet opened his own Pontiac agency. Domet decided that he wanted to beat his ex-partner, "whom he now hated," by getting feature films of his own for television and paying higher rates for them. So, he called "everybody in the business" and offered them $3,500 per film. Many distributors jumped at that deal, but Moran had "a lot of tax money" and decided to offer $7,500 per film, "which was unheard of." Moran eventually succeeded in putting Domet out of business, but when he tried to work the price per film back down again, it was not so easy. As Weintraub explained, "It is harder to get back than it is to go up, so he is now paying five to six thousand dollars out of a market that paid only two thousand or twenty-five hundred."[12] Although Weintraub described $7,500 as a large amount to pay for a feature film for television, a study conducted at Stanford had found that by 1954, some distributors paid between $25,000 and $50,000 for the top feature films.[13] By 1955, CBS was paying up to $10,000 per feature film; however, they would get six or seven broadcasts of each film that they paid that much money for.[14] This was because, whereas films were generally sold in single runs in 1950, by 1955 they were generally sold in multiple runs. So, television stations paid distributors a good deal more money for the films in 1955, but on a per-run basis, it was actually less expensive than it was in 1950.[15]

DISTRIBUTORS OF FILMS TO TV

In order to meet the increased demand for feature films on television, more distributors of films to television opened shop. Some of the more successful distributors at that time included Argyle and Hygo, Unity Films, General Teleradio, Associated Artists, the J. Arthur Rank organization, George Bagnall Associates, M. A. Alexander Productions, Inc., Artists Distributors, Inc., Combined Television Pictures, Inc., Howard C. Brown Productions, and Film Classics Exchange.[16] Most distributors were located in New York, a few were on the West Coast, and some had branch offices in other major cities. Films were typically rented from these distributors rather than directly from the various movie studios that had produced them.[17] Quality Films, for example, began operating in late 1949 from the General Service Studios in Hollywood. They got their product primarily from independent producers that had made features for theatrical release. They also got some films from the federal court as a result of bankruptcy settlements.[18] Since the television industry was still growing, and the distribution of feature films to television had not yet settled into an established system, the distributors often dealt with a range of people to get the films on air. Charles Weintraub of Quality Films described their clients at this time as including "primarily television stations, advertising agencies, occasionally a sponsor directly. There is a fourth one, however, which has sprung up lately, and that is station reps. They represent certain stations and they may do the buying at one central point."[19]

In addition to the more conventional distribution companies, some unusual players also distributed films to television. In some cases, managers functioned as distributors, as in May 1950, when Eddie Sherman's motion picture management firm leased thirty-nine old British features to KTSL for $9,750.[20] Television station WPIX in New York was also functioning as a local distributor and supplied twenty-six stations in twenty-two cities throughout the country with films for television.[21] Financial institutions also got in the business of distributing feature films to television. In January 1950, *Variety* reported that five "top banks" were "holding the sack for approximately $10,000,000 in bad motion picture loans to indie producers. Figure represents almost 15 percent of total $70,000,000 banks now have invested with Indie producers. . . . They are seriously considering taking over film negatives in several cases."[22] The banks planned to sell or license the films to television to try to recoup some of their lost money. The Bank of America (BOA) was one of the most established banks that distributed films to television at this time. When filmmakers, often independent filmmakers, borrowed money from the bank to finance their films, their agreements stipulated that if the filmmaker was unable to repay the loan, then the film and its rights would revert to the bank. Charles Weintraub of Quality Films recalled the story of one film's journey back to the BOA's possession: "There was, for instance, Enterprise Films, whose personnel were such men as David Loew, Charles Einfeld, who has a company. They were doing pretty well. They made a picture called *Body and Soul* with John Garfield that made an awful lot of money, but then they got trapped into making a picture called *Arch of Triumph* that cost millions of dollars, and as I understood from Tom Dean of the bank, never got its print cost back. Those pictures were all cross-collateralized so they all fell in one group back in the vaults of the bank."[23] So, the BOA had many films in their possession that had unsuccessfully exhausted their theatrical runs. With the advent of television, BOA finally had a way to recoup some of their money on those films. Channel 9, KHJ, in Los Angeles, for example, ran *Million Dollar Movie Theatre* with films acquired from the BOA, wherein the station broadcast a film every night for five or six consecutive nights. This program attracted a large, stable audience, which got the attention of other sponsors that wanted to emulate the success of that program.[24] All of those cases, whether or not they involved a more conventional distribution company, demonstrate the ways in which the major studios' failure to innovate in terms of distributing film to television allowed for newcomers of all types and from all backgrounds to fill that need. The studios had a major nationwide system of distribution in place that they could have utilized to distribute content to television stations throughout the country. Instead, the studios remained focused on their 35mm business and allowed these young upstarts to develop systems of distribution for television.

FILMS ON TELEVISION

By 1954, the prices paid for feature films on television were much higher, distribution channels were developing, and the number of films available to television had increased.[25] Feature films took up a huge amount of television time, but broadcasters needed even more films to sustain that rate of use. Despite their popularity, feature films were still primarily used during nonnetwork hours, which meant time other than prime time. From the studios' perspective, this was a problem because, as Peter Levathes, the head of television at Fox, described, it was not "a proper use" of feature films on television. He explained that "Columbia Broadcasting, or NBC, to my knowledge, has never put on the air, on a network basis, a motion picture feature film originating in New York at what is deemed to be prime time. . . . These are the choice times when . . . the number of sets in use is very large, the audiences are very large, and where advertisers are willing to pay more money than they are for other pieces of time."[26] Kenneth Beggs, of the Stanford Research Institute, after making a study of the television industry's expenditures on feature films, testified that he knew of "no case in which a feature film has been used, up to the end of 1954, on national network time as a network show. They are non-network program material."[27] When asked whether persons in the television industry could have spent more money on feature films, Beggs concluded that "if feature films had been used and were usable as network program material, there apparently were many more dollars that could have been paid for them, much more than what was actually expended by television for feature films."[28] The fact that many more dollars could have been spent may have been related, at least in part, to the fact that most of the major studios' higher-quality films were still not available to television. When, for example, Mr. Burke of *Radio TV Daily* spoke at a meeting of the National Television Film Council in 1953, he stated, "Television without movies would be nothing—they are the background of programming on the local level."[29] But Burke also mentioned one of the biggest gripes of the home viewer: "Why are so many of the features crime or class B rejects?"[30] As Steve Broidy of Monogram Pictures confirmed at the COMPO meeting, many of the films offered to television were independent films or B films. Don Fedderson, president of the Television Broadcasters Association and executive vice president and general manager of the KMTR Radio Corporation, which operated the KLAC radio and television stations, explained that B films were "excellent television fare, because of the comparative values to what is on television. When you go to a motion picture house and you see a 'B' picture, you may shrug your shoulders, because your comparative values are *Gone With The Wind* and great pictures. In television a 'B' picture is great television fare."[31] That was in part because many B films were shorter in length and more easily edited down to fit television's programming schedules.

Feature films had to be edited not only to adapt to the television schedule but also to accommodate one of the central differences between film and television: commercials. For feature films originally produced for theatrical release, organizing the story to naturally allow commercial breaks and avoid conflicts with sponsors had to be dealt with long after the films had been completed, which often made for awkwardly placed commercial breaks. For that reason, many advertisers had concluded that feature films were too long to be used as network programming.[32] Many advertisers feared that the drastic cuts necessary to fit a feature film in an hour-long time slot would damage the quality of the film itself. If the sponsor wanted to use the feature film for more than an hour, they had to purchase so much broadcast time that it was no longer an economic form of advertising. Joint sponsorship might have solved that problem, but many advertisers disliked joint advertising because they believed that it decreased the product identification of the program with a particular sponsor or their products. The importance of the link between the program and the sponsor's products was highlighted in a letter from Jack Devine, of the J. Walter Thompson Agency, in November 1953 to John K. Herbert, vice president of NBC. Devine warned NBC that JWT was very concerned that CBS was beating NBC in the ratings. Devine cautioned Herbert that "in the event the October and early November ratings do not show an improvement of the NBC position, a change in policy may be in order." Devine then suggested that NBC could improve by embracing "concentration, continuity, and frequency," which he argued were hallmarks of the most effective use of any medium. Devine continued, "Also, ideally, there should be developed an identity between program and product. Without this identity many advertisers feel that they can spend their money with greater concentration, continuity and frequency in places other than network television. There are many who feel that the chief weakness of the divided segment plan is just such lack of identity per dollar invested."[33] There were, however, still advertisers that would pay to be the sole sponsor for a feature film. KCEA in Los Angeles, for example, had a "Triple Theatre, Star One, Star Two, Star Three" on Monday nights starting at seven o'clock, in which they would air the three feature films in a row sponsored by Chevrolet Company Used Car Dealers. Another Los Angeles station, KTLA, had a "Movie Feature" that was sponsored by Murphy Motors. The films earned good ratings, which reportedly held up week after week.[34]

Regardless of who sponsored the films, even feature films that were simply bad films did very well on television. For example, a special film issue of *Television Magazine* reported in August 1950, "The surest bet in television programming is sponsorship of Hollywood movies and Westerns. No other category has consistently come up with such high ratings and at such a low cost. . . . The popularity of movies on television apparently is not affected to any marked degree by a specific feature film."[35] Since the ratings for feature films were consistently good, stations competed intensely to get the best feature films possible. Even John Balaban, owner of Balaban and Katz Theatres and television station WBKB in Chicago, testified that although he owned movie theaters, he still worked to acquire quality feature films for his television station, because "if it is a desirable picture, if I don't take it, someone else will, even at the expense of affecting our theatres. If I don't take the picture and one of the other stations takes it, it still affects our theatres."[36] Although Balaban's example only included his local Chicago theaters and television station, it reflected an early form of corporate conglomerate logic that considered what was best for the whole as opposed to narrowly focusing on any individual subsidiary.

LOCAL AND INDEPENDENT STATIONS

In the early 1950s, feature films that appeared on television were primarily used by local independent television stations or television stations during nonnetwork time. As Wayne Tiss described, "The network program structure is not the kind that they use films made in motion picture studios to any great degree at all. The programs are live and sent out over the network. However, in individual markets is where the films are, they are purchased by the local stations."[37] Milford Fenster, film manager for television station WOR-TV in New York, which was owned at that time by General Teleradio, Inc., explained that by 1955, the station used a "great deal more" film than it did in 1950. He said, "Film has become a more integral part of our programming and, as a matter of fact, constitutes our major programming. Hence the task of satisfying that need has become that much greater, and, in addition those handling films have come into more authority than they had back in

1950."[38] Fenster even described feature films as "the lifeblood of the programming of an independent station."[39] He explained the distinction between the financial models of the networks and those of the independent stations, and the economic advantages the networks enjoyed as a result:

> Say in New York, it is faced with the competition of the Columbia Broadcasting System, the National Broadcasting System, and the American Broadcasting System, all of whom originate programs in various cities and carry those programs to its member affiliated or owned stations throughout the entire country. In that way the cost of the production of the show is borne to a great extent by all of the stations that pick up the telecast, and by the sponsor who pays for the cost of that telecast. In the instance of a local station, it must originate every program that goes over its airways, as a result of which it gets no contribution in any shape or form from any other station. It absorbs the entire program cost and must live by the income it receives for the locally-originated broadcast.[40]

Fenster further explained that, unlike the networks, WOR-TV did not produce much of their own live programming because the costs would be too great, and with their lower budgets, the quality of the shows could not compete with the higher production values of the network shows. Those lower-quality shows would also negatively affect interest from sponsors, and a vicious cycle would ensue. WOR had great success with feature films on television, though, and it was the case that all of the stations in New York used feature films at that time. WCBS, for example, used feature films on their late show, early show, late-late show, and late matinee. Since the resolution of the Autry and Rogers lawsuits against Republic, WOR-TV had a Gene Autry and Roy Rogers show wherein they played Autry and Rogers features. Fenster argued that the Autry and Rogers films were particularly valuable since they had been produced with substantially higher budgets than typical westerns, and had more general appeal than the average western. Fenster explained that, "more than that, they are more family entertainment because they are in the nature of feature productions. But even more than that, they give you continuity of character throughout the entire series and employ the services of Gene Autry and Roy Rogers who today are the best known western stars."[41] The higher production values WOR looked for in their films may have contributed to the success of their program *Million Dollar Movie*, which earned ratings as high as 84 on the Telepulse Ratings Service. Such a rating meant that virtually everyone in New York with a television set viewed the program. Fenster said, "The ratings have been consistently high for the programs, and by far exceeded anything that we had anticipated when the program was first designed."[42]

WOR-TV had also shown a "considerable amount" of British films as well as independently produced films from the United States. The widespread use of foreign films on television during the late 1940s and early 1950s exposed American audiences to international locations and different filmmaking techniques. Although the increase in runaway productions after World War II has often been attributed to factors such as economic incentives and the preferences of soldiers who served in foreign locations during the war, the fact that American television regularly broadcast foreign films to home audiences certainly influenced studios' willingness to shoot in foreign locations and audiences' interest in seeing those films.

WOR-TV licensed their films from every one of the television distributors, and Fenster believed there were approximately 3,000 films available to television stations at that time; most of them had already been shown on television. But even that number of films was not enough to meet the demand of the stations. It was not unusual for a station to show a film six, seven, or eight times in the course of a year or eighteen months. However, that did not necessarily apply to smaller markets where there were only one or two stations. Stations in those smaller markets did not rerun as many films as did the multistation markets.[43] When WOR-TV obtained a feature film for broadcast, they were allowed to edit the film themselves in order to conform to their time segments. As Fenster explained, "We do have many skilled persons who can do the job. They screen the films first, re-screen them if they like, and then go through and take out the footage that must be taken out in order to program the film for an hour and a half time slot." In fact, they had eight men on their staff working as "re-editors."[44]

NETWORKS AND NETWORK FILM DEPARTMENTS

Although local and independent stations may have been the primary users of feature films, the networks also had film departments that worked to purchase or license feature films. CBS, for example, had a film department that had existed for years before 1951. They maintained files on sources of available film products and kept information on what other stations in their area had paid for films, which they used to negotiate for prices. They had facilities to "receive, screen, cut, repair, restore, and ship" the films they broadcast.[45] Alan Rhone, of the CBS film department, advocated for increasing the activities and power of the department, especially in terms of their control over feature films on their owned and operated (O&O) stations. Rhone argued that with such a relatively small number of feature films available to television, it required "constant observation of product sources, information through contacts and the power to buy in quantity or in size of bid."[46] If the CBS film department could purchase films for the network and their stations, they could better compete with other networks. This would also help keep the prices for films low because they could negotiate to buy in bulk and avoid driving up prices by competing with their own stations for films.[47] Rhone also argued that a stronger network film department would help the network and stations deal with inevitable last-minute programming changes. He lobbied for a film department that could provide the network and stations with suitable films at the last minute, if necessary. Rhone cited the example of WCBS-TV, which "in procuring for the Early Show and the Late Show has screened a number of films which the Film Dept.'s files and previous knowledge indicated were not suitable."[48] A centralized network film department would also streamline the process of procuring, handling, and returning the films, which was, according to Rhone, a problem. With a centralized film department, the time consumed in those processes was much less, because it was, as Rhone described, "one person with proper help, rather than a two location, four headed manoeuvre."[49] The CBS Film Department even proposed extending their services to their affiliate stations, as well as their O&O stations, "enabling all to share in the greater buying power."[50]

ABC, the relative newcomer to network broadcasting when it was born out of the Blue Network (formerly the NBC Blue Network) in 1945, also had a film department that would purchase film for four of the five O&O stations. The one exception was their station in Los Angeles. The benefit of the network buying the film for their stations was they could buy the films in bulk rather than put the films in competition with one another. It also made film directors at each O&O station unnecessary, which saved the network money.[51] Don Tatum, in charge of television in the Pacific region for ABC, recalled that feature films appeared on television under a variety of conditions: "There have been many feature-length motion pictures produced originally for theatre consumption which have been telecast in whole over many stations. . . . Many of the pictures have been made available for sponsorship and have been sponsored in whole. Many of the pictures have been made available for participating sponsorship, which means the insertion of individual announcements within the body of the motion picture as it is telecast. Many of the motion pictures are shown on a sustaining basis without any sponsorship."[52] In December 1955, ABC acquired an additional group of one hundred British films, produced by J. Arthur Rank, that were similar to those being used on ABC's Sunday evening *Famous Film Festival*.[53] Those films provided enough material for twenty weeks of ABC's afternoon series, after which time the films would be rerun once, and some twice. ABC sold the commercial sponsorship in sixty- and ninety-second spots, and there was a maximum of three sixty-second spots and one ninety-second commercial during each half hour. That was in addition to a five-second opening and closing "billboard" for each advertiser in that segment.[54]

CBS, on the other hand, played feature films between eight and nine o'clock on Tuesday nights as a sustaining program, and they paid an average of $2,500 per film. They had *Johnny Frenchman* (1945), for example, "one of the better Rank pictures," scheduled for one Tuesday in 1951. Other films CBS had scheduled for that time slot included *Miss Pilgrim's Progress* (1950), distributed by Unity; *Backdoor to Heaven* (1939), *Chelsea Story* (1951), *Dark Interval* (1950), and *One-Third of a Nation* (1939), distributed by Alexander; *The Outsider* (1948), distributed by Commonwealth; and *Carmen* (1944), distributed by Screencraft. The films ranged in price from $2,000 to $2,500 each, and they were all first runs on television with the exception of *Carmen* and *Walls of Malapaga* (1949), which had already been broadcast in Chicago.[55] CBS had a chance to get *The Walls of Malapaga*, which had recently won the Academy Award for Best Foreign Picture, for $4,000. They had screened the film and found that "the sub-titles are a minimum since most of the picture is pantomime. . . . We could probably get some special publicity on the Academy Award aspects of the film."[56] Jack Van Volkenburg, president of CBS Television, explained that although CBS still used primarily live and original programming for their prime-time hours, they were simply obtaining film "wherever it is possible to obtain it. There are many distributors of this type of product, both in New York and in other cities, and they have rather substantial sales forces, and they call upon our film buyers with great frequency, and offer the product that they have."[57] Van Volkenburg testified that they would always be "very interested" in the films of the major studios, and they were still "always after additional feature films," but no films from the majors had ever been offered to them.[58] As Van Volkenburg explained, "Well, we just never have solicited from the majors, because in the early days we had a very distinct feeling that if we could obtain them at all, that we just would not be able to afford the price, and weren't sure we could get them at all."[59] And as Spyros Skouras testified, "At no time the networks approached, at least, Twentieth Century-Fox to offer us sufficient money on a prime time. The impression we received from the inquiry from insignificant sources, not from the important people of the industry, they offered us off time, and not the prime time."[60]

Fox, Sol Wurtzel, and the British Films

Although up to this point studios had been dissatisfied with the offers for their films on television, they constantly surveyed the prices they could get for their films on television. Peter Levathes at Fox explained that before 1955, their primary hesitation had been the fact that releasing their films to television before it had become a truly national advertising medium would have been "a very wanton dissipation of pictures that would some day have great value for the company."[61] There were, however, a few points at which Fox tested the waters and found creative ways to release some of their films to television. For example, in 1951 an article appeared in the trades that stated that B films could gross $87,650 from their first showing on television, which was substantially more than Fox thought they could get.[62] Producer Sol Wurtzel and Al Lichtman, an executive at Fox, were very enthusiastic about what that might mean for their films, and contacted Peter Levathes to discuss their options.[63] Wurtzel was a producer who had worked at Fox from its earliest years until October 1945, when he left and formed Sol M. Wurtzel Productions, Inc. His company produced eighteen B motion pictures for double bills, which were all distributed by Fox. Wurtzel's deal with the studio was very common for independent production companies, wherein Wurtzel produced films for Fox, and Fox put up part of the money for their production. In return, Fox had the distribution rights, which included the television distribution rights. Many of the films Wurtzel produced did not do well at the box office, however, and Wurtzel owed money to both Fox and the bank.[64]

Since Fox had a financial interest in the Wurtzel films, Lichtman asked Levathes to have his department conduct a survey of possible prices they could get for the films.[65] At this point, the theatrical distribution of the films had, as Isidore Kornblum, a lawyer for Fox, explained, "slowed down to a walk."[66] Another of the reasons Fox pursued this deal so actively was because, as Levathes recalled, "Twentieth

Century-Fox was feeling the full effects of the various problems that had beset the industry, and it needed ready cash, it needed to show a better profit picture in that year."[67] They talked to several distributors of motion picture films for television, including Matthew Fox and Hygo Television Films, Inc.[68] Irving Kahn, the program manager of the television department at Fox, also contacted stations in New York. Ultimately, Levathes ended up negotiating a deal with Unity Television because they offered the largest cash advance for the films.[69]

Once Levathes and Unity had agreed on the terms, Fox canceled their distribution contract with Wurtzel, released the films to Wurtzel, and provided that Wurtzel would enter into the contract with Unity.[70] Unity paid a $250,000 advance, of which Fox received $200,000 and the Wurtzel Company executed a note for the $125,000 balance, payable in five years to Fox, and gave them a mortgage on the films to secure it. The contract also stated that the name and trademark of Fox and their affiliates had to be removed from each of the films.[71] This attempt to camouflage Fox's intellectual property would, in part, function to avoid any affiliation of these films on television with Fox, and thereby help them avoid the wrath of the theaters. As a judge in a later trial commented, "They had a complete bill of divorcement. All they wanted was their money, and they got it."[72] But Levathes insisted that he asked for the removal of the Fox name and logo from the films because "I knew that the feature films are mutilated by the stations. They re-edit them as they will, they try to accommodate their lengths to their own program requirements, and I was afraid the fact that the films would be mutilated, the fact that they would be adjacent to all kinds of products that we had no control over, that it would protect that trade-mark from a product that was going to be inferior. I didn't want any implied endorsement on the part of Twentieth Century-Fox for products that would be in the films themselves."[73] When asked whether this was an effort to conceal the deal from exhibitors, Levathes replied, "The minute the deal was made [exhibitors] knew the Wurtzel pictures were released by Fox, and this was something we couldn't conceal. This was an effort not to have the Twentieth Century-Fox trademark reach the public. The trade knew exactly what was going on."[74] It was also, practically speaking, likely an attempt to circumvent any contractual obligations they might have had to the unions and guilds and any other rights holders involved in the films. As B. B. Kahane, vice president of Columbia, later testified, "When Sol Wurtzel put his independent pictures—pictures to which he had title, on television, he was not concerned with the production of theatrical pictures, and, therefore, it did not make any difference to him whether the guilds cancelled their contracts. . . . Our company's business is primarily the production of theatrical pictures. Therefore, if we would have our contracts cancelled, we would destroy a very huge investment. We couldn't continue the production of the pictures without the services of the actors, obviously, or directors or writers."[75] So, the issue was twofold: in order to release their films to television, producers needed to own, free and clear, the rights to distribute those films to television, and they needed to have an agreement with the unions and guilds as to the terms by which those pictures could be released. If the producer did not have those things, they could distribute their films to television, but at risk of not being able in the future to make or release films theatrically. For some independent producers, that was a risk worth taking.

Around that same time in 1951, Levathes was busy negotiating for another package of films for television. He had been contacted by Fred Packard, J. Arthur Rank's son-in-law, who asked if Levathes could help him sell to television certain British films that Packard had acquired in England.[76] As Levathes later recalled, "Packard didn't know his way around in the television business, and he had come to us because we had a television department to help him. And we were to acquire an interest in these films. We were to get paid for making this arrangement."[77] Levathes met with Milford Fenster at WOR-TV in New York at the office of General Teleradio. Levathes had a group of approximately forty films, known as the "Packard group," that had been produced in England and that he wanted to license to television.[78] Fenster recalled, "[Levathes] said that Fox had decided in some way to get into television distribution, and thought that this might be the opening wedge. And, of course, if we made the deal we would be in a position of being favored on any other product that Fox offered for television."[79] But before they were able to make a deal, Fenster received a call from Levathes, who said he was withdrawing his offer. Apparently, Packard had returned to England and encountered difficulties in securing the rights for the films because the rights holders required a cash deposit and Packard did not have access to that amount of cash. He contacted Levathes and advised him to withdraw the films and cancel the negotiations, which Levathes did.[80] It then took almost two years to clear the titles, and it was not until 1953 that the films appeared on television courtesy of Atlas Television.[81]

In 1953, Twentieth Century-Fox licensed between ninety and one hundred feature films to television. There were, as Milford Fenster from WOR-TV described them, the "Fox groups," which included the "Wurtzel groups," the "Charley [sic] Chans," a group of English films, and others. Fox had begun negotiations for the licensing of these films to television in 1951, but it took their lawyers almost two years to resolve the many rights issues related to the films.[82] Spyros Skouras still saw television as an impudent upstart and was not a proponent of releasing all of Fox's feature films to television. In 1955 he argued, "They wanted to use an important industry, who is rendering great services, beyond that of the common man point of view, also from an information point of view, on the worst scale, as a makeshift to build up an industry, and to sell through advertisements, to sell other products, so the motion picture industry would become an instrument of merchandising other people's products."[83] But there were a number of reasons that Skouras decided to release these films to television, such as that Fox felt comfortable licensing these films to television because they "didn't feel that this type of product would have too serious an effect on theatre revenue. . . . Because they were, you might say, B pictures."[84] Skouras had concluded that those groups of films were about the same quality as the other films he had seen on television, and that, as Fox's lawyer described, "it wouldn't hurt his company any more to have a few more old dogs there than there were already, so he accomplished the purpose of getting some more money for his corporation without harming them."[85] They did, in fact, make a decent amount of money from the films. The Wurtzel films, for example, were licensed to Major Attractions for twenty-eight months, and the gross from stations was almost $600,000.[86]

Fox decided to release their Charlie Chan films because although they had at one point owned the literary rights to Charlie Chan, they decided to stop producing them and sold those rights to another producer. That producer made new films based on the stories and had already licensed those newer films to television. Since Fox no longer held the literary rights and could therefore not make any new Charlie Chan films, and the newer Charlie Chan films had already been released to television, Fox went ahead and licensed their old Charlie Chan films to television.[87] Skouras explained that even in this situation they still experienced resistance from theater owners. He recalled, "Now, we were opposed, by the way, by some of the exhibitors, but we didn't pay attention to them. I had sympathy for their position, I want you to understand that, I always felt the consequence of what could happen to these people if all the films would be available."[88] One of the most significant reasons that Fox decided to go ahead with the sale was that they needed to increase their profit and loss statement in order to make a good showing at the end of the fiscal year. Even though Skouras claimed he was "conscience-stricken" when he sold those films to television, he said he had to do it in order to make his year-end profit and loss statement look better.[89]

In addition to the financial returns that Fox enjoyed from these films, releasing them to television allowed Fox an opportunity to gain experience in the field. As Levathes explained, in all of the deals they not only received a percentage of the gross but also gained access to the distributors' contracts, giving them "a pulse on the market." This allowed them to get valuable information and determine just how large the market actually was. Levathes admitted, "We knew that there would come a time in the evolution of television when we would have to face up to the fact it would be advantageous for us to release other films to television, more valuable films."[90] As we have seen from the numerous surveys the studios conducted and commissioned on television, they were very interested in getting as much data as possible to support their decision-making. The direct experience and knowledge Fox gained from leasing these films to television was potentially more valuable than the money Fox made from the deals themselves.

COLUMBIA SCREEN GEMS

During this time, Columbia also more actively investigated the possibility of releasing their films to television. At the end of 1950, when Columbia abandoned their plan to recut and reframe their theatrical films for television, they turned their attention to licensing their films to television. Ralph Cohn, the head of Screen Gems, undertook a survey to determine the going rates for features on television. He surveyed John Mitchell, general sales manager of United Artists Television, a company that distributed motion pictures for television; Herb Gelbspan, who supervised the sale of Hal Roach's theatrical motion pictures to television; David

Savage, Beulah Jarvis, and Nat Fowler, the buyers of television films for, respectively, CBS, NBC, and ABC O&O stations; Tony Azzato, the film buyer for New York station WPIX; and Sy Weintraub and Sol Turrell, each of whom was a distributor of films for television.[91] In June 1951, Cohn concluded from the survey "that the prices of films on television were getting better, and that the expansion of the medium was continuing, that sets were being sold continuously at a very good rate, new stations were coming into existence, and if we waited for a while the value of this film to the stockholders of this company, and to this company, would be greater."[92]

Then in August of that year, Columbia shifted from surveying the landscape toward seriously considering releasing their films to television. This move was motivated in part by sentiment revealed in a report from B. B. Kahane to Ralph Cohn: "The revenue a company can realize today even from only the stations presently operating may be considerably more than might be realized for the same product from many more stations later, if all the other major companies also make available for television the thousands of films they have in their vaults."[93] That month, Columbia's officers met in Chicago and discussed the subject of motion pictures on television at great length. The president of Columbia, Harry Cohn, presented to the meeting a memorandum from Don Tatum, head of TV for ABC in Hollywood, on the residual value of Columbia's backlog as it pertained to television. B. B. Kahane presented a report on the many legal, union, and jurisdictional problems that they would face if they released their films to television.[94] Kahane later recalled that he believed that even if they could overcome the issues with the unions and guilds, "with the television industry, really, in embryo, and in its infancy, so to speak, it was a question whether it was advisable at that time to release pictures to television, or should it not be more prudent to wait until the industry grew, as it looked like it was destined to grow, and probably obtain a great deal more revenue if and when you decided to release your pictures on television."[95] Kahane's concerns reveal not only the level of uncertainty and anxiety that existed at the time about ensuring that they released their films to television before other studios flooded the market, but also the desire to wait until the television industry had grown to a point where they could pay prices for the films that the studios thought were fair. It was suggested at that August meeting that Columbia might be able to make $10–$20 million for the release of their films to television. Ralph Cohn subsequently investigated that figure and found "it was just a dream. There was nobody available. . . . It was purely an idea, but it didn't have any funds in back of it."[96]

Meanwhile, Ralph Cohn was releasing some of his own feature films to television. Cohn had been an independent producer before joining Columbia Screen Gems and had ownership in five films that he subsequently released to television. When he was later asked why he released his own films to television but advised Columbia to withhold theirs, he explained that his films had not earned back their costs by the time they exhausted their theatrical runs, and there were a "considerable number" of outstanding loans against the films. The interest on the loans was accruing, and, as Cohn recalled, "the people who held the mortgages for those loans forced us to put them into television in order to begin to liquidate the loan. I objected to their doing so. I felt that they were doing an uneconomic thing, because of the timing of the putting of the pictures into television, but they insisted they wanted to reduce the amount of the loans and the interest payments, and we had nothing to do but go along with them or face foreclosure."[97] Cohn's situation was a common one faced by independent producers in those days, and was one of the main reasons that independent feature films ended up on television. Although Cohn had released some of his films to television, albeit against his wishes, Columbia was still waiting for better prices before releasing their feature films to television.[98]

In early 1955, they began talks with NBC about licensing some of their catalog. Ralph Cohn explained that the company had noticed a rise in the use of "spectaculars" on television, and believed that the older films in their vaults were of higher quality than those being broadcast and "could make better spectaculars than the spectaculars."[99] They also believed that using their films as spectaculars on television would give them an opportunity to "bring to the attention of the public current theatrical features playing in theatres."[100] As a result, they began discussions with NBC about televising a group of thirteen of Columbia's films as monthly spectaculars.[101] But NBC did not see eye to eye with Columbia in terms of a price for the films, and as Cohn testified, "at the moment that [price] is the principal question, although there are still some doubts on the part of the networks as to the complete acceptability of these pictures in the role for which we see them."[102] B. B. Kahane, vice president of Columbia, argued of the companies that had put their feature films on television, "I think it was rather a matter of self-preservation. I understand from them that they were practically at the point of bankruptcy, and that they sought refuge by taking some of the revenue that was available to them from television."[103] Since Columbia had not reached a point of financial desperation, they did not feel compelled to make any deals they found less than optimal.

RKO

Things were somewhat different for RKO, which, by 1955, was experiencing a great deal of turmoil and financial difficulty. They had, since 1941, been in and out of discussions with television interests about selling or licensing their films for television. As RKO's lawyer, Fleming, described, their negotiations failed for two main reasons. First, buyers wanted RKO's films on a percentage basis, which meant they would make payments out of earnings if and when they were made. And second, RKO blamed "the attitude of the broadcasting companies themselves, who at this time appeared to look on motion pictures as an inferior form of entertainment, relegated to poor hours, and for which they would be willing to pay only minimum prices."[104] In 1951, for example, Creighton J. Tevlin, vice president in charge of studio operations for RKO, negotiated "very seriously" with CBS to sell the backlog of their films to CBS "in bulk." Tevlin had worked as an accountant for Howard Hughes during his most active period as a producer in the late 1920s and early 1930s. In 1943, Hughes hired Tevlin as his personal assistant, and in 1948, when Hughes took over RKO, he made Tevlin head of RKO's West Coast operations along with Bicknell Lockhart and Sid Rogell. Of the three, Tevlin was the one who functioned as the gatekeeper for Hughes, and anyone who wanted to communicate with Hughes had to go through Tevlin.[105] In June 1951, Tevlin and Noah Deitrich, then chairman of the board of RKO Radio Pictures, met in Chicago with Daniel O'Shea and Charles Glett of CBS. Tevlin brought with him all of the information he had on the films for which they had been able to clear the rights. They had some contracts, however, where although the language was clear, they still posed a problem. For example, as Tevlin explained, "a contract with Irving Berlin, where his compensation on some pictures is determined on the basis of 10 per cent of the gross. Frankly, applying that contract to a television exhibition, I don't know what the answer would be. I don't know whether the gross would be what we would receive or what a distributor who distributed for us would receive, or what the broadcaster might receive."[106] In order to resolve fundamental issues like this, RKO asked for a cash sale "in the neighborhood of 10 million dollars." They wanted that kind of bulk sale for a few different reasons. First, the company was financially unstable and needed an influx of cash. Second, they hoped that if they went to the unions with one large sum, it might allow them to negotiate for more favorable residual payments than the 5 percent or more per film that the unions demanded. Third, since advertising dollars spent on television still had not increased to a level the studios thought worth their while, the studios feared they might earn low returns from percentage deals, which were based on a percentage of the revenue from advertising. Although O'Shea told Tevlin that he considered $10 million a realistic value for RKO's film vault, Tevlin recalled, "[O'Shea] felt it would be a bad bargain for CBS, if they purchased these films that it might open the floodgates and the market would become flooded with motion pictures, and anybody who would have been the first one to buy would have a bad deal."[107] O'Shea suggested that instead of the bulk sale, RKO turn their films over to CBS on a percentage basis, which meant that RKO would receive a percentage of the amount that CBS earned for the broadcast of each film. Tevlin responded that "based on our knowledge of the money being paid by TV stations for pictures and the very second-rate time being devoted to motion pictures, that this was completely unrealistic and we weren't interested."[108]

The negotiations for the sale of RKO's library to CBS collapsed at that point, but they continued discussing the possibility of CBS exchanging "stock on a merger basis to either acquire control of all of RKO. But nothing ever came of that."[109] Tevlin left his negotiations with CBS convinced that the networks had resigned themselves to using feature films in secondary time slots because they were developing a majority of their own original programming for prime time, and "as far as they were concerned, the future appeared for motion pictures to be one in which these secondary time slots would always be employed."[110] Tevlin had also engaged in talks with other television networks and stations prior to CBS, and when the negotiations with CBS finally fell apart, Tevlin concluded that they would not be able to make a deal "involving any real money." He explained, "It looks just so hopeless that we decided, right after this Columbia Broadcasting negotiation, to adopt a policy of just forgetting television, let it go its way, let it get what pictures it could, and see if time wouldn't improve the situation as to values. So I would say for a period of at least six to eight months after these CBS meetings, we just forgot television completely."[111]

Then, in early 1952, parties that "appeared to be very substantial" approached RKO, so they moved forward with negotiations once again.[112] At that time, RKO had approximately 650 feature films that they considered for television. There were many films, however, where rights could not be cleared or copyrights had expired and could not be renewed, as well as films that were so dated that the studio believed they did not have any real value for television. After excluding those films, RKO believed they had between 400 and 450 "usable pictures."[113] Tevlin negotiated with Matty Fox, who had a television distribution company, but Fox ultimately could not put together a cash price or give guarantees that RKO would agree to. Later that year, Tevlin was negotiating with Eliot Hyman at Associated Artists, a company that began producing film for theatrical release but then moved to syndicating films to television, when, as Tevlin explained, Hughes sold the controlling interest of RKO to a Chicago group headed by Ralph Stolkin, a businessman who had reportedly made his money from shady business dealings and punchboard gambling. The Stolkin group controlled RKO for only a brief two-month period, and during that time Tevlin was not involved in the company. When Hughes officially regained control, Tevlin returned as vice president in charge of studio operations and learned that the Stolkin group had engaged in several negotiations with people in New York to sell their backlog of films to television. Even though Arnold Grant, chairman of RKO's board during the transition from Stolkin back to Hughes, had attempted to calm their exhibitors' nerves by assuring them that the company "had no plans for a sale of the library to television for the present or in the foreseeable future," negotiations continued to take place with potential buyers.[114] Once Hughes and Tevlin were back in charge, Tevlin negotiated "whenever, wherever we could find anyone who appeared to be a substantial buyer." These people included one man, a "well-known New York film man" named Harry Gold, who appeared to have substantial backing, but the negotiations finally folded because they were, according to Tevlin, "very complicated and impractical."[115]

Around that same time, Jules Levey, a film producer and distributor, approached Ned Depinet, then acting as president of RKO, and expressed interest in making a deal for televising some of RKO's "less important pictures," and he offered somewhere between $500,000 and $1 million. Depinet had a list put together of those less important pictures, but when Levey saw the list, he lost interest. Levey said that he wanted only the good films, and so the deal fell through. Depinet recalled that RKO had many applications for the use of their films on television, but "when it came to talking money, why, there was no money."[116] The "capricious decision making" of Howard Hughes, who controlled RKO at that time, also had a devastating effect on RKO's distribution and their relationship with their exhibitors, and endlessly frustrated Depinet.[117]

While many studios compared potential revenues from television and the theaters, those comparisons could be misleading. Studios still considered the offers they received from television for their films as a price for each "ticket" per audience member who might attend a theater. For example, as Tevlin explained, if a film was televised to 3 million people, but the studio was paid only $7,500 for the film, they were making only a quarter of a cent per viewer. Tevlin reasoned, "We felt that on an economic basis this was completely and utterly ridiculous, and we did not care to enter into that kind of a transaction at the risk of opening the doors so that many other pictures would enter, and our pictures eventually, then, would be lost in the shuffle. Our main economic consideration was to convert into dollars the value that this library represented."[118] The studios needed to readjust the basic financial model they were using to gauge the success and worth of their films. Ultimately, they had to decide between letting their films sit in their vaults, where they made zero revenue, and selling the films to television, where they would make a quarter of a cent per viewer. For a studio like RKO, which by 1955 was experiencing staggering losses, they could also benefit from using those losses to offset any tax liability from gains they made through a sale.[119] But studios clung to their old models and the hope of future success in theatrical reissues and rereleases, which had proved possible but were extremely rare.

Even though their negotiations continued to fail, Tevlin, then vice president of RKO, continued to meet with, as he described, "anybody who wanted to talk about these pictures." After their first attempt at a negotiation failed, he met with Dan O'Shea from CBS again, but O'Shea's "interest on behalf of CBS had not changed,"[120] meaning CBS still insisted on participation rather than cash payments for the films. Tevlin explained, "Anybody that would approach you, if they wanted to buy the library, when you started talking about $15,000,000, they had a token payment to make. Maybe they would pay $5,000,000 down, maybe they would pay $2,000,000 down. But the net final result would be that you would speculate on their efforts, and on what TV stations would pay them, to determine whether you would or would not get what you felt was the value of your product."[121] RKO felt that the value they had attached to their vault was fair and reasonable, and they did not feel it was wise to assume the risk of entering a deal based on speculation. Hughes had also carried on negotiations in Los Angeles, as Depinet described, "over a long period of time for the disposal of our library."[122] As Depinet argued, "If somebody wants to buy our library for television, let them put the money on the line. Maybe they can buy it. We never had to make the decision of whether we would sell it or not, because nobody ever made us a legitimate offer."[123] When claims were made that RKO had actually not engaged in negotiations to the extent they said they did, Depinet countered that most of their negotiations were not a part of the public record for two reasons. First is something we know to be true, that "Mr. Hughes was a pretty secretive man."[124] Second, as Depinet argued, "if you want to make a good deal to see your pictures to television, you don't go and parade around the world and tell everybody that you are going to sell your pictures to television. You try to be tough, thinking maybe you would get a better price. If you traded in business, you would know you would never get anywhere by telling anybody you can buy these pictures cheap, and we will sell you anything you want."[125] The studios' decision to largely keep the ongoing negotiations secret was motivated in part by their desire to avoid the wrath of their theaters, but this secrecy resulted in the cultivation and perpetuation of the myth that Hollywood was not interested in licensing or selling their features to television.

By 1954, RKO had made some progress, and as Creighton J. Tevlin recalled, it "was a very important year as far as negotiations were concerned."[126] Tevlin had been talking with David Baird, who was the head of the Baird Foundation, and Baird made an offer that involved the purchase of all of RKO's assets. Baird's plan was to separate RKO's film library from the physical assets of the company so that he could offer the films to television and merge the physical assets with another company. Tevlin recalled, "Well, this deal became complicated, again, based upon two things. One, the schedule of payments to be made; and, second, Mr. Hughes' desire that RKO as a company be perpetuated and not closed up and merged with some other distributor."[127] As a result, those negotiations fell through. When Tevlin's negotiations with Baird collapsed, Tevlin began talking with a group in New York that included the three largest theater circuits: the Stanley Warner Theatres, the Paramount Theatres, and National Theatres. They also made an offer to buy RKO, and as a part of the total purchase price, they had offered $12 million as the value of RKO's films on television. That deal also fell through, however, because it too was based on a partial payment up front, with the balance of the purchase price to come from future profits, and RKO would not accept those terms.[128]

By this time, word was getting around that RKO was interested in selling their film library. As Charles Weintraub of Quality Films recalled, he first learned that the RKO films were being made available for television when his friend came to Los Angeles from New York with a certified check for $5 million. When Weintraub asked his friend what the check was for, he replied, to "try to buy the RKO pictures."[129] Then, in late 1954, RKO, through an attorney representing Hughes, began negotiations in New York with Eliot Hyman and General Teleradio. General Teleradio had extensive holdings in broadcasting, including WOR-TV in New York, and the major interest in the Mutual Broadcasting System. In 1954 they had formed a syndication department, known as the Film Division, that obtained the rights to distribute films on a national basis and then contract with stations to license those features.[130]

Again, the terms of that deal were that a group would purchase RKO, RKO's films would be turned over to General Teleradio, and the remainder of the company would proceed as a film company.[131] General Teleradio had experienced great success with films on television through WOR-TV with shows like their *Million Dollar Movie*. The first package of films they used for that show they licensed from ROA. The package totaled thirty films and included *Magic Town* (1947), *Body and*

Soul (1947), *The Arch of Triumph* (1948), and *Ruthless* (1948). Milford Fenster, film manager for WOR-TV, claimed that the films were "very well received" by the public.[132] General Teleradio paid approximately $45,000 for the package of films, which, at the time, was the highest price paid for feature films for television. The films were a great success, though, and the station made a great deal of money on them.[133] As *Time* magazine reported, General Teleradio ultimately made more than $600,000 profit on the deal.[134] As Fenster explained, "It gave us a position in the city that we never had had before. It brought to the station advertisers of a caliber we never had before, and it made money and got us an audience and got people talking about us. It was a success from every possible angle."[135] That success significantly influenced General Teleradio's interest in buying RKO.[136]

Meanwhile, as the negotiations with General Teleradio continued, RKO decided to approach television networks directly to discuss possible deals for the use of their films on television. As Tevlin recalled, in late March or early April 1955, RKO's advertising agency made a presentation to Tevlin and others at RKO on Walt Disney's *Mickey Mouse Club* program that was airing on ABC. It aired for an hour, five days a week, at five o'clock. ABC had been able, based on the value of Disney's name, to attract national sponsors on a fifty-two-week-a-year basis. This successful deal gave RKO hope that they might be able to, as Tevlin explained,

> approach TV on some plan other than a program sale plan, because if the sponsorship of a program would be national sponsorship, and if it would be anything like a Disney program that could run five days—the same program five days a week, and four different sponsors every day, with the multiplication factor it meant 20 sponsors for a single program, and we examined this, and it was quite evident to us that this type of percentage, if you have something important enough to justify it, would give the program probably $100,000 worth of revenue, or at least $75,000 on the basis of a one-hour program, and perhaps $100,000, and as the program would increase in rating, if the time changes were fixed, then the program would earn more.[137]

So, RKO decided to approach NBC with a similar plan, wherein they would supply a quality film every week for a year, and the film would be broadcast on the same day in every market and rerun until "it had achieved saturation."[138] Tevlin and RKO began negotiations with the Foote, Cone & Belding advertising agency and Pat Weaver, president of NBC. Their proposed deal would allow for NBC to keep the time charges, and any program revenue would go to RKO. After their initial meeting, Foote, Cone & Belding reported to Tevlin that Pat Weaver was "very enthusiastic" about the idea. They had discussed running the films as an afternoon matinee program, and the films would run for two hours with time included for eight station breaks. Weaver asked Tevlin to put together a program that represented what they would deliver in the first year, and RKO did so. They hoped they might start their program in September 1955, but as Tevlin recalled, "Weaver was always busy, or away from his office, and would send messages through a local representative, and, finally, he passed on the information that it looked too difficult to him to line up affiliated stations, in that he was running into two difficulties."[139] One of those was that RKO was interested in broadcasting the film in each market on multiple days of the week, but the local stations did not want to have the same program more than one day because they feared that on the second or third day, viewers would change to another channel. RKO argued that viewers from other channels might shift over to the NBC station, but NBC also pointed out that if a station in one market ran the film two days a week and another station ran it three days a week, NBC was left with a very disorganized program schedule. Tevlin became frustrated that the negotiations were not progressing, and asked Weaver to simply quote RKO a price for the time because they would consider buying it and presenting the program as their own. If they went that route, they could have their own advertising agency work on getting different sponsors for them. As Tevlin recalled, "The reply to that was that that was completely out of order and against all the rules of television, that they only sell their own time, and that they didn't want anybody to be in some kind of a brokerage situation. So we got down to the point finally where this thing looked hopeless, and we were in the midst of negotiations with General Teleradio, that involved the sale of the whole company, so we just called off everything with NBC."[140] In July 1955, RKO was finally able to agree on terms with General Teleradio, which involved their purchase of all of Howard Hughes's stock in RKO, and he was the sole owner, for $25 million in cash.[141] That amount broke down to approximately $11 million for the book value of RKO, and the balance for the value of their film library,[142] which, at that time, consisted of approximately 945 feature films.[143]

By the end of 1955, RKO's films were owned in part by General Teleradio and in part by Matty Fox, who had distributed films to television since the late 1940s. He headed C&C Television, a subsidiary of the C&C Super Corporation, which controlled various businesses unrelated to the film industry, and he also had an interest in the Skiatron subscription television system.[144] After General Teleradio's purchase of RKO, Matty Fox offered them $12.5 million to purchase the rights to most of their feature films. In their deal, General Teleradio kept the rights to the library for the six markets where it owned TV stations, while Fox took the rights to the rest of the country. Additionally, General Teleradio was to retain for two years the right to license the 150 best films in the library to a nationally advertised sponsor for television, and Fox had the rights to the rest of the films in the library and the rest of the country.[145] At the time, the deals that Tom O'Neil, president of General Teleradio (a subsidiary of the General Tire and Rubber Company), had made in buying RKO from Hughes and then licensing RKO's vault to television were heralded as brilliant business coups.[146] Over time, however, the folly of licensing those television rights "in perpetuity" would become clear, as the value of RKO's vault on television eventually far exceeded the $12.5 million RKO had received for them.

Once RKO Teleradio released their films to television, other studios took notice. Two of the main reasons that the other studios began working in late 1954 and into 1955 to release their films to television were the belief that television had reached its saturation point, and the studios' fear of a buyer's market for films on television.

Economists had argued for years that there was a saturation point on the horizon when television would have infiltrated enough homes that the film industry would no longer experience any additional decline in their box office from television competition. Many studios believed they had hit that saturation point by the end of 1954, which was one of the primary factors that motivated them to sell or license some of their films to television.[147]

FEAR OF A BUYER'S MARKET

Studios felt increasingly nervous that if one studio sold their films to television and flooded the market with their product, a buyer's market would result that would lower the value of all films on television. As Spyros Skouras wrote in April 1954 to Samuel Goldstein of the Western Massachusetts Theatres, "We have no present intention of letting the ropes down, as you put it, but whether or not we do in the future will depend on what the other companies do since we do not, naturally, want to be martyrs."[148] Warner Bros., meanwhile, was making general inquiries as to the prices their films might garner from their release to television.[149] At that time, the Warner brothers, Benjamin Kalmenson (the president and domestic sales manager for Warner Bros. Pictures Distributing Corporation), and Samuel Schneider discussed their business decisions. Regarding their feature films on television, as Jack Warner explained, Kalmenson raised the possibility of "selling some of our older pictures in a group of, say, 52 pictures, a year's programs, one a week. . . . I know one company he probed with, and beyond that I don't know, ABC Television Company . . . And the money was so small an amount of money, so insignificant in amount in comparison with the monies we deal with in our practice in general that we decided not to sell the pictures."[150] Despite Warner's description of Kalmenson's probing, by the end of 1955 Warner Bros. had not made a serious effort to determine how much money their films might make from television. At that point, Jack Warner explained, "As of this day, we haven't any particular policy. Our policy is flexible. It is wide open, with whatever success to our company can be made."[151]

Universal had also never sold, leased, or licensed any 35mm or 16mm feature films for television.[152] They were, however, engaged in talks to do so. Charles Weintraub of Quality Films, for example, claimed that he was negotiating a deal with Universal for a series of approximately ninety-seven westerns that had been produced between 1933 and 1946.[153] Len White, of the JWT advertising agency, also said, in an internal JWT memo from November 1955, that he had heard from Luke Blumberg, the son of Nate Blumberg at Universal, that the studio planned to sell a block of ten pictures for about $375,000 for a seven-year lease. The films included an early Noel Coward film and some Abbott & Costello films, among others. White mentioned that "for reasons peculiar to Blumberg, they have not offered the pictures to Matty Fox," and thought that Norman Gluck at United World Films would handle the deal.[154]

By the beginning of 1956, many of the disruptions of the previous decade had begun to settle. The FCC had resolved many of the core technological issues that had caused conflict and chaos in the early years of television, and many of the industrial structures and programming forms had matured and stabilized. The studios had finally come out the other side of their long engagement with the *Paramount* antitrust case, and the corporate restructuring mandated by the courts had taken place. Many of the contract and residual disputes, lawsuits, and aesthetic and financial questions in relation to feature films on television had finally been resolved, so the studios had begun to license and sell their films to television and had become more involved in the production of television as well. The resolution of those issues, combined with the motivation provided by the threat of a guilty verdict in the antitrust case *U.S. vs. Twentieth Century-Fox, et al.* prompted what has been widely acknowledged as the studios' move into television in the mid-1950s. For example, William Boddy argued that the trigger for the flood of feature films to television in the mid-1950s was Howard Hughes's sale of the RKO film library, and while this may be true in part because RKO's sale certainly played into the other studios' fear of waiting too long and finding themselves in a buyer's market, the move by RKO and others to license or sell their films to television only happened once the forces aligned at the end of 1955 to resolve the aforementioned issues.

Although by the end of 1955 RKO had sold their library and Republic had licensed substantial portions of their film library to television, it would be six more years before all of the other major studios sold their pre- and post-1948 films to television. Some studios began selling portions of their libraries in 1956, because it was at that time that the AFM agreed to allow the studios to release their pre-1948 films to television if they paid 5 percent of the revenue from that sale or lease to the AFM. They did not, however, reach an agreement on their post-1948 films. The issues of royalty and residual payments were vigorously debated between the producers and all of the unions and guilds, including the AFM, through the remainder of the 1950s. This is one of the reasons that for a period of years after 1956, there was an influx of pre-1948 films to television, but not post-1948 films.

The year 1956 was, in fact, a very busy one in terms of feature films appearing on television. In January 1956, Matty Fox announced his plans, through his company C&C Television, to sell to television the RKO films he had purchased in 1955.[155] Fox held on to any films in the package that were less than three years old, and "sold the remaining features on an exclusive basis to one station in each broadcast market, enabling that station to maintain its own film library—in many cases with enough films to last for six years or more under normal scheduling practices. The stations would possess these rights in perpetuity, excluding syndication rights."[156] As of July 1956, fifty-eight stations across the United States had bought the C&C package, and by mid-1957, C&C estimated its revenues from the RKO library at $25 million.[157] Many of the films were sold to stations on a barter basis whereby C&C-affiliated advertisers would be allowed reduced prices for spots in each showing of the films.[158] Also in January 1956, Len White reported to his colleagues at

JWT that Republic was ready to lease another group of films to television for a price of about $125,000.[159] At that time, Eliot Hyman purchased the rights to the Warner Bros. library of pre-1948 films for $21 million. Warner Bros. chose to sell the library outright rather than licensing their films for two reasons. First, the cash infusion from the sale boosted the value of the company's stock for the brothers Warner, who were considering retirement. Second, it helped save them money on taxes as the revenue from a sale was taxed at a lower rate than the income from rentals because the profits from a sale were taxed as capital gains rather than income.[160]

Even Spyros Skouras, whose close ties with exhibitors had made him an opponent of releasing films to television, was by February 1956 working on a plan to release Fox's pre-1948 films to television. Irving Asher, Twentieth Century-Fox's television chief, had discussed with Bill Paley, Pat Weaver, and Tom McAvity "the possibility of doing ninety-minute film spectaculars." According to Len White at JWT, "While Asher is reluctant to go into any project of this type, he tells me Skouras is urging him to make such a deal with Paley. At the moment Asher does not know whether he will win his point but says Skouras is highly in favor of this idea."[161] In May 1956, Fox licensed fifty-two of the films they had produced between 1935 and 1947 to Eli Landau at National Telefilm Associated for a ten-year period. The terms included the payment of $2 million to Fox, with the possibility of future revenues if National Telefilm's profits reached a certain level. Fox was apparently happy with that deal, because in November 1956 they signed a much larger deal with National Telefilm. That deal included Fox licensing to National Telefilm 390 of their pre-1948 films for seven years at a minimum price of $30 million. Fox clearly wanted a piece of the lucrative business of films on television, because as part of the deal, they bought a 50 percent interest in National Telefilm's television syndication business and agreed to produce four television pilots. Skouras had not completely overcome his reluctance to release his films to television, however, and in 1958 he was quoted as arguing that the studios should not sell or lease their post-1948 films to television.[162]

Many of the television film distributors chose to sell or license their films directly to individual stations rather than go through the networks. As Michele Hilmes explained, there were two reasons for that strategy: "First, the networks took a stand against theatrical films on TV, claiming they could pay no more than $20,000 per picture at that time and instead preferred to concentrate on their own distinctive programming. Second, even should the networks change their policy, the distributors' method of 'blanketing hundreds of markets around the country' with a film package, according to *Business Week*, 'yields the distributors prices that the networks couldn't afford to meet, even although the price per station may be modest.'"[163] Those films that did make their way to television did very well financially.[164] In July 1956, *Television* reported that 2,500 feature films had been released to television in the previous thirteen months, and Columbia reported an income of almost $10 million on their feature sales to television. Warner Bros. said they had earned $15 million in television sales that year.[165] MGM, which had released

750 features and 900 shorts to television starting in June 1956, had grossed $34.5 million by 1957. MGM also used their film library to increase their broadcast holdings by accepting a 25 percent ownership interest in KTTV as payment for the television rights to their films, and MGM entered similar deals with KTVR-TV in Denver and KMGM in Minneapolis.[166]

Although Lew Wasserman has often been given credit for discovering the potential value of studios' film vaults on television,[167] it was not until years after other studios had started selling and licensing their films that Wasserman and MCA were able to make a deal for Paramount's films. In 1958, Paramount sold the rights to their pre-1948 feature film library to EMKA, a subsidiary of the Music Corporation of America, for $50 million. Paramount kept the theatrical rights to a few of their films, including those made by Cecil B. DeMille. One of the reasons Paramount had held on to their rights longer than the other studios was that they were especially interested in, and convinced of, the promise of pay television.[168]

In all of the above instances, the studios were forced to deal with the issues of rights and residuals, and it took until 1960 for the studios to negotiate a deal with the unions that covered both their pre- and post-1948 films. The studios' willingness in 1960 to agree to terms with the unions was largely because the networks were converting to color television, which would eventually diminish the value of black-and-white films the studios had in their libraries.[169] The Writers Guild, for example, went on strike in January 1960 and, as Miranda Banks detailed in her history of the WGA, "gained the right to a fixed percentage from the studios' royalties, and, later, won residuals on television reruns and on the broadcasting of cinematic films on television."[170] The guild also won "a percentage of post-1948 film sales to television, and compensation for pay television, just in case it would become a significant force in future markets."[171] In lieu of agreeing to residual payments for films made before 1960, the producers agreed to a onetime $600,000 payment for past service into the WGA's pension and welfare fund.[172] SAG and DGA were also negotiating contracts with the studios that covered television rights to their post-1948 films. The stopgap clause in SAG's 1948 contracts had, to that point, kept most of the studios' post-1948 films off television. In March 1960, after failed negotiations, the issue of television revenues led SAG to strike for the first time in its sixty-year history. Ronald Reagan, then SAG president, ended the strike in April 1960 and entered into a collective bargaining agreement with every major studio except MCA and Universal. SAG's agreement was similar to the one the studios reached with the WGA. The studios agreed to pay $2,625,000 to establish pension, health, and welfare plans for their actors, and they further agreed to contribute 6 percent of the net television revenues of films made after February 1, 1960, to those plans. In exchange, SAG agreed not to bring compensation claims for films made before February 1, 1960, that were released to free television.[173] Once the WGA and SAG strikes were resolved in 1960, Warner Bros. leased a large package of their post-1948 films to a television distributor, and in 1961, in what was the first release of major films to network television relatively soon after their first theatrical run, Fox announced a deal with NBC for a program called *Saturday Night at the Movies.* The deal included a package of thirty-five features that NBC purchased from Fox for $25 million. NBC debuted the series on September 23, 1961, with *How to Marry a Millionaire.*[174] ABC then followed suit in 1962 by programming a package of United Artists' feature films on Sunday nights as their "Hollywood Special."[175]

By the late 1960s, networks were spending almost $300 million a year for feature films, scheduling movies every night of the week, and closing deals for $800,000 per film. Those prices were average prices, and the big hits and blockbuster films often commanded much more. As historian William Boddy argued, "Television income became expected and planned for. Few new film projects were put into production without assessing their potential on TV, and a TV sale was used as collateral in obtaining financing."[176] In addition to affecting the business dealings of the film industry, the ancillary market of television also affected the look of feature films. As historian John Belton documented, "In 1962, the American Society of Cinematographers issued a series of recommendations to its members, advising them to compose their wide-screen images for TV's 'safe action area.' Camera manufacturers began to produce viewfinders that indicated this area with a dotted line, and cinematographers began to protect their compositions for TV by keeping essential narrative and/or aesthetic elements within this frame-within-a-frame."[177] By 1965, "faced with full-color network television, the major Hollywood studios cut black and white production to its lowest levels yet. Within three years black and white had become so rare that the only new monochrome films to appear in American theaters were infrequent documentaries."[178]

After that long and drawn-out struggle of over a decade's worth of conflicts, lawsuits, and strikes to get Hollywood's feature films on television, one might expect that Hollywood would have learned how to more successfully manage periods of disruption and convergence, and particularly to facilitate the migration of their content across platforms. But Hollywood was doomed to repeat many of these same conflicts at other moments of disruption. For example, the labor unions went on strike again in 1980–1981, 1985, and 2007–2008 over films and other programming appearing on cable television, on videocassette, and in digital media, respectively. While in each instance the details might have changed, many of the core obstacles remained the same. One of the hopes of this book is that in studying historical periods such as this when television was introduced, scholars and practitioners can gain a better understanding of the industries, their behaviors, and their creative output, and better understand and navigate future moments of disruption.

CONCLUSION

DISRUPTING A BIG MARKET CAN BE BUMPY

This book's analysis of the struggle over Hollywood's feature films on early television demonstrates how long and gradual Hollywood's sale process actually was, and the many ways that it involved all aspects of the film and television industries. It illustrates the extent to which moments of convergence are fraught with systematic, overlapping, institutional confusions that are eventually resolved through often-unpredictable methods. Some behaviors and conflicts were settled in the courts; some borne out of lengthy negotiations; some formed on the basis of personal relationships and affinities; and some determined by sheer habit and inertia. Discerning the industry's rationalizations about how media works gives us better insight into the contemporary period of media industry disruption and convergence. In the wake of the introduction of digital media, many of the same issues and obstacles faced by the film and television industries in the 1940s and 1950s returned to once again challenge the media industries. Just as television disrupted the film industry by introducing new screens that allowed audiences to enjoy content in the home, digital technologies introduced new screens in computers, tablets, and smartphones that allow audiences to enjoy their content anywhere, anytime. How and when that content migrated between legacy and new media platforms, just as was the case with the migration of feature films to television, has been a source of great conflict.

As we have seen, when legacy media is faced with a disruption like digital media or television, they often fail to smoothly adapt and take advantage of the opportunities presented by the newer technologies. Consider, for example, the prolonged period of floundering the film, television, and music industries endured after the introduction of the internet in the 1990s. Like other dominant firms facing disruptions, these industries were confronted with a significant issue: it does not make much sense for dominant companies to invest aggressively in disruptive technologies. The reason for this is largely economic: since disruptive technologies often offer a cheaper and simpler product or service, they often also have lower profit margins. Additionally, many of the dominant firms' existing, and most profitable, customers initially cannot use products based on disruptive technologies, which are, by contrast, often eagerly adopted by the least profitable customers in the market. As a result, companies that are interested in higher profit margins and that are beholden to their existing, and most profitable, customers often fail to see the logic in making a serious investment in disruptive technologies until the market is "large enough to be interesting."[1] By then, it is often too late. Ultimately, it is not necessarily about companies working harder or smarter, but about the way they are able, or not, to productively approach disruptions in their industries.

The film industry is unique in that it has, to a large extent, operated as a functioning oligopoly, which results in corporate behaviors that are largely inflexible and conservative and privilege proven methods of success over innovation and risk. As economist Andrew Currah explained in his study of the oligopolistic behavior of the media industry, "There is a tendency for oligopolists to neglect or even marginalize emerging markets, especially those that are seen to threaten the status quo. Therefore, the behaviour of oligopolistic firms tends to reflect, defend and enforce the prevailing structure of the industry, making any kind of radical change difficult to justify or initiate."[2] In the study of Hollywood's response to television, we certainly saw the film industry's reluctance to embrace radical change. Similarly, the contemporary film and television industries have been reluctant to make any radical accommodations for the challenges of digital media. A senior vice president of a studio, when asked about his company's resistance to adapting to the introduction of digital media, responded with a question often repeatedly asked in the industry over the past hundred years: "Why deliberately upset a system that works?"[3]

Not only are oligopolies resistant to relinquish the behaviors that have brought them success, but when confronted with challengers, they often invest more heavily in expanding their existing media. In the 1950s, this meant the investment by the studios in things like their widescreen technologies that made their existing business bigger and better. Today, for example, the media companies have spent large amounts of capital, not necessarily on radical innovations but on technologies like 3D and HD that improve on their existing offerings and differentiate their content from mobile or online content. Although the behavior of these companies may be rational and fiscally advisable in the short term because it seeks to minimize risk and maximize quarterly earnings, it is potentially damaging in the long term.[4] When oligopolies are institutionally incapable of exploring and defining the new parameters of a disruptive technology, they leave it, as Currah concluded, to the "creative and economic margins of the entertainment industry, with the support of 'independent' content, which is subject to fewer legal restrictions in a digital or physical commodity form."[5] This may eliminate risk, but it also eliminates potential successes.

Another characteristic of oligopolies is that the corporate executives have incentives to focus on their larger, proven markets, thereby sustaining growth and protecting the company's market capitalization.[6] This was evident in many of the studio heads' focus in the 1940s and 1950s on their larger theatrical market as opposed to the smaller market of television. As is the case for the CEOs of media companies today, those studio heads were responsible to shareholders who wanted to see increasing profits and steady growth. Those priorities create cultures wherein it is difficult to take risks or accept failure, even in the pursuit of future success. In a 2008 study, for example, Ernst & Young found that CEOs of the major media companies were more focused on protecting their traditional business than pursuing digital opportunities, largely because they saw greater profits coming in from their traditional businesses than they did from digital. For example, one CEO explained that "digital media may not be as economically attractive as old media." Another complained that "media is trading analog dollars for digital dimes."[7] The heads of existing media companies balk when confronted by the rates and profits for content in a new medium or platform largely because it is difficult to establish the value of content in the new medium. This is made more difficult because the heads of existing media companies often compare the values of the two mediums as though they are comparing apples to apples, which is not the case. For example, one CEO said, "The ability to persuade consumers to pay fair value for content is critical."[8] Another CEO took that one step further and argued, "The major challenge is getting people to pay for content—not what is 'fair' but what they used to pay."[9] We also saw that sentiment arise among studio heads when offered deals for their films on television. They did not believe they were getting the fair value for their work in the new medium. They expected to get at least the same amount for the content from television as they did from their theaters. They expected each audience member to pay the same amount for a "ticket" to view their films, whether the films were old or new, and whether they were at home in front of their television or in a movie theater.

One of the reasons that content providers complained in the 1940s and 1950s, and still do today, that they cannot make as much money for their content in the new medium as they would like is because advertisers are also unsure as to how to value the new medium and are therefore reluctant to spend large amounts of money. Just as advertisers in the early days of television waited for ratings information to show them where they could successfully spend their money, so too have advertisers today hesitated to take risks without better data analytics and audience measurement tools pointing them in the right direction. They want a clear measurement of their return on investment, or, as Ernst & Young described, "They need the tools to demonstrate that they are winning in the market."[10] Not only are there concerns about not getting enough value out of newer technologies, but there are also concerns about devaluing existing media properties if they are shown on the new platform. Just as in the 1940s and 1950s the theaters complained to the studios that showing films on television would ruin any potential value the films had in the theaters, Alisa Perren has observed that affiliate stations today object to streaming programming online "on the grounds that it devalues their status as the initial site for original network content."[11] Just as the studios argued to their theaters in the 1950s, "the networks have been able to mediate this issue to some extent by arguing that streaming serves primarily promotional purposes."[12]

Video games provide another example of this destructive mindset at work. In the case of Nintendo, for years they dug in their heels and insisted on developing and releasing games only for their own hardware systems. But as mobile devices increased in popularity, Nintendo's sales decreased. Their strategies so seriously backfired that in January 2014, they took a step that is almost unheard of and dramatically lowered their financial forecast, in large part because they expected to sell nearly 70 percent fewer Wii U consoles than expected.[13] Fewer console sales meant fewer sales of games. Although the sale of a $.99 app may not be as sexy as the sale of a $300-plus Wii U, if Nintendo embraced mobile gaming and developed versions of their games, both old and new, for devices such as the iPad, they could enjoy entirely new streams of revenue. In 2017, they took a step in that direction by introducing the Switch, which provided the mobility that many consumers wanted. But if we consider Chris Anderson's theory of the long tail, a million small sales can be much more profitable than a few larger sales,[14] and as Greg Richardson, CEO of online games company Rumble, observed of Nintendo's predicament: "It's a classic challenge of having to disrupt yourself. They have to fail against their old playbook fundamentally before they take a step back to assess, 'Who are we?' Clearly, the present is not the past."[15]

Another example of the very practical issues that prevent existing industries from taking advantage of newer technologies and media is the different financial models of the legacy media and the newer media. For example, when Chris Sacca, a venture investor, technology adviser, and entrepreneur who manages consumer web, mobile, and technology start-ups, was working at Google sometime around late 2005, he met with music company executives and offered to sell their music through Google, but at the music companies' prices and on their terms. He expected the executives to jump at the chance, but their response was to ask how much cash he could guarantee them in the first year. It was then that Sacca realized one of the fundamental differences between the two industries: Hollywood was used to getting paid yearly in cash, while Silicon Valley was used to getting paid every four years in equity. The stockholders of the publicly traded Hollywood studios expected to see healthy income every year, whereas the venture capitalists and owners of the Silicon Valley start-ups worked according to a fundamentally different value exchange that often assumed not to see a return on investment until a few years in the future.[16] Those key differences in their basic operational models and expectations of what "success" meant to their shareholders and investors created a significant enough obstacle to prevent them from working together. You could see that mindset at work in the difficulties RKO faced when trying to make a deal, in that they wanted a lump sum payment for their films, whereas the television industry wanted to pay them a percentage of future profits. That was emblematic of what media scholar Denise Mann observed in *Wired TV*, "Their tendency to return to old patterns and profit centers, which reinforces their reluctance to rethink their creative and business models."[17]

Another area of contention that demonstrates the need for existing media companies to fundamentally rethink their financial models to incorporate new technologies is piracy. As one CEO of a contemporary media company argued, "Absolutely need to restrict piracy—if everything is free, you can't make investments in the franchise."[18] The studios in the 1940s and 1950s were also on a crusade against their version of piracy: the unlicensed showing of 16mm films. That fight did not turn out particularly well for the studios, as it was a part of what prompted the DOJ's antitrust suit *U.S. vs. Twentieth Century-Fox, et al.* Considering piracy in light of the argument made by Chris Anderson in *Free*, however, what might appear to be given away "free" actually has the potential to create an incredible amount of revenue. However, realizing that potential would require producers to shift their view of their market and their notion of who their customers actually are.[19] When in the 1950s studio heads and theater owners saw television as content that was given away to customers for free, they had a difficult time understanding that the basic financial model of television was simply a different, more complex one than that for film. Similarly, producers today see the internet as the land of the free, where companies like Google and Facebook are clearly incredibly profitable. Existing media companies just have to figure out how to adapt to these new profit models.

Netflix has found great success in digital media, in part because when they first started their streaming service they considered piracy not as something that had to be defeated but as another tool to improve their business. That is not to say that they encouraged piracy, and since they have achieved market dominance and gained entry to most countries around the globe they have joined the Motion Picture Association of America and actively fought against piracy; but in their earlier years, they accepted that piracy was an unavoidable characteristic of digital media and decided to derive value from it by using it as a source of information and data gathering about their audience. As the *New York Times* described it: "Stopping online piracy is like playing the world's largest game of Whac-A-Mole."[20] Instead of wasting their energy and resources playing that game, Netflix used the information from pirating websites to determine the genre of shows and films their viewers might be interested in and therefore the type of content they would produce or license. As Kelly Merryman, vice president of content acquisition at Netflix, described, "With the purchase of a series, we look at what does well on piracy sites."[21] Merryman said, for example, that Netflix decided to license the show *Prison Break* because it had been popular on piracy sites. This is not to suggest that media companies should open their gates and offer all of their content for free, but they have to accept the qualities of a new technology—both good and bad—and try to find ways to use them to their advantage rather than trying to beat them into submission.

One of the central reasons that existing companies may be reluctant to invest early in new technologies is that they do not want to dilute the profitability of their portfolios in the short term, but economists have found that "companies that reallocate resources early to capture trends often have higher returns and are more likely to survive long term."[22] Unfortunately, today, as we saw in the 1940s and 1950s, many companies prefer to wait until newer markets are large enough to be interesting. For example, as Ned Depinet explained, "Our policy, frankly, about television has been one of watchful waiting. . . . And we figured there was a strong financial advantage to accrue to our company to await the development of this industry."[23] We see that same attitude today. As a senior vice president at one of the major Hollywood studios explained, "We need to open up our libraries and get legal content out there . . . onto the Internet . . . to drive consumer adoption, tackle piracy and grow the market. . . . The flipside is that the market is too small to warrant our investment. *But* and here's the Catch-22 . . . the market can't grow if we don't take that risk and license content. It's a real dilemma that will take a courageous move by one of the studios to resolve."[24] Just as the film industry waited for the saturation point for television, media companies today waited for the "media saturation index," which measures the level of adoption of broadband access and consumer internet-enabled devices. Ernst & Young found that for "every increase in the number of devices, there is a corresponding multiplicative increase in the amount of internet data traffic consumers generate. So while the number of devices grows by 20% annually, the amount of traffic in terms of usage that those devices consume is growing even faster at 32%."[25]

The problem with waiting until a market is large enough to be interesting, however, is that the companies that participate in those newer markets end up establishing themselves as leaders in that market, and they gain experience and expertise that later entrants find difficult to replicate.[26] Take the example of YouTube and Hulu. The studios did not launch Hulu until 2008—only a little over two years after YouTube went live. In those two years, YouTube was able to dominate the market for online video and, in terms of traffic to the site, was exponentially more successful than Hulu had been. This example shows how business leaders cannot wait until they witness success by other companies in newer technologies before they get involved. They need to think further into the future and be willing to take risks on smaller markets that might become larger markets tomorrow.[27]

One obstacle that prevented studios from putting their content online on sites like Hulu, however, was the enduring question over rights. For example, as Alisa Perren described, NBC had a difficult time gaining the rights to show *ER* on Hulu and NBC.com, which caused a long delay before that show appeared on streaming platforms.[28] Those same issues over the rights to content in a new medium were litigated in the early 1950s in the *Rogers* and *Autry* cases. In those cases, the studios tried to claim all television rights to Rogers's and Autry's films as early as the 1930s, but television was not a known quantity to all parties involved in the contract, and so it was subject to legal testing decades later. This inability to understand the exact nature of a future medium like television or digital media may make it nearly impossible for companies to claim the rights to a medium before it exists. Of course, they do try to claim those rights in their contracts, but whether those claims will hold up in court once companies are faced with the reality of the new medium is another matter. Take, for example, the case of Napster, which was fundamentally a case about what it meant to own and use the rights to a piece of music on the internet. The courts had to debate and determine the very nature of the internet as opposed to audio CDs or cassette tapes. So while the record labels' contracts contained language that protected their rights in all media, the fact that the internet presented wholly unimagined possibilities for the use of their content resulted in prolonged legal battles that delayed all parties from making progress in the new medium.

In terms of limitations from restrictive existing contracts, one of the best examples of the problems that can result is the demise of Blockbuster Video. Their bankruptcy is one of the most significant failures that occurred in the face of the introduction of digital technologies. From the outside, it seemed as though Blockbuster should have been perfectly positioned to innovate and take advantage of the introduction of digital media. If they had taken their physical rental business and moved it online, Netflix may never have had the opportunity to dominate the market in the way they eventually did. Blockbuster certainly made errors of judgment along the way, including their focus in the early years of the first decade of the twenty-first century on defending their turf against the young upstart Netflix rather than looking at how they could improve their own service.[29] There were more practical issues, however, such as legacy leases with studios for their rental videos, which forced Blockbuster to continue doing business as usual. Even if Blockbuster was interested in adjusting their business model, issues like their legacy leases and their overreliance on their investments in, and income from, their brick-and-mortar business would have made it extremely difficult, if not impossible, to innovate at a pace rapid enough for their survival. They needed to have identified the potentially disruptive technology early enough to have adapted their contracts before these technologies had begun to exert their disruptive powers in the economy and society.[30]

When you consider contracts in the media industries, you have to consider the contracts with the unions and guilds, and we have seen the central importance of those contracts in navigating times of change. The willingness to invest in both the proven and currently profitable technologies, as well as exploring new, and possibly disruptive, technologies, is a burden that rests not only with business leaders but with other groups such as unions and guilds. They also have a responsibility to prepare for disruptive technologies, because, as we saw highlighted in the AFM's struggle with "mechanized music," new media can upset the "older ways of doing things and [render] old skills and organizational approaches irrelevant."[31] The question of labor and training the labor force to work with the new technologies is another matter. As happened with the unions and guilds in the 1940s and 1950s, the introduction of television provided not only a challenge in terms of the value of their work when reused in another medium, but also the very real and potentially more dangerous fact that the disruptive technology of television displaced work and in many cases rendered performers of all types unnecessary. With the introduction of digital media, similar challenges appeared, albeit in a slightly different way. As Nicholas Carr observed, "Computerization, like electrification before it, simply continues the centuries-long trend of substituting machines for workers. . . . Whereas industrialization in general and electrification in particular created many new office jobs even as they made factories more efficient, computerization is not creating a broad new class of jobs to take the place of those it destroys."[32] The unions and guilds complained that the introduction of the mechanized medium of television was limiting their employment opportunities and reusing their work without compensation. Since the introduction of digital media, the media companies have asked writers, actors, and so on to produce content for the internet or mobile devices that was, at least initially, uncredited and unpaid. Once again union and guild members were faced with the basic questions of what employment looks like for them in the new media, and how they can ensure they are fairly compensated for it.

The WGA strike in 2007–2008 was a direct result of the standoff between the guild and producers over payment and credit for digital content. While the unions and guilds are understandably hesitant about entering into agreements with producers that they might later regret (e.g., the low rates they originally agreed to for their work on VHS and DVD), they must prepare as much as possible for the future so that they can ensure their financial security and better position themselves to deal successfully with new media and technologies. As scholars Michael Curtin and Kevin Sanson have observed, "Working conditions [for media workers] have been deteriorating since the 1990s if not earlier. . . . Today's increasingly mobile and globally dispersed mode of production thrives (indeed, depends) on interregional competition, driving down pay rates, benefits, and job satisfaction for media workers around the world."[33] The lower labor rates and fewer regulations in right-to-work states and overseas locations where unions have little to no clout are very appealing to producers that are primarily concerned with meeting their budgets. As scholar Mark Deuze has argued, "Across the manufacturing, service, and creative industries, a new world of work is taking shape that seems to be premised on individual rather than industry-level responsibility, requires a high degree of skill-set flexibility, and implicitly expects portfolio careerism. Media industries are notable in this context for their long history of manifesting these broader trends, and in some instances serving as an inspiration for management developments in other economic sectors."[34] In the era of post-Fordist flexibility, when there are so often conflicts between labor and management, the industry should also consider the more difficult question of what is the moral obligation of employers when their labor force is confronted with these types of challenges. The concept of Flexicurity, for example, as taken from European Labor Law, endorses flexible and reliable contractual agreements between management and labor, the availability of comprehensive lifelong learning strategies for workers, and sustainable systems that protect all members of society. This balance between the rights and responsibilities of all concerned is necessary to ensure a productive future for all.

Just as the unions and guilds need to work to better anticipate disruptive technologies, so do regulators and policy makers. As an example of the problems that can occur when regulators and policy makers do not stay ahead of the curve, one of the CEOs of a contemporary media company observed, "Structural and regulatory uncertainty is an understatement. Regulators are confused. They are looking at an evolving animal and saying, 'How do I tax it?'"[35] The FCC's debates over subscription television, and the FCC's behavior more generally in the early years of television, illustrated their confusion as to how best to proceed in terms of regulating the new media. Today one of the most salient examples of that confusion can be seen in the conflicts over net neutrality, and the basic questions of whether and how the FCC has the power to regulate the internet. The problems that arose around the issue of net neutrality provide a perfect example of how technicalities in regulation can determine the future use and limitations of media by existing media companies and consumers. A decision by a federal appeals court in January 2014 determined that regulations put in place in 2010 that limited internet service providers like Verizon from making deals with companies like Netflix or Amazon to allow those companies to pay more to stream their products to viewers through faster "express lanes" online were not legal because, the court argued, the internet was not considered a utility under federal law, and was therefore not subject to those kinds of common carrier regulations. Verizon told the court that if those rules had not been in place, they would already have explored those commercial arrangements.[36] As Jennifer Holt has argued, "Content companies can deal with today's turbulence most strategically, particularly as it exists in the policy realm, by thinking with tomorrow's logic."[37] The same could be said for regulators and policy makers, and since those who set policy have multiple responsibilities that often conflict when disruptive technologies emerge, citizens also need to educate themselves and advocate on their own behalf by engaging with policy makers on issues that matter to them. In the example of net neutrality, the cable and internet providers certainly lobbied Congress and the FCC, and citizens should make sure their interests are heard by lobbying for their own rights.

In examining these many parallels, the intention is not to develop a teleological history where media industry convergence in the 1950s leads to convergence in the first decade of the twenty-first century and reveals some magical truth about the obstacles presented by industrial and technological disruptions. It does seem, however, that lessons can be learned to help better account for subsequent changes and shifts. This historiographic process is less about distilling what "causes" any of the conflicts and problems than about understanding the nature of the recurrence of selective industrial blindness. In the course of that understanding, it may be possible to uncover keys to removing those blinders. The changes wrought by digital technologies have demonstrated that the rate of change has increased and made it all the more essential to understand its challenges. For traditional disruptive innovations required the "painstaking manipulation and alignment of physical resources. . . . This takes time. And it takes money—lots of it."[38] In something as complex as the media industries, there are so many moving parts and so much money at risk that the stakes are very high for a number of different factions that each have their own interests to protect. It is not unlike trying to turn the *Titanic*. You might all see the iceberg and have ideas as to how to avoid it, but actually getting that massive ship to quickly adapt and respond is an almost impossible task.

But in the digital space, where physical resources have become less of a concern, things move faster and can cost less, and one of the keys to success when faced with potentially disruptive technology is, as Christensen argued, the need for dominant firms to create autonomous organizations built around the disruptive technology. In that way, the dominant firms align themselves with the new technologies rather than ignoring or fighting them.[39] We saw examples of this tactic at work in the 1950s with the creation of Hollywood Television and Screen Gems, which were separate, but affiliated, companies of Republic and Columbia, respectively. Both of those companies allowed Republic and Columbia to more successfully converge their existing film businesses with television and enabled a smoother transition of their films to television. In today's Hollywood, many media companies are either, as a study by Ernst & Young of innovation in the media industry described them, "born-digital" or "born-again."[40] Born-digital companies include those like Facebook and Netflix, whereas born-again companies include the existing media companies that have to redefine themselves in the world of digital media. If an existing media company creates a subsidiary company that develops their business in the new media, the existing media company could benefit from its "born-digital" subsidiary and use the relationship with that subsidiary to help manage its own relationship with the disruptive media. Creating autonomous organizations to build business around new technologies can create an opportunity for a balance of risk and growth between the existing companies and their new, innovative offshoots.

Especially in light of the inertia inherent in oligopolies, independent companies today, just as with television in the 1950s, have seen some of the most success in being born-again in digital media. As Alisa Perren observed, smaller companies that have more modest financial expectations for their films, like Magnolia Pictures and IFC Direct, experimented more aggressively than major studios with releasing their films with day and date releasing.[41] Many observers believe that day and date releasing will be the future of film distribution, and these smaller companies will have experience and infrastructure accrued before the majors are able to take their first steps in that direction. Perren also found that Magnolia and IFC have been "among the most active buyers of completed films in recent years. They acquire a wide range of lower-budgeted American independents and imported films on the cheap from producers desperate to make even a small amount of money back on their investments."[42] This is exactly what happened in the 1950s with the rise of companies that distributed films to television. They were independent companies with modest financial expectations and would buy their films from desperate independent producers. Examples of these tendencies exist in even earlier periods of disruption. As Charles Musser observed in his overview of the American film industry before 1907, "Ironically, the very dynamics of change that favored consolidation and rationalization frequently worked against those in a dominant position. Change was commonly introduced by those companies or individuals who were at a competitive disadvantage."[43] Media companies today should look toward a more flexible model as practiced by independent companies as a way not only to expand their profits, even if minimally at first, but more importantly to get a foothold in the new system of distribution and exhibition that will eventually establish itself with or without them.

Denise Mann's work has found similar examples of success on the margins. She observed that "in the past decade, in particular, 'the industry' has expanded to include large numbers of younger, smaller, independent-minded sub-companies and units—transmedia production companies, digital marketing agencies, and even lone digital artists—that have intentionally aligned themselves with Silicon Valley's work ethos over Hollywood's."[44] Legacy media companies need to create smaller subsidiary companies that are charged with innovating—not just digital divisions that can be pushed aside and are still subject to the structure and culture of their larger corporate parent, but autonomous companies that are allowed to take risks and accept failure as the cost of experimentation. Those companies would be able to allocate resources to develop business in new technologies rather than focusing on making the business of the old media more profitable. This strategy would allow companies to balance the consistent improvement of their successful products with the adoption and promotion of new technologies.[45] Studying these smaller intermediaries offers a better understanding of their role in historical case studies, and it also allows a clearer understanding of the historical and contemporary media industries as a whole—from the bottom and middle up, as it were, rather than from the top down.

In the end, the key is the ability to anticipate future disruption and convergence, and being willing to adapt early enough to take advantage of it. As Christensen argued, that kind of anticipation and adaptation are especially difficult for successful firms because it fundamentally goes against the grain of what they have done to achieve success in the first place. He argued that when faced with disruptive technologies, good management itself is a root cause of failure among existing media companies because they play the game the way it has always been played. He explained that "the very decision-making and resource-allocation processes that are key to the success of established companies are the very processes that reject disruptive technologies: listening carefully to customers; tracking competitors' actions carefully; and investing resources to design and build higher-performance, higher-quality products that will yield greater profit."[46] Since it is virtually impossible for anyone to accurately predict future technological innovations and the ways consumers might use them, the key, then, is not to plan for a specific disruptor but to plan for flexibility.[47] Media companies should embrace the fact that they cannot and do not know where the technologies will go, but they should plan to adapt to working with whatever arises. Particularly today, when increased merger and acquisition activity has further reduced the number of media corporations dominating the industry, flexibility remains essential. Rethinking antitrust law to better address the contemporary marketplace and the challenges it and the laborers within it face would help to ensure a more competitive and successful future. As economist Orly Lobel pointed out in her study of the ways that people and skills are depleted when they are monopolized, "Introducing more competition, more products and related companies into a market, strengthens it. In fact, it is the lack of diversity that threatens an industry's future."[48]

With digital technologies in particular, the rate of change has been significantly faster, and that has made the need for flexibility and quick adaptation all the more essential. As Nicholas Carr noted in his history of the electrification of America and the switch to cloud computing, "History also suggests that the ultimate form of the World Wide Computer, as a communication system, a popular mass medium, and a commercial infrastructure, will be determined to a large degree through the wrangling of politicians, lawyers, judges, and diplomats. Technological revolutions tend to race ahead of institutional responses, creating all sorts of social and legal quandaries. In time, the institutions catch up, power shifts from the techies to the technocrats, and a new status quo emerges."[49] At each moment when a new disruptive technology is introduced, the existing media is faced with the challenge of adapting or perishing. As we have seen, the losers are often the ones that are least flexible, such as theater owners or Blockbuster Video, whose large investments in their brick-and-mortar operations left them unable to easily adapt and innovate. Even if existing media adapts, another disruptive technology may come along and devalue their adaptation. But if media companies can learn from the challenges, successes, and failures experienced in the history of media convergence and disruption, perhaps they can better adapt in the future.

Today, an additional challenge to the media industries is that contemporary industrial convergence and disruption, while in some ways confined by national borders and therefore determined by each nation's particular laws, policies, and labor conditions, are happening in an increasingly global media industry. In this global landscape, international laws and policies often dictate the behaviors of media conglomerates as much as, if not more than, the conditions of individual nations do. Take, for example, the influence of the 2018 European privacy mandates in the General Data Protection Regulation, of antitrust regulations and actions taken in 2015 by the European Union against Google, or Chinese policies regarding the content of media texts and copyright. In this climate, Hollywood's unions and guilds struggle against conglomerates that outsource labor to other countries in order to avoid more restrictive labor contracts and take advantage of more generous tax incentives. As media conglomerates increasingly look to locations around the world for growth potential, they will be influenced by international laws and policies. Considering this modern media landscape in the light of this book's historical analysis of disruption and convergence heightens Jennifer Holt's call to "update policy goals so that they are capable of addressing media industries as they exist and function today; and expand the paradigm to accommodate cultural concerns alongside those of economics and the law."[50]

One of the most significant lessons from this book, however, is the extent to which media studies have arbitrarily kept film, television, and digital media studies separate for too long, when, in reality, the histories of film and television are intricately and essentially interwoven. Even in a case study as seemingly specific as the struggle over the licensing and sale of Hollywood's feature films to television before 1955, the degree to which this story necessarily expanded to include the involvement of almost every aspect of the film and television industries clearly demonstrates the ways in which it is impossible to truly understand the behavior and content of one medium without the other. The complex relationships and interests in the media industries, both past and present, influence each other in often subtle but important ways, and only by moving forward with a coherent media history can we fully appreciate the awesome complexity of the media industries and their products.

ACKNOWLEDGMENTS

This book got its start in Vivian Sobchack's historiography class while I was studying at UCLA, and I thank her for inspiring me to appreciate history in a different way. I am forever indebted to John Caldwell, an all-around fantastic human who provided invaluable guidance in the early stages of this project, helped me navigate the publishing process, and supported me in the hellscape that is the academic job market. Denise Mann, Kathleen McHugh, and Jennifer Holt gave me insightful feedback on earlier drafts, and along with other faculty and staff at UCLA, supported me in the early stages of this work. My brilliant cohort mates Maya Montañez Smukler, David O'Grady, and Drew Morton have shared their wisdom and friendship with me since the beginnings of this project, and I am lucky to have met and worked with so many other wonderful Bruins over the years: Allyson Nadia Field, Erin Hill, Ross Melnick, Jonathan Cohn, Jaimie Baron, Jennifer Moorman, Andrew deWaard, Karrmen Crey, Bryan Wuest, Lindsay Giggey, Harrison Gish, Dawn Fratini, Emily Carman, Phil Wagner, Maja Manojlovic, Ben Harris, Samantha Sheppard, Ben Sher, and Ben Sampson, to name a few. In one way or another, they all made it possible for me to finish this project.

Completing this work required visits to many archives across the country, and I benefited from the generosity of many archivists and librarians who helped me navigate their collections, especially the fount of TV knowledge, Mark Quigley, manager of the UCLA Film and Television Archive Research and Study Center; Sandra Joy Lee and Jonathan Auxier at USC's Warner Bros. Archives; Julie Graham at the UCLA Library Special Collections; Monique Leahy Sugimoto and Paul Wormser at the National Archives at Laguna Niguel/Riverside; Valerie Yaros at the Screen Actors Guild; Jenny Romero and Barbara Hall at the Margaret Herrick Library; and Marva Felchin at the Autry Library.

My colleagues in the Department of Visual & Media Arts at Emerson College and in the Boston Media Collective made my formational time there a joy. I am particularly grateful for Eric Schaeffer's mentorship, Charlotte Howell's adventurousness, and for colleagues and friends like Rodolfo Fernandez, Cristina Kotz

Cornejo, Kim Icreverzi, Lindsay Hogan, Andy Owens, and Ben Aslinger, whose shared appreciation for cocktails helped make the winters warmer. Miranda Banks and Deborah Jaramillo were the best part of my two years in Boston, and I am incredibly fortunate that they have continued to be wonderful friends and constant sources of brilliance.

A huge thank-you to my fantastic colleagues and friends in the Media Arts Department at the University of North Texas for giving me the opportunity to move back to Texas. The administration supported this work with the College of Liberal Arts and Social Sciences' Scholarly and Creative Activity Award and the Office of the Provost and Vice President of Academic Affairs' Junior Faculty Summer Research Support Award. I am especially grateful for the ongoing support and friendship of Jacqueline Vickery, Harry Benshoff, Eugene Martin, Courtney Brannon Donoghue, Stephen Mandiberg, Melinda Levin, Tania Khalaf, and Andrea Miller. At UNT, I have been fortunate to have the opportunity to work out my ideas in the classroom, and I appreciate my students' openness to my insistence that learning about topics like antitrust and tax law can be interesting.

I also want to express my gratitude for the fellow academics whom I have gotten to know and learn from at our various conferences over the years: Ariel Rogers, Karen Petruska, Kristen Warner, Deron Overpeck, Christine Becker, Ethan Tussey, Phil Scepanski, Liz Elcessor, and Josh Gleich are some of the many colleagues who have made those often-exhausting conferences a pleasure. Erin Copple Smith was one of my earliest conference friends, and I am so lucky to have her as a fellow Texan.

At Rutgers University Press, Leslie Michner was incredibly supportive of me from the very early stages, and I have missed her guidance since she retired. Nicole Solano has since helped shepherd this project into the much stronger work that it is today. For Leslie, Nicole, and reviewers like the brilliant Michele Hilmes who provided helpful feedback on early drafts, and the design department who made this book look super cool, I am very grateful.

Last but certainly not least, I am blessed with family and nonacademic friends who have been a source of great joy: my parents, Barbara and Jim; stepparents, Hilton and Kathy; my many step-siblings, aunts, uncles, and cousins—I am very fortunate to have too many of you to name here; my brothers, Rich, Jim, and Michael; sisters-in-law, Michelle, Mary, and Krista; and my brilliant nieces and nephews, Madison, Stella, Asher, Griffin, Ellie, and Mikey; for Precious, Dignan, and Gidget, who have been my constant companions and brought me so much happiness. Thank you all for your kindness and love. Finally, for my grandparents, Rosemary and Dick Leach, whose support made all of this possible.

Abbreviations Used in Notes

DOJ NACP	DOJ Class 60 Antitrust Accession 57A60, National Archives at College Park, MD.
JMR	Jack Mathis/Republic—Research Files, L. Tom Perry Special Collections, Harold B. Lee Library, Brigham Young University, Provo, UT.
JWTCA	J. Walter Thompson Company Archives, Rare Book, Manuscript, and Special Collections Library, Duke University, Durham, NC.
NACP	National Archives, College Park, MD.
NAR 14354-Y	Civil Case 14354-Y, U.S. v. Twentieth Century-Fox, et al., Southern District of California, Central Division (Los Angeles), Records of the United States District Court, Record Group 21, National Archives at Riverside, Perris, CA.
NAR 13220-PH	Civil Case No. 13220-PH, Roy Rogers v. Republic Productions, Inc., Hollywood Television Service, Inc., et al., Southern District of California, Central Division (Los Angeles), Records of the United States District Court, Record Group 21, National Archives at Riverside, Perris, CA.
NAR 13596-BH	Civil Case No. 13596-BH, Gene Autry v. Republic Productions, Inc., et al., Southern District of California, Central Division (Los Angeles, CA), Records of the United States District Court, Record Group 21, National Archives at Riverside, Perris, CA.
NATO	NATO Collection, L. Tom Perry Special Collections, Harold B. Lee Library, Brigham Young University, Provo, UT.
SAGA	Screen Actors Guild Archive, Los Angeles, CA.
UCLA	Twentieth Century-Fox Film Corporation, Records of the Legal Department, UCLA Performing Arts Special Collections.
WBA	Warner Bros. Archives, School of Cinematic Arts, University of Southern California.

NOTES

INTRODUCTION

1. Kim Masters, "Kim Masters: Why Did Bob Iger's Disney Announcement Feel So Rushed?," *Hollywood Reporter*, 10 March 2020.
2. Kara Swisher, "Disney Channels the Force," *New York Times*, 15 November 2019.
3. Henry Jenkins, *Convergence Culture: Where Old and New Media Collide* (New York: New York University Press, 2006), 2.
4. Etan Vlessing, "Netflix Adds Far Fewer Subscribers during Second Quarter," *Hollywood Reporter*, 18 July 2016, https://www.hollywoodreporter.com/news/netflix-adds-far-subscribers-second-911968.
5. William Uricchio, "Historicizing Media in Transition," in *Rethinking Media Change: The Aesthetics of Transition*, ed. David Thorburn and Henry Jenkins (Cambridge, MA: MIT Press, 2003), 33.
6. Ibid., 32.
7. Mark Williams, "Rewiring Media History: Intermedial Borders," in *Convergence Media History*, ed. Janet Staiger and Sabine Hake (New York: Routledge, 2009), 46.
8. Ibid.
9. Christopher Anderson, *Hollywood TV: The Studio System in the Fifties* (Austin: University of Texas Press, 1994); Tino Balio, ed., *Hollywood in the Age of Television* (Boston: Unwin Hyman, 1990); Michele Hilmes, *Hollywood and Broadcasting: From Radio to Cable* (Urbana: University of Illinois Press, 1990); William Boddy, *Fifties Television: The Industry and Its Critics* (Urbana: University of Illinois Press, 1990); Edward Buscombe, "Thinking It Differently: Television and the Film Industry," 196–203; Robert Vianello, "The Rise of the Telefilm and the Networks' Hegemony over the Motion Picture Industry," 204–218; Douglas Gomery, "Failed Opportunities: The Integration of the U.S. Motion Picture and Television Industries," 219–228, all in *Quarterly Review of Film Studies* 9, no. 3 (Summer 1984).
10. David Pierce, "'Senile Celluloid': Independent Exhibitors, the Major Studios and the Fight over Feature Films on Television," *Film History* 10, no. 2 (1998): 141–164; Michele Hilmes, *Only Connect: A Cultural History of Broadcasting in the United States*, 3rd ed. (Boston: Wadsworth/Cengage Learning, 2011), 224–26; Amy Schnapper, "The Distribution of Theatrical Feature Films to Television" (Diss., University of Wisconsin–Madison,

1975); and Eric Hoyt, "Hollywood Vault: The Business of Film Libraries, 1915–1960" (PhD diss., University of Southern California, 2012).

11. Joseph Schumpeter, *Capitalism, Socialism, and Democracy* (New York: Harper Collins Publishers, 2008).

12. Orly Lobel, *Talent Wants to Be Free: Why We Should Learn to Love Leaks, Raids, and Free Riding* (New Haven, CT: Yale University Press, 2013), 242–243.

13. Clayton M. Christensen, *The Innovator's Dilemma: The Revolutionary Book That Will Change the Way You Do Business* (New York: Harper Business, 2011), xi.

14. Ibid., xviii.

15. James Manyika et al., "Disruptive Technologies: Advances That Will Transform Life, Business, and the Global Economy," McKinsey Global Institute, May 2013, https://www.mckinsey.com/business-functions/mckinsey-digital/our-insights/disruptive-technologies.

16. Andrew Currah, "Hollywood versus the Internet: The Media and Entertainment Industries in a Digital and Networked Economy," *Journal of Economic Geography* 6 (2006): 457.

17. James L. Baughman, "The Weakest Chain and the Strongest Link: The American Broadcasting Company and the Motion Picture Industry, 1952–60," in *Hollywood in the Age of Television*, ed. Tino Balio (Boston: Unwin Hyman, 1990), 100.

18. Tino Balio, "Part IV/Retrenchment, Reappraisal, and Reorganization, 1948–," in *The American Film Industry*, ed. Tino Balio (Madison: University of Wisconsin Press, 1985), 422–423.

19. Anderson, *Hollywood TV*, 2.

20. Quoted in Charles Musser, *The Emergence of Cinema: The American Screen to 1907*, vol. 1 of *History of the American Cinema* (Los Angeles: University of California Press, 1990), 11.

21. Jennifer Porst, "The Preservation of Competition: Hollywood and Antitrust," in *Hollywood and the Law*, ed. Paul McDonald, Philip Drake, Eric Hoyt, and Emily Carman (London: BFI Publishing, 2015).

22. Michele Hilmes, "Rethinking Radio," in *Radio Reader: Essays in the Cultural History of Radio*, ed. Michele Hilmes and Jason Loviglio (New York: Routledge, 2002), 3.

23. "TV's Time of Trouble," *Fortune*, August 1951, 131.

24. Michele Hilmes, "Nailing Mercury: The Problem of Media Industry Historiography," in *Media Industries: History, Theory, and Method*, ed. Jennifer Holt and Alissa Perren (Malden, MA: Wiley-Blackwell, 2009), 21.

25. Charles Acland, "Dirt Research for Media Industries," in *Media Industries: Perspectives on an Evolving Field*, ed. Amelia Arsenault and Alisa Perren (Austin, TX: Media Industries Editorial Board, 2016), 9.

26. Jennifer Holt, *Empires of Entertainment: Media Industries and the Politics of Deregulation, 1980–1996* (New Brunswick, NJ: Rutgers University Press, 2011), 5.

27. Eileen Meehan, "Watching Television: A Political Economic Approach," in *A Companion to Television*, ed. Janet Wasko (Malden, MA: Wiley-Blackwell, 2010), 238.

28. Ibid., 393–411.

29. Michele Hilmes, *Network Nations: A Transnational History of British and American Broadcasting* (New York: Routledge, 2012), 9.

30. Douglas Gomery, "The Centrality of Media Economics," in *Defining Media Studies: Reflections on the Future of the Field*, ed. Mark R. Levy and Michael Gurevitch (New York: Oxford University Press, 1994), 199.

31. Hilmes, *Hollywood and Broadcasting*, 1.

32. David Hesmondhalgh, *The Cultural Industries*, 2nd ed. (Los Angeles: Sage Publications, 2007), 6, 9, 42.

33. Brian Winston, "Breakages Limited," in *Electronic Media and Technoculture*, ed. John Thornton Caldwell (New Brunswick, NJ: Rutgers University Press, 2000), 78.

34. Jane Gaines, *Contested Culture: The Image, the Voice, and the Law* (Chapel Hill: University of North Carolina Press, 1991), 4, 14.

35. John Thornton Caldwell, *Production Culture: Industrial Reflexivity and Critical Practice in Film and Television* (Durham, NC: Duke University Press, 2008), 2.

36. Uricchio, "Historicizing Media in Transition," 33.

37. Testimony of Alexander Kenneth Beggs, Reporter's Transcript of Proceedings, vol. 14, p. 1416, 18 October 1955, NAR 14354-Y.

38. Des Freedman, "Media Policy Research and the Media Industries," in *Media Industries: Perspectives on an Evolving Field*, ed. Amelia Arsenault and Alisa Perren (Austin, TX: Media Industries Editorial Board, 2016), 19.

39. Manyika et al., "Disruptive Technologies," 21.

40. David Thorburn and Henry Jenkins, "Introduction: Towards an Aesthetics of Transition," in *Rethinking Media Change: The Aesthetics of Transition*, ed. David Thorburn and Henry Jenkins (Cambridge, MA: MIT Press, 2004), 2.

CHAPTER 1 — SYSTEMS OF AUTHORITY AND EVALUATION

1. Anderson, *Hollywood TV*, 5.

2. Philip W. Sewell, *Television in the Age of Radio: Modernity, Imagination, and the Making of a Medium* (New Brunswick, NJ: Rutgers University Press, 2014), 1.

3. Ibid.

4. Timothy White, "Hollywood's Attempt at Appropriating Television: The Case of Paramount Pictures," in *Hollywood in the Age of Television*, ed. Tino Balio (Boston: Unwin Hyman, 1990), 146.

5. Hilmes, *Hollywood and Broadcasting*.

6. Ibid., 50.

7. Testimony of Thomas Hutchinson, Reporter's Transcript of Proceedings, pp. 1361, 1388, 28 September 1951, NAR 13220-PH.

8. Reporter's Transcript of Proceedings, p. 480, 19 September 1951, NAR 13220-PH.

9. *Hearings on the Restrictive Practices of the American Federation of Musicians* (testimony of Frank E. Mullen, Executive Vice President, NBC), 263.

10. Tino Balio, "Introduction to Part I," in Balio, *Hollywood in the Age of Television*, 14–15.

11. James L. Baughman, *Same Time, Same Station: Creating American Television, 1948–1961* (Baltimore: Johns Hopkins University Press, 2007), 58–59.

12. Ibid., 60.

13. FCC, "Eighteenth Annual Report of the Federal Communications Commission for Fiscal Year Ended June 30, 1952," NACP, 107.

14. Testimony of Peter G. Levathes, Reporter's Transcript of Proceedings, p. 2224, 26 October 1955, NAR 14354-Y.

15. Reporter's Transcript of Proceedings, p. 80, 22 September 1955, NAR 14354-Y.

16. "Address by Wayne Coy, Chairman, Federal Communications Commission," p. 5, 25 September 1948, MSS 1446, folder 5, box 40, NATO.

17. "Television Outlook Is Bright," *Radio Age*, July 1949, 21–22.

18. "New Coaxial Cable Service Begins Today," *Radio Daily*, 1 September 1949, 1, 7.

19. FCC, "Sixteenth Annual Report of the Federal Communications Commission for Fiscal Year Ended June 30, 1950," NACP, 102–104.

20. "NBC Sets Saturday Nite Buildup: 3-Hour Program to Be Opened to 12 Sponsors," *Radio Daily*, 31 August 1949, 7.

21. Ibid.
22. "J. Walter Thompson Co.—Chicago—Television Department Report—Nov. 1955," folder "1953, Feb—1956, Sept," box 1, Dan Seymour Papers, JWTCA.
23. "Lack of Outlets Hurting Nets: Only One Station in 13 Cities on Cable," *Radio Daily*, 1 August 1949, 7.
24. "The Future of the Networks," *Television Magazine*, April 1950, 11.
25. FCC, "Eighteenth Annual Report," 109.
26. Affidavit of Wayne Tiss, pp. 3–4, 5 July 1951, NAR 13220-PH.
27. Excerpts from Minutes of Board of Directors of Republic—April 24, 1952, Reprinted in "Answers of the Defendant Republic Pictures Corporation (Hereinafter called 'Republic') to the Interrogatories Dated March 4, 1953 Propounded by the Plaintiff Herein," Schedule 5, pp. 1–2, 22 September 1953, NAR 14354-Y.
28. Testimony of Alexander Kenneth Beggs, Reporter's Transcript of Proceedings, vol. 14, p. 1456, 18 October 1955, NAR 14354-Y.
29. "Big 7 Gross $952 Million: Profits Are Cut 25 Pct. by Rising Prod. Costs," *Daily Variety*, 5 May 1948, 1.
30. Testimony of Alexander Kenneth Beggs, Reporter's Transcript of Proceedings, 1731–1732, 19 October 1955.
31. Testimony of Ned E. Depinet, Reporter's Transcript of Proceedings, p. 1831, 21 October 1955, NAR 14354-Y.
32. Ibid.
33. Reporter's Transcript of Proceedings, pp. 90–91, 22 September 1955, NAR 14354-Y.
34. Herbert J. Yates's Deposition, p. 20, 7 September 1951, NAR 13220-PH.
35. Ibid., 21.
36. Reporter's Transcript of Proceedings, p. 149, 11 March 1952, NAR 13596-BH.
37. Testimony of Peter G. Levathes, Reporter's Transcript of Proceedings, 2208.
38. Testimony of Ned E. Depinet, Reporter's Transcript of Proceedings, 1786–1787.
39. "Lasky Warns Pix to Get Close to Television," *Daily Variety*, 19 March 1948, 1.
40. "Plans for Pix-TV Alliance Reaffirmed by Johnston," *Radio Daily*, 15 September 1949, 7.
41. "Full-Time Aide," *Radio Daily*, 18 May 1949, 7.
42. Reporter's Transcript of Proceedings, pp. 90–91, 22 September 1955, NAR 14354-Y.
43. Reporter's Transcript of Proceedings, p. 3022, 31 October 1955, NAR 14354-Y.
44. Attorneys for Columbia Pictures, Screen Gems Inc., and RKO Radio Pictures, "Trial Memorandum for Columbia Pictures Corporation, Screen Gems, Inc. and RKO Radio Pictures, Inc.," pp. 7–8, 21 September 1955, NAR 14354-Y.
45. Gael Sullivan, letter to Ted R. Gamble, 30 March 1949, folder: Theatre Owners of America 6 to 599, box 1, DOJ NACP.
46. Ibid.
47. "Biography of Balabans," *Television Daily*, 15 June 1949, 6.
48. Office Communication from Alan Rhone to Grant Theis, Columbia Broadcasting System, Inc., 23 April 1951, folder "Columbia Broadcasting Co. 60-6-99 N-1 to N-16," box 8, DOJ NACP.
49. Wayne Coy, Chairman of the FCC, letter to Attorney General, 29 June 1948, folder 60-6-98, box 89, Department of Justice Class 60 Litigation Case Files, NACP; Reporter's Transcript of Proceedings, p. 2176, 26 October 1955, NAR 14354-Y.
50. Wayne Coy, Chairman of the FCC, letter to Attorney General.
51. Wayne Coy, letter to Gael Sullivan, 4 March 1949, folder: Theatre Owners of America 6 to 599, box 1, DOJ NACP.
52. Reporter's Transcript of Proceedings, p. 154, 11 March 1952, NAR 13596-BH.

53. Sidney N. Strotz, "Hollywood and Television," *Radio Age*, January 1944, 15.

54. Hilmes, *Hollywood and Broadcasting*, 143.

55. Balio, "Introduction to Part I," 17–18.

56. Alison Perlman, *Public Interests: Media Advocacy and Struggles over U.S. Television* (New Brunswick, NJ: Rutgers University Press, 2016), 4.

57. "Tele Topics," *Radio Daily*, 1 July 1949, 7.

58. Testimony of Jack L. Van Volkenburg, President of the Television Division of CBS, Reporter's Transcript of Proceedings, 585–586, NAR 14354-Y.

59. Baughman, "The Weakest Chain and the Strongest Link."

60. Hilmes, *Hollywood and Broadcasting*, 143.

61. "FCC Cuts Tele Time to 12 Hrs.: Minimum Will Be Stepped Up Every 6 Mos," *Daily Variety*, 7 May 1948, 6.

62. Balio, "Introduction to Part I," 30.

63. Testimony of Peter G. Levathes, Reporter's Transcript of Proceedings, 2225.

64. Reporter's Transcript of Proceedings, p. 174, 11 March 1952, NAR 13596-BH.

65. "3 Hail Hollywood's TV Future: Ad Club Briefed on New Phases of Industry Here," *Daily Variety*, 21 March 1950, 4.

66. "Tele-Type," *Daily Variety*, 10 May 1950, 8.

67. "Television: The Local Businessman's Most Powerful Sales Medium," *Television*, February 1950, 25.

68. "Double Features on TV," *Radio Daily*, 1 July 1949, 7.

69. "Old Pix Keep L.A. TV in Biz: 7 Stations Spend $1,000,000 for Films This Year," *Daily Variety*, 31 May 1950, 11.

70. Testimony of Milford Fenster, Reporter's Transcript of Proceedings, vol. 9, pp. 858–859, 6 October 1955, NAR 14354-Y.

71. "Hollywood Films Pay Off in High Ratings," *Television Magazine*, May 1950, 20.

72. Ibid.

73. Ibid.

74. Boddy, *Fifties Television*, 103–104.

75. Hilmes, *Only Connect*, 126.

76. Paul Alley, "Films for Television," *Radio Age*, October 1946, 24.

77. "Roach Makes Video Deal for 32 Pix," *Daily Variety*, 8 March 1948, 2.

78. "24 Korda Pix Sold for Tele," *Daily Variety*, 27 April 1948, 1, 6.

79. Ibid., 6.

80. "Rank, RCA Talk Tele Deal: 10 Year Pact for Pix Use Under Way," *Daily Variety*, 28 April 1948, 1, 8.

81. Unsigned letter to Mrs. Frank J. Lowell, 17 January 1950, folder "Columbia Broadcasting Co. 60-6-99 N-1 to N-16," box 8, DOJ NACP.

82. "CBS Begins Film Syndication; Affiliates to Get First Call," *Radio Daily*, 11 March 1949, 7.

83. Quoted in Baughman, *Same Time, Same Station*, 89.

84. Wayne Tiss's Testimony, Reporter's Transcript of Proceedings, p. 670, 20 September 1951, NAR 13220-PH.

85. "Pix Serials Given Boot by KTLA; Too Gruesome," *Daily Variety*, 12 May 1948, 8.

86. Unsigned letter to Mrs. Frank J. Lowell.

87. Quoted in "Tele Topics," *Radio Daily*, 7 February 1949, 7.

88. Thomas Doherty, *Hollywood's Censor: Joseph I. Breen & the Production Code Administration* (New York: Columbia University Press, 2007).

89. "Would Eliminate Pix If Censorship Upheld," *Radio Daily*, 11 May 1949, 7.

90. Deborah L. Jaramillo, *The Television Code: Regulating the Screen to Safeguard the Industry* (Austin: University of Texas Press, 2018), 1.
91. Reporter's Transcript of Proceedings, p. 323, 13 March 1952, NAR 13596-BH.
92. "Fine Grain Positive Urged for Movies," *Radio Daily*, 15 February 1949, 7.
93. Testimony of Jack L. Van Volkenburg, Reporter's Transcript of Proceedings, 590.
94. Testimony of Peter G. Levathes, Reporter's Transcript of Proceedings, 2209.
95. Ibid., 2218.
96. Ibid., 2219, 2223–2224.
97. Ibid., 2219–2220.
98. Ibid., 2221.
99. Spyros Skouras, letter to Arthur Lockwood, 27 October 1948, Reporter's Transcript of Proceedings, pp. 2148–2149, 26 October 1955, NAR 14354-Y.
100. Testimony of Spyros Skouras, Reporter's Transcript of Proceedings, 2121–2122, NAR 14354-Y.
101. Norman Moray to Jack L. Warner, 6 April 1948, *United States v. 20th Century-Fox, et al.*, box 12545A, Warner Brothers Legal Department Files, WBA.
102. Jack Warner, Western Union Telegram, 1 March 1948, U.S. v. 20th Century Fox et al., box 12545A, Records of the Warner Bros. Legal Department, WBA.
103. Testimony of Jack L. Warner, Reporter's Transcript of Proceedings, vol. 22, pp. 3006–3007, 31 October 1955, NAR 14354-Y.
104. Wayne Coy, "Address," 6.
105. Testimony of Abe Montague, Reporter's Transcript of Proceedings, vol. 21, pp. 2465–2466, 28 October 1955, NAR 14354-Y.
106. Reporter's Transcript of Proceedings, pp. 125–126, 22 September 1955, NAR 14354-Y.
107. Testimony of Ralph Morris Cohn, Reporter's Transcript of Proceedings, pp. 2381–2384, NAR 14354-Y.
108. Ibid., 2389–2390.
109. Reporter's Transcript of Proceedings, pp. 125–126, 22 September 1955, NAR 14354-Y.
110. Testimony of Ralph Morris Cohn, Reporter's Transcript of Proceedings, 2444–2445.
111. Ibid., 2438.
112. Ibid., 2384–2385.
113. John Ellis, *Visible Fictions* (London: Routledge and Kegan Paul, 1982).
114. Testimony of Ralph Morris Cohn, Reporter's Transcript of Proceedings, 2386–2387.
115. Boddy, *Fifties Television*, 81.
116. Quoted in Vance Kepley Jr., "From 'Frontal Lobes' to the 'Bob-and-Bob' Show: NBC Management and Programming Strategies, 1949–65," in *Hollywood in the Age of Television*, ed. Tino Balio (Boston: Unwin Hyman, 1990), 47.
117. Reporter's Transcript of Proceedings, pp. 125–126, 22 September 1955, NAR 14354-Y.
118. Testimony of Ralph Morris Cohn, Reporter's Transcript of Proceedings, 2389–2390, 2393.
119. Ibid., 2399–2401.
120. Ibid.
121. Ibid., 2484–2485.
122. Advertisement for Twentieth Century-Fox, *Daily Variety*, 11 May 1950, 6–7; Herbert J. Yates's Testimony, Reporter's Transcript of Proceedings, p. 2107, 9 October 1951, NAR 13220-PH.
123. Testimony of Spyros Skouras, Reporter's Transcript of Proceedings, 2112–2113.
124. Testimony of Ned E. Depinet, Reporter's Transcript of Proceedings, 1753–1754.
125. Ibid., 1767.

126. Ibid., 1829.

127. Speech by Spyros Skouras at TOA Convention, p. 6, 31 October 1950, folder 2, box 41, MSS 1446, NATO.

128. Ibid., 7–8.

129. "Green Light for COMPO," *Daily Variety*, 10 May 1950, 3.

130. Testimony of Ned E. Depinet, Reporter's Transcript of Proceedings, 1822.

131. Objections to COMPO Transcription of Defendants RKO Radio Pictures, Inc., Columbia Pictures Corporation and Screen Gems, Inc., 23 September 1955, NAR 14354-Y.

132. "COMPO Arming for Drive to Wholly Abolish Admish Tax," *Daily Variety*, 18 May 1950, 3.

133. "Appendix 'E' Remarks of Arthur Lockwood, president, Theatre Owners of America," p. 1, 30 August 1950, folder "Council of Motion Picture Organizations Inc (COMPO) U1 to U218," box 8, DOJ NACP.

134. Ibid., 2.

135. "Minutes of Special Meeting: Executive Board of Council of Motion Picture Organizations, Inc.," p. 25, 9 August 1950, folder "Council of Motion Picture Organizations Inc (COMPO) U1 to U218," box 8, DOJ NACP.

136. Ibid., 26–27.

137. Spyros Skouras telegram to Attendees of COMPO Meeting, p. 6, 26 July 1952, folder "Testimony of Ronald Reagan," box 11, DOJ NACP.

138. Thomas M. Pryor, "Roy Rogers Suing on Video Problem: Cowboy Star Wins Temporary Injunction against Republic on TV Use of Old Films," *New York Times*, 24 July 1951, 21.

139. Testimony of Benjamin B. Kahane, Reporter's Transcript of Proceedings, vol. 21, pp. 2595–2596, 28 October 1955, NAR 14354-Y.

140. Testimony of Ned E. Depinet, Reporter's Transcript of Proceedings, 1836–1838.

141. Testimony of Howard A. McDonnell, Reporter's Transcript of Proceedings, pp. 947–949, 7 October 1955, NAR 14354-Y.

142. Ronald Reagan speech to COMPO Meeting, p. 11, 26 July 1952, folder "Testimony of Ronald Reagan," box 11, DOJ NACP.

143. Testimony of Howard A. McDonnell, Reporter's Transcript of Proceedings, 947–949.

144. Ibid., 947–949.

145. Ronald Reagan speech to COMPO Meeting, 10–11.

146. Fred Schwartz speech to COMPO Meeting, p. 13, 26 July 1952, folder "Testimony of Ronald Reagan," box 11, DOJ NACP.

147. Ibid., 14.

148. Testimony of Howard A. McDonnell, Reporter's Transcript of Proceedings, 947–949.

149. Reporter's Transcript of Proceedings, pp. 973–974, 7 October 1955, NAR 14354-Y.

150. Ibid., 975–976.

151. Ibid.

152. Testimony of Benjamin B. Kahane, Reporter's Transcript of Proceedings, 2595–2596.

153. Reporter's Transcript of Proceedings, p. 970, 7 October 1955, NAR 14354-Y; and Amended Answer of Columbia Pictures Corporation to Plaintiff's Interrogatory No. 5, 29 July 1955, NAR 14354-Y.

154. Reporter's Transcript of Proceedings, pp. 976–977, 7 October 1955, NAR 14354-Y.

155. Richard B. Jewell, "RKO Film Grosses, 1929–1951: The C.J. Tevlin Ledger," *Historical Journal of Film, Radio & Television* 14, no. 1 (March 1994): 37–38.

156. Reporter's Transcript of Proceedings, pp. 968–969, 7 October 1955, NAR 14354-Y.

157. Testimony of Ned E. Depinet, Reporter's Transcript of Proceedings, 1836–1838.

158. Reporter's Transcript of Proceedings, pp. 954–955, 7 October 1955, NAR 14354-Y.
159. S. H. Fabian speech to COMPO Meeting, p. 23, 26 July 1952, folder "Testimony of Ronald Reagan," box 11, DOJ NACP.
160. Fred Schwartz speech to COMPO Meeting, 14.
161. Testimony of Howard A. McDonnell, Reporter's Transcript of Proceedings, 947–949.
162. Testimony of Ned E. Depinet, Reporter's Transcript of Proceedings, 1789.
163. Testimony of Ralph Morris Cohn, Reporter's Transcript of Proceedings, 2417.
164. Timothy R. White, "Life after Divorce: The Corporate Strategy of Paramount Pictures Corporation in the 1950s," *Film History* 2, no. 2 (1988): 112–113.
165. Arthur Levey, President of Skiatron Electronics & Television Corporation, letter to Barney Balaban, President of Paramount Pictures, p. 1, 19 December 1951, folder 60-6-98, box 89, DOJ NACP.
166. Levey, letter to Barney Balaban, 2; Arthur Levey, letter to Harry Warner, 19 December 1951, U.S. v. 20th Century Fox, et al., box 12545A, Warner Bros. Legal Department Files, WBA.
167. Fred Schwartz speech to COMPO Meeting, 15.
168. Barney Balaban, letter to Arthur Levey, President Skiatron Electronics & Television Corporation, 27 December 1951, folder 60-6-98, box 89, DOJ NACP.
169. Answers of Defendant RKO Radio Pictures, Inc. to Certain Interrogatories Propounded by Plaintiff, Pursuant to Stipulation of the Parties, pp. 4–5, 14 September 1953, NAR 14354-Y; and Answers by Columbia Pictures Corporation to Certain Interrogatories Propounded by Plaintiff, p. 5, 18 September 1953, NAR 14354-Y.
170. "TV's Time of Trouble," *Fortune*, August 1951, 79.
171. Cited in ibid.
172. Ibid.
173. Testimony of Ralph Morris Cohn, Reporter's Transcript of Proceedings, 2494–2495.
174. "TV's Time of Trouble," 79.
175. Ibid.
176. FCC, "Nineteenth Annual Report," NACP, 98.
177. Answers of Defendant RKO Radio Pictures, Inc., 4.
178. Testimony of Ralph Morris Cohn, Reporter's Transcript of Proceedings, 2460.
179. FCC, "Twenty First Annual Report," NACP, 98.
180. Ibid., 99.
181. Report of Mr. Alfred Starr before the Meeting of the Theatre Owners of America, p. 7, 6 October 1955, folder 2, box 43, MSS 1446, NATO.
182. Ibid.
183. William Lafferty, "Feature Films on Prime-Time Television," in *Hollywood in the Age of Television*, ed. Tino Balio (Boston: Unwin Hyman, 1990), 235.

CHAPTER 2 — EXHIBITION, AUDIENCES, AND MEDIA CONSUMPTION

1. Lynn Spigel, *Make Room for TV: Television and the Family Ideal in Postwar America* (Chicago: University of Chicago Press, 1992), 1.
2. Ibid., 106.
3. Gael Sullivan, letter to Theatre Owners of America members, 7 April 1950, folder: Theatre Owners of America 6 to 599, box 1, DOJ NACP.
4. "Exhib-Prod TV Showdown Due: Explosion Now Expected within Next 12 Months," *Daily Variety*, 14 February 1950, 5.
5. Hilmes, *Hollywood and Broadcasting*, 2.
6. Ibid., 42.

7. "The Reaction of Exhibitors to Television," p. 3, folder "M (2 of 4) Reaction of Exhibitors to TV," box 1, Department of Justice Class 60 Litigation Case Files, NACP.

8. Hilmes, *Hollywood and Broadcasting*, 42.

9. Janet Staiger, "Combination and Litigation: Structures of U.S. Film Distribution, 1896–1917," *Cinema Journal* 23 (Winter 1983), 61.

10. Hilmes, *Hollywood and Broadcasting*, 60.

11. Testimony of Alexander Kenneth Beggs, Reporter's Transcript of Proceedings, vol. 14, p. 1456, 18 October 1955, NAR 14354-Y.

12. Testimony of Ned E. Depinet, Reporter's Transcript of Proceedings, p. 1833, 21 October 1955, NAR 14354-Y.

13. Testimony of Spyros Skouras, Reporter's Transcript of Proceedings, pp. 2177–2178, 26 October 1955, NAR 14354-Y.

14. Mitchell Wolfson, Chairman TOA Television Committee, "Report of Theatre Owners of America Television Committee," p. 3, October 1950, folder 2, box 41, MSS 1446, NATO.

15. Porst, "The Preservation of Competition."

16. "Report of Theatre Owners of America National Convention," 6.

17. Arthur Ungar, "Keep Step or Fall Out," *Daily Variety*, 21 May 1948, 3.

18. Peter Lev, *Twentieth Century-Fox: The Zanuck-Skouras Years, 1935–1965* (Austin: University of Texas Press, 2013), 109, 162; Reporter's Transcript of Proceedings, pp. 75–76, 22 September 1955, NAR 14354-Y.

19. Attorneys for Columbia Pictures, Screen Gems Inc., and RKO Radio Pictures, "Trial Memorandum for Columbia Pictures Corporation, Screen Gems, Inc. and RKO Radio Pictures, Inc.," p. 7, 21 September 1955, NAR 14354-Y.

20. "Par Holds Off Video; More Value in Reissues, Says Prez Balaban," *Daily Variety*, 12 May 1948, 6.

21. Testimony of Jack L. Warner, Reporter's Transcript of Proceedings, vol. 22, p. 3008, 31 October 1955, NAR 14354-Y.

22. Testimony of Spyros Skouras, Reporter's Transcript of Proceedings, 2111–2112.

23. Ibid., 2113.

24. Ibid., 2114.

25. "TV's Time of Trouble," *Fortune*, August 1951, 132.

26. "Par Survey Finds Vid Hits Pix 20 to 30 Pct," *Daily Variety*, 15 February 1950, 1, 5.

27. "Yates Making U.S. Survey of Video Effect on B.O.," *Daily Variety*, 21 March 1950, 1.

28. "Don't Blame B.O. Blues on TV, Sez African Exhib," *Daily Variety*, 11 May 1950, 4.

29. Gael Sullivan, draft of TV speech for TOA meeting in Atlanta, 17 May 1950, folder: Theatre Owners of America 6 to 599, box 1, DOJ NACP.

30. Testimony of Alexander Kenneth Beggs, Reporter's Transcript of Proceedings, 1384.

31. Ibid., 1460–1461, 1464.

32. Reporter's Transcript of Proceedings, pp. 1461, 1464, 18 October 1955, NAR 14354-Y.

33. Lynn Spigel, *Welcome to the Dreamhouse: Popular Media and the Postwar Suburbs* (Durham, NC: Duke University Press, 2001).

34. Testimony of Alexander Kenneth Beggs, Reporter's Transcript of Proceedings, 1502–1503.

35. Ibid., 1504–1508, 1511.

36. Testimony of Peter G. Levathes, Reporter's Transcript of Proceedings, pp. 2275–2276, 26 October 1955, NAR 14354-Y.

37. "Address of Barney Balaban, President of Paramount Pictures, Inc. before the Annual Convention of Theatre Owners of America," p. 1, 25 September 1948, folder 5, box 40, MSS 1446, NATO.

38. Reporter's Transcript of Proceedings, p. 92, 22 September 1955, NAR 14354-Y.

39. Ibid., 2200–2201.
40. "Fite Pix Sales for Video; Exhibs in Protest to TOA," *Daily Variety*, 29 April 1948, 1, 10.
41. Frederic H. Sturdy's Testimony, Reporter's Transcript of Proceedings, p. 2193, 10 October 1951, NAR 13220-PH.
42. "24 Korda Pix Sold for Tele," *Daily Variety*, 27 April 1948.
43. Hilmes, *Hollywood and Broadcasting*, 43.
44. "Ban on Film Sales for Video Urged," *Daily Variety*, 5 May 1948, 8.
45. Ibid., 8.
46. Wayne Coy, "Address to the Theater Owners of America," Drake Hotel, Chicago, IL, 25 September 1948, U.S. v. 20th Century Fox et al., box no. 12545A, Records of the Warner Bros. Legal Department, WBA.
47. Ibid.
48. Ibid.
49. Ibid.
50. Arthur H. Lockwood, letter to Herbert Yates, President, Republic Pictures Corp, 7 October 1948, Schedule 2 of the "Answers of the Defendant Republic Pictures Corporation to the Interrogatories Dated March 4, 1953 Propounded by the Plaintiff Herein," filed 22 Sept. 1953, NAR 14354-Y.
51. Spyros Skouras, letter to Arthur Lockwood, 27 October 1948, NAR 14354-Y.
52. Theatre Owners of America Special Bulletin, pp. 2–3, 12 November 1948, folder 60-6-99, box 1, Department of Justice Class 60 Litigation Case Files, NACP.
53. Porst, "The Preservation of Competition."
54. Testimony of Peter G. Levathes, Reporter's Transcript of Proceedings, 2227.
55. Gael Sullivan, draft of TV speech for TOA meeting in Atlanta.
56. Arthur H. Lockwood, letter to Ben Strosier, Capitol Theatre, 26 May 1949, folder: Theatre Owners of America 6 to 599, box 1, DOJ NACP.
57. Theatre Owners of America Special Bulletin, vol. 4, no. 19, 25 April 1949, folder 3, box 1, DOJ NACP.
58. Ibid.
59. Mitchell Wolfson, letter to Charles E. Lewis, 20 April 1949, folder: Theatre Owners of America 6 to 599, box 1, DOJ NACP.
60. "The Reaction of Exhibitors to Television," 6.
61. Dave Wallerstein, letter to Stanley W. Prenosil, Theatre Owners of America, 15 November 1949, folder: Theatre Owners of America 6 to 599, box 1, DOJ NACP.
62. Stanley Prenosil, letter to the Director of Publicity-Television Department, ABC, 25 March 1949, folder: Theatre Owners of America 6 to 599, box 1, DOJ NACP.
63. Harry Vinnicof, letter to Gael Sullivan, 17 May 1949, folder: Theatre Owners of America 6 to 599, box 1, DOJ NACP.
64. Hilmes, *Hollywood and Broadcasting*, 56.
65. Bob Rains, letter to Duke Wales, 7 September 1950, AMPTP file 617, "Television," Special Collections, Margaret Herrick Library, Los Angeles, CA.
66. Bonwick, President Pictorial Pictures, letter to Arel, Inc., p. 17, 3 June 1949, cited in "Restrictions Imposed by the Conspiracy," folder: Enclosure File 60-6-99 Serial No. 7, box 1, DOJ NACP.
67. Herbert J. Yates's Testimony, Reporter's Transcript of Proceedings, p. 2093, 9 October 1951, NAR 13220-PH.
68. "The Reaction of Exhibitors to Television," 17.
69. Ibid., 17–20.
70. Ibid., 17–20.

71. Ibid., 21.

72. Walter Reade Jr., letter to Herbert J. Yates, 11 May 1953, folder: Theatre Owners of America 6 to 599, box 1, DOJ NACP.

73. Robert V. Newman's Testimony, Reporter's Transcript of Proceedings, p. 2016, 5 October 1951, NAR 13220-PH.

74. Herbert J. Yates's Testimony, Reporter's Transcript of Proceedings, 2090–2091.

75. Ibid., 2092.

76. Ibid., 2093.

77. "TOA Pressing B.O. Tax Cut," *Daily Variety*, 10 January 1950, 5.

78. Baughman, "The Weakest Chain and the Strongest Link."

79. Paul Lazarus Jr., letter to Myron Blank, quoted in "Theatre Owners of America Special Bulletin," p. 5, 27 April 1949, folder: Theatre Owners of America 6 to 599, box 1, DOJ NACP.

80. Testimony of Abe Montague, Reporter's Transcript of Proceedings, vol. 21, p. 2466, 28 October 1955, NAR 14354-Y.

81. Gladys Penrod, letter to Nate Blumberg, 15 January 1952, folder: Theatre Owners of America 6 to 599, box 1, DOJ NACP; Reporter's Transcript of Proceedings, p. 33, 22 September 1955, NAR 14354-Y.

82. Reporter's Transcript of Proceedings, pp. 35–37, 22 September 1955, NAR 14354-Y.

83. "Allied Praises Hollywood for Withholding Product from TV," *Daily Variety*, 25 May 1950, 3.

84. "Report of Theatre Owners of America National Convention," p. 2, 24–25 September 1948, folder 5, box 40, MSS 1446, NATO.

85. Wayne Coy, "Address," 3.

86. Gael Sullivan, letter to James Coston, 13 May 1949, folder: Theatre Owners of America 6 to 599, box 1, DOJ NACP.

87. Ibid.

88. Wolfson, "Report of Theatre Owners of America Television Committee," 1, 5.

89. Mitchell Wolfson, letter to A. M. Zarem, Stanford Research Institute, 21 April 1949, folder: Theatre Owners of America 6 to 599, box 1, DOJ NACP; Mitchell Wolfson, letter to Charles E. Lewis, 20 April 1949, folder: Theatre Owners of America 6 to 599, box 1, DOJ NACP.

90. Wolfson, "Report of Theatre Owners of America Television Committee," 5.

91. Suggested Agenda for TOA Television Committee Meeting, 4 May 1949, folder: Theatre Owners of America 6 to 599, box 1, DOJ NACP.

92. Wolfson, "Report of Theatre Owners of America Television Committee," 3.

93. Ibid., 3017.

94. S. H. Fabian speech to COMPO Meeting, p. 24, 26 July 1952, folder "Testimony of Ronald Reagan," box 11, DOJ NACP.

95. Brad Chisolm, "Red, Blue, and Lots of Green: The Impact of Color Television on Feature Film Production," in *Hollywood in the Age of Television*, ed. Tino Balio (Boston: Unwin Hyman, 1990), 213–215.

96. Testimony of Alexander Kenneth Beggs, Reporter's Transcript of Proceedings, 1570–1571.

97. Testimony of Ralph Morris Cohn, Reporter's Transcript of Proceedings, 2427.

98. Testimony of Alexander Kenneth Beggs, Reporter's Transcript of Proceedings, 1570–1571.

99. Chisolm, "Red, Blue, and Lots of Green," 225.

100. Testimony of Jack L. Warner, Reporter's Transcript of Proceedings, 3013.

101. Testimony of Ralph Morris Cohn, Reporter's Transcript of Proceedings, 2428.

102. Testimony of Benjamin B. Kahane, Reporter's Transcript of Proceedings, 2559.

103. Testimony of Ned E. Depinet, Reporter's Transcript of Proceedings, 1755–1757.

104. John Belton, "Glorious Technicolor, Breathtaking CinemaScope, and Stereophonic Sound," in *Hollywood in the Age of Television*, ed. Tino Balio (Boston: Unwin Hyman, 1990), 187.

105. Testimony of Spyros Skouras, Reporter's Transcript of Proceedings, 2168.

106. "The Reaction of Exhibitors to Television," 16.

107. Spyros Skouras, letter to Robert A. Weil, Executive Secretary of the Independent Theatre Owners of Ohio, 15 May 1953, Reporter's Transcript of Proceedings, p. 2171, 26 October 1955, NAR 14354-Y.

108. Testimony of Spyros Skouras, Reporter's Transcript of Proceedings, 2166–2167.

109. Ibid., 2166–2167.

110. White, "Hollywood's Attempt at Appropriating Television," 149.

111. Gael Sullivan, draft of TV speech for TOA meeting in Atlanta.

112. Quoted in White, "Life after Divorce," 111.

113. "Testimony of Spyros Skouras to an FCC hearing in 1948," Reporter's Transcript of Proceedings, pp. 2183–2184, 26 October 1955, NAR 14354-Y.

114. "NBC Calls Meeting of 31 Affiliates on Television," *Daily Variety*, March 8, 1948, 8.

115. Memorandum of Messrs. Halpern and O'Brien to Gael Sullivan on TOA Requirements for Theatre Television, 1 March 1950, folder: Theatre Owners of America 6 to 599, box 1, DOJ NACP.

116. Ibid.

117. "Memorandum of Meeting of MPAA concerning Theatre Television on Friday, April 14, 1950," p. 40, folder: Theatre Owners of America 6 to 599, box 1, DOJ NACP.

118. Ibid.

119. Richard Krolik, letter to Nathan L. Halpern, TOA, 8 May 1950, folder: Theatre Owners of America 6 to 599, box 1, DOJ NACP.

120. Gael Sullivan to Theatre Owners of America members, 7 April 1950.

121. Memorandum of Messrs. Halpern and O'Brien to Gael Sullivan on TOA Requirements for Theatre Television.

122. Speech by Spyros Skouras at TOA Convention, p. 5, 31 October 1950, folder 2, box 41, MSS 1446, NATO.

123. Testimony of Ralph Morris Cohn, Reporter's Transcript of Proceedings, 2436.

124. Balio, "Introduction to Part I," 22.

125. Marcus Cohn to S. H. Fabian, Fabian Theatres, 26 March 1952, folder: Theatre Owners of America 6 to 599, box 1, DOJ NACP.

126. Balio, "Introduction to Part I," 22.

127. FCC, "Nineteenth Annual Report of the Federal Communications Commission for Fiscal Year Ended June 30, 1953," NACP, 34–35.

128. Ibid.

129. Testimony of Spyros Skouras, Reporter's Transcript of Proceedings, 2182–2183.

130. White, "Hollywood's Attempt at Appropriating Television," 155.

131. Testimony of Ralph Morris Cohn, Reporter's Transcript of Proceedings, pp. 2482–2483, Vol. 21, 28 October 1955, NAR 14354-Y.

132. "20th Salesmen Get Bonus for Booking Oldies," *Daily Variety*, 15 February 1950, 5.

133. "Lloyd Refuses a Quarter Million from Video for 70 Old Pictures," *Daily Variety*, 23 February 1950, 1, 5.

134. Testimony of Alexander Kenneth Beggs, Reporter's Transcript of Proceedings, 1558.

135. Reporter's Transcript of Proceedings, pp. 87–89, 22 September 1955, NAR 14354-Y.

136. Testimony of Alexander Kenneth Beggs, Reporter's Transcript of Proceedings, 1559–1560.

137. Testimony of Ned E. Depinet, Reporter's Transcript of Proceedings, 1778–1779.

138. Ibid., 1779–1780.

139. Reporter's Transcript of Proceedings, pp. 133–136, 22 September 1955, NAR 14354-Y.

140. Testimony of Ned E. Depinet, Reporter's Transcript of Proceedings, 1781–1782.

141. Testimony of Spyros Skouras, Reporter's Transcript of Proceedings, 2106–2107.

142. Testimony of Peter G. Levathes, Reporter's Transcript of Proceedings, 2228–2229.

143. Ibid., 2362.

144. Testimony of Ralph Morris Cohn, Reporter's Transcript of Proceedings, 2431, 2488.

145. Ibid., 2431, 2488.

146. Testimony of Alexander Kenneth Beggs, Reporter's Transcript of Proceedings, 1689.

147. Ibid., 1568.

148. Testimony of Spyros Skouras, Reporter's Transcript of Proceedings, 2111–2112.

149. Testimony of Jack L. Warner, Reporter's Transcript of Proceedings, 3009–3010.

150. Ibid., 3016–3017.

151. James McQuivey, *Digital Disruption: Unleashing the Next Wave of Innovation* (Cambridge, MA: Forrester Research, Inc., 2013), 8.

152. Christensen, *Innovator's Dilemma*, xv.

153. Deron Overpeck, "Splitsville: Independent Exhibitors Court Federal Intervention in the American Film Industry, 1975–1988," in *Film History* 26, no. 1 (2014): 137.

154. William Boddy, "Redefining the Home Screen: Technological Convergence as Trauma and Business Plan," in *Rethinking Media Change: The Aesthetics of Transition*, ed. David Thorburn and Henry Jenkins (Cambridge, MA: MIT Press, 2004), 191.

CHAPTER 3 — CONTRACTS, RIGHTS, RESIDUALS, AND LABOR

1. Catherine L. Fisk, *Writing for Hire: Unions, Hollywood, and Madison Avenue* (Cambridge, MA: Harvard University Press, 2016), 9.

2. Ibid., 14.

3. Argument of Herman F. Selvin, Reporter's Transcript of Proceedings, p. 2424, 16 October 1951, NAR 13220-PH.

4. Affidavit of Earl R. Collins, pp. 2–3, 2 July 1951, NAR 13220-PH.

5. Meyer H. Lavenstein's Testimony, Reporter's Transcript of Proceedings, p. 1547, 2 October 1951, NAR 13220-PH.

6. Laurence M. Weinberg, Inter-Office Memorandum to Republic's Contract Department, 18 November 1954, vol. 1, folder R-1, drawer 25B, MSS 2389, JMR.

7. Memo from the Republic Contract Department to Gordon T. Kay, 9 March 1955, vol. 1, folder R-1, drawer 25B, MSS 2389, JMR.

8. Testimony of Creighton J. Tevlin, Reporter's Transcript of Proceedings, vol. 18, pp. 2048–2050, 25 October 1955, NAR 14354-Y.

9. Ibid.

10. Answers of Defendant RKO Radio Pictures, Inc., to Certain Interrogatories Propounded by Plaintiff, Pursuant to Stipulation of the Parties, pp. 11–15, 14 September 1953, NAR 14354-Y.

11. Testimony of Creighton J. Tevlin, Reporter's Transcript of Proceedings, 2050.

12. Attorneys for Columbia Pictures, Screen Gems, Inc., and RKO Radio Pictures, "Trial Memorandum for Columbia Pictures Corporation, Screen Gems, Inc. and RKO Radio Pictures, Inc.," p. 9, 21 September 1955, NAR 14354-Y.

13. Testimony of Ralph Morris Cohn, Reporter's Transcript of Proceedings, vol. 21, pp. 2442–2443, 28 October 1955, NAR 14354-Y.

14. Ibid., 2429.

15. Ibid., 2430.

16. Reporter's Transcript of Proceedings, p. 1201, 12 October 1955, NAR 14354-Y.

17. Reporter's Transcript of Proceedings, p. 135, 22 September 1955, NAR 14354-Y.

18. Testimony of Creighton J. Tevlin, Reporter's Transcript of Proceedings, 2046–2047.

19. Reporter's Transcript of Proceedings, p. 2451, 28 October 1955, NAR 14354-Y.

20. Reporter's Transcript of Proceedings, pp. 133–134, 28 October 1955, NAR 14354-Y.

21. "Screen Producers Guild Sets Up Shop, Officers and By-Laws," *Daily Variety*, 3 May 1950, 3.

22. Unsigned letter to Mrs. Frank J. Lowell, 17 January 1950, folder "Columbia Broadcasting Co. 60-6-99 N-1 to N-16," box 8, DOJ NACP.

23. Saul N. Rittenberg, Inter-Office Memorandum to Republic Productions, Inc. Contract Department, p. 1, 24 March 1955, vol. 1, folder R-1, drawer 25B, JMR.

24. Ibid.

25. Reporter's Transcript of Proceedings, pp. 133–134, 28 October 1955, NAR 14354-Y.

26. "High-Lights of the Convention," *International Musician*, July 1949, 7.

27. Miranda Banks, *The Writers: A History of American Screen Writers and Their Guild* (New Brunswick, NJ: Rutgers University Press, 2015), 186–187.

28. Ronald Reagan and Richard G. Hubler, *Where's the Rest of Me?* (New York: Duell, Sloan and Pearce, 1965), 221.

29. Ibid., 222.

30. Ibid., 227.

31. Ibid., 229–230.

32. Screen Actors' Guild press release, 20 June 1950, AMPTP file 617, "Television," Special Collections, Margaret Herrick Library, Los Angeles, CA.

33. Reagan and Hubler, *Where's the Rest of Me?*, 230.

34. Screen Actors' Guild press release.

35. Minutes of meeting of the MPAA Radio and Television Subcommittee, 15 September 1947, Reporter's Transcript of Proceedings, vol. 19, pp. 2089–2090, 26 October 1955, NAR 14354-Y.

36. Ibid.

37. *Rooney*, 538 F. Supp. at 211, as cited in Scott L. Whiteleather, "Rebels with a Cause: Artists' Struggles to Escape a Place Where Everybody Owns Your Name," *Loyola of Los Angeles Entertainment Law Review* 21, no. 2 (2001): 3.

38. Hilmes, *Hollywood and Broadcasting*, 55.

39. "Actress Sues to Bar Use of Her Film by Television," *Daily Variety*, 23 April 1948, 3.

40. "Pact Talks Opened by Actors," *Daily Variety*, 12 March 1948.

41. Reagan and Hubler, *Where's the Rest of Me?*, 276.

42. "SAG Breaks Off Parley; Actors Strike Threat," *Daily Variety*, 12 April 1948, 1, 8.

43. "SAG Prods Clash on Tele," *Daily Variety*, 17 March 1948, 1, 9.

44. Ibid.

45. "Hollywood Inside," *Daily Variety*, 18 March 1948, 2.

46. Testimony of Benjamin B. Kahane, Reporter's Transcript of Proceedings, vol. 21, pp. 2566–2567, 28 October 1955, NAR 14354-Y.

47. Reagan and Hubler, *Where's the Rest of Me?*, 198.

48. Testimony of Benjamin B. Kahane, Reporter's Transcript of Proceedings, 2566–2567.

49. Ronald Reagan Speech at COMPO Meeting, p. 1, 25 July 1951, folder "Testimony of Ronald Reagan," box 11, DOJ NACP.

50. Hollywood AFL Film Council Press Release, 26 May 1954, folder "January 1953–December 1955," SAGA.

51. *Intelligence Report*, 25 November 1953, folder "January 1953–December 1955," SAGA.

52. Loan-out Agreement between Columbia and Universal, 11 May 1953, NAR 14354-Y.

53. Attorneys for Columbia Pictures, Screen Gems Inc., and RKO Radio Pictures, "Trial Memorandum," 6.

54. Darryl Zanuck to Spyros Skouras, telegram summary, 4 January 1951, *"United States v. Twentieth Century-Fox Film Corporation, et al.*, Digest of Documents, 16mm B," UCLA.

55. Attorneys for Columbia Pictures, Screen Gems Inc., and RKO Radio Pictures, "Trial Memorandum," 11.

56. Fisk, *Writing for Hire*, 145.

57. Ibid., 147.

58. Ibid., 155.

59. Ibid., 156–157.

60. Ibid., 158.

61. "Directors Meet Prods on Pact," *Daily Variety*, 12 May 1948, 4.

62. *Hearings on the Investigation of James C. Petrillo, the American Federation of Musicians, et al, Vol. 1, Before the Special Subcommittee of the Committee on Education and Labor*, 80th Cong., 1st Sess. (1947), 370, 568.

63. Ibid., 178.

64. Ibid., 200; "Petrillo, Nets Sign Peace; Music Okayed for Televish," *Daily Variety*, 19 March 1948, 1.

65. *Hearings on the Investigation of James C. Petrillo* (testimony of Ed Fishman), 139.

66. *Hearings on the Restrictive Practices of the American Federation of Musicians* (testimony of Justin Miller, President of the National Association of Broadcasters), 3.

67. *Hearings on the Investigation of James C. Petrillo* (Allen Weiss, Chairman of the Board of Directors of the Mutual Broadcasting System and vice president and general manager of the Don Lee Broadcasting System), 543–544.

68. *Hearings on the Restrictive Practices of the American Federation of Musicians* (testimony of J. N. "Bill" Bailey, Executive Director of the FM Association), 81.

69. *Hearings on the Restrictive Practices of the American Federation of Musicians* (testimony of James C. Petrillo), 377.

70. *Hearings on the Investigation of James C. Petrillo* (testimony of Burton A. Zorn, special labor-relations counsel for the majors during their negotiations with the AFM in 1946), 506.

71. Robert V. Newman's Testimony, Reporter's Transcript of Proceedings, p. 2016, 5 October 1951, NAR 13220-PH.

72. James C. Petrillo, "International Executive Board Consummates Agreement with Eight Major Motion Picture Producers," *International Musician*, August 1946, 7.

73. Ibid. The language used here is substantially the same as the language in the agreement itself. Agreement between the American Federation of Musicians and Republic Productions, Inc., p. 6, 1 April 1946, NAR 13220-PH; Agreement between the American Federation of Musicians and Republic Productions, Inc., p. 4, 1 September 1948, NAR 13220-PH.

74. *Hearings on the Investigation of James C. Petrillo* (testimony of Burton A. Zorn, special labor-relations counsel for the majors during their negotiations with the AFM in 1946), 506–507.

75. *Hearings on the Investigation of James C. Petrillo* (testimony of Charles Boren, Vice President of the Motion Picture Producers Association), 472–473.

76. *Hearings on the Investigation of James C. Petrillo* (testimony of Burton A. Zorn, special labor-relations counsel for the majors during their negotiations with the AFM in 1946), 504–505.

77. Ibid., 507.

78. Samuel Flatow memo to Victor H. Kramer, Chief of the General Litigation Section, "American Federation of Musicians," pp. 1, 29, 10 September 1956, folder 60-6-98, box 89, DOJ NACP.

79. "Petrillo Okay on Films for Tele Due in 10 Days," *Daily Variety*, 5 May 1948, 1, 8.

80. Flatow, "American Federation of Musicians," 1.

81. *Hearings on the Investigation of James C. Petrillo* (testimony of Charles Boren, Vice President of the Motion Picture Producers Association), 459.

82. *Hearings on the Investigation of James C. Petrillo* (testimony of Isaac Chadwick, President of the Independent Motion Picture Producers and Distributors Association), 497.

83. Ibid., 498.

84. *Hearings on the Investigation of James C. Petrillo* (testimony of Anthony J. O'Rourke, Chairman, Labor Advisory Committee, Society of Independent Motion-Picture Producers), 482.

85. *Hearings on the Investigation of James C. Petrillo* (testimony of C. L. Bagley, Vice President of the AFM), 463–464.

86. *Hearings on the Investigation of James C. Petrillo* (testimony of James C. Petrillo), 190, 198.

87. Ibid., 189–190.

88. *Hearings on the Restrictive Practices of the American Federation of Musicians* (testimony of James C. Petrillo), 389.

89. *Hearings on the Investigation of James C. Petrillo* (testimony of Burton A. Zorn, special labor-relations counsel for the majors during their negotiations with the AFM in 1946), 506–507.

90. Robert V. Newman's Deposition, pp. 52–54, 56, 28 August 1951, NAR 13220-PH.

91. *Hearings on the Investigation of James C. Petrillo* (statements of Carroll D. Kearns, Chairman of the Subcommittee), 479.

92. Victor A. Altman, Office Memorandum to Richard K. Decker, "American Federation of Musicians—Labor Contract Provision Prohibiting Use of Film Sound Track on Television," p. 11, 26 October 1951, folder 60-6-98, box 89, Department of Justice Class 60 Litigation Case Files, NACP.

93. *Hearings on the Investigation of James C. Petrillo* (statements of Irving G. McCann, General Counsel to the Committee on Education and Labor), 488–489.

94. *Hearings on the Investigation of James C. Petrillo* (testimony of Joseph A. Padway), 336.

95. *Hearings on the Restrictive Practices of the American Federation of Musicians* (statement of Hon. Fred A. Hartley, Chairman, Committee on Education and Labor), 1.

96. *Hearings on the Investigation of James C. Petrillo* (statements of Carroll D. Kearns, Chairman of the Subcommittee), 177.

97. *Hearings on the Restrictive Practices of the American Federation of Musicians* (statement of Hon. Fred A. Hartley, Chairman, Committee on Education and Labor), 351–352.

98. *Hearings on the Restrictive Practices of the American Federation of Musicians* (Findings of Fact), 573.

99. *Hearings on the Investigation of James C. Petrillo* (statements of Irving G. McCann, General Counsel to the Committee on Education and Labor), 459.

100. *Hearings on the Restrictive Practices of the American Federation of Musicians* (testimony of J. R. Poppele, President, Television Broadcasters Association, Director of the Mutual Network, and Vice President, Chief Engineer, and Secretary of the Bamberger Broadcasting Service), 165.

101. James C. Petrillo, "James C. Petrillo, President of the American Federation of Musicians of the United States and Canada, Explains Why Members of the American Federation of Musicians Have Not Been Making Recordings since January 1, 1948," *International Musician*, February 1948, 9.

102. James C. Petrillo, "Why Members of the American Federation of Musicians Are Not Working for Television and Frequency Modulation Radio," *International Musician*, April 1946, 1.

103. Milton Diamond, "Petrillo's Case: New Light on an Age-Old Problem—Man vs. Machine," *International Musician*, March 1948, 7.

104. *Hearings on the Investigation of James C. Petrillo*, 189.

105. Petrillo, "James C. Petrillo, President," 3.

106. *Hearings on the Restrictive Practices of the American Federation of Musicians* (testimony of J. R. Poppele, President, Television Broadcasters Association, Director of the Mutual Network, and Vice President, Chief Engineer, and Secretary of the Bamberger Broadcasting Service), 165.

107. *Hearings on the Investigation of James C. Petrillo* (Allen Weiss, Chairman of the Board of Directors of the Mutual Broadcasting System and Vice President and General Manager of the Don Lee Broadcasting System), 543.

108. *Hearings on the Restrictive Practices of the American Federation of Musicians* (testimony of Frank E. Mullen, Executive Vice President, NBC), 264.

109. Murray Forman, *One Night on TV Is Worth Weeks at the Paramount: Popular Music on Early Television* (Durham, NC: Duke University Press, 2012), 41.

110. "Federation Reaches Fiftieth Milestone," *International Musician*, February 1946, 13.

111. *Hearings on the Restrictive Practices of the American Federation of Musicians*, 212–214.

112. "Official Proceedings of the Fifty-Third Annual Convention of the American Federation of Musicians, Fourth Day," *International Musician*, December 1950, 17.

113. "High-Lights of the Convention," 10.

114. Samuel R. Rosenbaum, letter to James C. Petrillo, "Administration of Recording Fund," *International Musician*, July 1949, 11.

115. Ibid.

116. Hilmes, *Hollywood and Broadcasting*, 158.

117. "From the President's Office," *International Musician*, April 1951, 6.

118. "Music by Outlook," *International Musician*, February 1951, 8.

119. "The Fifty-Fourth Annual Convention," *International Musician*, July 1951, 6.

120. "Official Proceedings of the Fifty-Fifth Convention of the American Federation of Musicians. Third Day," *International Musician*, September 1952, 11.

121. James C. Petrillo, "Dim Future for Musicians in TV," *International Musician*, August 1952, 10.

122. James L. McDevitt, Director, Labor's League for Political Education, "Progress Report from Labor's League," *International Musician*, September 1952, 11.

123. "Minutes of the Mid-winter Meeting of the International Executive Board, American Federation of Musicians," *International Musician*, February 1952, 6.

124. Testimony of Benjamin B. Kahane, Reporter's Transcript of Proceedings, 2573.

125. Supplementary Affidavit of Zachary J. Rottman, pp. 3–4, 6 July 1951, NAR 13220-PH; Testimony of Howard A. McDonnell, Reporter's Transcript of Proceedings, pp. 954–955, 7 October 1955, NAR 14354-Y.

126. James M. McGrath, Acting Chief of the Los Angeles Office, Interoffice Memorandum to George B. Haddock, Chief of the Trial Section, "American Federation of Musicians," pp. 1–2, 23 June 1953, folder 60-6-98, box 89, Department of Justice Class 60 Litigation Case Files, NACP; Television Film Labor Agreement between the American Federation of Musicians and Republic Productions, Inc., p. 3, 14 May 1951, NAR 13220-PH.

127. Morton Scott's Testimony, Reporter's Transcript of Proceedings, p. 1209, 27 September 1951, NAR 13220-PH.

128. Ibid., 1142.

129. Herbert J. Yates's Deposition, pp. 81–83, 7 September 1951, NAR 13220-PH.

130. Television Film Labor Agreement, 3.

131. Testimony of Benjamin B. Kahane, Reporter's Transcript of Proceedings, 2563, 2565.

132. Testimony of Howard A. McDonnell, Reporter's Transcript of Proceedings, 952.

133. Testimony of Benjamin B. Kahane, Reporter's Transcript of Proceedings, 2573.

134. Ibid., 2570–2571.

135. "Minutes of Special Meeting of the International Executive Board of the American Federation of Musicians," International Musician, April 1953, 22.

136. Ibid.

137. "Motion Picture Agreement," International Musician, March 1954, 6.

138. "Special Meeting of the International Executive Board of the American Federation of Musicians. New York, NY. February 15–19, 1954," International Musician, May 1954, 32.

139. Ibid.

140. Testimony of Benjamin B. Kahane, Reporter's Transcript of Proceedings, 2565–2566.

141. Petrillo, "Man, Machine, Music and Musicians," International Musician, June 1955, 10.

142. Petrillo, "The Musician's Fight," International Musician, October 1955, 31.

143. Arthur J. Goldberg, Attorney and Counselor, "Following Is a Report and Recommendations of Referee Arthur J. Goldberg Who Was Appointed by President Petrillo at the Direction of the International Executive Board to Hear the Charges of President te Groen and Financial Secretary G. R. Hennon of Local 47, Los Angeles, Calif., against Certain Members of That Local," International Musician, May 1956, 12.

144. "Minutes of the Mid-Winter Meeting," International Musician, March 1956, 11.

145. Ibid., 12.

146. Goldberg, "Following Is a Report and Recommendations," 12, 45.

147. Don Tatum's Testimony, Reporter's Transcript of Proceedings, pp. 1694–1695, 3 October 1951; NAR 13220-PH.

148. Testimony of Creighton J. Tevlin, Reporter's Transcript of Proceedings, 2046.

149. Reporter's Transcript of Proceedings, pp. 2584–2585, 28 October 1955, NAR 14354-Y.

150. Testimony of Creighton J. Tevlin, Reporter's Transcript of Proceedings, 2044–2045.

151. Reporter's Transcript of Proceedings, pp. 133–134, 28 October 1955, NAR 14354-Y.

152. Testimony of Creighton J. Tevlin, Reporter's Transcript of Proceedings, 2038–2039, 2048.

153. Testimony of Benjamin B. Kahane, Reporter's Transcript of Proceedings, 2579.

154. Ibid., 2569.

155. H. A. McDonell, Inter-Office Memorandum to Zack Rottman, 14 May 1953, vol. 1, folder R-1, drawer 25B, MSS 2389, JMR.

156. "Proposed Changes of SEG Agreement," 2 October 1953, folder "January 1953-December 1955," SAGA.

157. Fisk, Writing for Hire, 161.

158. Quoted in Fisk, *Writing for Hire*, 137.

159. Mark Deuze, "Work in the Media," in *Media Industries: Perspectives on an Evolving Field*, ed. Amelia Arsenault and Alisa Perren (Austin, TX: Media Industries Editorial Board, 2016), 13.

CHAPTER 4 — ROY ROGERS, GENE AUTRY, AND THE INTERVENTION OF THE COURTS

1. Gaines, *Contested Culture*, 4.

2. Ibid., 239.

3. Michael Kackman, "Nothing on but Hoppy Badges: *Hopalong Cassidy*, William Boyd Enterprises, and Emergent Media Globalization," *Cinema Journal* 47, no. 4 (Summer 2008): 77; "66 'Hopalongs' for Television Serials," *Daily Variety*, 21 May 1948, 1.

4. Baughman, *Same Time, Same Station*, 11.

5. "Old Pix Keep L.A. TV in Biz: 7 Stations Spend $1,000,000 for Films This Year," *Daily Variety*, 31 May 1950, 11.

6. Roy Rogers's Testimony, Reporter's Transcript of Proceedings, p. 723, 21 September 1951, NAR 13220-PH; Kackman, "Nothing on but Hoppy Badges," 79.

7. Reporter's Transcript of Proceedings, p. 725, 21 September 1951, NAR 13220-PH.

8. Quoted in Kackman, "Nothing on but Hoppy Badges," 81.

9. "Moppet Viewers Rout 'Hoppy' at Oklahoma Dept. Store," *Radio Daily*, 25 August 1949, 135.

10. Christine Becker, *It's the Pictures That Got Small: Hollywood Film Stars on 1950s Television* (Middletown, CT: Wesleyan University Press, 2008), 7–8.

11. "Hopalongs' Getting $Million a Year from Television," *Daily Variety*, 26 January 1950, 1, 10.

12. "TV Trove in Them Thar Oaters: Pre-1946 Saddle-Sagas Gilt-Edge Studio Shelves," *Daily Variety*, 27 April 1950, 1.

13. Ibid., 11.

14. "Focus," *Television Magazine*, September 1950, 5.

15. Gaines, *Contested Culture*, 171–174.

16. William Arthur Rush's Testimony, Reporter's Transcript of Proceedings, p. 1001, 26 September 1951, NAR 13220-PH.

17. William Arthur Rush, letter to Herbert Yates, Republic, 20 January 1950, quoted in Reporter's Transcript of Proceedings, p. 1069, 26 September 1951, NAR 13220-PH.

18. Herbert J. Yates's Testimony, Reporter's Transcript of Proceedings, pp. 2087–2089, 9 October 1951, NAR 13220-PH.

19. Ibid.

20. Memorandum from Harry L. Gershon to Bob Newman, Re. Republic adv. Rogers, 18 August 1951, folder P-1, drawer 25, MSS 2389, Jack Mathis Collection (Legal Battles—Suits . . .), L. Tom Perry Special Collections, Harold B. Lee Library, Brigham Young University, Provo, UT.

21. William Arthur Rush's Testimony, Reporter's Transcript of Proceedings, 973–974.

22. Roy Rogers's Testimony, Reporter's Transcript of Proceedings, 756–757.

23. William Arthur Rush's Testimony, Reporter's Transcript of Proceedings, 954.

24. Balio, "Introduction to Part I," 4; Richard M. Hurst, *Republic Studios: Between Poverty Row and the Majors* (Lanham, MD: Scarecrow Press, 2007).

25. Maureen Rogers, "Remaking the B Film in 1940s Hollywood: Producers Releasing Corporation and the Poverty Row Programmer," *Film History: An International Journal* 29, no. 2 (2017): 138–164.

26. Ibid., 956–957.

27. Arthur Rush's Deposition, pp. 113–114, 6 September 1951, NAR 13220-PH.

28. Herbert J. Yates's Deposition, p. 75, 7 September 1951, NAR 13220-PH.

29. "Million Vid Tag on Autrys: Rep Turns Down 750G for 50 Pix," *Daily Variety*, 21 February 1950, 1.

30. Reporter's Transcript of Proceedings, p. 393, 13 March 1952, NAR 13596-BH.

31. Ibid., 393–394.

32. "Autry Sells Half Interest in KOWL in Santa Monica," *Radio Daily*, 20 September 1949, 1, 5.

33. "Gene Autry No Longer Seeks to Buy KTSA," *Radio Daily*, 25 May 1949, 1.

34. Frederic H. Sturdy's Testimony, Reporter's Transcript of Proceedings, p. 2221, 10 October 1951, NAR 13220-PH.

35. Ibid.

36. William Arthur Rush's Testimony, Reporter's Transcript of Proceedings, 959.

37. Frederic H. Sturdy's Testimony, Reporter's Transcript of Proceedings, 2221.

38. Robert V. Newman's Testimony, Reporter's Transcript of Proceedings, pp. 1996–1997, 5 October 1951, NAR 13220-PH.

39. Morton Scott's Testimony, Reporter's Transcript of Proceedings, pp. 1132, 1136, 1148, 27 September 1951, NAR 13220-PH.

40. Ibid., 1135, 1150.

41. Reporter's Transcript of Proceedings, p. 844, 21 September 1951, NAR 13220-PH.

42. Morton Scott's Testimony, Reporter's Transcript of Proceedings, 1185–1186.

43. Ibid.

44. Robert V. Newman's Testimony, Reporter's Transcript of Proceedings, 1998; Herbert J. Yates's Testimony, Reporter's Transcript of Proceedings, 2098–2099.

45. Herbert J. Yates's Testimony, Reporter's Transcript of Proceedings, 2098–2099.

46. Ibid.

47. Robert V. Newman's Testimony, Reporter's Transcript of Proceedings, 1999–2000.

48. Herbert J. Yates's Testimony, Reporter's Transcript of Proceedings, 2098–2099.

49. Fred Schwartz speech to COMPO Meeting, p. 17, 26 July 1952, folder "Testimony of Ronald Reagan," box 11, DOJ NACP.

50. Ronald Reagan speech to COMPO Meeting, p. 48, 26 July 1952, folder "Testimony of Ronald Reagan," box 11, DOJ NACP.

51. Arthur Marquette's Deposition, Reporter's Transcript of Proceedings, p. 1415, 28 September 1951, NAR 13220-PH.

52. Arthur Rush's Deposition, p. 63, 6 September 1951, NAR 13220-PH.

53. William Arthur Rush's Testimony, Reporter's Transcript of Proceedings, 808.

54. Arthur Marquette's Deposition, Reporter's Transcript of Proceedings, 1430.

55. Arthur Rush's Deposition, 132–134.

56. Ibid.

57. Herbert J. Yates's Testimony, Reporter's Transcript of Proceedings, 2100.

58. Arthur Marquette's Deposition, Reporter's Transcript of Proceedings, 1406.

59. Herbert J. Yates's Deposition, 66.

60. Herbert J. Yates's Testimony, Reporter's Transcript of Proceedings, 2101.

61. Ibid., 2103.

62. William Arthur Rush's Testimony, Reporter's Transcript of Proceedings, 808.

63. Roy Rogers's Testimony, Reporter's Transcript of Proceedings, 119–123.

64. Arthur Marquette's Deposition, Reporter's Transcript of Proceedings, 1395–1396.

65. Ibid.

66. William Arthur Rush's Testimony, Reporter's Transcript of Proceedings, 1076, 1078.
67. Arthur William Rush's Testimony, Reporter's Transcript of Proceedings, p. 1836, 4 October 1951, NAR 13220-PH.
68. Walter Frank Craig's Testimony, Reporter's Transcript of Proceedings, p. 2338, 11 October 1951, NAR 13220-PH.
69. Roy Rogers's Testimony, Reporter's Transcript of Proceedings, 746–747.
70. Walter Frank Craig's Testimony, Reporter's Transcript of Proceedings, 2329.
71. Arthur William Rush's Testimony, Reporter's Transcript of Proceedings, 1843–1845.
72. Earl R. Collins, Pres. Hollywood Television Service, Inc., letter to J. J. Van Nostrand Jr., Vice Pres. Tel. Dir. Sullivan, Stauffer, Colwell & Bales, Inc., p. 8, 8 June 1951, NAR 13220-PH; also Roy Rogers's Testimony, Reporter's Transcript of Proceedings, 126–129; Affidavit of Morton Scott, p. 1, 2 July 1951, NAR 13220-PH; and Herbert J. Yates's Testimony, Reporter's Transcript of Proceedings, 2108.
73. Frederic H. Sturdy's Testimony, Reporter's Transcript of Proceedings, 2222.
74. Morton Scott's Testimony, Reporter's Transcript of Proceedings, 1155–1157.
75. Ibid., 1193; and Affidavit of Morton Scott, 2–3.
76. Reporter's Transcript of Proceedings, pp. 151–152, 11 March 1952, NAR 13596-BH.
77. Morton Scott's Testimony, Reporter's Transcript of Proceedings, 1158, 1160, 1162, 1167, 1174, 1176.
78. Excerpts from Minutes of Board of Directors of Republic—June 21, 1951, Reprinted in "Answers of the Defendant Republic Pictures Corporation (Hereinafter called 'Republic') to the Interrogatories Dated March 4, 1953 Propounded by the Plaintiff Herein," Schedule 5, p. 1, 22 September 1953, NAR 14354-Y.
79. Motion for Issuance of Temporary Restraining Order, pp. 1–2, 23 June 1951, NAR 13220-PH.
80. Preliminary Injunction, p. 3, 24 July 1951, NAR 13220-PH.
81. Affidavit of Herbert J. Yates, pp. 3–4, 2 July 1951, NAR 13220-PH.
82. Ibid.
83. Affidavit of Wayne Tiss, pp. 3–4, 5 July 1951, NAR 13220-PH.
84. Morton Scott's Testimony, Reporter's Transcript of Proceedings, 1199.
85. Affidavit of Herbert J. Yates, 3–4.
86. Herbert J. Yates's Deposition, 76–78.
87. William Arthur Rush's Testimony, Reporter's Transcript of Proceedings, 1082–1084.
88. Ibid., 1091.
89. Morton Scott's Testimony, Reporter's Transcript of Proceedings, 1218; Herbert J. Yates's Testimony, Reporter's Transcript of Proceedings, 2108.
90. Morton Scott's Testimony, Reporter's Transcript of Proceedings, 1219–1221, 1223.
91. Ibid., 1226–1227.
92. Ibid., 1228–1229, 1183.
93. Ibid., 1145, 1165–1166, 1213–1214.
94. Reporter's Transcript of Proceedings, pp. 223, 434, 18 September 1951, NAR 13220-PH.
95. Molly Selvin, "The Loeb Firm and the Origins of Entertainment Law Practice in Los Angeles, 1908–1940," California Legal History 10 (2015): 135–173.
96. Roy Rogers's Testimony, Reporter's Transcript of Proceedings, 434.
97. Opening statements of Herman F. Selvin, Reporter's Transcript of Proceedings, p. 18, 13 September 1951, NAR 13220-PH.
98. Opening statements of Frederic H. Sturdy, Reporter's Transcript of Proceedings, p. 10, 13 September 1951, NAR 13220-PH.
99. Roy Rogers's Testimony, Reporter's Transcript of Proceedings, 166–167.

100. Argument of Herman F. Selvin, Reporter's Transcript of Proceedings, p. 2425, 16 October 1951, NAR 13220-PH.

101. Roy Rogers's Testimony, Reporter's Transcript of Proceedings, 353.

102. Emily Carman and Philip Drake, "Doing the Deal: Talent Contracts in Hollywood," in *Hollywood and the Law*, ed. Paul McDonald et al. (London: BFI Palgrave, 2015), 211–212.

103. Robert V. Newman's Testimony, Reporter's Transcript of Proceedings, 2053.

104. Saul N. Rittenberg's Testimony, Reporter's Transcript of Proceedings, p. 1962, 5 October 1951, NAR 13220-PH.

105. Roy Rogers's Testimony, Reporter's Transcript of Proceedings, 266.

106. Ibid., 342.

107. Ibid., 331–332.

108. Ibid., 267–268.

109. Reporter's Transcript of Proceedings, p. 2542, 17 October 1951, NAR 13220-PH.

110. Ibid., 1890.

111. Gaines, *Contested Culture*, 161–165.

112. Argument of Frederic H. Sturdy, Reporter's Transcript of Proceedings, p. 2370, 16 October 1951, NAR 13220-PH.

113. Reporter's Transcript of Proceedings, p. 1888, 4 October 1951, NAR 13220-PH.

114. Roy Rogers's Testimony, Reporter's Transcript of Proceedings, 361–362.

115. Opening statements of Frederic H. Sturdy, Reporter's Transcript of Proceedings, 11–12.

116. Reporter's Transcript of Proceedings, pp. 423–424, 13 March 1952, NAR 13596-BH.

117. Roy Rogers's Testimony, Reporter's Transcript of Proceedings, 430.

118. Ibid., 458.

119. Opening statements of Frederic H. Sturdy, Reporter's Transcript of Proceedings, 14.

120. Roy Rogers's Testimony, Reporter's Transcript of Proceedings, 273–274.

121. Gaines, *Contested Culture*, 161.

122. Opening statements of Frederic H. Sturdy, Reporter's Transcript of Proceedings, 14.

123. Balio, "Introduction to Part I," 4; Hurst, *Republic Studios*.

124. Opening statements of Frederic H. Sturdy, Reporter's Transcript of Proceedings, 15.

125. Affidavit of W. Arthur Rush, p. 2, 5 July 1951, NAR 13220-PH.

126. Opening statements of Frederic H. Sturdy, Reporter's Transcript of Proceedings, 15.

127. Ibid., 15–16.

128. Wayne Tiss's Testimony, Reporter's Transcript of Proceedings, p. 526, 20 September 1951, NAR 13220-PH.

129. Herbert J. Yates's Deposition, 74; William R. Golden's Testimony, Reporter's Transcript of Proceedings, p. 1510, 2 October 1951, NAR 13220-PH.

130. Opening statements of Herman F. Selvin, Reporter's Transcript of Proceedings, 23.

131. Roy Rogers's Testimony, Reporter's Transcript of Proceedings, 46.

132. Ibid., 48–49.

133. Kristin J. Lieb, *Gender, Branding, and the Modern Music Industry* (New York: Routledge, 2013), 16.

134. Barry King, "Articulating Stardom," *Screen* 26, no. 5 (September–October 1985): 27–50.

135. Roy Rogers's Testimony, Reporter's Transcript of Proceedings, 155.

136. Ibid., 144.

137. Avi Santo, *Selling the Silver Bullet: The Lone Ranger and Transmedia Brand Licensing* (Austin: University of Texas Press, 2015), 83.

138. Wayne Tiss's Testimony, Reporter's Transcript of Proceedings, 510, 522.

139. Wayne Tiss's Affidavit, Reporter's Transcript of Proceedings, pp. 1427–1428, 28 September 1951, NAR 13220-PH.

140. Roy Rogers's Testimony, Reporter's Transcript of Proceedings, 142–143.

141. Reporter's Transcript of Proceedings, p. 30, 13 September 1951, NAR 13220-PH.

142. Roy Rogers's Testimony, Reporter's Transcript of Proceedings, 324.

143. Arthur William Rush's Testimony, Reporter's Transcript of Proceedings, 1823.

144. William Arthur Rush's Testimony, Reporter's Transcript of Proceedings, 881.

145. Roy Rogers's Testimony, Reporter's Transcript of Proceedings, 296.

146. William Arthur Rush's Testimony, Reporter's Transcript of Proceedings, 915.

147. Roy Rogers's Testimony, Reporter's Transcript of Proceedings, 320.

148. Judge Peirson M. Hall's Memorandum Opinion, Reporter's Transcript of Proceedings, p. 2580, 18 October 1951, NAR 13220-PH.

149. Reporter's Transcript of Proceedings, p. 24, 13 September 1951, NAR 13220-PH.

150. Reporter's Transcript of Proceedings, p. 2, 18 October 1951, NAR 13220-PH; Roy Rogers v. Republic Production, Inc. and Hollywood Television Service, folder P-1, drawer 25, MSS 2389, Jack Mathis Collection (Legal Battles—Suits . . .), L. Tom Perry Special Collections, Harold B. Lee Library, Brigham Young University, Provo, UT.

151. Ibid., 8.

152. Ibid., 8–9.

153. Ibid., 9.

154. Gaines, *Contested Culture*, 14.

155. Harry L. Gershon, Attorney from Loeb and Loeb, "Notice of Appeal," 25 February 1952, NAR 13220-PH.

156. Judgment for Defendants, 14 January 1952, Roy Rogers vs. Republic Productions, Inc. et al., folder P-1, drawer 25, MSS 2389, Jack Mathis Collection (Legal Battles—Suits . . .), L. Tom Perry Special Collections, Harold B. Lee Library, Brigham Young University, Provo, UT.

157. Excerpts from Minutes of Board of Directors of Republic—October 25, 1951, Reprinted in "Answers of the Defendant Republic Pictures Corporation (Hereinafter called 'Republic') to the Interrogatories Dated March 4, 1953 Propounded by the Plaintiff Herein," Schedule 5, pp. 1–2, 22 September 1953, NAR 14354-Y.

158. Larry Weinberg, Republic Productions Inter-Office Memorandum to Gordon T. Kay, 4 March 1952, folder R-1, drawer 25B, MSS 2389, JMR.

159. "Answer," p. 4, 5 November 1951, NAR 13596-BH.

160. "Complaint for Unfair Competition, for Declaratory Relief, and for Injunction," 30 October 1951, Gene Autry vs. Republic Productions, Inc., Hollywood Television Service, Inc., et al., folder "13595 13596," box 260, Records of the District Court of the United States for the Southern District of California, Central Division, 1938–1961, Civil Case Files 13590–13596, National Archives, Pacific Region, Perris, CA, 12 November 2010.

161. Reporter's Transcript of Proceedings, p. 1, 11 March 1952, NAR 13596-BH.

162. Ibid., 467–468.

163. Ibid., 4.

164. Ibid., 5.

165. "Answer," pp. 3, 7, Gene Autry vs. Republic Productions, Inc., Hollywood Television Service, Inc., et al.

166. Reporter's Transcript of Proceedings, p. 35, 11 March 1952, NAR 13596-BH.

167. Ibid., 14.

168. Gene Autry's Testimony, Reporter's Transcript of Proceedings, p. 35, 11 March 1952, NAR 13596-BH.
169. Reporter's Transcript of Proceedings, p. 464, 13 March 1952, NAR 13596-BH.
170. Gene Autry's Testimony, Reporter's Transcript of Proceedings, 71.
171. Reporter's Transcript of Proceedings, p. 41, 11 March 1952, NAR 13596-BH.
172. Ibid., 83.
173. Ibid., 82.
174. Autry v. Republic Productions, Inc. et al., No. 13522, United States Court of Appeals, Ninth Circuit, 213 F.2d 667, 1954 U.S. App. LEXIS 3561, 101 U.S.P.Q. (BNA) 478, 4 June 1954.
175. Ibid.
176. Reporter's Transcript of Proceedings, pp. 339–340, 13 March 1952, NAR 13596-BH.
177. Ibid., 341.
178. Ibid., 217, 221–222.
179. Ibid., 285–287.
180. "Autry Gets OK on Ariz. Station Buy," *Daily Variety*, 9 April 1948, 3.
181. "CBS Plans Video Pic Deal with Gene Autry," *Daily Variety*, 26 May 1948, 14.
182. Opinion, p. 6, 13 May 1952, Gene Autry v. Republic Production, Inc. et al., folder P-1, drawer 25, MSS 2389, Jack Mathis Collection (Legal Battles—Suits . . .), L. Tom Perry Special Collections, Harold B. Lee Library, Brigham Young University, Provo, UT.
183. Thomas M. Pryor, "TV-Movie Tie-Ins Remain Confused: Conflicting Decisions by Two Jurists on Coast Make New Problem on Issue," *New York Times*, 15 May 1952, 39.
184. Opinion, p. 12, 13 May 1952, Gene Autry v. Republic Production, Inc. et al.
185. Ibid.
186. Laura Wittern-Keller, "Controlling Content: Government Censorship, the Production Code and the Ratings System," in *Hollywood and the Law*, ed. Paul McDonald, Emily Carman, Eric Hoyt, and Philip Drake (London: BFI Palgrave, 2015), 130–153.
187. "Appellant's Opening Brief," p. 3, 17 April 1953, Gene Autry vs. Republic Productions, Inc., Hollywood Television Service, et al., United States Court of Appeals for the Ninth Circuit, No. 13522, Gene Autry Collection, Autry National Center of the American West, Los Angeles, CA.
188. Thomas M. Pryor, "Roy Rogers Tests TV Deal for Films," *New York Times*, 15 September 1951. 7.
189. Harry L. Gershon, Memo of Conversation with Don Fedderson, 23 August 1951, folder P-1, drawer 25, MSS 2389, Jack Mathis Collection (Legal Battles—Suits . . .), Tom Perry Special Collections, Harold B. Lee Library, Brigham Young University, Provo, UT.
190. Pryor, "Roy Rogers Tests TV Deal for Films."
191. Thomas M. Pryor, "Hollywood Edict: Ruling on Use of Autry, Rogers Films May Set Pattern—of Best Sellers," *New York Times*, 13 June 1954. X5.
192. Thomas M. Pryor, "Roy Rogers Suing on Video Problem: Cowboy Star Wins Temporary Injunction against Republic on TV Use of Old Films," *New York Times*, 24 July 1951, 21.
193. "Roy Rogers Ruling Bars Film Sale to TV," *New York Times*, 19 October 1951, 24.
194. Reporter's Transcript of Proceedings, p. 8, 18 October 1951, Roy Rogers v. Republic Production, Inc. and Hollywood Television Service, folder P-1, drawer 25, MSS 2389, Jack Mathis Collection (Legal Battles—Suits . . .), L. Tom Perry Special Collections, Harold B. Lee Library, Brigham Young University, Provo, UT.
195. Opinion of Judge Bone, 4 June 1954, Republic Pictures Corp. et al. v. Rogers, No. 13314, United States Court of Appeals, Ninth Circuit, 213 F.2d 662, 1954 U.S. App. Lexis 4737, 101 U.S.P.Q. (BNA) 475.

196. Ibid.

197. Supreme Court Decision, p. 1, 29 November 1954, NAR 13220-PH.

198. Statements of Harry L. Gershon, Esq., Reporter's Transcript of Proceedings, pp. 13–14, 13 December 1954, NAR 13220-PH.

199. Further Answers of Defendants Republic Pictures Corporation to the Interrogatories Dated March 4, 1953 Propounded by the Plaintiff Herein, 28 December 1953, NAR 14354-Y.

200. Order of Judge Peirson M. Hall, p. 1, 23 December 1954, NAR 13220-PH.

201. Republic Pictures Corporation et al., Appellants, v. Roy Rogers, Appellee, 222 F.2d 950, United States Court of Appeals Ninth Circuit, San Francisco, 19 May 1955, Reporter's Transcript of Proceedings, pp. 2–3, 1 August 1955, NAR 13220-PH.

202. Pryor, "TV-Movie Tie-Ins Remain Confused."

203. Opinion, p. 12, 13 May 1952, Gene Autry v. Republic Production, Inc. et al.

204. Pryor, "Hollywood Edict."

205. Autry v. Republic Productions, Inc. et al., No. 13522, United States Court of Appeals, Ninth Circuit, 213 F.2d 667, 1954 U.S. App. LEXIS 3561, 101 U.S.P.Q. (BNA) 478, 4 June 1954.

206. Opinion of Judge Bone, 4 June 1954, Autry v. Republic Productions, Inc. et al., No. 13522, United States Court of Appeals, Ninth Circuit, 213 F.2d 667, 1954 U.S. App. LEXIS 3561, 101 U.S.P.Q. (BNA) 478.

207. Peter Decherney, *Hollywood's Copyright Wars: From Edison to the Internet* (New York: Columbia University Press, 2012), 121–122.

208. Pryor, "Hollywood Edict."

209. Gaines, *Contested Culture*, 164–171.

210. Decherney, *Hollywood's Copyright Wars*, 116–122.

211. Pryor, "Hollywood Edict."

CHAPTER 5 — ANTITRUST, MARKET DOMINANCE, AND EMERGING MEDIA

1. Currah, "Hollywood versus the Internet," 440.

2. Testimony of Benjamin Kalmenson, Reporter's Transcript of Proceedings, p. 3031, 31 October 1955, NAR 14354-Y.

3. Meyer H. Lavenstein's Testimony, Reporter's Transcript of Proceedings, p. 1549, 2 October 1951, NAR 13220-PH.

4. Michael Conant, *Antitrust in the Motion Picture Industry: Economic and Legal Analysis* (Los Angeles: University of California Press, 1960).

5. Augustus N. Hand, "Opinion," United States v. Paramount Pictures, Inc., et al., United States District Court for the Southern District of New York, 66 F. Supp. 323, 11 June 1946.

6. Porst, "The Preservation of Competition."

7. Tino Balio, *Grand Design: Hollywood as a Modern Business Enterprise, 1930–1939*, History of the American Cinema, ed. Charles Harpole, vol. 5 (Berkeley: University of California Press, 1993).

8. "TOA Legal Eagles Brief Exhibs on Court Decision," *Daily Variety*, 10 March 1948, 9.

9. Reporter's Transcript of Proceedings, p. 162, 11 March 1952, NAR 13596-BH.

10. "Supreme Court Decision: Divorcement Delayed; Competitive Bids Out; Divestiture Sent Back with 'Get Tough' Order," *Daily Variety*, 4 May 1948, 1, 12.

11. "Indies Hail High Court for 'Breaking Backbone of Trust,'" *Daily Variety*, 5 May 1948, 3.

12. *West's Encyclopedia of American Law*, 2nd ed. (Detroit: Gale Group, 2004).

13. "Zenith Seeks Phonevision Trial: Ask FCC Approval for Three-Month Chicago Run," *Radio Daily*, 5 August 1949, 7.

14. "Phonevision Gets OK for Paid Tests," *Daily Variety*, 10 February 1950, 1.

15. "DeMille Sees Pix, Vid Joining; Phonevision Claims Test Films," *Daily Variety*, 14 March 1950, 3.

16. Ibid.

17. Ibid.

18. Memorandum of Messrs. Halpern and O'Brien to Gael Sullivan on TOA Requirements for Theatre Television, 1 March 1950, folder: Theatre Owners of America 6 to 599, box 1, DOJ NACP.

19. Herbert A. Ferguson, Assistant Attorney General, letter to Warner Bros. Pictures, Inc., 1 June 1950, U.S. v. 20th Century Fox et al., box no. 12545A; Records of the Warner Bros. Legal Department, WBA.

20. "Film Firms Roughed Up at FCC Sesh," *Daily Variety*, 25 April 1950, 1, 6.

21. Reporter's Transcript of Proceedings, p. 2153, 26 October 1955, NAR 14354-Y.

22. "20th Test: S. Skouras Tells Plan; Scoffs at Phonevision," *Daily Variety*, 25 April 1950, 3.

23. Richard Krolik, letter to Nathan L. Halpern, TOA, 8 May 1950, folder: Theatre Owners of America 6 to 599, box 1, DOJ NACP.

24. T. R. Gilliam, letter to Spyros Skouras, April 1950, Reporter's Transcript of Proceedings, pp. 2154–2155, 26 October 1955, NAR 14354-Y.

25. Reporter's Transcript of Proceedings, pp. 2155–2156, 26 October 1955, NAR 14354-Y.

26. "20th Test: S. Skouras Tells Plan; Scoffs at Phonevision."

27. Spyros Skouras, letter to E. F. McDonald, 8 May 1950, Quoted in Digest of Defendants Rebuttal Documents—Films, Inc. (Continued), p. 65, folder: Enclosure File 60-6-99 Serial No. 7, box 1, DOJ NACP.

28. "The Reaction of Exhibitors to Television," pp. 23–24, folder "M (2 of 4) Reaction of Exhibitors to TV," box 1, Department of Justice Class 60 Litigation Case Files, NACP.

29. Summary of a letter from Walter Reade Jr. to Spyros Skouras, 26 May 1952, "United States v. Twentieth Century Fox Film Corporation, et al. Digest of Documents; 16mm B," box FX-LR-1377, USA v. Twentieth 16mm TV Suit, 8216-A, UCLA.

30. "The Reaction of Exhibitors to Television," 23.

31. Dave Wallerstein, letter to Marcus Cohn, 9 December 1949, folder: Theatre Owners of America 6 to 599, box 1, DOJ NACP.

32. Answer of Defendant Universal Pictures Company, Inc. to Plaintiff's Interrogatories, vol. 1, p. 18, 4 March 1953, NAR 14354-Y.

33. "Phonevision Postpones Test: Chi Unveiling Is Blocked, Majors Refuse Product," *Daily Variety*, 26 May 1950, 7.

34. "The Reaction of Exhibitors to Television," 26.

35. Mitchell Wolfson, Chairman TOA Television Committee, "Report of Theatre Owners of America Television Committee," p. 1, October 1950, folder 2, box 41, MSS 1446, NATO.

36. Ferguson, letter to Warner Bros. Pictures, Inc.

37. For more information on the Sherman Antitrust Act and its relationship to Hollywood, see Porst, "The Preservation of Competition."

38. George B. Haddock, Interoffice Memorandum to Worth Rowley, Chief, Trial Section of the DOJ, "American Federation of Musicians," p. 3, 16 June 1954, folder 60-6-98, box 89, Department of Justice Class 60 Litigation Case Files, NACP.

39. Ibid., 4.

40. James M. McGrath, Office Memorandum to William C. Dixon, Chief of the DOJ's Southern California Office, "American Federation of Musicians," p. 1, 25 July 1951, folder 60-6-98, box 89, Department of Justice Class 60 Litigation Case Files, NACP.

41. William C. Dixon, Chief of the DOJ's Southern California Office, Office Memorandum to Honorable H. G. Morison, Assistant Attorney General, "American Federation of Musicians," p. 1, 31 July 1951, folder 60-6-98, box 89, Department of Justice Class 60 Litigation Case Files, NACP.

42. Richard K. Decker, Acting Chief of the Trial Section of the DOJ, Office Memorandum to George B. Haddock, Acting Second Assistant Attorney General, 13 November 1951, folder 60-6-98, box 89, Department of Justice Class 60 Litigation Case Files, NACP.

43. George B. Haddock, Office Memorandum to Richard K. Decker, Acting Chief of the Trial Section of the DOJ, 14 December 1951, folder 60-6-98, box 89, Department of Justice Class 60 Litigation Case Files, NACP.

44. William C. Dixon, Chief of the DOJ's Southern California Office, Office Memorandum to George B. Haddock, Chief of the DOJ's Trial Section, p. 1, 22 December 1952, folder 60-6-98, box 89, Department of Justice Class 60 Litigation Case Files, NACP.

45. George B. Haddock, Chief of the Trial Section, Memorandum to William C. Dixon, Chief of the Los Angeles Office of the DOJ, "American Federation of Musicians— Labor Contract Provision Relating to Use of Film Sound Track on Television," p. 1, 16 February 1953, folder 60-6-98, box 89, Department of Justice Class 60 Litigation Case Files, NACP; Haddock, Interoffice Memorandum to Worth Rowley, 1; and James M. McGrath, Acting Chief of the Los Angeles Office, Interoffice Memorandum to Worth Rowley, Chief of the Trial Section, "American Federation of Musicians," 17 June 1954, folder 60-6-98, box 89, Department of Justice Class 60 Litigation Case Files, NACP.

46. Haddock, Interoffice Memorandum to Worth Rowley, 4.

47. James M. McGrath, Interoffice Memorandum to Victor H. Kramer, "American Federation of Musicians," p. 5, 21 September 1956, folder 60-6-98, box 89, Department of Justice Class 60 Litigation Case Files, NACP.

48. Ferguson, letter to Warner Bros. Pictures, Inc.

49. Ray Engle Jr., Manager, Strand Theatre, letter to Justice Department, 28 July 1952, folder "60-6-99 Section 2," box 89, DOJ Class 60 Litigation Case Files, NACP.

50. Samuel Flatow, "Pre-trial Memorandum for the United States," 15 September 1955, NAR 14354-Y; Statement of Samuel Flatow, Special Assistant to the Attorney General, Reporter's Transcript of Proceedings, 22 September 1955, NAR 14354-Y.

51. Paul Wormser (Regional Archives Director, National Archives and Records Administration, Pacific Region. Laguna Niguel, CA) in discussion with the author, May 2009.

52. Flatow, "Pre-trial Memorandum for the United States," 5.

53. Testimony of Harrison F. Houghton (Economist with Antitrust Division of U.S. Department of Justice), p. 1310, Reporter's Transcript of Proceedings, vol. 13, 13 October 1955, NAR 14354-Y.

54. Ibid., 1315.

55. Testimony of Charles Weintraub, President of Quality Films, Reporter's Transcript of Proceedings, vol. 14, pp. 838–840, 6 October 1955, NAR 14354-Y.

56. William C. Dixon, Special Assistant to the Attorney General, "Complaint," 22 July 1952, vol. 1, NAR 14354-Y.

57. Testimony of Ned E. Depinet, Reporter's Transcript of Proceedings, pp. 1757–1758, 21 October 1955, NAR 14354-Y.

58. Testimony of Peter G. Levathes, Reporter's Transcript of Proceedings, pp. 2255–2256, 26 October 1955, NAR 14354-Y.

59. Ibid., 2257.
60. Testimony of Sidney Kramer, Reporter's Transcript of Proceedings, vol. 17, p. 1851, 21 October 1955, NAR 14354-Y.
61. Testimony of Bernard Lowenthal, Reporter's Transcript of Proceedings, vol. 7, p. 599, 4 October 1955, NAR 14354-Y.
62. Department of Justice Press Release, 22 July 1952, AMPTP File 617, "Television," Special Collections, Margaret Herrick Library, Los Angeles.
63. Flatow, "Pre-trial Memorandum for the United States," 1.
64. Ibid., 4.
65. Department of Justice Press Release, 22 July 1952.
66. Statement of Issues, Department of Justice, 11 October 1954, NAR 14354-Y.
67. Dixon, "Complaint," 9.
68. Statement of Issues.
69. Dixon, "Complaint," 11.
70. Ibid., 10–11.
71. Editorial, *Los Angeles Examiner*, 18 August 1952, AMPTP file 617, "Television," Special Collections, Margaret Herrick Library, Los Angeles.
72. John Dales Jr., Executive Secretary of the Screen Actors Guild, letter to George Meany, Secretary-Treasurer of the American Federation of Labor, 29 August 1952, SAGA.
73. Screen Actors Guild Press Release, 23 September 1952, SAGA.
74. Ibid.
75. Los Angeles City Council Resolution, 18 August 1952, AMPTP file 617, "Television," Special Collections, Margaret Herrick Library, Los Angeles, CA.
76. "U.S. Sues to Release Newer Movies for TV," *Los Angeles Times*, 23 July 1952.
77. Meredith Parker, letter to Samuel Schneider, Warner Brothers, 24 October 1950, U.S. v. 20th Century Fox, et al., box no. 12545A, Records of the Warner Bros. Legal Department, WBA.
78. Ray Engle Jr., Manager, Strand Theatre, letter to Justice Department.
79. J. C. Mohrstadt, letter to James McGranery, Attorney General, 28 July 1952, folder "60-6-99 Section 2," box 89, DOJ Class 60 Litigation Case Files, NACP.
80. Frank Lesmeister, letter to James McGranery, 28 July 1952, folder "60-6-99 Section 2," box 89, DOJ Class 60 Litigation Case Files, NACP.
81. Resolution of the Southern California Theatre Owners Association, 23 September 1952, AMPTP file 617, "Television," Special Collections, Margaret Herrick Library, Los Angeles, CA.
82. Ibid.
83. Ibid.
84. Ibid.
85. Trueman Rembusch, letter to James P. McGranery, U.S. Attorney General, 1 August 1952, folder "60-6-99 Section 4," box 90, DOJ Class 60 Litigation Files, NACP.
86. Memo to George H. Schueller re. Conference on 16 Millimeter Film—United States v. Twentieth Century-Fox Film Corp., et al., pp. 1–2, 14 August 1952, folder "60-6-99 Section 3," box 90, DOJ Class 60 Litigation Files, NACP.
87. "U.S. v. 20th Century Fox et al., Government's Objections to Interrogatories," 26 October 1954, U.S. v. 20th Century Fox et al., folder 30–34, box no. 12545A, Records of the Warner Bros. Legal Department, WBA.
88. Reporter's Transcript of Proceedings, p. 1368, 10 December 1954, NAR 14354-Y.
89. Reporter's Transcript of Proceedings, p. 1368, 13 October 1955, NAR 14354-Y.
90. Notice of Motion to Amend Complaint, 20 January 1955, NAR 14354-Y.

91. Reporter's Transcript of Proceedings, p. 951, 7 October 1955, NAR 14354-Y.

92. Judge Leon R. Yankwich, Consent Judgment for Republic Pictures Corp. and Republic Productions, Inc., 12 September 1955, NAR 14354-Y.

93. Reporter's Transcript of Proceedings, p. 5, 22 September 1955, NAR 14354-Y.

94. Ibid., 7.

95. Notice of Motion of Loeb and Loeb to Withdraw as Attorneys of Record for Pictorial Film, Inc., 29 November 1954, NAR 14354-Y.

96. Final Judgment as to Pictorial Film, Inc. and Final Judgment as to Films, Inc., 21 September 1955, NAR 14354-Y.

97. Justice Douglas, Opinion of the Court, United States v. Paramount Pictures, Inc. et al., Supreme Court of the United States, 334 U.S. 131, 68 S. Ct. 915, 92 L. Ed. 1260, 3 May 1948.

98. Reporter's Transcript of Proceedings, pp. 14–15, 22 September 1955, NAR 14354-Y.

99. Ibid., 2294–2295.

100. Fanchon & Marco, Inc. v. Paramount Pictures, Inc. et al., 215 F.2d 167 (United States Court of Appeals, Ninth Circuit, 11 August 1954).

101. Reporter's Transcript of Proceedings, pp. 2123–2124, 26 October 1955, NAR 14354-Y.

102. Answer of T.C.F. Film Corporation, 16 February 1953; Answer of Defendant United World Films, Inc., to Amended Complaint, 17 February 1953; Answer of Defendant Universal Pictures Company, Inc. to Amended Complaint, 18 February 1953; Answer of Defendants Republic Pictures Corporation and Republic Productions, Inc. to the Amended Complaint, 18 February 1953; Answer, Warner Bros., 18 February 1953; Answer, Films, Inc., 19 February 1953; Answer of Defendants Columbia Pictures Corporation and Screen Gems, Inc., 10 March 1953; Answer of RKO Pictures, Inc., 10 March 1953, NAR 14354-Y.

103. Answer of Defendant Universal Pictures Company, Inc., 20.

104. Answer of the Defendant Republic Pictures Corporation (Hereinafter Called "Republic") to the Interrogatories Dated March 4, 1953 Propounded by the Plaintiff Herein, p. 15, 22 September 1953, NAR 14354-Y.

105. Defendants' Amended Answers to Plaintiff's Interrogatories, September 1955, NAR 14354-Y.

106. Testimony of Ned E. Depinet, Reporter's Transcript of Proceedings, 1766–1767.

107. Ibid., 1825–1826.

108. Testimony of Spyros Skouras, Reporter's Transcript of Proceedings, pp. 2105–2106, 26 October 1955, NAR 14354-Y.

109. Reporter's Transcript of Proceedings, p. 2223, 26 October 1955, NAR 14354-Y.

110. Testimony of Ned E. Depinet, Reporter's Transcript of Proceedings, 2454–2455.

111. "Opinion" and "Decision and Directions for Findings," 5 December 1955, NAR 14354-Y.

112. Case Summary, "United States of America, Plaintiff, v. Twentieth Century-Fox Film Corporation, et al.," 5 December 1955, No. 14354, United States District Court for the Southern District of California, Central Division, 137 F. Supp. 78, 1955 U.S. Dist. Lexis 2288, 1955 Trade Cas. (CCH) P68,205.

113. Herman M. Levy, TOA Press Release, p. 5, 15 December 1955, folder 2, box 43, MSS 1446, NATO.

114. Stipulation for Stay of Operation of Judgment, 27 December 1955, NAR 14354-Y.

115. "Department of Justice Files Motion to Terminate Paramount Consent Decrees," Department of Justice, Office of Public Affairs, 22 November 2019, https://www .justice.gov/opa/pr/department-justice-files-motion-terminate-paramount-consent -decrees.

CHAPTER 6 — FEATURE FILMS MAKE THEIR WAY TO TELEVISION

1. "NBC, CBS Working to Get Film Studios," *Hollywood Reporter*, 15 December 1955, 1.
2. Don J. Fedderson's Testimony, Reporter's Transcript of Proceedings, p. 1738, 3 October 1951, NAR 13220-PH.
3. Testimony of Alexander Kenneth Beggs, Reporter's Transcript of Proceedings, vol. 14, pp. 1397, 1405–1407, 1412, 18 October 1955, NAR 14354-Y.
4. FCC, "Twenty First Annual Report of the Federal Communications Commission for Fiscal Year Ended June 30, 1955," NACP, 120
5. "Memorandum Re Television as Discussed at Finance Committee Meeting—May 4, 1956," folder "Administrative: Dept. Organizations 1955–1960 and undated," box 1, John F. Devine Papers, 1952–1974, JWTCA.
6. Testimony of Alexander Kenneth Beggs, Reporter's Transcript of Proceedings, 1485–1486.
7. Ibid., 1425–1426, 1428.
8. Testimony of Charles Weintraub, President of Quality Films, Reporter's Transcript of Proceedings, vol. 14, pp. 841–842, 6 October 1955, NAR 14354-Y.
9. Ibid., 842–843, 851.
10. Ibid., 847–848.
11. Ibid., 843–846.
12. Ibid., 849–850.
13. Testimony of Alexander Kenneth Beggs, Reporter's Transcript of Proceedings, 1440.
14. Testimony of Jack L. Van Volkenburg, President of the Television Division of CBS, Reporter's Transcript of Proceedings, p. 585, 4 October 1955, NAR 14,354-Y.
15. Testimony of Milford Fenster, Reporter's Transcript of Proceedings, vol. 9, pp. 886, 896, 6 October 1955, NAR 14354-Y.
16. Testimony of Alexander Kenneth Beggs, Reporter's Transcript of Proceedings, 1432.
17. Unsigned letter to Mrs. Frank J. Lowell, 17 January 1950, folder "Columbia Broadcasting Co. 60-6-99 N-1 to N-16," box 8, DOJ NACP.
18. Testimony of Charles Weintraub, Reporter's Transcript of Proceedings, 833, 840, 842.
19. Ibid., 833.
20. "Eddie Sherman Sells KTSL 39 Old Films," *Daily Variety*, 19 May 1950, 5.
21. "26 Stations Airing WPIX Film Packages," *Radio Daily*, 22 November 1949, 7.
22. "Banks Hold $10 Million Indie Sack," *Daily Variety*, 18 January 1950, 1, 9.
23. Testimony of Charles Weintraub, Reporter's Transcript of Proceedings, 843–846.
24. Ibid.
25. Testimony of Alexander Kenneth Beggs, Reporter's Transcript of Proceedings, 1421, 1488.
26. Testimony of Peter G. Levathes, Reporter's Transcript of Proceedings, p. 2225, 26 October 1955, NAR 14354-Y.
27. Testimony of Alexander Kenneth Beggs, Reporter's Transcript of Proceedings, 1415.
28. Ibid., 1482.
29. Minutes of Meeting of the National Television Film Council, 1953, folder "National Television Film Council W1 to W22," box 8, DOJ NACP.
30. Ibid.
31. Don J. Fedderson's Testimony, Reporter's Transcript of Proceedings, 1761.
32. Testimony of Alexander Kenneth Beggs, Reporter's Transcript of Proceedings, 1484.
33. Jack Devine, letter to John K. Herbert, Vice President, NBC, 4 November 1953, folder "Review Board: National Broadcasting Company, 1953 and undated," box 36, John F. Devine Papers, 1954–1974, JWTCA.

34. Wayne Tiss's Testimony, Reporter's Transcript of Proceedings, pp. 660–661, 664, 20 September 1951, NAR 13220-PH.

35. "The State of Film," *Television Magazine*, August 1950, 15.

36. Transcript of John Balaban's testimony at the UPT-ABC Hearings, Copy included in letter from Marcus Cohn to S. H. Fabian, Fabian Theatres, 18 March 1952, folder: Theatre Owners of America 6 to 599, box 1, DOJ NACP.

37. Wayne Tiss's Testimony, Reporter's Transcript of Proceedings, 592–593.

38. Testimony of Milford Fenster, Reporter's Transcript of Proceedings, 857.

39. Ibid., 871–872, 893.

40. Ibid., 871–872.

41. Ibid., 861, 873, 875.

42. Ibid., 873–874.

43. Ibid., 862, 863–864, 866–867, 868.

44. Ibid., 879.

45. Office Communication from Alan Rhone to Grant Theis, Columbia Broadcasting System, Inc., 23 April 1951, folder "Columbia Broadcasting Co. 60-6-99 N-1 to N-16," box 8, DOJ NACP.

46. Ibid.

47. Ibid.

48. Ibid.

49. Ibid.

50. Ibid.

51. Ibid.

52. Don Tatum's Testimony, Reporter's Transcript of Proceedings, pp. 1693–1694, 3 October 1951, NAR 13220-PH.

53. "New ABC-TV Daytime Program 'Afternoon Film Festival,'" 13 December 1955, folder "Networks, National Broadcasting Company, 1955–1957," box 9, Dan Seymour Papers, JWTCA.

54. Ibid.

55. Office Communication from Alan Rhone to Grant Theis.

56. Interoffice Communication from Mr. Underhill to Mr. Robinson, Columbia Broadcasting System, Inc., 23 April 1951, folder "Columbia Broadcasting Co. 60-6-99 N-1 to N-16," box 8, DOJ NACP.

57. Testimony of Jack L. Van Volkenburg, Reporter's Transcript of Proceedings, 576.

58. Ibid., 578.

59. Ibid., 590.

60. Testimony of Spyros Skouras, Reporter's Transcript of Proceedings, vol. 19, p. 2108, 26 October 1955, NAR 14354-Y.

61. Testimony of Peter G. Levathes, Reporter's Transcript of Proceedings, 2363.

62. Testimony of Isidore B. Kornblum, Reporter's Transcript of Proceedings, vol. 12, pp. 1195–1196, 12 October 1955, NAR 14354-Y; Testimony of Peter G. Levathes, Reporter's Transcript of Proceedings, 2244.

63. Testimony of Peter G. Levathes, Reporter's Transcript of Proceedings, 2244.

64. Testimony of Isidore B. Kornblum, Reporter's Transcript of Proceedings, 1182, 1192–1194.

65. Testimony of Peter G. Levathes, Reporter's Transcript of Proceedings, 2243.

66. Testimony of Isidore B. Kornblum, Reporter's Transcript of Proceedings, 1192.

67. Testimony of Peter G. Levathes, Reporter's Transcript of Proceedings, 2232–2233.

68. Ibid., 2231–2232; Testimony of Isidore B. Kornblum, Reporter's Transcript of Proceedings, 1185–1186, 1197–1198.

69. Testimony of Peter G. Levathes, Reporter's Transcript of Proceedings, 2232, 2243–2244.
70. Testimony of Isidore B. Kornblum, Reporter's Transcript of Proceedings, 1185–1186; Testimony of Peter G. Levathes, Reporter's Transcript of Proceedings, 2231–2232.
71. Testimony of Isidore B. Kornblum, Reporter's Transcript of Proceedings, 1185–1186, 1203.
72. Ibid.
73. Testimony of Peter G. Levathes, Reporter's Transcript of Proceedings, 2233.
74. Ibid., 2234.
75. Testimony of Benjamin B. Kahane, Reporter's Transcript of Proceedings, vol. 21, pp. 2571–2572, 28 October 1955, NAR 14354-Y.
76. Testimony of Peter G. Levathes, Reporter's Transcript of Proceedings, 2229–2230.
77. Ibid., 2229–2230.
78. Testimony of Milford Fenster, Reporter's Transcript of Proceedings, 891, 893.
79. Ibid.
80. Testimony of Peter G. Levathes, Reporter's Transcript of Proceedings, 2229–2230.
81. Testimony of Spyros Skouras, Reporter's Transcript of Proceedings, 2164; Testimony of Milford Fenster, Reporter's Transcript of Proceedings, 894.
82. Testimony of Spyros Skouras, Reporter's Transcript of Proceedings, 2164.
83. Ibid., 2108.
84. Testimony of Peter G. Levathes, Reporter's Transcript of Proceedings, 2236.
85. Reporter's Transcript of Proceedings, pp. 93–94, 22 September 1955, NAR 14354-Y.
86. Defendants' Exhibit CV, "Television Statistics," Reporter's Transcript of Proceedings, p. 2338, 27 October 1955, NAR 14354-Y.
87. Testimony of Peter G. Levathes, Reporter's Transcript of Proceedings, 2236.
88. Testimony of Spyros Skouras, Reporter's Transcript of Proceedings, 2116.
89. Ibid., 1227, 2120.
90. Testimony of Peter G. Levathes, Reporter's Transcript of Proceedings, 2237–2238.
91. Testimony of Ralph Morris Cohn, Reporter's Transcript of Proceedings, vol. 21, pp. 2410–2411, 28 October 1955, NAR 14354-Y.
92. Ibid.
93. Testimony of Benjamin B. Kahane, Reporter's Transcript of Proceedings, 2587.
94. Testimony of Ralph Morris Cohn, Reporter's Transcript of Proceedings, 2412–2413, 2416.
95. Testimony of Benjamin B. Kahane, Reporter's Transcript of Proceedings, 2561.
96. Testimony of Ralph Morris Cohn, Reporter's Transcript of Proceedings, 2486–2487.
97. Ibid., 2425.
98. Reporter's Transcript of Proceedings, pp. 125–126, 22 September 1955, NAR 14354-Y.
99. Testimony of Ralph Morris Cohn, Reporter's Transcript of Proceedings, 2432.
100. Ibid.
101. Ibid.
102. Ibid., 2433.
103. Testimony of Benjamin B. Kahane, Reporter's Transcript of Proceedings, 2575–2576.
104. Reporter's Transcript of Proceedings, p. 138, 22 September 1955, NAR 14354-Y.
105. Richard B. Jewell, *Slow Fade to Black: The Decline of RKO Radio Pictures* (Oakland: University of California Press, 2016), 87–88.
106. Testimony of Creighton J. Tevlin, Reporter's Transcript of Proceedings, vol. 18, pp. 2054–2056, 25 October 1955, NAR 14354-Y.
107. Ibid., 2056.
108. Ibid.
109. Ibid., 2056–2057.

110. Ibid., 2057–2058.

111. Ibid., 2057.

112. Ibid.

113. Ibid., 2061.

114. Jewell, *Slow Fade to Black*, 145–150.

115. Testimony of Creighton J. Tevlin, Reporter's Transcript of Proceedings, 2058–2059.

116. Testimony of Ned E. Depinet, Reporter's Transcript of Proceedings, pp. 1775–1776, 21 October 1955, NAR 14354-Y.

117. Jewell, *Slow Fade to Black*, 107–112.

118. Testimony of Creighton J. Tevlin, Reporter's Transcript of Proceedings, 2076.

119. Jewell, *Slow Fade to Black*, 157.

120. Testimony of Creighton J. Tevlin, Reporter's Transcript of Proceedings, 2059.

121. Ibid., 2060.

122. Testimony of Ned E. Depinet, Reporter's Transcript of Proceedings, 1828.

123. Ibid., 1829.

124. Ibid.

125. Ibid.

126. Testimony of Creighton J. Tevlin, Reporter's Transcript of Proceedings, 2062–2063.

127. Ibid.

128. Ibid.

129. Testimony of Charles Weintraub, Reporter's Transcript of Proceedings, 854.

130. Testimony of Milford Fenster, Reporter's Transcript of Proceedings, 858, 900.

131. Testimony of Creighton J. Tevlin, Reporter's Transcript of Proceedings, 2062–2063.

132. Testimony of Milford Fenster, Reporter's Transcript of Proceedings, 859–860.

133. Ibid., 897–898.

134. Jewell, *Slow Fade to Black*, 189.

135. Testimony of Milford Fenster, Reporter's Transcript of Proceedings, 898.

136. Ibid.

137. Testimony of Creighton J. Tevlin, Reporter's Transcript of Proceedings, 2064–2066.

138. Ibid.

139. Ibid., 2066–2068.

140. Ibid.

141. Ibid., 2063; Reporter's Transcript of Proceedings, p. 895, 6 October 1955, NAR 14354-Y.

142. Testimony of Creighton J. Tevlin, Reporter's Transcript of Proceedings, 2069.

143. Testimony of Alexander Kenneth Beggs, Reporter's Transcript of Proceedings, 1960.

144. Hilmes, *Hollywood and Broadcasting*, 161; and Kerry Segrave, *Movies at Home: How Hollywood Came to Television* (Jefferson, NC: McFarland, 1999), 40.

145. Hoyt, "Hollywood Vault," 309n96; also Jewell, *Slow Fade to Black*.

146. Jewell, *Slow Fade to Black*, 194.

147. Reporter's Transcript of Proceedings, pp. 125–126, 22 September 1955, NAR 14354-Y.

148. Spyros Skouras, letter to Samuel Goldstein, 28 April 1954, Reporter's Transcript of Proceedings, pp. 2174–2175, 26 October 1955, NAR 14354-Y.

149. Testimony of Jack L. Warner, Reporter's Transcript of Proceedings, vol. 22, pp. 3004–3005, 31 October 1955, NAR 14354-Y.

150. Ibid., 3014–3015.

151. Ibid., 3017–3018, 3027.

152. Answer of Defendant Universal Pictures Company, Inc., vol. 1, p. 9, 4 March 1953, NAR 14354-Y.

153. Testimony of Charles Weintraub, Reporter's Transcript of Proceedings, 838, 840–841.

154. Memo from Len White to Bob Ballin, 29 November 1955, folder "Hollywood: Memoranda/Reports on TV Related Subjects, including Screenings from Len White, 1955, Oct—1956, Nov," box 3, Dan Seymour Papers, JWTCA.

155. Hoyt, "Hollywood Vault," 312.

156. Hilmes, *Hollywood and Broadcasting*, 161.

157. Boddy, *Fifties Television*, 138.

158. Hilmes, *Hollywood and Broadcasting*, 161.

159. Memo from Len White to Jack Devine, Cornwell Jackson, et al., 9 January 1956, folder "Hollywood: Memoranda/Reports on TV Related Subjects, including Screenings from Len White, 1955, Oct—1956, Nov," box 3, Dan Seymour Papers, JWTCA.

160. Hoyt, "Hollywood Vault," 315–317.

161. Memo from Len White to Peter Cavallo, Jack Devine, et al., 14 February 1956, folder "Hollywood: Memoranda/Reports on TV Related Subjects, including Screenings from Len White, 1955, Oct—1956, Nov," box 3, Dan Seymour Papers, JWTCA.

162. Lev, *Twentieth Century-Fox*, 182–183.

163. Hilmes, *Hollywood and Broadcasting*, 160.

164. Eric Hoyt, *Hollywood Vault: Film Libraries before Home Video* (Oakland: University of California Press, 2014).

165. Boddy, *Fifties Television*, 138.

166. Hilmes, *Hollywood and Broadcasting*, 162.

167. *The Last Mogul: The Life and Times of Lew Wasserman*, directed by Barry Avich (New York: Kino Video, 2005).

168. White, "Life after Divorce," 113–114.

169. Balio, "Introduction to Part I," 37.

170. Banks, *The Writers*, 193.

171. Ibid., 224.

172. Ibid., 231.

173. Whiteleather, "Rebels with a Cause," 3–4.

174. Hilmes, *Hollywood and Broadcasting*, 166.

175. Balio, "Introduction to Part I," 37–38; Lev, *Twentieth Century-Fox*, 182–183.

176. Balio, "Introduction to Part I," 38–39.

177. Belton, "Glorious Technicolor," 206.

178. Chisolm, "Red, Blue, and Lots of Green," 228.

CONCLUSION — DISRUPTING A BIG MARKET CAN BE BUMPY

1. Christensen, *The Innovator's Dilemma*, xx and xxv.

2. Currah, "Hollywood versus the Internet," 440.

3. Quoted in Ibid., 459.

4. Ibid., 442.

5. Ibid., 464.

6. Ibid., 440.

7. "Opportunity and Optimism: How CEOs are Embracing Digital Growth," Ernst & Young (2012), 5., https://www.ey.com/us/en/newsroom/news-releases/opportunity-and -optimism--global-media-and-entertainment-ceos-see-digital-media-as-a-significant -driver-of-future-growth.

8. Ibid., 31.

9. Ibid., 37.

10. Ibid., 39.

11. Alisa Perren, "Business as Unusual: Conglomerate-Sized Challenges for Film and Television in the Digital Arena," *Journal of Popular Film and Television*, 8 August 2010, 74.

12. Ibid.

13. Nick Wingfield, "Resisting Mobile Hurts Nintendo's Bottom Line," *New York Times*, 17 January 2014.

14. Chris Anderson, *The Long Tail: Why the Future of Business Is Selling Less of More* (New York: Hyperion, 2006).

15. Quoted in Wingfield, "Resisting Mobile Hurts."

16. Chris Sacca's comments as part of the panel "Follow the Money: Where Investment Is Headed in Technology, Content" (TheGrill 2012 Media Leadership Conference, sponsored by *The Wrap*, West Hollywood, CA, 1 October 2012).

17. Denise Mann, "Introduction: When Television and New Media Work Worlds Collide," in *Wired TV: Laboring over an Interactive Future*, ed. Denise Mann (New Brunswick, NJ: Rutgers University Press, 2013), 2.

18. "Opportunity and Optimism," 34.

19. Chris Anderson, *Free: The Future of a Radical Price* (New York: Hyperion, 2009).

20. Nick Bilton, "Content Creators Use Piracy to Gauge Consumer Interest," *New York Times*, 17 September 2013.

21. Ibid.

22. Manyika et al., "Disruptive Technologies," 149.

23. Testimony of Ned E. Depinet, Reporter's Transcript of Proceedings, pp. 1766–1767, 21 October 1955, NAR 14354-Y.

24. Currah, "Hollywood versus the Internet," 458.

25. "Opportunity and Optimism," 13.

26. Christensen, *Innovator's Dilemma*, 152.

27. Manyika et al., "Disruptive Technologies," 1.

28. Perren, "Business as Unusual," 74.

29. James B. Stewart, "Netflix Looks Back on Its Near-Death Spiral," *New York Times*, 26 April 2013.

30. Manyika et al., "Disruptive Technologies."

31. Ibid.

32. Nicholas Carr, *The Big Switch: Rewiring the World from Edison to Google: The Definitive Guide to the Cloud Computing Revolution* (New York: W. W. Norton, 2013), 135–136.

33. Michael Curtin and Kevin Sanson, "Precarious Creativity: Global Media, Local Labor," in *Precarious Creativity: Global Media, Local Labor*, ed. Michael Curtin and Kevin Sanson (Oakland: University of California Press, 2016), 1–2.

34. Mark Deuze, "Work in the Media," in *Media Industries: Perspectives on an Evolving Field*, ed. Amelia Arsenault and Alisa Perren (Austin, TX: Media Industries Editorial Board, 2016), 14.

35. "Opportunity and Optimism," 34.

36. Edward Wyatt, "Rebuffing F.C.C. in 'Net Neutrality' Case, Court Allows Streaming Deals," *New York Times*, 14 January 2014.

37. Jennifer Holt, "Regulating Connected Viewing: Media Pipelines and Cloud Policy," in *Connected Viewing Initiative Final Report*, Carsey-Wolf Center Media Industries Project, UC Santa Barbara, 7 September 2012, 12.

38. McQuivey, *Digital Disruption*, 8–9.

39. Christensen, *Innovator's Dilemma*, xxiii–xxiv.

40. Ernst & Young, *Sustaining Digital Leadership! Agile Technology Strategies for Growth, Business Models and Customer Engagement*, EY's Global Technology Center and Global

Media & Entertainment Center, Report No. 2, 2014, 6–7, https://www.ey.com/Publication
/vwLUAssets/EY-Sustaining-digital-leadership/$FILE/EY-Sustaining-digital-leadership
.pdf.

41. Perren, "Business as Unusual," 76.
42. Ibid.
43. Musser, *The Emergence of Cinema*, 492.
44. Mann, "Introduction," 6.
45. Christensen, *Innovator's Dilemma*, 258–260.
46. Ibid., 112.
47. Ibid., 165.
48. Orly Lobel, *Talent Wants to Be Free: Why We Should Learn to Love Leaks, Raids, and Free Riding* (New Haven, CT: Yale University Press, 2013), 244.
49. Carr, *The Big Switch*, 241–242.
50. Holt, *Empires of Entertainment*, 177.

BIBLIOGRAPHY

ARCHIVAL COLLECTIONS

AMPTP File 617, "Television." Special Collections, Margaret Herrick Library. Los Angeles, CA.

DOJ Class 60 Antitrust Accession 57A60. National Archives. College Park, MD.

Gene Autry Collection. Autry National Center of the American West. Los Angeles, CA.

Gene Autry v. Republic Productions, Inc., et al. Case No. 13596-BH Civil. United States District Court. Southern District of California. Central Division. Los Angeles, CA. National Archives, Pacific Region.

J. Walter Thompson Special Collection. Rare Book, Manuscript, and Special Collections Library, Duke University. Durham, NC.

Jack Mathis Collection. MSS 2389. L. Tom Perry Special Collections. Harold B. Lee Library. Brigham Young University. Provo, UT.

National Association of Theatre Owners Collection. MSS 1446. L. Tom Perry Special Collections. Harold B. Lee Library. Brigham Young University. Provo, UT.

Roy Rogers v. Republic Productions, Inc., Hollywood Television Service, Inc., et al. Case No. 13220-PH Civil. United States District Court. Southern District of California. Central Division. Los Angeles, CA. National Archives, Pacific Region.

Screen Actors Guild Archive. Los Angeles, CA.

USA v. Twentieth 16mm TV Suit. 8216-A. Twentieth Century-Fox Film Corporation. Records of the Legal Department. UCLA Performing Arts Special Collections.

U.S. v. Twentieth Century-Fox, et al. Records of the District Court of the United States for the Southern District of California, Central Division (Los Angeles). Civil Case Files 14354. National Archives and Records Administration, Pacific Region.

U.S. v. 20th Century-Fox, et al. Records of the Warner Bros. Legal Department. Warner Bros. Archives. School of Cinematic Arts. University of Southern California.

CONGRESSIONAL HEARINGS AND FCC REPORTS

Federal Communications Commission Annual Reports. National Archives at College Park, MD.

Hearings on the Investigation of James C. Petrillo, the American Federation of Musicians, et al, Vol. 1, Before the Special Subcommittee of the Committee on Education and Labor, 80th Congress, First Session (1947).

Hearings on the Restrictive Practices of the American Federation of Musicians, Vol. 1, Before the Committee on Education and Labor, 80th Congress, Second Session (1948).

BOOKS AND JOURNAL ARTICLES

Acland, Charles. "Dirt Research for Media Industries." In *Media Industries: Perspectives on an Evolving Field*, edited by Amelia Arsenault and Alisa Perren, 5–12. Austin, TX: Media Industries Editorial Board, 2016.

Allen, Robert C. "Contra the Chaser Theory." In *Film before Griffith*, edited by John Fell, 105–115. Los Angeles: University of California Press, 1983.

Anderson, Chris. *Free: The Future of a Radical Price*. New York: Hyperion, 2009.

———. *The Long Tail: Why the Future of Business Is Selling Less of More*. New York: Hyperion, 2006.

Anderson, Christopher. *Hollywood TV: The Studio System in the Fifties*. Austin: University of Texas Press, 1994.

Balio, Tino. *Grand Design: Hollywood as a Modern Business Enterprise, 1930–1939*. History of the American Cinema, edited by Charles Harpole, vol. 5. Berkeley: University of California Press, 1993.

———, ed. *Hollywood in the Age of Television*. Boston: Unwin Hyman, 1990.

———. "Part IV/Retrenchment, Reappraisal, and Reorganization, 1948- ." In *The American Film Industry*, edited by Tino Balio. Madison: University of Wisconsin Press, 1985.

Banks, Miranda. *The Writers: A History of American Screen Writers and Their Guild*. New Brunswick, NJ: Rutgers University Press, 2015.

Baughman, James L. *Same Time, Same Station: Creating American Television, 1948–1961*. Baltimore: Johns Hopkins University Press, 2007.

———. "The Weakest Chain and the Strongest Link: The American Broadcasting Company and the Motion Picture Industry, 1952–60." In *Hollywood in the Age of Television*, edited by Tino Balio, 91–114. Boston: Unwin Hyman, 1990.

Becker, Christine. *It's the Pictures That Got Small: Hollywood Film Stars on 1950s Television*. Middletown, CT: Wesleyan University Press, 2008.

Belton, John. "Glorious Technicolor, Breathtaking CinemaScope, and Stereophonic Sound." In *Hollywood in the Age of Television*, edited by Tino Bailo, 185–212. Boston: Unwin Hyman, 1990.

Boddy, William. *Fifties Television: The Industry and Its Critics*. Urbana: University of Illinois Press, 1990.

———. "Redefining the Home Screen: Technological Convergence as Trauma and Business Plan." In *Rethinking Media Change: The Aesthetics of Transition*, edited by David Thorburn and Henry Jenkins, 191–202. Cambridge, MA: MIT Press, 2004.

Buscombe, Edward. "Thinking It Differently: Television and the Film Industry," *Quarterly Review of Film Studies* 9, no. 3 (Summer 1984): 196–203.

Caldwell, John Thornton. "Critical Industrial Practice: Branding, Repurposing, and the Migratory Patterns of Industrial Texts." *Television & New Media* 7, no. 2 (May 2006): 99–134.

———. *Production Culture: Industrial Reflexivity and Critical Practice in Film and Television*. Durham, NC: Duke University Press, 2008.

———. "Welcome to the Viral Future of Cinema (Television)," *Cinema Journal* 45, no. 1 (Fall 2005): 90–97.

Carman, Emily, and Philip Drake. "Doing the Deal: Talent Contracts in Hollywood." In *Hollywood and the Law*, edited by Paul McDonald, Emily Carman, Eric Hoyt, and Philip Drake, 209–234. London: BFI Palgrave, 2015.

Carr, Nicholas. *The Big Switch: Rewiring the World from Edison to Google: The Definitive Guide to the Cloud Computing Revolution.* New York: W.W. Norton, 2013.

Chisolm, Brad. "Red, Blue, and Lots of Green: The Impact of Color Television on Feature Film Production." In *Hollywood in the Age of Television*, edited by Tino Balio, 213–234. Boston: Unwin Hyman, 1990.

Christensen, Clayton M. *The Innovator's Dilemma: The Revolutionary Book That Will Change the Way You Do Business.* New York: Harper Business, 2011.

Conant, Michael. *Antitrust in the Motion Picture Industry: Economic and Legal Analysis.* Los Angeles: University of California Press, 1960.

Currah, Andrew. "Hollywood versus the Internet: The Media and Entertainment Industries in a Digital and Networked Economy." *Journal of Economic Geography* 6, no. 4 (2006): 439–468.

Curtin, Michael, and Kevin Sanson. "Precarious Creativity: Global Media, Local Labor." In *Precarious Creativity: Global Media, Local Labor*, edited by Michael Curtin and Kevin Sanson, 1–18. Oakland: University of California Press, 2016.

Decherney, Peter. *Hollywood's Copyright Wars: From Edison to the Internet.* New York: Columbia University Press, 2012.

Deuze, Mark. "Work in the Media." In *Media Industries: Perspectives on an Evolving Field*, edited by Amelia Arsenault and Alisa Perren, 13–18. Austin, TX: Media Industries Editorial Board, 2016.

Doherty, Thomas. *Hollywood's Censor: Joseph I. Breen & the Production Code Administration.* New York: Columbia University Press, 2007.

Ellis, John. *Visible Fictions.* London: Routledge and Kegan Paul, 1982.

Fisk, Catherine L. *Writing for Hire: Unions, Hollywood, and Madison Avenue.* Cambridge, MA: Harvard University Press, 2016.

Forman, Murray. *One Night on TV Is Worth Weeks at the Paramount: Popular Music on Early Television.* Durham, NC: Duke University Press, 2012.

Freedman, Des. "Media Policy Research and the Media Industries." In *Media Industries: Perspectives on an Evolving Field*, edited by Amelia Arsenault and Alisa Perren, 19–24. Austin, TX: Media Industries Editorial Board, 2016.

Gaines, Jane. *Contested Culture: The Image, the Voice, and the Law.* Chapel Hill: University of North Carolina Press, 1991.

Gomery, Douglas. "The Centrality of Media Economics." In *Defining Media Studies: Reflections on the Future of the Field*, edited by Mark R. Levy and Michael Gurevitch, 198–206. New York: Oxford University Press, 1994.

———. "Failed Opportunities: The Integration of the U.S. Motion Picture and Television Industries." *Quarterly Review of Film Studies* 9, no. 3 (Summer 1984): 219–228.

Hesmondalgh, David. *The Cultural Industries.* 2nd ed. Los Angeles: Sage Publications, 2007.

Hilmes, Michele. *Hollywood and Broadcasting: From Radio to Cable.* Urbana: University of Illinois Press, 1990.

———. "Nailing Mercury: The Problem of Media Industry Historiography." In *Media Industries: History, Theory, and Method*, edited by Jennifer Holt and Alissa Perren, 21–33. Malden, MA: Wiley-Blackwell, 2009.

———. *Network Nations: A Transnational History of British and American Broadcasting.* New York: Routledge, 2012.

———. *Only Connect: A Cultural History of Broadcasting in the United States.* 3rd ed. Boston: Wadsworth/Cengage Learning, 2011.

———. "Rethinking Radio." In *Radio Reader: Essays in the Cultural History of Radio*, edited by Michele Hilmes and Jason Loviglio, 1–20. New York: Routledge, 2002.

Holt, Jennifer. *Empires of Entertainment: Media Industries and the Politics of Deregulation, 1980–1996*. New Brunswick, NJ: Rutgers University Press, 2011.
———. "Regulating Connected Viewing: Media Pipelines and Cloud Policy." In *Connected Viewing Initiative Final Report*, Carsey-Wolf Center Media Industries Project, UC Santa Barbara, 7 September 2012.
Hoyt, Eric. "Asset or Liability? Hollywood and Tax Law." In *Hollywood and the Law*, edited by Paul McDonald, Emily Carman, Eric Hoyt, and Philip Drake, 183–208. London: British Film Institute, 2015.
———. *Hollywood Vault: Film Libraries before Home Video*. Oakland: University of California Press, 2014.
———. "Hollywood Vault: The Business of Film Libraries, 1915–1960." PhD diss., University of Southern California, 2012.
Hurst, Richard M. *Republic Studios: Between Poverty Row and the Majors*. Lanham, MD: Scarecrow Press, 2007.
Jaramillo, Deborah L. *The Television Code: Regulating the Screen to Safeguard the Industry*. Austin: University of Texas Press, 2018.
Jenkins, Henry. *Convergence Culture: Where Old and New Media Collide*. New York: New York University Press, 2006.
Jewell, Richard B. "RKO Film Grosses, 1929–1951: The C.J. Tevlin Ledger." *Historical Journal of Film, Radio & Television* 14, no. 1 (March 1994): 51–58.
———. *Slow Fade to Black: The Decline of RKO Radio Pictures*. Oakland: University of California Press, 2016.
Kackman, Michael. "Nothing on but Hoppy Badges: *Hopalong Cassidy*, William Boyd Enterprises, and Emergent Media Globalization," *Cinema Journal* 47, no. 4 (Summer 2008): 76–101.
Kepley, Vance, Jr. "From 'Frontal Lobes' to the 'Bob-and-Bob' Show: NBC Management and Programming Strategies, 1949–65." In *Hollywood in the Age of Television*, edited by Tino Balio, 41–62. Boston: Unwin Hyman, 1990.
King, Barry. "Articulating Stardom," *Screen* 26, no. 5 (September–October 1985): 27–50.
Lafferty, William. "Feature Films on Prime-Time Television." In *Hollywood in the Age of Television*, edited by Tino Balio, 235–258. Boston: Unwin Hyman, 1990.
Lev, Peter. *The Fifties: Transforming the Screen, 1950–1959*. History of the American Cinema, edited by Charles Harpole, vol. 7. Berkeley: University of California Press, 2003.
———. *Twentieth Century-Fox: The Zanuck-Skouras Years, 1935–1965*. Austin: University of Texas Press, 2013.
Lieb, Kristin J. *Gender, Branding, and the Modern Music Industry*. New York: Routledge, 2013.
Lobel, Orly. *Talent Wants to Be Free: Why We Should Learn to Love Leaks, Raids, and Free Riding*. New Haven, CT: Yale University Press, 2013.
Mann, Denise. "Introduction: When Television and New Media Work Worlds Collide." In *Wired TV: Laboring over an Interactive Future*, edited by Denise Mann, 1–31. New Brunswick, NJ: Rutgers University Press, 2013.
Manyika, James, Michael Chui, Jacques Bughin, Richard Dobbs, Peter Bisson, and Alex Marrs. "Disruptive Technologies: Advances That Will Transform Life, Business, and the Global Economy." McKinsey Global Institute, May 2013. https://www.mckinsey.com/business-functions/mckinsey-digital/our-insights/disruptive-technologies.
McQuivey, James. *Digital Disruption: Unleashing the Next Wave of Innovation*. Cambridge, MA: Forrester Research, 2013.
Meehan, Eileen. "Critical Theorizing on Broadcast History." *Journal of Broadcasting & Electronic Media* 30, no. 4 (Fall 1986): 393–411.

———. "Watching Television: A Political Economic Approach." In *A Companion to Television*, edited by Janet Wasko, 238–255. Malden, MA: Wiley-Blackwell, 2010.

Musser, Charles. *The Emergence of Cinema: The American Screen to 1907*. Vol. 1 of *History of the American Cinema*. Los Angeles: University of California Press, 1990.

Overpeck, Deron. "Splitsville: Independent Exhibitors Court Federal Intervention in the American Film Industry, 1975–1988." *Film History* 26, no. 1 (2014): 136–157.

Perlman, Alison. *Public Interests: Media Advocacy and Struggles over U.S. Television.* New Brunswick, NJ: Rutgers University Press, 2016.

Perren, Alisa. "Business as Unusual: Conglomerate-Sized Challenges for Film and Television in the Digital Arena." *Journal of Popular Film and Television* 38, no. 2 (8 August 2010): 72–78.

Pierce, David. "'Senile Celluloid': Independent Exhibitors, the Major Studios and the Fight over Feature Films on Television." *Film History* 10, no. 2 (1998): 141–164.

Porst, Jennifer. "The Preservation of Competition: Hollywood and Antitrust." In *Hollywood and the Law*, edited by Paul McDonald, Emily Carman, Eric Hoyt, and Philip Drake, 103–129. London: BFI Publishing, 2015.

Reagan, Ronald, and Richard G. Hubler. *Where's the Rest of Me?* New York: Duell, Sloan and Pearce, 1965.

Rogers, Maureen. "Remaking the B Film in 1940s Hollywood: Producers Releasing Corporation and the Poverty Row Programmer." *Film History: An International Journal* 29, no. 2 (2017): 138–164.

Santo, Avi. *Selling the Silver Bullet: The Lone Ranger and Transmedia Brand Licensing.* Austin: University of Texas Press, 2015.

Schnapper, Amy. "The Distribution of Theatrical Feature Films to Television." Diss., University of Wisconsin–Madison, 1975.

Schumpeter, Joseph. *Capitalism, Socialism, and Democracy.* New York: Harper Collins Publishers, 2008.

Segrave, Kerry. *Movies at Home: How Hollywood Came to Television.* Jefferson, NC: McFarland, 1999.

Selvin, Molly. "The Loeb Firm and the Origins of Entertainment Law Practice in Los Angeles, 1908–1940," *California Legal History* 10 (2015): 135–173.

Sewell, Philip W. *Television in the Age of Radio: Modernity, Imagination, and the Making of a Medium.* New Brunswick, NJ: Rutgers University Press, 2014.

Spigel, Lynn. *Make Room for TV: Television and the Family Ideal in Postwar America.* Chicago: University of Chicago Press, 1992.

———. *Welcome to the Dreamhouse: Popular Media and the Postwar Suburbs.* Durham, NC: Duke University Press, 2001.

Staiger, Janet. "Combination and Litigation: Structures of U.S. Film Distribution, 1896–1917," *Cinema Journal* 23 (Winter 1983): 41–72.

Thorburn, David, and Henry Jenkins. "Introduction: Towards an Aesthetics of Transition." In *Rethinking Media Change: The Aesthetics of Transition*, edited by David Thorburn and Henry Jenkins, 1–18. Cambridge, MA: MIT Press, 2004.

Uricchio, William. "Historicizing Media in Transition." In *Rethinking Media Change: The Aesthetics of Transition*, edited by David Thorburn and Henry Jenkins, 23–38. Cambridge, MA: MIT Press, 2003.

Vianello, Robert. "The Rise of the Telefilm and the Networks' Hegemony over the Motion Picture Industry." *Quarterly Review of Film Studies* 9, no. 3 (Summer 1984): 204–218.

West's Encyclopedia of American Law. 2nd ed. Detroit: Gale Group, 2004.

White, Timothy. "Hollywood's Attempt at Appropriating Television: The Case of Paramount Pictures." In *Hollywood in the Age of Television*, edited by Tino Balio, 145–164. Boston, MA: Unwin Hyman, 1990.

White, Timothy R. "Life after Divorce: The Corporate Strategy of Paramount Pictures Corporation in the 1950s." *Film History* 2, no. 2 (1988): 99–119.

Whiteleather, Scott L. "Rebels with a Cause: Artists' Struggles to Escape a Place Where Everybody Owns Your Name." *Loyola of Los Angeles Entertainment Law Review* 21, no. 2 (2001): 253–287.

Williams, Mark. "Rewiring Media History: Intermedial Borders." In *Convergence Media History*, edited by Janet Staiger and Sabine Hake, 46–56. New York: Routledge, 2009.

Winston, Brian. "Breakages Limited." In *Electronic Media and Technoculture*, edited by John Thornton Caldwell, 77–89. New Brunswick, NJ: Rutgers University Press, 2000.

Wittern-Keller, Laura. "Controlling Content: Government Censorship, the Production Code and the Ratings System." In *Hollywood and the Law*, edited by Paul McDonald, Emily Carman, Eric Hoyt, and Philip Drake, 130–153. London: BFI Palgrave, 2015.

INDEX

About the Author

JENNIFER PORST is an assistant professor in the Department of Media Arts at the University of North Texas. Her work on the media industries has been published in journals and anthologies including *Film History, Television & New Media, Hollywood and the Law,* and the *Routledge Companion to Media Industries.* She also co-edited with Jonathan Cohn the anthology *Very Special Episodes: Televising Industrial and Social Change* (Rutgers University Press, 2021).